History of Budapest

Compiled by
Karyn Lavender

Scribbles

Year of Publication 2018

ISBN : 9789387513112

Book Published by

Scribbles

(An Imprint of Alpha Editions)

email - alphaedis@gmail.com

Produced by: PediaPress GmbH
Limburg an der Lahn
Germany
http://pediapress.com/

The content within this book was generated collaboratively by volunteers. Please be advised that nothing found here has necessarily been reviewed by people with the expertise required to provide you with complete, accurate or reliable information. Some information in this book may be misleading or simply wrong. Alpha Editions and PediaPress does not guarantee the validity of the information found here. If you need specific advice (for example, medical, legal, financial, or risk management) please seek a professional who is licensed or knowledgeable in that area.

Sources, licenses and contributors of the articles and images are listed in the section entitled "References". Parts of the books may be licensed under the GNU Free Documentation License. A copy of this license is included in the section entitled "GNU Free Documentation License"

The views and characters expressed in the book are those of the contributors and his/her imagination and do not represent the views of the Publisher.

Contents

Articles 1

Prehistory and Roman era 1
    Hungarian prehistory 1
    Aquincum 32

Middle Ages 37
    Kingdom of Hungary (1526–1867) 37

Renaissance 53
    Buda Castle 53
    Ottoman Hungary 115

19th century 129
    Hungarian Revolution of 1848 129
    Austria-Hungary 159

20th century 239
    Hungary in World War II 239

Hungarian Revolution 259
    Hungarian Revolution of 1956 259

Timeline 297
    Timeline of Budapest 297

Appendix 309

References 309

Article Sources and Contributors 329

Image Sources, Licenses and Contributors 331

Article Licenses 337

Index 339

Prehistory and Roman era

Hungarian prehistory

<indicator name="good-star"> ⊕ </indicator>

Part of a series on the
History of Hungary

Hungary portal

- v
- t
- e[1]

Hungarian prehistory (Hungarian: *magyar őstörténet*) spans the period of history of the Hungarian people, or Magyars, which started with the separation of the Hungarian language from other Finno-Ugric or Ugric languages around 800 BC, and ended with the Hungarian conquest of the Carpathian Basin around 895 AD. Based on the earliest records of the Magyars in Byzantine, Western European, and Hungarian chronicles, scholars considered them for centuries to have been the descendants of the ancient Scythians and Huns. This historiographical tradition disappeared from mainstream history after the realization of similarities between the Hungarian language and the Uralic languages in the late 18th century. Thereafter, linguistics became the principal source of the study of the Hungarians' ethnogenesis. In addition, chronicles written between the 9th and 15th centuries, the results of archaeological research and folklore analogies provide information on the Magyars' early history.

Study of pollen in fossils based on cognate words for certain trees – including larch and elm – in the daughter languages suggests the speakers of the Proto-Uralic language lived in the wider region of the Ural Mountains, which were inhabited by scattered groups of Neolithic hunter-gatherers in the 4th millennium BC. They spread over vast territories, which caused the development of a separate Proto-Finno-Ugric language by the end of the millennium. Linguistic studies and archaeological research evidence that those who spoke this language lived in pit-houses and used decorated clay vessels. The expansion of marshlands after around 2600 BC caused new migrations. No scholarly consensus on the *Urheimat*, or original homeland, of the Ugric peoples exists: they lived either in the region of the Tobol River or along the Kama River and the upper courses of the Volga River around 2000 BC. They lived in settled communities, cultivated millet, wheat, and other crops, and bred animals – especially horses, cattle, and pigs. Loan words connected to animal husbandry from Proto-Iranian show that they had close contacts with their neighbors. The southernmost Ugric groups adopted a nomadic way of life by around 1000 BC, because of the northward expansion of the steppes.

The development of the Hungarian language started around 800 BC with the withdrawal of the grasslands and the parallel southward migration of the nomadic Ugric groups. The history of the ancient Magyars during the next thousand years is uncertain; they lived in the steppes but the location of their *Urheimat* is subject to scholarly debates. According to one theory, they initially lived east of the Urals and migrated west to "Magna Hungaria" by 600 AD at the latest. Other scholars say Magna Hungaria was the Magyars' original homeland, from where they moved either to the region of the Don River or towards the Kuban River before the 830s AD. Hundreds of loan words adopted from Chuvash-type Turkic languages prove the Magyars were closely connected to Turkic peoples. Byzantine and Muslim authors regarded them as a Turkic people in the 9th and 10th centuries.

An alliance between the Magyars and the Bulgarians in the late 830s was the first historical event that was recorded with certainty in connection with the Magyars. According to the Byzantine Emperor Constantine VII Porphyrogenitus, the Magyars lived in Levedia in the vicinity of the Khazar Khaganate in the early 9th century and supported the Khazars in their wars "for three years". The Magyars were organized into tribes, each headed by their own

Figure 1: *A fastener from the 9th century, unearthed in Kirovohrad Oblast, Ukraine; the finding belongs to the "Subotcy horizon", attributed to the pre-conquest Hungarians*

"voivodes", or military leaders. After a Pecheneg invasion against Levedia, a group of Magyars crossed the Caucasus Mountains and settled in the lands south of the mountains, but the majority of the people fled to the steppes north of the Black Sea. From their new homeland, which was known as Etelköz, the Magyars controlled the lands between the Lower Danube and the Don River in the 870s. The confederation of their seven tribes was led by two supreme chiefs, the *kende* and the *gyula*. The Kabars – a group of rebellious subjects of the Khazars – joined the Magyars in Etelköz. The Magyars regularly invaded the neighboring Slavic tribes, forcing them to pay a tribute and seizing prisoners to be sold to the Byzantines. Taking advantage of the wars between Bulgaria, East Francia, and Moravia, they invaded Central Europe at least four times between 861 and 894. A new Pecheneg invasion compelled the Magyars to leave Etelköz, cross the Carpathian Mountains, and settle in the Carpathian Basin around 895.

Sources

Archaeology

Since the 1830s, archaeology has played an important role in the study of the Magyar prehistory.[2] Archaeologists have applied two methods; the so-called

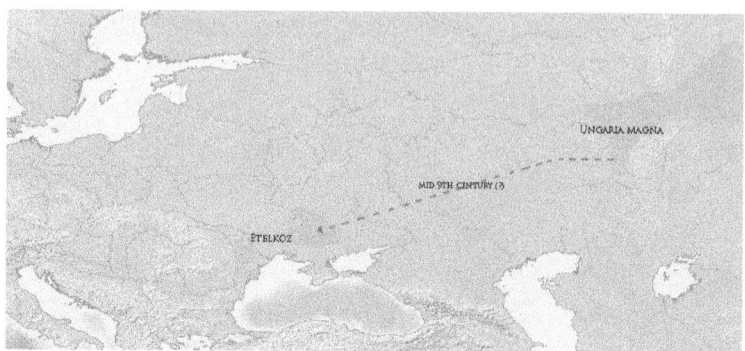

Figure 2: *Migration of Hungarians*

"linear method" attempts to determine the route of the migrating Magyars from their original homeland to the Carpathian Basin, while the "retrospective method" tries to discover the antecedents of 10th-century assemblages from the Carpathian Basin in the Eurasian steppes.[3,4] However, only twelve cemeteries in the steppes have yielded finds that show similarities to assemblages unearthed in the Carpathian Basin.[5] The dating of those cemeteries is also controversial.[5,6]

Both the scarcity of published archaeological material and the misdating of some sites may have contributed to the low number of archaeological sites that can be attributed to the Hungarians in the steppes, according to archaeologist László Kovács.[7] Kovács also says that the Hungarians' migration from the steppes and their settlement in the Carpathian Basin may have caused the development of a new material culture, rendering the identification of pre-conquest Hungarians difficult.[7] Archaeological research has demonstrated that the material culture of the Avars and other steppe peoples who settled in the Carpathian Basin before the Hungarians experienced a similarly significant change after they left the steppes and settled in their new homeland.[8]

Buckles, belt mounts, and other objects of the so-called "Subotcy horizon", which were unearthed at Caterinovca, Slobozia, and other sites along the middle course of the Dniester show similarities with archaeological finds from the 10th-century Carpathian Basin.[9] These objects were carbon dated to the late 9th century.[9] The same archaeological sites also yielded vessels similar to the pottery of the neighboring Slavic territories.[9]

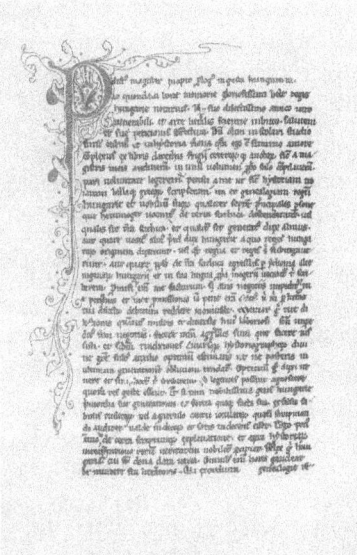

Figure 3: *The first page of the sole manuscript preserving the text of the Gesta Hungarorum, the earliest extant Hungarian chronicle*

Linguistics

The study of the Hungarian language is one of the main sources of the research on the ethnogenesis of the Hungarian people because a language shows the circumstances of its own development and its contacts with other idioms.[10,11] According to a scholarly theory, the oldest layers of Hungarian vocabulary show features of the territory in which the language emerged.[12] The study of loan words from other languages is instrumental in determining direct contacts between the ancient speakers of the Hungarian language and other peoples.[13,14] Loan words also reflect changes in the way of life of the Magyars.[15]

Written sources

Written sources on the prehistoric Hungarians may begin with Herodotus, who wrote of the Iyrcae, a people of equestrian hunters who lived next to the Thyssagetae.[16,17,18] Based on the location of the homeland of the Iyrcae and their ethnonym, Gyula Moravcsik, János Harmatta, and other scholars identify them as Hungarians; their view has not been universally accepted.[16,17,19,20] The 6th-century Byzantine historian John Malalas referred to a Hunnic tribal leader called Muageris, who ruled around 527 AD.[21] Moravcsik, Dezső Pais, and other historians connect Muageris's name to the Hungarians' endonym (Magyar); they say Malalas's report proves the presence of Magyar tribes in the region of the Sea of Azov in the early 6th century AD. This identification is rejected by most scholars.[20,22,23]

The Continuation of the Chronicle by Friar George, which was written in the middle of the 10th century, recorded the first historical event – an alliance between the Magyars and the Bulgarians in the late 830s – that can without doubt be connected to the Magyars.[24,25,26] The Byzantine Emperor Leo the Wise's *Tactics*, a book written around 904, contained a detailed description of their military strategies and way of life.[27] Emperor Constantine Porphyrogenitus's *De administrando imperio* ("On Governing the Empire"), which was completed between 948 and 952, preserves most information on the Magyars' early history.[28] Abu Abdallah al-Jayhani, the minister of Nasr II, ruler of the Samanid Empire, collected the reports of merchants who had traveled in the western regions of the Eurasian steppes in the 870s and 880s.[29,30,31] Although Al-Jayhani's work was lost, later Muslim scholars Ibn Rusta, Gardizi, Abu Tahir Marwazi, and Al-Bakri used his book, preserving important facts about the late 9th-century Magyars.[31,32] However, their works also contain interpolations from later periods.[31] Among the sources written in Western Europe, the longer version of the *Annals of Salzburg*, Regino of Prüm's *Chronicon*, the *Annals of Fulda*, and Liutprand of Cremona's *Antapodosis* ("Retribution"), provide contemporaneous or near-contemporaneous information of the 9th-century Magyars.[33] There are also references to the Magyars dwelling in the Pontic steppes in the legends of Cyril, Methodius and other early Slavic saints.[34] According to historian András Róna-Tas, information preserved in the *Russian Primary Chronicle*, which was completed in the 1110s, has to be "treated with extreme caution".[35]

The first Hungarian chronicles were written in the late 11th or early 12th centuries but their texts were preserved in manuscripts compiled in the 13th to 15th centuries.[36,37] Most extant chronicles show that the earliest works contained no information on the history of the Hungarians before their conversion to Christianity in the 11th century.[36] The only exception is the *Gesta Hungarorum*, which is the earliest extant Hungarian chronicle, whose principal subject is the Magyars' pagan past.[38] However, the reliability of this work, which was written by a former royal notary now known as Anonymus, is suspect.[39] In his monograph of medieval Hungarian historians, Carlile Aylmer Macartney describes it as "the most famous, the most obscure, the most exasperating and most misleading of all the early Hungarian texts".[40]

Ethnonyms

The Hungarians were mentioned under various ethnic names in Arabic, Byzantine, Slavic, and Western European sources in the 9th and 10th centuries.[41,42] Arabic scholars referred to them as *Magyars*, *Bashkirs*, or *Turks*; Byzantine authors mentioned them as *Huns*, *Ungrs*, *Turks*, or *Savards*; Slavic sources used the ethnonyms *Ugr* or *Peon*, and Western European authors wrote of *Hungrs*, *Pannons*, *Avars*, *Huns*, *Turks*, and *Agaren*.[42] According to the linguist Gyula Németh, the multiple ethnonyms – especially *Ungr*, *Savard*, and *Turk* – reflect that the Magyars had been integrated in various empires of the Eurasian steppes – the tribal confederations of the Onogurs and of the Sabirs, and the Turkic Khaganate – before gaining their independence.[43]

Ibn Rusta was the first to record a variant of the Hungarians' self-designation; *(al-Madjghariyya)*.[41] According to a scholarly theory, the ethnonym "Magyar" is a composite word.[44] The first part of the word *(magy-)* is said to have been connected to several recorded or hypothetical words, including the Mansi's self-designation *(mānśi)* and a reconstructed Ugric word for man *(*mańća)*.[45,46] The second part *(-er* or *-ar)* may have developed from a reconstructed Finno-Ugrian word for man or boy *(*irkä)* or from a Turkic word with a similar meaning *(eri* or *iri)*.[42] Alan W. Ertl writes that the ethnonym was initially the name of a smaller group, the Megyer tribe; it developed into an ethnonym because Megyer was the most powerful tribe within the people.[47] Most scholars agree that the Hungarian exonym and its variants were derived from the Onogurs' name.[41] This form started spreading in Europe with Slavic mediation.[48]

Legend of the Wondrous Hind

Most historians agree that the legend of the wondrous hind preserved the Hungarians' own myth of their origins.[49] The late 13th-century chronicler Simon of Kéza was the first to record it.[49] The legend says two brothers, Hunor and Magor, were the forefathers of the Huns and Hungarians.[49] They were the sons of Ménrót and his wife, Eneth.[49] While chasing a hind, they reached as far as the marches of the Sea of Azov, where they abducted the wives of Belar's sons and two daughters of Dula, the prince of the Alans.[49,50] According to historian Gyula Kristó, Eneth's name derived from the Hungarian word for hind *(ünő)*, showing that the Magyars regarded this animal as their totemistic ancestor.[51] Kristó also says the four personal names mentioned in the legend personify four peoples: the Hungarians (Magor), the Onogurs (Hunor), the Bulgars (Belar) and the Dula – kindred of the Alans or Bulgars (Dulo).[52] The hunt for a beast, ending with the arrival in a new homeland, was a popular legend among the peoples of the Eurasian steppes, including the Huns and the

Figure 4: *The "legend of the wondrous hind" depicted in the Illuminated Chronicle*

Mansi.[52] The myth that a people were descended from two brothers was also widespread.[53] Consequently, it is possible that Simon of Kéza did not record a genuine Hungarian legend, but borrowed it from foreign sources.[54]

> *After the confusion of tongues the giant [Ménrót] entered the land of Havilah, which is now called Persia, and there he begot two sons, Hunor and Mogor, by his wife Eneth. It was from them that the Huns, or Hungarians, took their origins. ... [A]s Hunor and Mogor were Ménrót's first born, they journeyed separately from their father in tents. Now it happened one day when they had gone out hunting in the Meotis marshes that they encountered a hind in the wilderness. As they went in pursuit of it, it fled before them. Then it disappeared from their sight altogether, and they could not find it no matter how long they searched. But as they were wandering through these marshes, they saw that the land was well suited for grazing cattle. They then returned to their father, and after obtaining his permission they took all their possessions and went to live in the Meotis marshes. ... So they entered the Meotis marshes and remained there for five years without leaving. Then in the sixth year they went out, and when by chance they discovered that the wives and children of the sons of Belar were camped in tents in a lonely place without their menfolk, they carried them off with all their belongings as fast as they could into the*

Meotis marshes. Two daughters of Dula, prince of the Alans, happened to be among the children who were seized. Hunor took one of them in marriage and Mogor the other, and to these women all the Huns owe their origin.

—Simon of Kéza: *Gesta Hunnorum et Hungarorum*[55]

Historiography

Medieval theories

According to the *Annals of St. Bertin*, the Magyars who invaded East Francia in 862[56] were enemies "hitherto unknown"[57] to the local population.[58] Likewise, Regino of Prüm wrote that the Magyars had been "unheard of in the previous centuries because they were not named".[59] in the sources.[58] Both remarks evince that late 9th-century authors had no knowledge of the Magyars' origins.[58,60] However, the Magyar raids reminded the Western European and Byzantine scholars of earlier historians' descriptions of the Scythians or Huns, which gave rise to their identification with those peoples.[58,61] For instance, Leo the Wise listed the Hungarians among the "Scythian nations".[62,63] The similarity between the Latin ethnonyms *Huni* and *Hungari* strengthened the identification of the two peoples, which became commonplace in Western Europe in the 11th century.[63] The *Chronicon Eberspergense* was the first source that clearly stated that the Huns and the Hungarians were the same people.[63]

The earliest Hungarian chronicles adopted the idea that the Huns and Hungarians were closely related.[64] Anonymus did not mention the Huns, but he referred to Attila the Hun as a ruler "from whose line Prince Álmos",[65] the supreme head of the Magyar tribes, descended.[66] However, Simon of Kéza explicitly identified the Huns and the Hungarians in the 1280.[67,68] He started his chronicle with a book of the history of the Huns, thus presenting the Hungarian conquest of the Carpathian Basin as the reoccupation of a land inherited from their ancestors.[38] Thereafter the identification of the two peoples was the basic theory of the origins of the Hungarians for centuries.[61]

Modern scholarship

Scholarly attempts in the early 18th century to prove a relationship between the Finns and the Huns led to the realization of the similarities between the Finnish and Hungarian languages.[69] János Sajnovics's *Demonstratio*, the first systematic comparative study of Hungarian and the Saami languages, was published in 1770.[70,71] Three decades later, Sámuel Gyarmathi demonstrated similarities between a larger group of languages that are now known as Uralic languages.[71] However, the majority of Hungarian scholars only gradually adopted

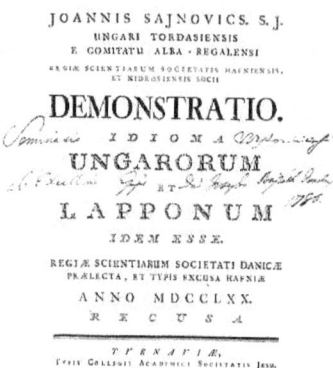

Figure 5: *The title page of János Sajnovics's Demonstratio, the first systematic study of the comparison of the Hungarian and Saami languages*

Sajnovics's and Gyarmathi's views.[72,73] In the 1830s, Pál Hunfalvy still wrote that Hungarian had an intermediate position between the Finnish and Turkic languages, but later accepted that Hungarian is closely related to the Mansi and Khanty languages.[72] Hereafter linguistics played a pre-eminent role in the research of the Magyars' prehistory because it was always the dominant linguistic theory that determined the interpretation of historical and archaeological evidence.[73] Consequently, as historian Nóra Berend writes, Hungarian prehistory is "a tenuous construct based on linguistics, folklore analogies, archaeology, and later written evidence", because there are no certain records of the Magyars before the 9th century and the identification of archaeological cultures with peoples is highly debatable.[74] Historian László Kontler identifies "the history of Hungarian origins" as "the history of a community whose genetic composition and cultural character has been changing, but which has assuredly spoken Hungarian or its predecessor language".[75]

According to mainstream scholarly consensus, the Hungarians are not the autochthonous population of the Carpathian Basin.[76] Their ancestors arrived there through a series of westward migrations across the Eurasian steppes around 894, centuries after their departure from their original homeland located somewhere in the East.[76] Many details of the Magyars' prehistory – the location of their original homeland, the ancient Magyars' connections with

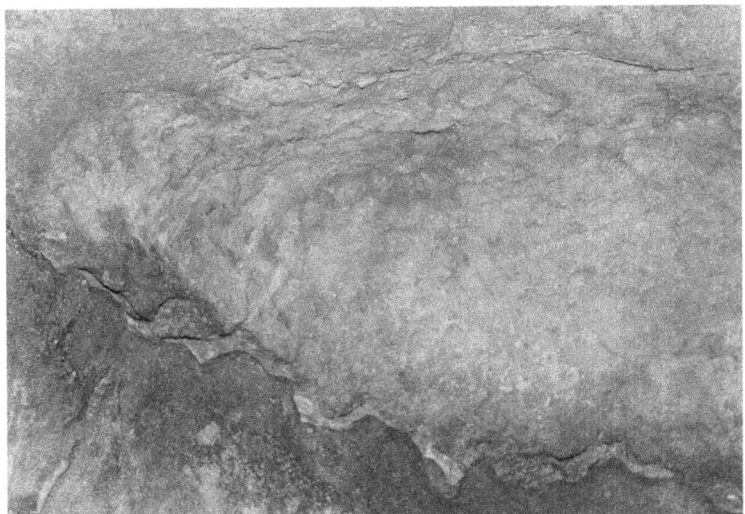

Figure 6: *Cave painting in the Ignateva Cave in the Ural Mountains*

the Turkic peoples and the Khazar Khaganate, their lifestyle and political organization, and the background of their conquest of the Carpathian Basin – are still subject to scholarly debates.[77] With regard of the connections between the Magyars and the Turkic tribes, archaeologist Gyula László mooted an alternative theory in the 1960s.[78] According to his theory of the "double conquest", a large group of people who spoke a Finno-Ugrian language arrived in the Carpathian Basin in 670, and a Turkic-speaking people conquered the same territory in the late 9th century.[78] László's theory has never been widely accepted.[79]

Formation of the Magyar people

Before the separation of the Hungarian language (before c. 800 BC)

Hungarian has traditionally been classified as an Ugric language within the family of Uralic languages, but alternative views exist.[75,80,81] For instance, linguist Tapani Salminen rejects the existence of a Proto-Ugric language, saying Hungarian was a member of an "areal genetic unit" that also included Permic languages. Paleolinguistic research suggests the speakers of the Proto-Uralic language lived in a territory where four trees – larch, silver fir, spruce, and elm – grew together.[82,83] The study of pollen in fossils shows these trees could be found on both sides of the Ural Mountains along the rivers Ob, Pechora, and Kama in the 4th millennium BC.[84,85] The land between the Urals and the Kama was sparsely inhabited during this period.[86] From around 3600 BC, the Neolithic material culture of the wider region of the Urals spread over vast territories to the west and east.[87] Regional variants emerged, showing the appearance of groups of people who had no close contact with each other.[87]

About 1000 basic words of the Hungarian language – including the names of the seasons and natural phenomena, and the most frequently used verbs – had cognates in other Finno-Ugric languages, suggesting the temporary existence of a Proto-Finno-Ugric language.[88] Between around 2600 and 2100 BC, climatic changes caused the spread of swamps on both sides of the Urals, forcing groups of inhabitants to leave their homelands.[89] The Finno-Ugric linguistic unity disappeared and new languages emerged around 2000 BC.[90,91] Whether the groups speaking the language from which Hungarian emerged lived to the east or to the west of the Urals in this period is debated by historians.[88]

Further climate changes occurring between 1300 and 1000 BC caused the northward expansion of the steppes by about 200–300 kilometres (120–190 mi), compelling the southernmost Ugric groups to adopt a nomadic lifestyle.[88,92,93] Around 800 BC, the climate again changed with the beginning of a wetter period, forcing the nomadic Ugric groups to start a southward migration, following the grasslands.[88,94] Their movement separated them from the northern Ugric groups, which gave rise to the development of the language from which modern Hungarian emerged.[95] According to historian László Kontler, the concept of the "sky-high tree" and some other elements of Hungarian folklore seem to have been inherited from the period of the Finno-Ugric unity.[96] The melodies of the most common Hungarian funeral songs show similarities to tunes of Khanty epic songs.[97]

Original homeland (c. 800 BC – before 600 AD)

The stag and the eagle, which are popular motifs of 10th-century Magyar art, have close analogies in Scythian art.[98] The Scythians, Sarmatians, and other peoples who spoke Iranian languages dominated the Eurasian steppes between around 800 BC and 350 AD.[99,100] During this period, all ethnic groups in the steppes were nomads with almost identical material cultures, for which the certain identification of the Magyars is impossible.[100] Consequently, the location of their original homeland is subject to scholarly debates.[101] Róna-Tas says the development of Hungarian started in the region of the rivers Kama and Volga, west of the Urals.[102] Archaeologist István Fodor writes that the original homeland lay to the east of the Urals.[103] He says that some features of the *tumuli* erected at Chelyabinsk in the 4th century BC, including the northward orientation of the heads of the deceased and the geometric motifs on the clay

Hungarian prehistory

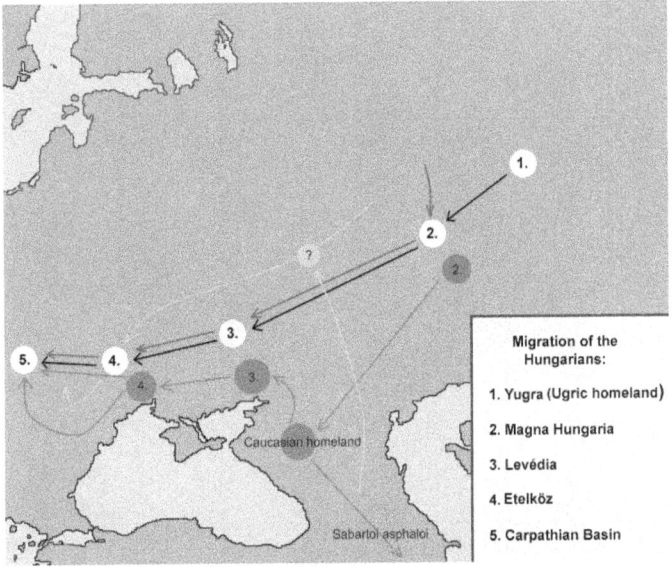

Figure 7: *A map depicting the theories of the Magyars' proposed Urheimats and their migrations*

vessels put in the graves, are similar to older burials that he attributes to Ugric peoples.[104]

Migrations

Early westward migrations (before 600 AD – c. 750 or 830 AD)

In the 1230s, Friar Julian went to search for the Magyars' legendary homeland Magna Hungaria after reading about it and a group of Magyars who had remained there in a Hungarian chronicle.[105,106] He met a Hungarian-speaking group "beside the great Etil river" (the Volga or the Kama) in the land of the Volga Bulgars, in or in the wider region of present-day Bashkortostan in Eastern Europe.[107,108] Whether Magna Hungaria was the original homeland of the Magyars, or whether the Magyars' ancestors settled in Magna Hungaria after their migration to Europe from their Western Siberian original homeland is still subject to scholarly debates.[109,103,110] According to a third scholarly theory, Magna Hungaria was neither the Magyars' original homeland nor their first homeland in Europe. Instead, the ancestors of the Eastern Magyars whom Friar Julian met had moved to Magna Hungaria from the south.[111]

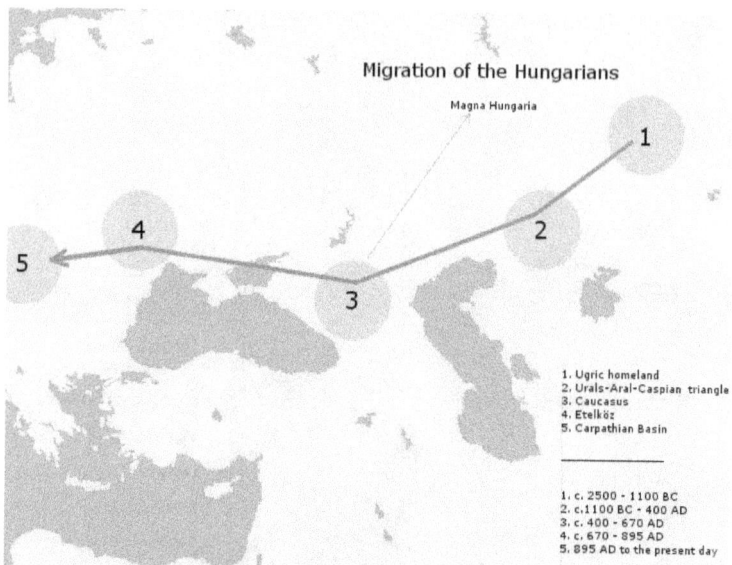

Figure 8: *A map depicting Péter Veres's theory of the Magyars' Urheimat and of their migrations, including their staying in the region of the Kuban River*

According to a scholarly theory, the name of at least one Magyar tribe, Gyarmat, is connected to the name of a Bashkir group, Yurmatï.[112] Specific burial rites – the use of death masks and the placing of parts of horses into the graves – featuring a 9th- or 10th-century cemetery at the confluence of the Volga and Kama near present-day Bolshie Tigany in Bashkortostan are also evidenced among the Magyars who lived in the Carpathian Basin in the 10th century.[113,114] Most specialists say that the cemetery at Bolshie Tigany was used by Magyars who either remained in Magna Hungaria when other Magyar groups left the territory, or who moved there from other regions which were inhabited by the Magyars during their migrations.[113,114]

If the Magyars' original homeland was situated in Western Siberia, instead of being identical with Magna Hungaria, their ancestors moved from Western Siberia to Eastern Europe.[101] This must have happened between 500 BC and 700 AD, because there were several major movements of peoples across the steppes during this period.[115] The "Prohorovo culture" spread towards modern-day Bashkortostan around 400 BC.[115] The westward migration of the Huns forced many groups of people of Western Siberia to depart for Europe between about 350 and 400 AD.[115] The Avars' attack against the Sabirs in Siberia set in motion a number of migrations in the 460s.[101] Between around

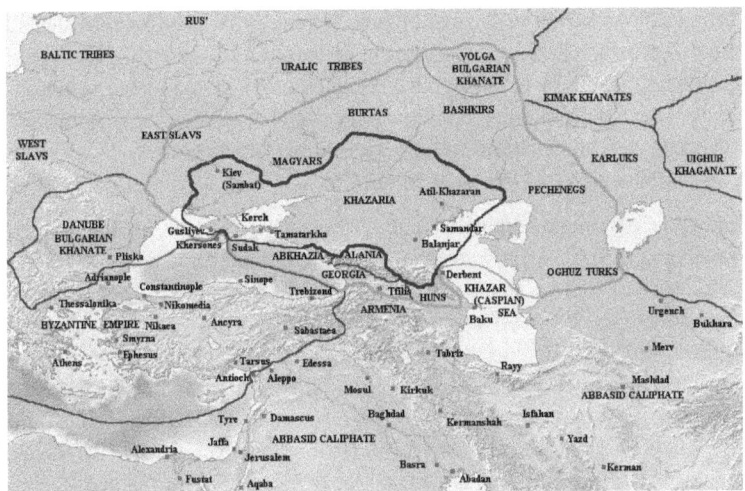

Figure 9: *The Khazar Khaganate around 830*

550 and 600, the migration of the Avars towards Europe compelled many nomadic groups to move.[116]

The arrival of the Huns ended the dominance of Iranian peoples in the Eurasian steppes.[117] Thereafter the Sabirs, Avars, Onoghurs, Khazars, and other Turkic peoples controlled the grasslands of Eastern Europe for centuries.[118] Gardizi described the Magyars as "a branch of the Turks"; Leo the Wise and Constantine Porphyrogenitus called them Turks.[56] About 450 Hungarian words were borrowed from Turkic languages before around 900.[119] The oldest layer of Hungarian folk songs show similarities to Chuvash songs.[97] These facts show the Magyars were closely connected to the Turks while they stayed in the Pontic steppes.[120]

Gyula Németh, András Róna-Tas and other scholars write that for centuries, the Magyars lived around the Kuban River, to the north of the Caucasus Mountains.[121,122] They say it was there that the Magyars adopted the Turkic terminology of viticulture, including *bor* ("wine") and *seprő* ("dregs"), and the Turkic names of cornel *(som)*, grapes *(szőlő)* and some other fruits.[123] According to these scholars, the Hungarian words of Alanic origin – including *asszony* ("lady", originally "noble or royal lady") – were also borrowed in the same region.[50]

Levedia (c. 750 or 830 – c. 850)

The Khazar Khaganate was the dominant power in the steppes between the rivers Dnieper and Volga after around 650.[124,125] Archaeological finds show that the Khagans controlled a multi-ethnic empire.[126,127] The "Saltovo-Mayaki culture", which flourished in the same region around 750 and 900, had at least seven variants.[128] In the Hungarian chronicles, the legend of the wondrous hind seems to have preserved the memory of the Magyars' "close symbiosis, intermarriages, and incipient fusion" with various ethnic groups – Alans, Bulgars, and Onogurs – of this large region.[126]

Emperor Constantine Porphyrogenitus wrote that the Magyars "had of old their dwelling next to Chazaria, in the place called Levedia,"[129] adding that "a river Chidmas, also called Chingilous" ran through this territory.[130] The identification of the (one or two) rivers is uncertain.[131,132] Porphyrogenitus associated Levedia with the whole territory dominated by the Magyars, but most modern historians agree that he only described a smaller region situated on the Don River.[133] The period when the Magyars settled in Levedia is also uncertain; this happened either before 750 (István Fodor) or around 830 (Gyula Kristó).[134,135] Porphyrogenitus said that the Magyars had been named "Sabartoi asphaloi", or "steadfast Savarts", while staying in Levedia.[131,136] Róna-Tas says the ethnonym is an invented term with no historical credibility.[136] Based on the same denomination, Károly Czeglédy, Dezső Dümmerth, Victor Spinei, and other historians associated the Magyars either with the late 6th-century Sabirs or with the Suvar tribe of the Volga Bulgars.[136,137,138]

Porphyroneitus wrote that the Magyars "lived together with the Chazars for three years, and fought in alliance with the Chazars in all their wars", which suggests that the Magyars were subjugated to the Khazar Khagan, according to a scholarly view.[139,140] On the other hand, historian György Szabados says, the emperor's words prove the equal position of the Magyars and the Khazars, instead of the Magyars' subjugation to the Khagan.[141] Although the emperor said that the Magyars' cohabitation with the Khazars lasted only for three years, modern historians tend to propose a longer period (20, 30, 100, 150, 200 or even 300 years).[139,142]

According to a memorial stone erected in or before 831, a Bulgarian military commander named Okorsis drowned in the Dnieper during a military campaign.[143] Florin Curta says this inscription may be the "'first clue' to the upheaval on the steppes created by the migration of the Magyars into the lands between the Dnieper and the Danube".[144] The earliest certainly identifiable events of the Magyars' history occurred in the 830s.[145] The Bulgarians hired them to fight against their Byzantine prisoners, who rebelled and tried to return to Macedonia in the late 830s, but the Byzantines routed them on the banks on the Lower Danube.[24] According to the *Annals of St. Bertin*, Rus' envoys who visited Constantinople in 839 could only return to their homeland through the Carolingian Empire because "the route by which they had reached Constantinople had taken them through primitive tribes that were very fierce and

Figure 10: *The "seven captains" of the Magyars depicted in the Illuminated Chronicle*

savage";[146] Curta and Kristó identify those tribes with the Magyars.[147,148] Ibn Rusta wrote that the Khazars "used to be protected from attack by the Magyars and other neighboring peoples" by a ditch.[149,150] According to a scholarly theory, Ibn Rusta's report shows that the Khazar fort at Sarkel, which was built in the 830s, was one of the forts protecting the Khazars against the Magyars.[151,150]

According to Porphyrogenitus, In Levedia, the Magyars "were seven clans, but they had never had over them a prince either native or foreign, but there were among them 'voivodes'", or chiefs.[152,153] Although the exact meaning of the term the emperor used *(genea)* cannot be exactly determined, scholars have traditionally considered the Magyar "clans" or "tribes" as ethnic and territorial units.[154] In the Hungarian chronicles, references to "seven leading persons"[155] or "seven captains"[156] denote the existence of seven Magyar tribes.[157]

Porphyrogenitus said the tribes did not "obey their own particular [voivodes], but [had] a joint agreement to fight together with all earnestness and zeal ... wheresoever war breaks out",[158] suggesting the tribal chiefs were military rather than political leaders.[159] According to Kristó, the emperor's report also shows the tribal confederation was not a "solid political formation with strong cohesion" in the early 9th century.[152] The *Gesta Hungarorum* referred to the seven Magyar chiefs as "Hetumoger", or "Seven Magyars".[157,160] Similar ethnonyms – including Toquz Oghuz ("Nine Oghuzes") and Onogur ("Ten Ogurs") – suggest the *Gesta* preserved the name of the confederation of the Magyar tribes.[157,161] According to Porphyrogenitus, Levedia was named after Levedi, one of the Magyar voivodes.[162,163] During Levedi's life, the Kangars, a distinct group within the Pechenegs' tribal confederation whom the Khazars had expelled from their homeland, invaded Levedia and forced the Magyars to cede the territory.[164,165] A Magyar group fled across the Caucasus Mountains as far as Persia.[166] However, the masses departed for the West and settled in a region called Etelköz.[138] Most historians agree the Magyars' forced exodus from Levedia occurred around 850.[167]

> [T]*he Pechenegs who were previously called "Kangar" (for this "Kangar" was a name signifying nobility and valour among them), these, then, stirred up war against the [Khazars] and, being defeated, were forced to quit their own land and to settle in that of the [Magyars]. And when battle was joined between the [Magyars] and the Pechenegs who were at that time called "Kangar", the army of the [Magyars] was defeated and split into two parts. One part went eastwards and settled in the region of Persia, and they to this day are called by the ancient denomination of the [Magyars] "Sabartoi asphaloi"; but the other part, together with their voivode and chief [Levedi], settled in the western regions, in places called [Etelköz] ... .*
>
> —Constantine Porphyrogenitus: De Administrando Imperio[168]

Etelköz (c. 850 – c. 895)

Constantine Porphyrogenitus identified **Etelköz** with the lands where the rivers "Barouch", "Koubou", "Troullos", "Broutos", and "Seretos"[169] run.[170] The identification of the last three rivers with the Dniester, the Prut, and the Siret is without debate, but the traditional identification of the Barouch with the Dnieper and the Koubou with the Southern Bug is refuted by Spinei.[170,171] Al-Jayhani wrote that the Magyars' territory was located between two rivers named *"tl"* and *"dwb"* in the 870s.[172] According to modern scholars, *tl* may refer to the Volga, the Don, or the Dnieper; *dwb* is identified as the Danube.[172,173,50] According to the *Gesta Hungarorum*, the Magyars lived in "Scythia" or "Dentumoger";[174] the latter name, which refers to the Don River, suggests the Magyars inhabited the eastern regions of the Pontic steppes, according to Spinei.[175]

The Khazar Khagan sent his envoys to the Magyars shortly after they fled from Levedia and settled in Etelköz, according to Porphyrogenitus. The Khagan invited Levedi to a meeting, proposing to make Levedi the supreme head

Figure 11: *Álmos depicted in the Illuminated Chronicle: he was the first head of the federation of the Magyar tribes, according to the Hungarian chronicles*

of the confederation of the Magyar tribes in exchange for the acceptance of his suzerainty.[176,177,177] Instead of accepting the offer, Levedi suggested the new rank should be offered to another voivode, Álmos, or the latter's son, Árpád.[177] The Khagan accepted Levedi's proposal and upon his demand the Magyar chiefs proclaimed Árpád their head.[177,178] According to Kristó and Spinei, Porphyrogenitus' report preserved the memory of the creation of a central office within the federation of the Magyar tribes.[178,179] Róna-Tas says the story relates only a "change of dynasty"; the fall of Levedi's family and the emergence of the Árpád dynasty.[180] In contrast with Porphyrogenitus's story, the *Gesta Hungarorum* says it was not Árpád, but his father who was elected the first supreme prince of the Magyars.[181]

According to Muslim scholars, the Magyars had two supreme leaders, the *kende* and the *gyula*, the latter being their ruler in the 870s.[182] Their report implies the Khagan granted a Khazar title to the head of the federation of the Magyar tribes; Ibn Fadlan recorded that the third Khazar dignitary was styled *kündür* in the 920s.[183] The Muslim scholar's report also implies the Magyars adopted the Khazar system of "dual kingship", whereby supreme power was divided between a sacred ruler (the *kende*) and a military leader (the *gyula*).[178,184,185]

Figure 12: *Álmos's son, Árpád, depicted in the Illuminated Chronicle: he was the first head of the federation of the Magyar tribes, according to the Byzantine Emperor Constantine VII Porphyrogenitus*

> *Between the country of the [Pechenegs] and the country of the Iskil, which belongs to the [Volga Bulgars], lies the first of the Magyar frontiers. ... Their chief rides at the head of 20,000 horsemen. He is named kundah, but the one who actually rules them is called jilah. All the Magyars implicitly obey this ruler in wars of offence and defence. ... Their territory is vast, extending to the Black Sea, into which two rivers flow, one larger than the Oxus. Their campsites are located between these two rivers.*
>
> *—Ibn Rusta: On the Magyars*

Porphyrogenitus wrote that the Kabars – a group of Khazars who rebelled against the Khagan – joined the Magyars in Etelköz at an unspecified time,[186,187] suggesting that the Magyars had got rid of the Khagan's suzerainty.[188] The Kabars were organized into three tribes, but a single chieftain commanded them.[189,188] Porphyrogenitus also wrote that the Kabars "were promoted to be first" tribe, because they showed themselves "the strongest and most valorous"[190] of the tribes.[191] Accordingly, the Kabars formed the Magyars' vanguard, because nomadic peoples always placed the associated tribes in the most vulnerable position.[191,188]

Ibn Rusta wrote that the Magyars subjected the neighboring Slavic peoples, imposing "a heavy tribute on them" and treating them as prisoners.[192] The Magyars also "made piratical raids on the Slavs" and sold those captured during these raids to the Byzantines in Kerch on the Crimean peninsula.[192,138] A band of Magyar warriors attacked the future Saint Cyril the Philosopher "howling like wolves and wishing to kill him"[193] in the steppes near the Crimea, according to the saint's legend.[147] However, Cyril convinced them to "release him and his entire retinue in peace".[147] The inhabitants of the regions along the left bank of the Dniester – whom the *Russian Primary Chronicle* identified as Tivertsi – fortified their settlements in the second half of the 9th century, which seems to be connected to the Magyars' presence.[194]

A plundering raid in East Francia in 862 was the Magyars' first recorded military expedition in Central Europe.[195,56] This raid may have been initiated by Rastislav of Moravia, who was at war with Louis the German, according to Róna-Tas and Spinei.[196,197] The longer version of the *Annals of Salzburg* said the Magyars returned to East Francia and ransacked the region of Vienna in 881.[196,56] The same source separately mentioned the *Cowari*, or Kabars, plundering the region of Kulmberg or Kollmitz in the same year, showing that the Kabars formed a distinct group.[198,199] In the early 880s, a "king" of the Magyars had an amicable meeting with Methodius, Archbishop of Moravia, who was returning from Constantinople to Moravia, according to Methodius' legend.[200,147,201,202,203]

> When the King of Hungary came to the lands of the Danube, Methodius wished to see him. And though some were assuming and saying: "He will not escape torment," Methodius went to [the king]. And as befits a sovereign, [the king] received [Methodius] with honor, solemnity, and joy. Having conversed with [Methodius] as befits such men to converse, [the king] dismissed [Methodius] with an embrace and many gifts. Kissing him, [the king] said: "O venerable Father, remember me always in your holy prayers."
>
> — *The Life of Methodius*[204]

The Hungarian Conquest (c. 895 – 907)

The Magyars returned to Central Europe in July 892, when they invaded Moravia in alliance with Arnulf, king of East Francia.[205,206,207] Two years later, they stormed into the March of Pannonia.[205,188] According to the *Annals of Fulda*, they "killed men and old women outright, and carried out the young women alone with them like cattle to satisfy their lusts".[208,209] Although this source does not refer to an alliance between the Magyars and Svatopluk I of Moravia, most historians agree the Moravian ruler persuaded them to invade

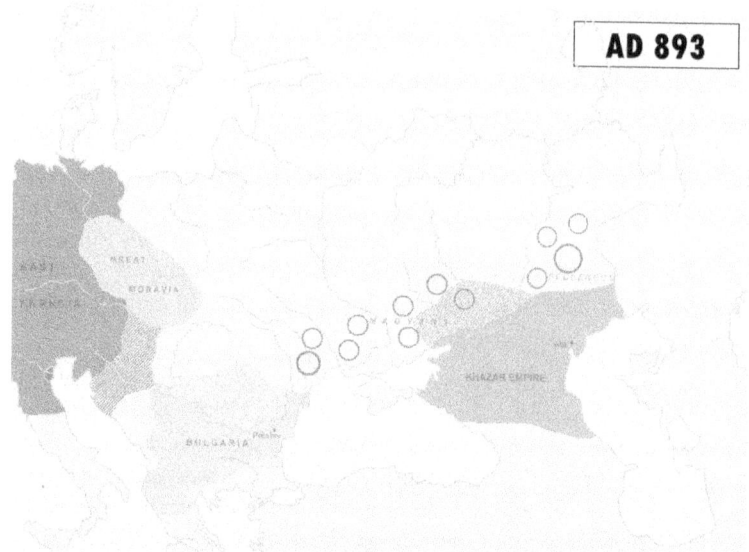

Figure 13: *The Hungarian conquest of the Carpathian Basin*

East Francia.[205,188,209] During their raids in the Carpathian Basin, the Magyars had several opportunities to collect information on their future homeland.[188]

The Samanid emir, Isma'il ibn Ahmad, launched an expedition against the Oghuz Turks in 893, forcing them to invade the Pechenegs' lands between the Volga and Ural rivers.[199,210,211] After being expelled from their homeland, the Pechenegs departed for the west in search of new pastures.[211] The Magyars had in the meantime invaded Bulgaria in alliance with the Byzantine Emperor Leo the Wise.[212] Simeon I of Bulgaria sent envoys to the Pechenegs and persuaded them to storm into Etelköz.[213] The unexpected invasion destroyed the unguarded dwelling places of the Magyars, forcing them to leave the Pontic steppes and seek refuge over the Carpathian Mountains.[214] The Magyars occupied their new homeland in several phases,[215] initially settling the lands east of the Danube[216] and only invading the March of Pannonia after Arnulf of East Francia died in 899.[217] They destroyed Moravia before 906 and consolidated their control of the Carpathian Basin through their victory over a Bavarian army in the Battle of Brezalauspurc in 907.[218]

Figure 14: *Traditional Khanty fishing equipment*

Way of life

Economy

Most Neolithic settlements were situated on the banks of rivers and lakes in the proposed original homeland of the Uralic peoples, but no houses have been excavated there.[219] The local inhabitants primarily used tools made of stone – especially jasper from the southern Urals – , bone and wood, but baked clay vessels decorated with broken or wavy lines were also found.[220] Their economy was based on fishing, hunting, and gathering.[221] The basic Hungarian words connected to these activities – *háló* (net), *íj* (bow), *nyíl* (arrow), *ideg* (bowstring), and *mony* (egg) – are inherited from the Proto-Uralic period.[222,223] Paleolithic drawings on rocks in the Urals depict scenes of hunting for reindeer and moose.[75] The Hungarian words for house *(ház)*, dwelling *(lak)*, door *(ajtó)*, and bed *(ágy)* are of Proto-Finno-Ugric origin.[224] Houses built in the presumed Finno-Ugric homeland in the wider region of the Urals in the 3rd millennium BC show regional differences; in the valley of the Sosva River, square pit-houses were dug deep into the ground; along the Kama River, rectangular semi-pit houses were built.[225] The local people were hunter-gatherers.[88] They used egg-shaped, baked clay vessels that were decorated with rhombuses, triangles, and other geometrical forms.[226] They buried their dead in shallow graves and showered the bodies with red ochre.[227] They

Figure 15: *10th-century artifacts from a grave of a wealthy woman, unearthed at Szeged-Bojárhalom*

also placed objects including tools, jewels made of pierced boar tusks, and small pendants in the form of animal heads into the graves.[228] Copper objects found in the graves, which were manufactured in the Caucasus Mountains, indicate that the inhabitants of the lands on both sides of the Ural Mountains had trading contacts with faraway territories around 2000 BC.[229] Words from the Proto-Ugric period – *ló* ("horse"), *nyereg* ("saddle"), *fék* ("bridle"), and *szekér* ("wagon") – show that those who spoke this language rode horses.[230] Animal husbandry spread on both sides of the Urals from around 1500 BC.[231] The bones of domestic animals – cattle, goats, sheep, pigs, and horses – comprised 90% of all animal bones excavated in many settlements.[232] Loan words from Proto-Iranian suggest the Ugric-speaking populations adopted animal husbandry from neighboring peoples.[88,233] For instance, the Hungarian words for cow *(tehén)* and milk *(tej)* are of Proto-Iranian origin.[88] Archaeological finds – including seeds of millet, wheat, and barley, and tools including sickles, hoes, and spade handles – prove the local population also cultivated arable lands.[234]

The Magyars' ancestors gave up their settled way of life because of the northward expansion of the steppes during the last centuries of the 2nd millennium BC.[88,93] Ethnographic studies of modern nomadic populations suggest cyclic migrations – a year-by-year movement between their winter and summer camps – featured in their way of life, but they also cultivated arable lands around their winter camps.[235] Most historians agree the Magyars had a mixed nomadic or semi-nomadic economy, characterized by both the raising of cattle and the cultivation of arable lands.[11] Turkic loanwords in the Hungarian language show the Magyars adopted many practices of animal husbandry and agriculture from Turkic peoples between the 5th and 9th centuries.[236] For instance, the Hungarian words for hen (tyúk), pig *(disznó)*, castrated hog *(ártány)*, bull *(bika)*, ox *(ökör)*, calf *(borjú)*, steer *(tinó)*, female cow *(ünő)*, goat *(kecske)*, camel *(teve)*, ram *(kos)*, buttermilk (író), shepherd's cloak *(köpönyeg)*, badger *(borz)*, fruit *(gyümölcs)*, apple *(alma)*, pear *(körte)*, grape *(szőlő)*, dogwood *(som)*, sloe *(kökény)*, wheat *(búza)*, barley *(árpa)*, pea *(borsó)*, hemp *(kender)*, pepper *(borz)*, nettle *(csalán)*, garden *(kert)*, plough *(eke)*, ax *(balta)*, scutcher *(tiló)*, oakum *(csepű)*, weed *(gyom)*, refuse of grain *(ocsú)*, fallow land *(tarló)*, and sickle *(sarló)* are of Turkic origin.[236] Most loanwords were borrowed from Bulgar or other Chuvash-type Turkic language, but the place and the time of the borrowings are uncertain.[237] The Magyars' connections with the people of the Saltovo-Mayaki culture may have contributed to the development of their agriculture, according to Spinei.[238]

According to Ibn Rusta, the late 9th-century Magyars "dwell in tents and move from place to place in search of pasturage", but during the winters they settled along the nearest river, where they lived by fishing.[239,240] He also said their "land is well watered and harvests abundant", showing they had arable lands, although it is unclear whether those lands were cultivated by the Magyars themselves or by their prisoners.[238] Taxes collected from the neighboring peoples, a slave trade, and plundering raids made the Magyars a wealthy people.[241] Gardezi wrote that they were "a handsome people and of good appearance and their clothes are of silk brocade and their weapons are of silver and are encrusted with pearls",[242] proving their growing wealth.[203] However, 9th-century Byzantine and Muslim coins have rarely been found in the Pontic steppes.[243]

Archaeological finds from the Carpathian Basin provide evidence of the crafts practiced by the Magyars.[244] 10th-century warriors' graves yielding sabres, arrow-heads, spear-heads, stirrups, and snaffle bits made of iron show that blacksmiths had a pre-eminent role in the militarized Magyar society.[245,244] Engraved or gilded sabres and sabretache plates – often decorated with precious stones – and golden or silver pectoral disks evidence the high levels of skills of Magyar gold- and silversmiths.[246,247] Cemeteries in the Carpathian Basin also yielded scraps of canvas made of flax or hemp.[248] The positioning of metal buttons in the graves shows the Magyars wore clothes that either opened down the front or were fastened at the neck.[249] Ear-rings were the only accessories worn above the belt by Magyar warriors; jewelry on their upper bodies would have hindered them from firing arrows.[250] In contrast, Magyar women wore head jewelry decorated with leaf-like pendants, ear-rings, decorated pectoral disks, and rings with gemstones.[251]

A man seeking a bride was expected to pay a bride price to her father before the marriage took place, according to Gardizi's description of the late 9th-century Magyars.[252] The Hungarian word for bridegroom – *vőlegény* from *vevő legény* ("purchasing lad") – and the expression *eladó lány* (verbatim, "bride for sale") confirm the reliability of the Muslim author's report.[253,254] A decree of Stephen I of Hungary prohibiting the abduction of a girl without her parents' consent implies that pretended abduction of the bride by her future husband was an integral part of ancient Magyar matrimonial ceremonies.[253,254]

Military

The Magyars' military tactics were similar to those of the Huns, Avars, Pechenegs, Mongols, and other nomadic peoples.[255,256] According to Emperor Leo the Wise, the main components of Magyar warfare were long-distance arrow-fire, surprise attack, and feigned retreat.[257,258] However, the contemporaneous Regino of Prüm said the Magyars knew "nothing about ... taking besieged cities".[259,239] Archaeological research confirms Leo the Wise's report of the use of sabres, bows, and arrows.[260] However, in contrast with the emperor's report, spears have rarely been found in Magyar warriors' tombs.[261] Their most important weapons were bone-reinforced reflex bows,[262] with which they could shoot at a specific target within 60–70 metres (200–230 ft).[263]

> *In battle [the Magyars] do not line up as do the [Byzantines] in three divisions, but in several units of irregular size, linking the divisions close to one another although separated by short distances, so that they give the impression of one battle line. Apart from their battle line, they maintain an additional force that they send out to ambush careless adversaries of theirs or hold in reserve to support a hard-pressed section. ... Frequently they tie the extra horses together to the rear, that is, behind their battle line, as protection for it. They make the depth of the files, that is, the rows, of their battle line irregular because they consider it more important that the line should be thick than deep, and they make their front even and dense. They prefer battles fought at long range, ambushes, encircling their adversaries, simulated withdrawals and wheeling about, and scattered formations.*
>
> —*Leo the Wise: Tactics*[264]

Religion

Modern scholarly theories of the Magyars' pagan religious beliefs and practices are primarily based on reports by biased medieval authors and prohibitions enacted during the reigns of Christian kings.[265] Both Christian and Muslim sources say the Magyars worshipped forces of nature.[265] They gave offering to trees, fountains, and stones, and made sacrifices at wells; these are evidenced by the prohibition of such practices during the reign of Ladislaus I of Hungary in the late 11th century.[266] In accordance with the custom of the peoples of the Eurasian steppes, the pagan Magyars swore oaths on dogs, which were bisected to warn potential oathbrakers of their fate.[265] Simon of Kéza also wrote about the sacrifice of horses.[267] According to the *Gesta Hungarorum*, the seven Magyar chiefs confirmed their treaty "in pagan manner with their own blood spilled in a single vessel".[267]

Scholars studying the Magyars' religion also take into account ethnographic analogies, folklore, linguistic evidence, and archaeological research.[268] Artifacts depicting a bird of prey or a tree of life imply both symbols were important elements of the Magyar religion.[267] Trepanation – the real or symbolic wounding of the cranium – was widely practiced by 10th-century Magyars.[269] Gyula László writes that real trepanations – the opening of the skull with a chiesel and the closing of the wound with a sheet of silver – were actually surgical operations similarly to those already practiced by Arab physicians, whereas symbolic trepanations – the marking of the skull with an incised circle – were aimed at the disposal of a protective talisman on the head.[270] According to Róna-Tas, a Hungarian word for cunning, *(agyafúrt)* – verbatim "with a drilled brain" – may reflect these ancient practices.[271]

The Magyars buried their dead, laying the deceased on their backs with the arms resting along their bodies or upon their pelvises.[272,273] A deceased warrior's tomb always contained material connected with his horse.[274] These are most frequently its skin, skull, and the lower legs; these were put into its master's grave, but occasionally only the harness was buried together with the warrior, or the horse's skin was stuffed with hay.[273,275] The Magyars rolled the corpses in textiles or mats and placed silver plates on the eyes and the mouth.[276]

Scholarly theories note the similarities between the *táltos* of Hungarian folklore and Siberian shamans, but the existence of shamans among the ancient Magyars cannot be proven.[265,277] Many elements of the Hungarian religious vocabulary, including *boszorkány* ("witch"), *elbűvöl* ("to charm"), and the ancient Hungarian word for holy (*igy* or *egy*), are of Turkic origin.[278] Many of these loanwords were adopted into their Christian vocabulary: *búcsú* (indulgence), *bűn* (sin), *gyón* (confess), *isten* (god), and *ördög* (devil).[279,266] According to Gyula László, a Hungarian children's verse that refers to a fife, a drum, and a reed violin preserves the memory of a pagan ritual for expelling harmful spirits by raising great noise.[280] The refrain of another children's verse, which mentions three days of the week in reverse order, may have preserved an ancient belief in the existence of an afterlife world where everything is upside-down.[281]

> *Stork, oh stork, oh little stork,*
> *What has made your leg bleed so?*
> *A Turkish child made the cut,*
> *A Magyar child will cure it*
> *With fife and drum and a reed violin.*
>
> —*A Hungarian children's song.*[281]

Sources

Primary sources

- *Anonymus, Notary of King Béla: The Deeds of the Hungarians* (Edited, Translated and Annotated by Martyn Rady and László Veszprémy) (2010). In: Rady, Martyn; Veszprémy, László; Bak, János M. (2010); *Anonymus and Master Roger*; CEU Press; ISBN 978-963-9776-95-1.
- *Constantine Porphyrogenitus: De Administrando Imperio* (Greek text edited by Gyula Moravcsik, English translation by Romillyi J. H. Jenkins) (1967). Dumbarton Oaks Center for Byzantine Studies. ISBN 0-88402-021-5.
- "Ibn Rusta on the Magyars 903–913" (2012). In: *Ibn Fadlān: Ibn Fadlān on the Land of Darkness: Arab Travellers in the Far North* (Translated with an Introduction by Paul Lunde and Caroline Stone) (2012) ; Penguin Books; ISBN 978-0-140-45507-6.
- *Simon of Kéza: The Deeds of the Hungarians* (Edited and translated by László Veszprémy and Frank Schaer with a study by Jenő Szűcs) (1999). CEU Press. ISBN 963-9116-31-9.
- *The Annals of Fulda (Ninth-Century Histories, Volume II)* (Translated and annotated by Timothy Reuter) (1992). Manchester University Press. ISBN 0-7190-3458-2.
- *The Annals of St-Bertin (Ninth-Century Histories, Volume I)* (Translated and annotated by Janet L. Nelson) (1991). Manchester University Press. ISBN 978-0-7190-3426-8.
- "The *Chronicle* of Regino of Prüm (2009). In: *History and Politics in Late Carolingian and Ottonian Europe: The* Chronicle *of Regino of Prüm and Adalbert of Magdeburg* (Translated and annotated by Simon MacLean); Manchester University Press; ISBN 978-0-7190-7135-5.

- *The Hungarian Illuminated Chronicle:* Chronica de Gestis Hungarorum (Edited by Dezső Dercsényi) (1970). Corvina, Taplinger Publishing. ISBN 0-8008-4015-1.
- *The Taktika of Leo VI* (Text, translation, and commentary by George T. Dennis) (2010). Dumbarton Oaks. ISBN 978-0-88402-359-3.
- "The Life of Constantine"; "The Life of Methodius" (1983). In: Kantor, Marvin (1983); *Medieval Slavic Lives of Saints and Princes*; pp. 23–161. University of Michigan; ISBN 0-930042-44-1.

Secondary sources

- Berend, Nora; Urbańczyk, Przemysław; Wiszewski, Przemysław (2013). *Central Europe in the High Middle Ages: Bohemia, Hungary and Poland, c. 900-c. 1300.* Cambridge University Press. ISBN 978-0-521-78156-5.
- Brook, Kevin Alan (2006). *The Jews of Khazaria.* Rowman & Littlefield. ISBN 978-0-7425-4982-1.
- Cartledge, Bryan (2011). *The Will to Survive: A History of Hungary.* C. Hurst & Co. ISBN 978-1-84904-112-6.
- Csorba, Csaba (1997). *Árpád népe* [Árpád's People] (in Hungarian). Kulturtrade. ISBN 963-9069-20-5.
- Curta, Florin (2006). *Southeastern Europe in the Middle Ages, 500–1250.* Cambridge University Press. ISBN 978-0-521-89452-4.
- Engel, Pál (2001). *The Realm of St Stephen: A History of Medieval Hungary, 895–1526.* I.B. Tauris Publishers. ISBN 1-86064-061-3.
- Ertl, Alan W. (2008). *Toward an Understanding of Europe: A Political Economic Précis of Continental Integration.* Universal-Publishers. ISBN 9781599429830.
- Fodor, István (1975). *In Search of a New Homeland: The Prehistory of the Hungarian People and the Conquest.* Corvina Kiadó. ISBN 963-13-1126-0.
- Gulya, János (1997). "A magyarok önelnevezésének eredete [Origin of the self-designation of the Hungarians]". In Kovács, László; Veszprémy, László. *Honfoglalás és nyelvészet* [The Hungarian Conquest and Linguistics]. Balassi Kiadó. pp. 85–97. ISBN 963-506-108-0.
- Harmatta, János (1997). "A magyarok nevei görög nyelvű forrásokban [The Hungarians' ethnonyms in Greek sources]". In Kovács, László; Veszprémy, László. *Honfoglalás és nyelvészet* [The Hungarian Conquest and Linguistics]. Balassi Kiadó. pp. 119–140. ISBN 963-506-108-0.
- Klima, László (2004). "The history of research on the ancestral Uralic homeland". In Nanovfszky, György. *The Finno-Ugric World.* Teleki László Foundation. pp. 15–24. ISBN 963-7081-01-1.

- Kontler, László (1999). *Millennium in Central Europe: A History of Hungary.* Atlantisz Publishing House. ISBN 963-9165-37-9.
- Kovács, László (2005). "Remarks on the archaeological remains of the 9th–10th century Hungarians". In Mende, Balázs Gusztáv. *Research on the Prehistory of the Hungarians: Review: Papers Presented at the Meetings of the Institute of Archaeology of the HAS, 2003–2004.* Archaeological Institute of the HAS. pp. 351–368. ISBN 963-7391-87-8.
- Kristó, Gyula (1996). *Hungarian History in the Ninth Century.* Szegedi Középkorász Muhely. ISBN 963-482-113-8.
- Langó, Péter (2005). "Archaeological research on the conquering Hungarians: a review". In Mende, Balázs Gusztáv. *Research on the Prehistory of the Hungarians: Review: Papers Presented at the Meetings of the Institute of Archaeology of the HAS, 2003–2004.* Archaeological Institute of the HAS. pp. 175–340. ISBN 963-7391-87-8.
- László, Gyula (1996). *The Magyars: Their Life and Civilisation.* Corvina. ISBN 963-13-4226-3.
- Macartney, C. A. (1953). *The Medieval Hungarian Historians: A Critical & Analytical Guide.* Cambridge University Press. ISBN 978-0-521-08051-4.
- Molnár, Miklós (2001). *A Concise History of Hungary.* Cambridge University Press. ISBN 978-0-521-66736-4.
- Róna-Tas, András (1999). *Hungarians and Europe in the Early Middle Ages: An Introduction to Early Hungarian History (Translated by Nicholas Bodoczky).* CEU Press. ISBN 978-963-9116-48-1.
- Spinei, Victor (2003). *The Great Migrations in the East and South East of Europe from the Ninth to the Thirteenth Century (Translated by Dana Badulescu).* ISBN 973-85894-5-2.
- Szabados, György (2011). *Magyar államalapítások a IX-X. században* [Foundations of the Hungarian States in the 9th–10th Centuries] (in Hungarian). Szegedi Középkorász Műhely. ISBN 978-963-08-2083-7.
- Szíj, Enikő (2005). "The past and present of the research on the prehistory of the Hungarians:Historiography". In Mende, Balázs Gusztáv. *Research on the Prehistory of the Hungarians: Review: Papers Presented at the Meetings of the Institute of Archaeology of the HAS, 2003–2004.* Archaeological Institute of the HAS. pp. 115–156. ISBN 963-7391-87-8.
- Tóth, Sándor László (1998). *Levédiától a Kárpát-medencéig* [From Levedia to the Carpathian Basin] (in Hungarian). Szegedi Középkorász Műhely. ISBN 963-482-175-8.
- Tóth, Sándor László (2005). "The past and present of the research on the prehistory of the Hungarians:Historiography". In Mende, Balázs Gusztáv. *Research on the Prehistory of the Hungarians: Review: Papers Presented at the Meetings of the Institute of Archaeology of the HAS, 2003–2004.*

Archaeological Institute of the HAS. pp. 45–86. ISBN 963-7391-87-8.
- Türk, Attila (Summer 2012). "The new archaeological research design for early Hungarian history"[282] (PDF). *Hungarian Archaeology*. hungarianarchaeology.hu. Retrieved 9 December 2014.
- Veres, Péter (2004). "The Uralic and Hungarian ancestral homeland: the state of current research". In Nanovfszky, György. *The Finno-Ugric World*. Teleki László Foundation. pp. 31–36. ISBN 963-7081-01-1.
- Zimonyi, István (2005). "The state of the research on the prehistory of the Hungarians: Historiography (Oriental sources, history of the Steppe)". In Mende, Balázs Gusztáv. *Research on the Prehistory of the Hungarians: Review: Papers Presented at the Meetings of the Institute of Archaeology of the HAS, 2003–2004*. Archaeological Institute of the HAS. pp. 87–102. ISBN 963-7391-87-8.

Further reading

- Bowlus, Charles R. (1994). *Franks, Moravians and Magyars: The Struggle for the Middle Danube, 788–907*. University of Pennsylvania Press. ISBN 0-8122-3276-3.
- Makkai, László (1994). "The Hungarians' prehistory, their conquest of Hungary and their raids to the West to 955". In Sugar, Peter F.; Hanák, Péter; Frank, Tibor. *A History of Hungary*. Indiana University Press. pp. 8–14. ISBN 0-253-35578-8.

External links

- Hofer, Tamás (Fall 1996). "Ethnography and Hungarian Prehistory (Edited version of a lecture held at the conference "Ethnography and Prehistory," organized by the Hungarian Prehistoric Committee of the Hungarian Academy of Sciences on December 5, 1995)"[283]. *Budapesti Könyvszemle – BUKSZ*. Retrieved 9 December 2014.

 Wikimedia Commons has media related to *Prehistory of Hungary*.

Aquincum

Aquincum

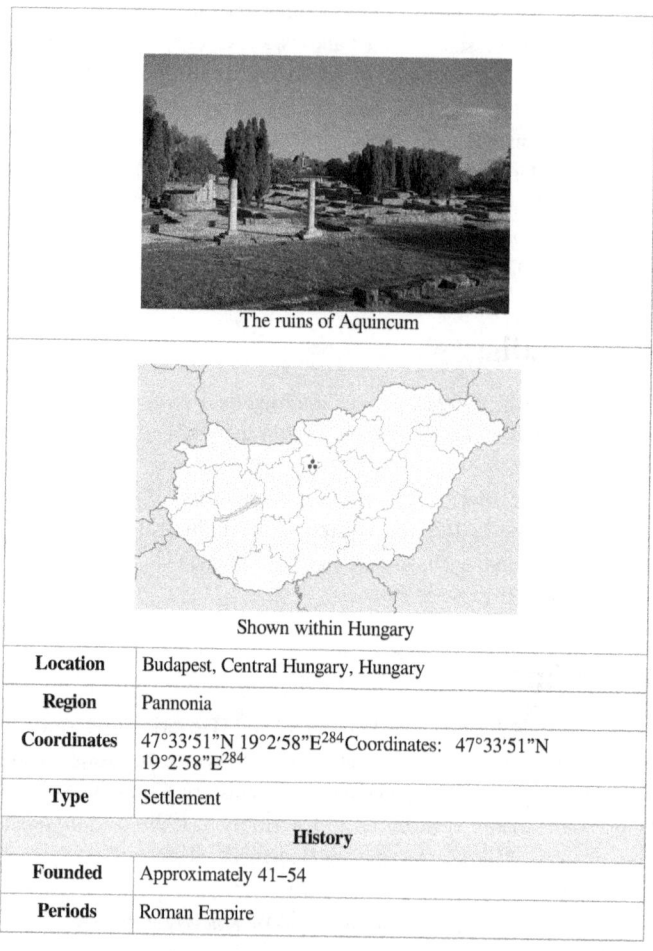

Location	Budapest, Central Hungary, Hungary
Region	Pannonia
Coordinates	47°33′51″N 19°2′58″E[284]Coordinates: 47°33′51″N 19°2′58″E[284]
Type	Settlement
History	
Founded	Approximately 41–54
Periods	Roman Empire

Aquincum was an ancient city, situated on the northeastern borders of the Pannonia province within the Roman Empire. The ruins of the city can be found today in Budapest, the capital city of Hungary. It is believed that Marcus Aurelius wrote at least part of his book *Meditations* at Aquincum.

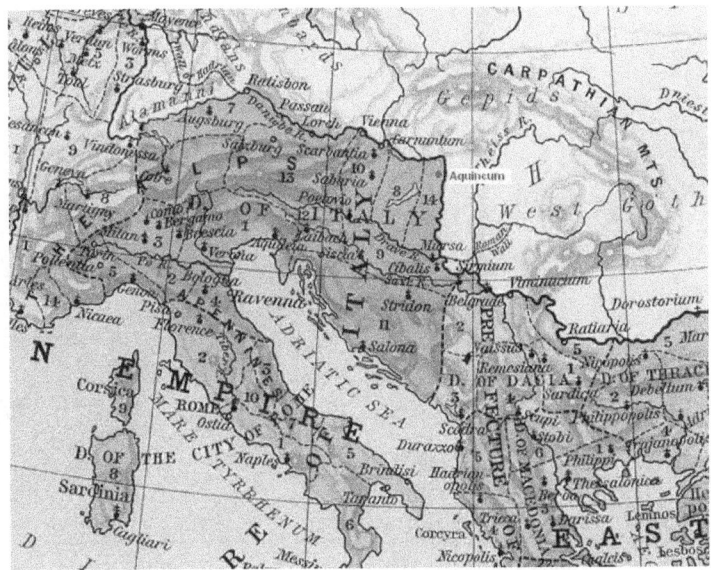

Figure 16: *Location of the city within the Roman Empire*

History

Aquincum was originally settled by the Eravisci, a Celtic tribe. Aquincum served as a military base (*castrum*), having been part of the Roman border protection system called *limes*. Around AD 41-54, a 500-strong cavalry unit arrived, and a Roman legion of 6,000 men was stationed here by AD 89. The city gradually grew around the fortress, and after Pannonia was reorganised by the Romans in AD 106, Aquincum became the capital city of the Roman province of Pannonia Inferior. The city had around 30,000 to 40,000 inhabitants by the end of the 2nd century, and covered a significant part of the area today known as the Óbuda district within Budapest. Ruins from the old Roman settlement can be seen in other parts of Budapest as well, notably Contra-Aquincum. These Roman structures were, during the 2nd and 3rd century AD, the heart of the commercial life of the Pannonia province. The excavations show evidence of the lifestyle of this period. The most important monuments in Aquincum are the two amphitheatres the Aquincum Civil Amphitheatre and the Aquincum Military Amphitheatre built in the 1st century AD.[285]

Figure 17: *Aquincum Amphitheatre, Budapest, 1996*

Settlement buildings

People living in the settlement could enjoy the achievements of the Empire, like central heating in the houses, public baths, a Mithraeum and palaces, as well as two amphitheatres, the Aquincum Civil Amphitheatre and the larger Aquincum Military Amphitheatre for gladiatorial combats and beast fights.

Aquincum Museum

Many historic artifacts from the city now appear in the Aquincum Museum. The museum exhibits a reconstruction of the hydraulic system, Roman houses and paintings that have been recovered on site. The ruins of a three-level aqueduct have been discovered around the city.

External links

 Wikimedia Commons has media related to *Aquincum*.

- Aquincum museum[286]
- Aquincum - Aerial photography[287]
- Video footage of ancient city of Aquincum of the Roman Empire.[288]
- Aquincum Ruins[289]

Middle Ages

Kingdom of Hungary (1526–1867)

\multicolumn{2}{c}{**Kingdom of Hungary**}
\multicolumn{2}{c}{*Königreich Ungarn* (de) *Regnum Hungariae* (la) *Magyar Királyság* (hu)}
\multicolumn{2}{c}{Crownland of Habsburg Monarchy and Austrian Empire}
\multicolumn{2}{c}{1526–1867}
\multicolumn{2}{c}{Flag}
\multicolumn{2}{c}{Coat of arms}
\multicolumn{2}{c}{**Motto** *Regnum Mariae Patrona Hungariae*[290] "Kingdom of Mary, the Patron of Hungary"}
\multicolumn{2}{c}{**Anthem** *Himnusz* Hymn}
Capital	Buda (1526–1536) Pressburg (1536–1848) Pest (1848–1867)

Languages	Official languages: Latin (before 1784; 1790–1844) German (1784–1790; 1849–1867) Hungarian (1844–1849)	
	Other spoken languages: Romanian, Slovak, Croatian, Slovene, Serbian, Italian, Ruthenian	
Religion	Catholic, Reformed, Lutheranism, Orthodox, Unitarianism, Judaism	
Government	Absolute monarchy	
Apostolic King		
•	1526–1564	Ferdinand I (first)
•	1848–1867	Franz Joseph I (last)
Palatine		
•	1526–1530	Stephen Báthory (first)
•	1847–1848	Stephen Francis (last)
Legislature	Royal Diet	
Historical era	Medieval / Early Modern	
•	Battle of Mohács	29 August 1526
•	Treaty of Nagyvárad	24 February 1538
•	Treaty of Karlowitz	26 January 1699
•	War of Independence	1703–1711
•	Hungarian Revolution	15 March 1848
•	Compromise of 1867	30 March 1867
Currency	Forint	

Preceded by	Succeeded by
Kingdom of Hungary (1301–1526)	Kingdom of Hungary (1867–1918)

Kingdom of Hungary (1526–1867)

Part of a series on the
History of Hungary

Hungary portal

- v
- t
- e²⁹¹

Part of a series on the
History of Slovakia

Prehistoric Slovakia

- Roman era
- Lombard state

Medieval Slavic states

- Avar Khaganate
- Samo's Empire
- Principality of Nitra
- Great Moravia
- Lower Pannonia

Kingdom of Hungary
(10th century – 1526)

- High Middle Ages
- Domain of Máté Csák
- Domain of Amade Aba
- Late Middle Ages

Ottoman Empire
(16th–17th century)

- Uyvar Eyalet
- Budin Eyalet
- Eğri Eyalet
- Principality of Transylvania
- Principality of Imre Thököly

Habsburg Monarchy
(1526–1918)

- Habsburg Kingdom of Hungary
- 1848–49 Slovak Uprising
- Military District of Preßburg
- Military District of Kaschau

Czechoslovakia

Slovaks in Czechoslovakia	1918–1938
Slovak Soviet Republic	1919
Slovak Republic	1939–1945
Slovak National Uprising	1944
Slovaks in Czechoslovakia	1948–1989
Slovak Socialist Republic	1969–1990
Velvet Revolution	1989

Modern Slovakia

Slovak Republic

▦ Slovakia portal

- v
- t
- e[292]

The **Kingdom of Hungary** between 1526 and 1867 was, while outside the Holy Roman Empire, part of the lands of the Habsburg Monarchy, that became the Empire of Austria in 1804. After the Battle of Mohács of 1526, the country was ruled by two crowned kings (John I and Ferdinand I). Initially the exact territory under Habsburg rule was disputed because both rulers claimed the whole kingdom. This unsettled period lasted until 1570 when John Sigismund Zápolya (John I) abdicated as King of Hungary in Emperor Maximilian II's favor.

In the early stages, the lands that were ruled by the Habsburg Hungarian kings were regarded both as "the Kingdom of Hungary" and "Royal Hungary".[293,294,295] Royal Hungary was the symbol of the continuity of formal law[296] after the Ottoman occupation, because it could preserve its legal traditions.[297] however in general it was *de facto* a Habsburg province.[298] The Hungarian nobility forced Vienna to admit that Hungary was a special unit of the Habsburg lands and had to be ruled in conformity with her own special laws.[299] Although, Hungarian historiography positioned Transylvania in a direct continuity with Medieval Kingdom of Hungary in pursuance of the advancement of Hungarian interests.[300]

Kingdom of Hungary (1526–1867)

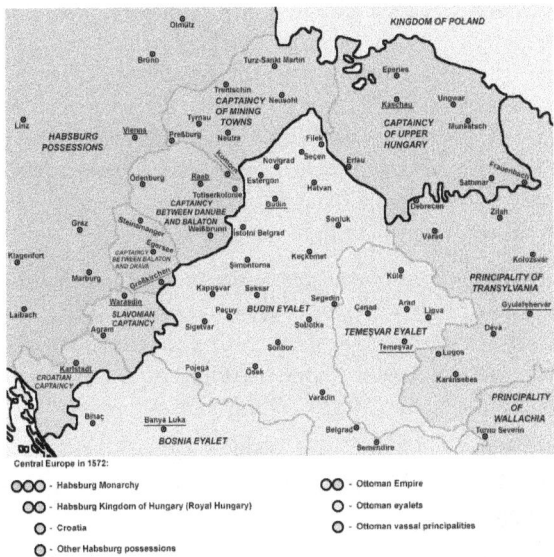

Figure 18: *Captaincies of the Kingdom of Hungary around 1572.*

Under the terms of the Treaty of Karlowitz, which ended the Great Turkish War in 1699, the Ottomans ceded nearly all of Ottoman Hungary. The new territories were united with the territory of Kingdom of Hungary, and, although its powers were mostly formal,Wikipedia:Accuracy dispute#Disputed statement a Diet seated in Pressburg ruled these lands.

Two major Hungarian rebellions as the Rákóczi's War of Independence in the beginning of the 18th century and the Hungarian Revolution of 1848 marked important shifts in the evolution of the polity. The kingdom became a dual monarchy in 1867 known as the Austro-Hungarian Empire.

Royal Hungary (1526–1699)

Royal Hungary (1526–1699),[301] (Hungarian: *Királyi Magyarország*, German: *Königliches Ungarn*), was the name of the portion of the medieval Kingdom of Hungary where the Habsburgs were recognized as Kings of Hungary[302] in the wake of the Ottoman victory at the Battle of Mohács (1526) and subsequent partition of the country.

Temporary territorial division between the rival rules (John I and Ferdinand I) occurred only in 1538 at Treaty of Nagyvárad,[303] when the Habsburgs got the north and west parts of the country (Royal Hungary), with the new capital Pressburg (Pozsony, now Bratislava). John I secured the eastern part of the kingdom (known as Eastern Hungarian Kingdom). Habsburg monarchs needed the economic power of Hungary for the Ottoman wars. During the Ottoman wars the territory of former Kingdom of Hungary was reduced by around 70%; despite these enormous territorial and demographic losses, the smaller heavily war-torn Royal Hungary remained economically more important than Austria or Kingdom of Bohemia even by the end of 16th century.

Territory of present-day Slovakia and northwestern Transdanubia were constant parts of this polity while the control was often switched at region of northeastern Hungary between Royal Hungary and Principality of Transylvania. The central territories of the medieval Hungarian kingdom were annexed by the Ottoman Empire for 150 years (see Ottoman Hungary).

In 1570, John Sigismund Zápolya, the rival Hungarian king, abdicated as King of Hungary in Emperor Maximilian II's favor, which was expressed in the Treaty of Speyer.[304]

The term "Royal Hungary" fell into disuse after 1699, and the Habsburg Kings referred to the newly enlarged country by the more formal term "Kingdom of Hungary".

Habsburg Kings

The Habsburgs, an influential dynasty of the Holy Roman Empire were elected Kings of Hungary.

Royal Hungary became a part of the Habsburg Monarchy and enjoyed little influence in Vienna. The Habsburg King directly controlled Royal Hungary's financial, military, and foreign affairs, and imperial troops guarded its borders. The Habsburgs avoided filling the office of palatine to prevent the holder's amassing too much power. In addition, the so-called Turkish question divided the Habsburgs and the Hungarians: Vienna wanted to maintain peace with the Ottomans; the Hungarians wanted the Ottomans ousted. As the Hungarians recognized the weakness of their position, many became anti-Habsburg. They complained about foreign rule, the behaviour of foreign garrisons, and the Habsburgs' recognition of Turkish sovereignty in Transylvania (Principality of Transylvania was usually under the suzerainty of the Ottoman Empire, however it often had dual vassalage -Ottoman Turkish sultans and the Habsburg Hungarian kings- in the 16th and 17th centuries).[305] Protestants, who were persecuted in Royal Hungary, considered the Counter-Reformation a greater menace than the Turks, however.

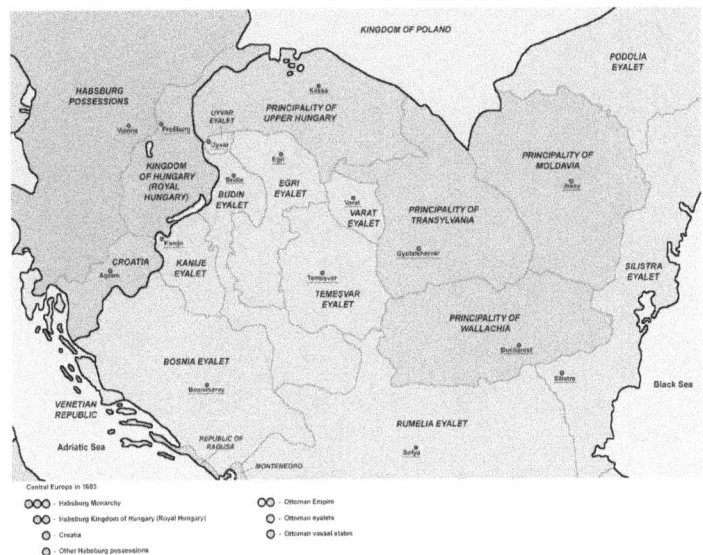

Figure 19: *Royal Hungary, Principality of Upper Hungary, Principality of Transylvania and Ottoman eyalets around 1683.*

Reformation

The Reformation spread quickly, and by the early 17th century hardly any noble families remained Catholic. In Royal Hungary, the majority of the population became Lutheran by the end of the 16th century.

Archbishop Péter Pázmány reorganized Royal Hungary's Roman Catholic Church and led a Counter-Reformation that reversed the Protestants' gains in Royal Hungary, using persuasion rather than intimidation. The Reformation caused rifts between Catholics, who often sided with the Habsburgs, and Protestants, who developed a strong national identity and became rebels in Austrian eyes. Chasms also developed between the mostly Catholic magnates and the mainly Protestant lesser nobles.

Figure 20: *Growth of Habsburg territories*

Kingdom of Hungary in the late modern period until 1848

18th century

As the Habsburgs' control of the Turkish possessions started to increase, the ministers of Leopold I argued that he should rule Hungary as conquered territory.Wikipedia:Citation needed At the Diet of "Royal Hungary" in Pressburg, in 1687, the Emperor promised to observe all laws and privileges.Wikipedia:Citation needed Nonetheless, hereditary succession of the Habsburgs was recognized, and the nobles' right of resistance was abrogated. In 1690 Leopold began redistributing lands freed from the Turks. Protestant nobles and all other Hungarians thought disloyal by the Habsburgs lost their estates, which were given to foreigners.Wikipedia:Citation needed Vienna controlled the foreign affairs, defense, tariffs, and other functions.Wikipedia:Citation needed

The repression of Protestants and the land seizures frustrated the Hungarians, and in 1703 a peasant uprising sparked an eight-year rebellion against Habsburg rule. In Transylvania, which became the part of Hungary again at the end of the 17th century[306] (as a province, called "Principality of Transylvania" with the Diet seated at Gyulafehérvár), the people united under Francis II Rákóczi, a Roman Catholic magnate. Most of Hungary soon supported Rákóczi, and the Hungarian Diet voted to annul the Habsburgs' right to the throne. Fortunes turned against the Hungarians, however, when the Habsburgs made peace in the West and turned their full force against them. The war ended in 1711, when Count Károlyi, General of the Hungarian Armies agreed to the Treaty of Szatmár.[307] The treaty contained the emperor's agreement to reconvene the Diet in Pressburg and to grant an amnesty for the rebels.

Leopold's successor, King Charles III (1711–40), began building a workable relationship with Hungary after the Treaty of Szatmár. Charles asked the Budapest Diet's approval for the Pragmatic Sanction, under which the Habsburg monarch was to rule Hungary not as Emperor, but as a King subject to the restraints of Hungary's constitution and laws. He hoped that the Pragmatic Sanction would keep the Habsburg Empire intact if his daughter, Maria Theresa, succeeded him. The Diet approved the Pragmatic Sanction in 1723, and Hungary thus agreed to become a hereditary monarchy under the Habsburgs for as long as their dynasty existed. In practice, however, Charles and his successors governed almost autocratically, controlling Hungary's foreign affairs, defense, and finance but lacking the power to tax the nobles without their approval.

Charles organized the country under a centralized administration and in 1715 established a standing army under his command, which was entirely funded and manned by the non-noble population. This policy reduced the nobles' military obligation without abrogating their exemption from taxation. Charles also banned conversion to Protestantism, required civil servants to profess Catholicism, and forbade Protestant students to study abroad.

Maria Theresa (1741–80) faced an immediate challenge from Prussia's Frederick II when she became head of the House of Habsburg. In 1741 she appeared before the Diet of Budapest holding her newborn son and entreated Hungary's nobles to support her. They stood behind her and helped secure her rule. Maria Theresa later took measures to reinforce links with Hungary's magnates. She established special schools to attract Hungarian nobles to Vienna.

Under Charles and Maria Theresa, Hungary experienced further economic decline. Centuries of Ottoman occupation and war had reduced Hungary's population drastically, and large parts of the country's southern half were almost deserted. A labor shortage developed as landowners restored their estates. In response, the Habsburgs began to colonize Hungary with large numbers of peasants from all over Europe, especially Slovaks, Serbs, Croatians, and Germans. Many Jews also immigrated from Vienna and the empire's Polish lands near the end of the 18th century. Hungary's population more than tripled to 8 million between 1720 and 1787. However, only 39 percent of its people were Magyars, who lived mainly in the center of the country.

In the first half of the 18th century, Hungary had an agricultural economy that employed 90 percent of the population. The nobles failed to use fertilizers, roads were poor and rivers blocked, and crude storage methods caused

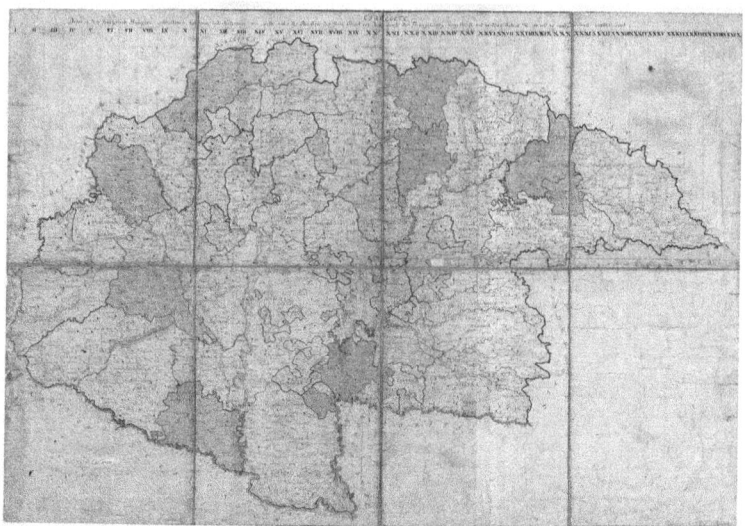

Figure 21: *Kingdom of Hungary on the Josephinische Landesaufnahme Original Map 1782-1785*

huge losses of grain. Barter had replaced money transactions, and little trade existed between towns and the serfs. After 1760 a labor surplus developed. The serf population grew, pressure on the land increased, and the serfs' standard of living declined. Landowners began making greater demands on new tenants and began violating existing agreements. In response, Maria Theresa issued her Urbarium of 1767 to protect the serfs by restoring their freedom of movement and limiting the corvée. Despite her efforts and several periods of strong demand for grain, the situation worsened. Between 1767 and 1848, many serfs left their holdings. Most became landless farm workers because a lack of industrial development meant few opportunities for work in the towns.

Joseph II (1780–90), a dynamic leader strongly influenced by the Enlightenment, shook Hungary from its malaise when he inherited the throne from his mother, Maria Theresa. In the framework of Josephinism, Joseph sought to centralize control of the empire and to rule it by decree as an enlightened despot. He refused to take the Hungarian coronation oath to avoid being constrained by Hungary's constitution. In 1781–82 Joseph issued a Patent of Toleration, followed by an Edict of Tolerance which granted Protestants and Orthodox Christians full civil rights and Jews freedom of worship. He decreed that German replace Latin as the empire's official language and granted the peasants the freedom to leave their holdings, to marry, and to place their children in trades. Hungary, Slavonia, Croatia, the Military Frontier and Transylvania became a single imperial territory under one administration, called the Kingdom of Hungary or "Lands of the Crown of St. Stephen". When the Hungarian nobles again refused to waive their exemption from taxation, Joseph banned imports of Hungarian manufactured goods into Austria and began a survey to prepare for imposition of a general land tax.

Joseph's reforms outraged nobles and clergy of Hungary, and the peasants of country grew dissatisfied with taxes, conscription, and requisitions of supplies. Hungarians perceived Joseph's language reform as German cultural hegemony, and they reacted by insisting on the right to use their own tongue. As a result, Hungarian lesser nobles sparked a renaissance of the Hungarian language and culture, and a cult of national dance and costume flourished. The lesser nobles questioned the loyalty of the magnates, of whom less than half were ethnic Hungarians, and even those had become French- and German-speaking courtiers. The Hungarian national reawakening subsequently triggered national revivals among the Slovak, Romanian, Serbian, and Croatian minorities within Hungary and Transylvania, who felt threatened by both German and Hungarian cultural hegemony. These national revivals later blossomed into the nationalist movements of the 19th and 20h centuries that contributed to the empire's ultimate collapse.

Late in his reign, Joseph led a costly, ill-fated campaign against the Turks that weakened his empire. On January 28, 1790, three weeks before his death, the emperor issued a decree canceling all of his reforms except the Patent of Toleration, peasant reforms, and abolition of the religious orders.

Joseph's successor, Leopold II (1790–92), re-introduced the bureaucratic technicality which viewed Hungary as a separate country under a Habsburg king. In 1791 the Diet passed Law X, which stressed Hungary's status as an independent kingdom ruled only by a king legally crowned according to Hungarian laws. Law X later became the basis for demands by Hungarian reformers for statehood in the period from 1825 to 1849. New laws again required approval of both the Habsburg king and the Diet, and Latin was restored as the official language. The peasant reforms remained in effect, however, and Protestants remained equal before the law. Leopold died in March 1792 just as the French Revolution was about to degenerate into the Reign of Terror and send shock waves through the royal houses of Europe.

First half of the 19th century

Enlightened absolutism ended in Hungary under Leopold's successor, Francis II (ruled 1792–1835), who developed an almost abnormal aversion to change, bringing Hungary decades of political stagnation. In 1795 the Hungarian police arrested Ignác Martinovics and several of the country's leading thinkers for plotting a Jacobin kind of revolution to install a radical democratic, egalitarian political system in Hungary. Thereafter, Francis resolved to extinguish any spark of reform that might ignite revolution. The execution of the alleged plotters silenced any reform advocates among the nobles, and for about three decades reform ideas remained confined to poetry and philosophy. The magnates, who also feared that the influx of revolutionary ideas might precipitate a popular uprising, became a tool of the crown and seized the chance to further burden the peasants.

In 1804 Francis II, who was also the Holy Roman Emperor and ruler of the other dynastic lands of the Habsburg dynasty, founded the Empire of Austria in which Hungary and all his other dynastic lands were included. In doing so he created a formal overarching structure for the Habsburg Monarchy, that had functioned as a composite monarchy for about three hundred years before. He himself became **Francis I** (*Franz I.*), the first Emperor of Austria (*Kaiser von Österreich*), ruling from 1804 to 1835, so later he was named the one and only *Doppelkaiser* (double emperor) in history.[308] The workings of the overarching structure and the status of the new *Kaiserthum*'s component lands at first stayed much as they had been under the composite monarchy that existed before 1804. This was especially demonstrated by the status of the Kingdom of Hungary, whose affairs remained to be administered by its own institutions (King and Diet) as they had been under the composite monarchy, in which it had always been considered a separate Realm. Article X of 1790, that was added to Hungary's constitution during the phase of the composite monarchy uses the Latin phrase "Regnum Independens". In the new situation therefore, no Imperial institutions were involved in its internal government.[309,310,311]

By the start of the 19th century, the aim of Hungary's agricultural producers had shifted from subsistence farming and small-scale production for local trade to cash-generating, large-scale production for a wider market. Road and waterway improvements cut transportation costs, while urbanization in Austria, Bohemia, and Moravia and the need for supplies for the Napoleonic wars boosted demand for foodstuffs and clothing. Hungary became a major grain and wool exporter. New lands were cleared, and yields rose as farming methods improved. Hungary did not reap the full benefit of the boom, however, because most of the profits went to the magnates, who considered them not as capital for investment but as a means of adding luxury to their lives. As expectations rose, goods such as linen and silverware, once considered luxuries, became necessities. The wealthy magnates had little trouble balancing their earnings and expenditures, but many lesser nobles, fearful of losing their social standing, went into debt to finance their spending.

Napoleon's final defeat brought recession. Grain prices collapsed as demand dropped, and debt ensnared much of Hungary's lesser nobility. Poverty forced

Figure 22: *István Széchenyi, the first great figure of the reform era*

Figure 23: *Arms of Hungary (1849)*

Figure 24: *Lajos Kossuth, The most popular of Hungary's great reform leaders*

many lesser nobles to work to earn a livelihood, and their sons entered education institutions to train for civil service or professional careers. The decline of the lesser nobility continued despite the fact that by 1820 Hungary's exports had surpassed wartime levels. As more lesser nobles earned diplomas, the bureaucracy and professions became saturated, leaving a host of disgruntled graduates without jobs. Members of this new intelligentsia quickly became enamored of radical political ideologies emanating from Western Europe and organized themselves to effect changes in Hungary's political system.

Francis rarely called the Diet into session (usually only to request men and supplies for war) without hearing complaints. Economic hardship brought the lesser nobles' discontent to a head by 1825, when Francis finally convoked the Diet after a fourteen-year hiatus. Grievances were voiced, and open calls for reform were made, including demands for less royal interference in the nobles' affairs and for wider use of the Hungarian language.

The first great figure of the reform era came to the fore during the 1825 convocation of the Diet. Count István Széchenyi, a magnate from one of Hungary's most powerful families, shocked the Diet when he delivered the first speech in Hungarian ever uttered in the upper chamber and backed a proposal for the creation of a Hungarian academy of arts and sciences by pledging a year's income to support it. In 1831 angry nobles burned Szechenyi's book Hitel (Credit), in which he argued that the nobles' privileges were both morally indefensible and economically detrimental to the nobles themselves. Szechenyi called for an economic revolution and argued that only the magnates were capable of implementing reforms. Szechenyi favored a strong link with the Habsburg Empire and called for abolition of entail and serfdom, taxation of landowners, financing of development with foreign capital, establishment of a national bank, and introduction of wage labor. He inspired such projects as the construction of the suspension bridge linking Buda and Pest. Szechenyi's reform initiatives ultimately failed because they were targeted at the magnates, who were not inclined to support change, and because the pace of his program was too slow to attract disgruntled lesser nobles.

The most popular of Hungary's great reform leaders, Lajos Kossuth, addressed passionate calls for change to the lesser nobles. Kossuth was the son of a landless, lesser nobleman of Protestant background. He practiced law with his father before moving to Pest. There he published commentaries on the Diet's activities, which made him popular with young, reform-minded people. Kossuth was imprisoned in 1836 for treason. After his release in 1840, he gained quick notoriety as the editor of a liberal party newspaper. Kossuth argued that only political and economic separation from Austria would improve Hungary's plight. He called for broader parliamentary democracy, industrialization, general taxation, economic expansion through exports, and abolition of privileges and serfdom. But Kossuth was also a Hungarian patriotic whose rhetoric provoked the strong resentment of Hungary's minority ethnic groups. Kossuth gained support among liberal lesser nobles, who constituted an opposition minority in the Diet. They sought reforms with increasing success after Francis's death in 1835 and the succession of Ferdinand V (1835–48). In 1843 a law was enacted making Hungarian the country's official language over the strong objections of the Croats, Slovaks, Serbs, and Romanians.

1848–1867

After the revolution, the emperor revoked Hungary's constitution and assumed absolute control. Franz Joseph divided the country into four distinct territories: Hungary, Transylvania, Croatia-Slavonia, and Vojvodina. German and Bohemian administrators managed the government, and German became the language of administration and higher education. The non-Magyar minorities of Hungary received little for their support of Austria during the turmoil. A Croat reportedly told a Hungarian: "We received as a reward what the Magyars got as a punishment."

Hungarian public opinion split over the country's relations with Austria. Some Hungarians held out hope for full separation from Austria; others wanted an accommodation with the Habsburgs, provided that they respected Hungary's constitution and laws. Ferenc Deák became the main advocate for accommodation. Deak upheld the legality of the April laws and argued that their amendment required the Hungarian Diet's consent. He also held that the dethronement of the Habsburgs was invalid. As long as Austria ruled absolutely, Deak argued, Hungarians should do no more than passively resist illegal demands.

The first crack in Franz Joseph's neo-absolutist rule developed in 1859, when the forces of Sardinia-Piedmont and France defeated Austria at the Battle of Solferino. The defeat convinced Franz Joseph that national and social opposition to his government was too strong to be managed by decree from Vienna. Gradually he recognized the necessity of concessions towards Hungary, and Austria and Hungary thus moved towards a compromise.

In 1866 the Prussians defeated the Austrians, further underscoring the weakness of the Habsburg Empire. Negotiations between the emperor and the Hungarian leaders were intensified and finally resulted in the Compromise of 1867, which created the Dual Monarchy of Austria-Hungary, also known as the Austro-Hungarian Empire.

Renaissance

Buda Castle

Buda Castle	
 Buda Castle aerial view with Matthias Church	
Location	Budapest, Hungary
Coordinates	47°29′46″N 19°02′23″E[312]Coordinates: 47°29′46″N 19°02′23″E[312]
Area	4.73 km² (1.8 sq mi)
Built	14–20th century
Architect	Jean Nicolas Jadot, Miklós Ybl, Alajos Hauszmann
Architectural style(s)	Medieval, Baroque, Baroque Revival, Modernist
UNESCO World Heritage Site	
Official name: Budapest, including the Banks of the Danube, the Buda Castle Quarter and Andrássy Avenue	
Type	Cultural
Criteria	ii, iv
Designated	1987 (11th session)
Reference no.	400[313]
State Party	Hungary
Region	Hungary

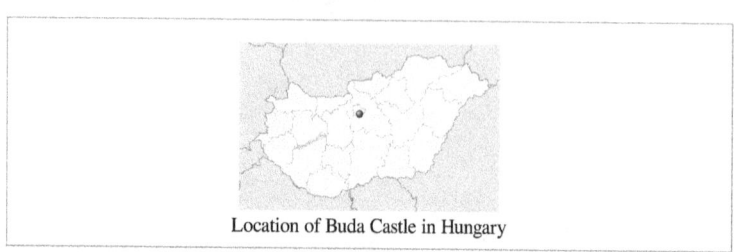

Location of Buda Castle in Hungary

Buda Castle (Hungarian: *Budavári Palota*, German: *Burgpalast*) is the historical castle and palace complex of the Hungarian kings in Budapest. It was first completed in 1265, but the massive Baroque palace today occupying most of the site was built between 1749 and 1769. The complex in the past was referred to as either the **Royal Palace** (Hungarian: *Királyi-palota*) or the **Royal Castle** (Hungarian: *Királyi Vár*, German: *Königliche Burg*).

Buda Castle sits on the south tip of Castle Hill, bounded on the north by what is known as the Castle District (*Várnegyed*), which is famous for medieval, Baroque and 19th-century houses, churches and public buildings. The hill is linked to Clark Ádám Square and the Széchenyi Chain Bridge by the Castle Hill Funicular. The castle is a part of the Budapest World Heritage Site, so declared in 1987.

History

Middle Ages

The first royal residence on the Castle Hill was built by King Béla IV of Hungary between 1247 and 1265. It is uncertain whether it was situated on the southern tip of the hill or on the northern elevation, near the Kammerhof.

The oldest part of the present-day palace was built in the 14th century by Stephen, Duke of Slavonia, who was the younger brother of King Louis I of Hungary. Only the foundations remain of the castle keep, which was known as **Stephen's Tower** (Hungarian: *István-torony*). The Gothic palace of King Louis I was arranged around a narrow courtyard next to the keep.

King Sigismund significantly enlarged the palace and strengthened its fortifications. Sigismund, as a Holy Roman Emperor, needed a magnificent royal residence to express his prominence among the rulers of Europe. He chose Buda Castle as his main residence, and during his long reign it became probably the largest Gothic palace of the late Middle Ages. Buda was an important artistic centre of the International Gothic style.

Figure 25: *Buda Castle in the Nuremberg Chronicle, 1493*

Figure 26: *Eastern view of the Medieval Royal palace (1490s)*

Construction began in the 1410s and was largely finished in the 1420s, although some minor works continued until the death of the king in 1437. The palace was first mentioned in 1437, under the name *"fricz palotha"*.

The most important part of Sigismund's palace was the northern wing, known as the Fresh Palace (Hun: *Friss-palota*). On the top floor was a large hall called the Roman Hall (70 × 20 m or 230 × 66 ft) with a carved wooden ceiling. Great windows and balconies faced toward the city of Buda. The façade of the palace was decorated with statues, a and coat-of-arms. In front stood the bronze equestrian statue of Sigismund, later repaired by King Matthias Corvinus.

The southern part of the royal residency was surrounded with narrow *zwingers*. Two parallel walls, the so-called "cortina walls", run down from the palace

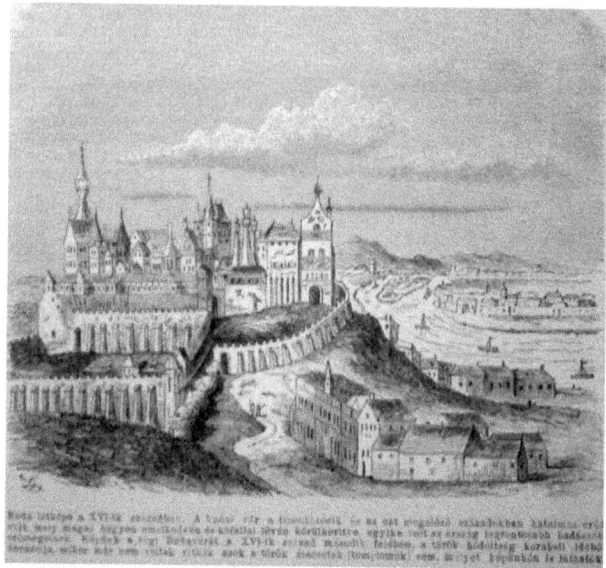

Figure 27: *Southern view of the Medieval Royal palace (1520s)*

to the River Danube across the steep hillside. The most imposing structure, the Broken Tower (Hun: *Csonka-torony*), on the western side of the *cour d'honneur*, remained unfinished. The basement of the tower was used as a dungeon; the top floors were probably the treasury of the royal jewels.

The last phase of large-scale building activity took place under King Matthias Corvinus. During the first decades of his reign the king finished the work on the Gothic palace. The Royal Chapel, with the surviving Lower Church, was likely built at that time.

After the marriage of Matthias and Beatrice of Naples in 1476, Italian humanists, artists and craftsmen arrived at Buda. The Hungarian capital became the first centre of Renaissance north of the Alps. The king rebuilt the palace in an early Renaissance style. The *cour d'honneur* was modernised and an Italian *loggia* was added. Inside the palace were two rooms with golden ceilings: the Bibliotheca Corviniana and a passage with the frescoes of the twelve signs of the Zodiac. The façade of the palace was decorated with statues of John Hunyadi, László Hunyadi and King Matthias. In the middle of the court there was a fountain with a statue of Pallas Athene.

Only fragments remain of this Renaissance palace: some red marble balustrades, lintels and decorative glazed tiles from stoves and floors.

Figure 28: *The reconstructed medieval fortifications and the Great Rondella*

In the last years of his reign Matthias Corvinus started construction of a new Renaissance palace on the eastern side of the Sigismund Courtyard, next to the Fresh Palace. The **Matthias Palace** remained unfinished because of the king's early death. The palace had a monumental red marble stairway in front of the façade. Matthias Corvinus was usually identified with Hercules by the humanists of his court; the bronze gates were decorated with panels depicting the deeds of Hercules, and a great bronze statue of the Greek hero welcomed the guests in the forecourt of the palace complex, where jousts were held.

The walled gardens of the palace were laid out on the western slopes of the Castle Hill. In the middle of the enclosure, a Renaissance villa was built by Matthias. Only one column survives of this so-called *Aula Marmorea*.

After the death of Matthias Corvinus, his successor, King Vladislaus II, carried on the works of the **Matthias Palace**, especially after his marriage with Anna of Foix-Candale in 1502.

Under the reign of King John Zápolya (the last national ruler of Hungary) the palace was repaired. On the southern tip of the Castle Hill, the Great Rondella was built by Italian military engineers. The circular bastion is one of the main surviving structure of the old palace.

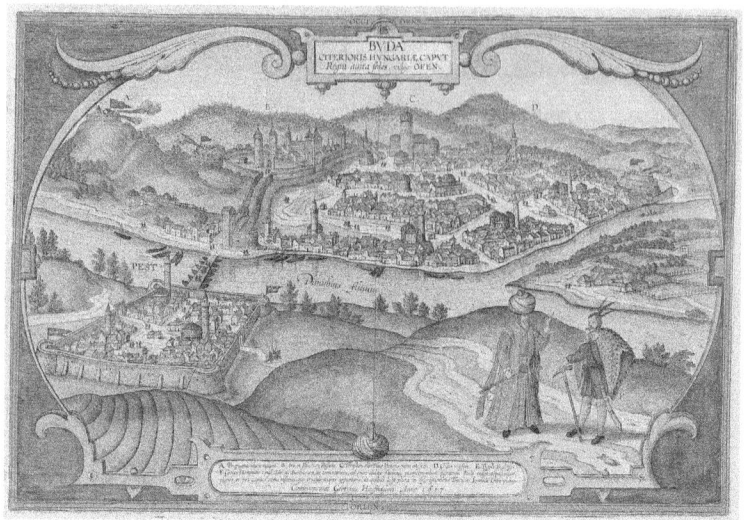

Figure 29: *Georg Houfnagel's view of Buda in 1617*

Ottoman Era

After the Battle of Mohács, the medieval Kingdom of Hungary collapsed. The Ottoman Turks occupied the evacuated town on 11 September 1526. Although Buda was sacked and burned, the Royal Palace was not damaged. Sultan Suleiman the Magnificent carried away all the bronze statues (the Hunyadis, Pallas Athene and Hercules) with him to Constantinople. The statues were destroyed there in a rebellion a few years later. The Sultan also took many volumes from the Corvina library.

In 1529 the Ottoman army besieged and occupied Buda again, and the palace was badly damaged. On 29 August 1541 Buda was occupied again by the Ottomans, without any resistance. Buda became part of Ottoman Empire and the seat of the Eyalet of Budin.

Although Turkish travel writers wrote enthusiastically about the beauty of the palace of the Hungarian kings, the new Ottoman government let the palace decay. It was partially used as barracks, a storage place and stables, and otherwise it stood empty.

The palace was called *Iç Kala* ("Inner Castle") and *Hisar Peçe* ("Citadel") by the Turks. The name of the *cour d'honneur* was *"Seray meydani"*. The favourite nickname of the complex was "Palace of the Golden Apples".

The economic decline of Buda the capital city during the Ottoman conquest characterised by the stagnation of population, the population of Buda was not

Figure 30: *The Holy League took Buda after a long siege in 1686*

larger in 1686, than the population of the city two centuries earlier in the 15th century. The Ottomans allowed the Hungarian royal place to fall into ruins. The amortised palace was later transformed into a gunpowder storage and magazine by the Ottomans, which caused its detonation during the siege in 1686. The original Christian Hungarian population didn't feel secure during the Ottoman conquest, their numbers significantly shrank in the next decades, due to their fleeing to the Habsburg ruled Royal Hungary. The number of Jews and Gypsy immigrants became dominant during the Ottoman rule in Buda.

In the era between 1541 and 1686, the Habsburgs tried to re-capture Buda several times. Unsuccessful sieges in 1542, 1598, 1603 and 1684 caused serious damage. The Ottoman authorities repaired only the fortifications. According to 17th-century sources, many buildings of the former Royal Palace were roofless and their vaults collapsed. Nonetheless the medieval palace mostly survived until the great siege of 1686.

Destruction of the medieval castle

The medieval palace was destroyed in the great siege of 1686 when Buda was captured by allied Christian forces.

In 1686, two years after the unsuccessful siege of Buda, a renewed Western European Christian campaign was started to take the city. This time the Holy League's army was much larger, consisting of 65,000–100,000 men, including German, Hungarian, Croat, Dutch, English, Spanish, Czech, Italian, French,

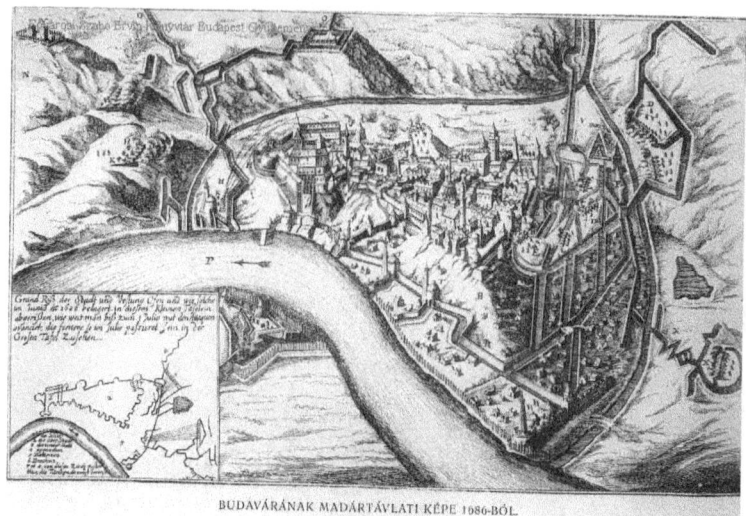

Figure 31: *The great siege of Buda (1686); contemporary drawing*

Burgundian, Danish and Swedish soldiers and other Europeans as volunteers, artillerymen and officers. The Turkish defenders consisted of 7,000 men.

In a heavy artillery bombardment, many buildings burned and collapsed. The Stephen's Tower, used as a gunpowder store by the Ottomans, exploded when hit by a single cannon, said to have been fired by a friar called Gábor, also referred as Tüzes Gábor ("Gabriel Fiery"). According to contemporary sources, the explosion killed as many as 1,500 Turkish soldiers and caused a wave on the Danube that washed away artillery batteries and guards standing on the opposite shore.Wikipedia:Citation needed

Habsburg military engineers made several plans and drawings of the buildings in subsequent decades. Although the walls mainly survived, the burned-out shell rapidly decayed from a lack of maintenance. Between 1702 and 1715, Stephen's Tower disappeared completely, and the palace was beyond repair. In 1715, King Charles III ordered the demolition of the ruins. Johann Hölbling surveyed the still-existing structures. The king ordered the surviving marble statues, antiquities, inscriptions and coins should be spared (there is no evidence about the realization of the royal decree). The main part of the palace and the Broken Tower were totally demolished, the hollows and moats were filled and a new flat terrace was established. The southern fortifications, zwingers and rooms were buried under tons of rubbish and earth.

Figure 32: *The royal castle built under King Charles III (1733)*

Early Baroque palace

In 1715 a small Baroque palace was built according to the plans of Johann Hölbling. It was a simple rectangular building, with an inner court and a shorter side wing, which was later demolished. The Hölbling palace is identical with the core of the present-day palace, where the Baroque Court of the Budapest Historical Museum is now located.

The interior of the palace was left unfinished when work stopped in 1719. The Hofkriegsrat commissioned Fortunato di Prati to make several plans for the palace, but lack of money hindered their implementation.

In 1723 the palace was accidentally burned down and the windows were walled up in order to stop further deterioration. Several drawings from the 1730s and 1740s show the unfinished decaying shell of the simple two-storey blockhouse. Some engravings show an idealised finished version which never existed. Sometime around 1730 the roof was repaired.

Era of Maria Theresa

In 1748 Count Antal Grassalkovich, President of the Hungarian Chamber, appealed to the public to finish the derelict palace by means of public subscription. Palatine János Pálffy called upon the counties and cities to award grants for the project. The moment was favourable because relations between the Hungarian nobility and the Habsburgs were exceptionally good. The Hungarians supported Queen Maria Theresa in the dire need of the War of the Austrian Succession. The queen was grateful for this, and the new Royal Palace became the symbol of peace and friendship between the dynasty and the nation.

The plans of the splendid, U-shaped Baroque palace with a *cour d'honneur* were drawn by Jean Nicolas Jadot, chief architect of the Viennese court. After 1753 the plans were modified by his successor, Nicolaus Pacassi. Ignác Oraschek, master builder, who guided the works, and modified the plans according to his own ideas. The foundation stone of the palace was laid on 13

Figure 33: *The façade of the cour d'honneur constructed under Hillebrandt in the 1760s*

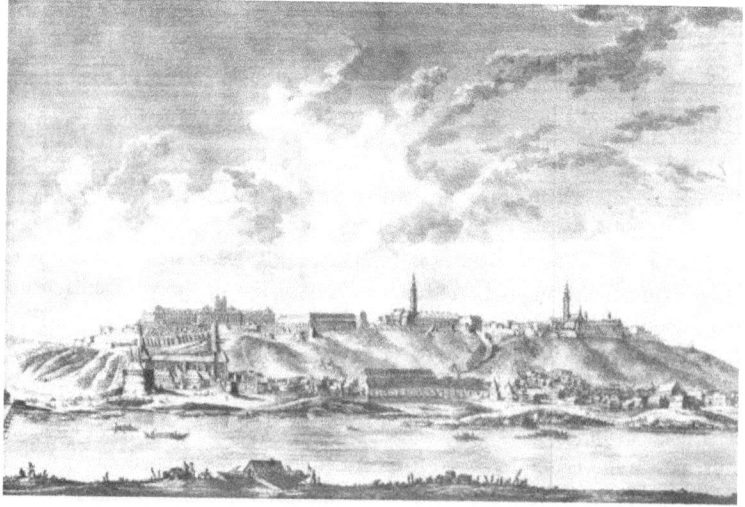

Figure 34: *The royal castle during the reign of Maria Theresa (1777)*

May 1749, which was the Queen's birthday. The work continued at a good pace until 1758, when financial difficulties caused a seven-year break. By that time only the interiors were left unfinished.

According to surviving historical documents, the layout of the palace followed Jadot's signed plans of 1749. The façades, some interior elements and the St. Sigismund Chapel are the works of Nicolò Pacassi, while the special double false domes were probably planned by Oraschek, formerly the master builder of Count Grassalkovich. Double false domes were typical features of the so-called Grassalkovich-type Baroque castles like Gödöllő. However, this feature was later removed from the palace.

In 1764 the Queen visited the palace and allotted 20,000 thalers a year for the work, which recommenced in 1765 according to the plans of Franz Anton Hillebrandt. Hillebrand altered the *cour d'honneur* façade of the central wing in Rococo style. In 1769 the St. Sigismund Chapel was consecrated and the palace was finished the same year. According to the aggregate statement of Grassalkovich, the costs were 402,679 forints.

Nuns and scholars

The future of the complex was uncertain; the Queen had no intention to use it as a royal residence, because she did not spend much time in Buda. In 1769 she gave one wing to the Sisters of Loreto, who came from Sankt Pölten. The building was handed over on 13 May 1770, but the elegant Baroque rooms were considered unsuitable for a nunnery. Alexander Keglevich, rector of the Eötvös Loránd University,[314] had provided financing to Maria Theresa, which supposedly should have been repaid, according to her letters to her children and friends.[315] In 1777 the Queen decided that the University of Nagyszombat should move to Buda.

The nuns moved out and the palace was hastily adapted to use as a university. The work was guided by Farkas Kempelen and led to classrooms, teacher's cabinets, museums, a library and a university press being built. In the front, the false dome was removed and a four-storey observatory tower, planned by Alfred Hillebrandt or Karl Georg Zillack was erected.

In 1778 Hillebrandt built a new chapel for the first king of Hungary, Saint Stephen's, the mummified right hand, which was recovered by Queen Maria Theresa from the Republic of Ragusa in 1771.[316,317] The Chapel of the Holy Right was situated near the St Sigismund Chapel, in the middle of an inner court. The outer form was octagonal and the inside was oval, crowned by a dome. The altar-piece was painted by Joseph Hauzinger.

The ribbon-cutting ceremony of the university was held on 25 June 1780, the 40th anniversary of the coronation of the Queen. The throne room became

Figure 35: *Archduke Joseph Anton, Palatine of Hungary, resided in the castle.*

a splendid aula decorated with frescoes depicting the four faculties. In 1953, two grisaille frescoes were discovered on the shorter sides of the room.

Residence of the Palatines

Functional problems of the university remained unresolved, which led to the faculties being moved to Pest in 1783. In 1791 the palace became the residence of the new Habsburg palatine of the Kingdom of Hungary, Archduke Alexander Leopold of Austria. After the early death of the palatine in 1795, his younger brother Archduke Joseph succeeded him, followed by Archduke Stephen. The palatinal court in Buda Castle was the centre of fashionable life and high society in the Hungarian capital.

In 1810 the palatinal palace was damaged by fire, but in the next decades, plans were made to raise the building with an upper storey, but they were not implemented, although the observatory tower, which hindered the work, was removed. In 1838 the crypt of the St. Sigismund Chapel was rebuilt according to the plans of Franz Hüppmann: the Palatinal Crypt was the burial place of Palatine Joseph and his family. The crypt is the only part of the palace that survived the Second World War.

Figure 36: *Buda Castle before its remodeling in the 1880s*

Palatine Joseph established gardens on the southern and eastern hillsides of the Castle Hill according to the plans of Antal Tost. The gardens of Buda Castle were among the most famous English-style landscape gardens in Hungary.

Palatine Stephen left the palace on 23 September 1848 when a break between the liberal Hungarian government and the dynasty became inevitable.

On 5 January Buda was occupied by the Austrian army led by Alfred I, Prince of Windisch-Grätz. The chief commander lodged in the royal palace.

On 4 May 1849, the Hungarian army, led by Artúr Görgey, laid siege on Buda Castle, which was being defended by General Heinrich Hentzi. On 20 May the Hungarians captured Buda with an assault. The palace was the last stronghold of the Austrian troops, and became a site of heavy artillery fighting. The ensuing fire consumed the central and southern wings; they were completely burned out and their interiors were destroyed.

Era of Franz Joseph

The palace was rebuilt between 1850 and 1856 by Josef Weiss and Carl Neuwirth. The 13-axis central wing was raised with a third storey and a squat attic-tower. The central risalit was decorated with a balcony of six colossal columns. With these changes, the former Viennese Baroque palace of Maria Theresa became considered a more austere Neoclassical Baroque building.

The ballroom was redecorated with marbles and stuccoes. After 1853 stately rooms were designed in a French Rococo style, with white-gold stuccoes and furniture from the Hofburg. The palace was already too small for the needs of the royal court, so the kitchens and service rooms were housed in the neighbouring Zeughaus. The palace was connected with the Zeughaus by a glassed passageway.

Figure 37: *View of the castle before its remodeling, as seen from the Danube*

On the western side of the *cour d'honneur* two smaller buildings were erected, using plans by Weiss and Neuwirth in 1854. The two-storey *Stöckl* housed the apartments of the archdukes and imperial officials, whereas the Wachlokal was built for the royal guards.

Emperor Franz Joseph I of Austria visited Buda Castle in 1856 and 1857. After the Austro-Hungarian Compromise of 1867, Franz Joseph was crowned king of Hungary. The palace played an important part in the lavish ceremony and was a symbol of peace between the dynasty and the nation.

In the last decades of the 19th century Budapest experienced rapid economic development. Ambitious urban planning projects were carried out to express the growing wealth and higher status of the Hungarian capital, with special attention being paid to the rebuilding of Buda Castle. The autonomous Hungarian government intended to create a royal palace to match any famous European royal residence (especially their old rival, Vienna's Hofburg). The rebuilding spanned forty years, between 1875 and 1912, and caused sweeping changes in topography of the entire area.

First the Várkert-bazár (Royal Garden Pavilion) was built on the embankment of the Danube, at the foot of the Castle Hill, between 1875 and 1882. This Neo-Renaissance gateway was designed by an Hungarian architect named Miklós Ybl. The structure was an open arcade, with pavilions, stairways and ramps, and two blocks of flats. Ybl also built a new waterworks pumping station, named Várkert-kioszk (Royal Garden Kiosk), and two stair towers against the medieval cortina walls. The southern stair tower followed French Renaissance style, resembling a small turreted castle, while the northern stair tower

Figure 38: *The Danube terrace with Eugene of Savoy's monument*

was similar to a Gothic brick donjon (a fortified main tower from a castle, also called a keep). Only Várkert-bazár and Várkert-kioszk survive currently.

In 1882 Prime Minister Kálmán Tisza charged Ybl with drawing a master plan for rebuilding the palace. In his 1885 plan, Ybl preserved the old Baroque palace, but mirrored it on the western side of the *cour d'honneur*, which doubled the size of the residence. He also planned a new carriageway on the western hillside, demolishing the medieval walls and towers of the Újvilág-kert terrace. The narrowness of the natural plateau of the Castle Hill meant there was not enough space for the new Krisztinaváros wing, which Ybl solved by erecting a substructure down to the foot of the hill. The monumental western façade sits on this windowless, three storey high substructure. The whole block covered almost the entire hill, but the main façade on the *cour d'honneur* had the same modest height as the Baroque palace. The façade was clad with stone slabs, while the old parts are stuccoed; hence, the difference between the original Baroque and the Neo-Renaissance wings is obvious. The formerly open *cour d'honneur* became a closed court with an arched gateway, guarded by the four lions of the sculptor, János Fadrusz. The court is called Lions Court (or *Oroszlános udvar*).

The work began on 1 May 1890, but Ybl died on 22 January 1891. His successor, Alajos Hauszmann, slightly modified the plans of the Krisztinaváros

Figure 39: *Royal procession in the western courtyard (1880s)*

wing. In 1896 the building reached the level of the court, and King Franz Joseph ceremoniously laid down the foundation stone of the palace, which was soon completed.

In 1893, the 25th anniversary of King Franz Joseph's coronation was celebrated in the Royal Palace. However, the old banqueting hall proved to be too small, so Hauszmann enlarged the room by knocking down and reconstructing the wall towards the *cour d'honneur* (which additionally had the Hillebrandt façade).

In spite of this expansion and Ybl's new wing, the palace was still deemed insufficient for great royal celebrations, so another round of construction began. The north wing, standing on the site of the old Zeughaus, was completely designed by Hauszmann. The architect doubled the Baroque palace on the Danube side, generally imitating its traditional architectural style. At the meeting point of the old and the new wings, a colonnaded portico was erected, with a lavishly-decorated tympanum (with allegorical statues by Károly Sennyey) and a flight of stairs called the *Habsburg Stairs*. The whole palace was crowned with a dome with a copy of the Crown of St. Stephen at its apex. The dome, like other details of the north wing, shows German *Jugendstil* influences, as does the rear façade towards the western forecourt. This forecourt also contains the Matthias Fountain (Hungarian: *Mátyás kútja*) by sculptor Alajos Stróbl. Above the main gate, towards Szent György tér, stood a statue

Buda Castle

Figure 40: *The western forecourt with the facade of the Grand Ballroom*

of the Goddess Hungaria. This side was the main façade of the complex, but it was much shorter and less characteristic than the long Danube façade. The old Chapel of the Holy Right was demolished to make room for a carriageway.

Hauszmann designed a new riding school in the former Újvilág terrace, which was now named the *Csikós* court, after the Csikós statue of György Vastagh (now in the western forecourt). In front of the long Danube façade, an equestrian statue was erected in honour of Prince Eugene of Savoy, the victorious leader of the Habsburg army in the Battle of Zenta. The eastern forecourt was closed off with a lavish wrought-iron rail, which ended in a pillar crowned by a statue of the legendary Turul, the sacred bird of the Magyars, spreading its wings above Budapest. Two flights of stairs led up to the Szent György tér, which was on much higher ground.

In the western forecourt, Hauszmann designed a new neo-Baroque guardhouse and rebuilt the old Royal Stables. The Royal Gardens on the southern hillside were famous for their precious plants, glass houses and picturesque terraces. In the middle of the gardens stood the Swiss House of Queen Elisabeth, furnished with Hungarian folk art objects. The house was built above the ruins of the medieval gatehouse, partially making use of them.

The interior of the palace was decorated and furnished exclusively with works of the leading Hungarian artists of the age. The Royal Palace was officially inaugurated in 1912. Contemporary critics praised it as the most outstanding Hungarian building of the turn of the 20th century.

Figure 41: *View of the dome and the terrace with Prince Eugene's monument (1926)*

Interbellum years and World War II

The Hauszmann palace existed for around three decades: on 30 December 1916, the building played a part in the coronation ceremony of the last Hungarian king, Charles IV of Hungary. After the 1918 revolution and the removal of the Habsburg dynasty, the Royal Palace became the seat of the new regent of the Kingdom of Hungary, Miklós Horthy. Horthy lived in the Krisztinaváros wing with his family between the years of 1920 and 1944. In this era the palace was the centre of Hungarian political and social life. Famous guests entertained by Horthy in the palace included King Victor Emmanuel III of Italy in 1937 and Cardinal Eugenio Pacelli (later Pope Pius XII) in 1938.

On 16 October 1944 a Nazi German commando unit, led by Otto Skorzeny, occupied the Royal Palace and forced the regent to abdicate. Buda Castle was the last major stronghold of Budapest held by Axis forces during the siege of Budapest between 29 December 1944 and 13 February 1945. The German and Hungarian forces defending the castle attempted to break the Soviet blockade on 11 February 1945, but failed. Allegedly the Soviet Red Army knew about their plans and had aimed heavy weapons at the possible escape routes hours earlier. This is considered one of the biggest disasters of Hungarian military history.

Figure 42: *The Royal Palace in the 1930s*

Heavy fights and artillery fire rendered the palace into ruins. The furniture vanished, roofs and vaults collapsed and the southern and western wings were burned out. The destruction was comparable to that of the great siege of 1686.

Reconstruction

Immediately after the war, archeological research was begun in order to unearth the remains of the medieval castle. The research, led by László Gerő (1946–1966) and László Zolnay (1967–1979), was likely the biggest castle excavation in Europe. The former Royal Gardens stairways, pavilions and glass houses, which dated from the turn of the 20th century, had to be sacrificed. Important parts of the former Sigismund and Matthias Palace had survived under the thick earth fill.

The first reconstruction plan of the medieval remains was written by László Gerő in 1950 and finalised in 1952. The reconstruction work was finished in 1966. Contrary to the generally accepted principles of historic reconstruction, the medieval fortification system was rebuilt in its entirety. Important elements like the 16th century Great Rondella and the medieval Gatehouse, the Mace Tower, the walls and the zwingers were reconstructed according to the results of the archaeological research and contemporary pictorial evidence. The low-lying southern wing of the Gothic palace was also reconstructed, together with the vaulted Gothic Hall and the Lower Church of the former Royal Chapel. Medieval-style gardens were planted in the zwingers. The foundation

Figure 43: *The burned-out ruins of the Royal Palace and the Chain Bridge (1946)*

of the Stephen's Tower was unearthed, but as archaeological evidence was lacking, the tower was not reconstructed. The remains of the Broken Tower were covered again.

The large-scale reconstruction of the medieval fortifications substantially changed the cityscape of Budapest. At the time it was considered a highly successful project, reconciling historical authenticity with urban-planning demands.

In the 1970s, archeological research continued on the northern and western side of the palace, led by László Zolnay. It produced many important achievements, including the Late Gothic Buda Castle Statues. The Karakash Pasha Tower, in the *Újvilág Garden*, was a Turkish-era tower demolished at the end of the 19th century. Photographic evidence enabled its reconstruction, but the new tower was only a copy of the original, and the details are not considered authentic.

Modernization

The government made a decision about reconstruction only in 1948. According to contemporary photos, all the important interiors were in a damaged state, but their reconstruction was technically possible. The new communist government of Hungary considered the Royal Palace a symbol of the former

Figure 44: *The modernist dome designed by Lajos Hidasi in 1961. Vast amounts of art work and sculpture on the exterior and almost all of the interior that survived the war were intentionally destroyed during the postwar reconstruction.*

Figure 45: *Aerial view of the castle today*

regime. Therefore, Hungarian leaders chose to thoroughly modernise the interior and exterior of the palace. Architectural trends played a part in the decision, as modernist architects had condemned the Hauszmann style as "too ornate".

The first modernist reconstruction plan was made by architect István Janáky in 1950. His controversial concept was later modified. In 1952 the Hungarian government asked for help from Poland, because they had successfully rebuilt Warsaw and, indeed, other cities. A delegation of Polish experts, led by the architectural historian Jan Zachwatowicz, proposed the rebuilding of the Hauszmann palace.

During the 1950s the palace was gutted and all the remaining interior, including the rooms and halls that were undamaged, were destroyed. Important exterior details, such as the main entrance, the Habsburg Steps, the dome, the Royal Stables, the guardhouse and the riding school were demolished, and the remaining façades were simplified. In Lions Court the ornate gates of *King's Stairs* and *Diplomat's Stairs* were demolished. The doorway of the castle church disappeared, as did the chapel. The detailed Neo-Baroque roofs were simplified and plain new windows were installed. The allegorical sculpture group of the tympanum was destroyed.

At the same time however, medieval elements that were uncovered were reconstructed in what was thought their appearance was. No precise drawings existed of the medieval elements, therefore an approximate reconstruction of their appearance was done.

The modernist dome was designed by Lajos Hidasi in 1961 after Italian Baroque models. The palace was rebuilt by 1966, but the interior spaces were ready only in the 1980s. Buda Castle became a cultural centre, home to three museums and the National Széchényi Library.

21st century

In March 2006 the National Office of Cultural Heritage finalised the long-term development plan of Buda Castle. Asserting that the modernisation in 1952–66 caused irreversible damage, they proposed the partial reconstruction of the façades, including the dome and the Habsburg Steps. No decision has been reached about the realization of the development plan.

On 25 July 2007 Prime Minister Ferenc Gyurcsány chose the medieval King's Cellar in Buda Castle as the place to announce the list of the "most important public works projects", which was financed by European Union funds between 2007–2013.

In 2008 an international consortium began to build an underground garage for 700 cars under the former Csikós Court. The developer was granted permission to demolish a 4.5-metre-long (15 ft) section of the 15th-century castle wall. The demolition was carried out in spite of criticism from archeologists and the public. The area had been previously excavated by archeologists, who discovered many important finds, including medieval children's toys and a tooth from the pet leopard of King Matthias Corvinus. Additionally, the area outside the inner walls was used as a garbage dump during the 15th–17th centuries. However, financial difficulties interrupted the construction of the garage in 2009; work resumed for a short time in November 2011 but stopped again after the completion of the concrete basement slab. The government granted 1.3 billion forint for the completion of the project in 2015 after the half-built garage was bought by the state. The castle courtyard was also used as the setting for Katy Perry's 2010 music video, "Firework", part of her *Teenage Dream* album.

Medieval wing

In 1958–1962, architect László Gerő partially recreated the façades of the Gothic castle facing the narrow southern, western and eastern courts. Only the ground and first floors were reconstructed; the castle was originally much higher. The unfinished façade stops at the level of the Baroque terrace above, with two windows opening towards the southern court and another two opening towards the eastern court. The four almost-identical windows are square, four-panel stone constructions of very fine Gothic craftsmanship, with their outer frames decorated with small columns. One window, which had been walled up, was discovered *in situ* during archeological research, and the others were reconstructed from fragments by the sculptor Ernő Szakál by means of anastylosis. The ground floor openings are simpler. An arched stone doorway gives access to the southern court from the cellar under the Gothic Hall.

The façade was originally plastered. The whitewashed surface was decorated with a painted pattern in a rusty hue, resembling rustication. Fragments of painted geometrical decoration, a common feature on the medieval buildings of Buda, were discovered on the eastern façade, but it was not restored.

A Gothic balcony tower projects from the wall at the end of the eastern façade. Its reconstruction was a much debated issue, because the balcony tower goes above the level of the Baroque terrace, disturbing the harmonious panorama of the palace. On the other hand, it clearly indicates that there are higher, missing floors.

The balcony tower is a two-storey structure standing on a wide stone basement. The first floor is a solid stone wall without any openings and the niche behind it belongs to the Gothic Hall. The second floor has a balcony with three windows; it is now closed off by a glass wall. Originally it would have been part of an important ceremonial room. The balcony is in the shape of half an octagon. The three Gothic double lancet windows are considered the most important architectural elements of the tower and the profiles; frames and mullions were restored in a simplified form, using many of the original stones. The tower is covered with a flat metal roof.

The Gothic Hall is connected to Stephen's Castle (*István vár*) on the western side. It was named after Prince Stephen, Duke of Slavonia, the younger brother of King Louis I of Hungary. Built in the 1340s–1370s, it is the oldest part of the medieval royal palace. Only the foundation and three interconnected barrel-vaulted rooms survive.

Stephen's Tower (*István torony*) was the keep of Stephen's Castle. However, it was destroyed by an explosion in 1686. The ground floor walls were discovered a little time after 1946. It was a square building (11.7 × 11.1 m), built upon the rock surface of Castle Hill. The walls are 2.31 to 2.7 m thick with narrow arrowslits on the southern, western and northern sides. The original doorway, on the eastern side, was walled up after the Gothic Hall was built in the 15th century.

Stephen's Tower was originally a free-standing structure, sited differently from later buildings. The triangle in front of it was walled up to create a continuous southern façade for the palace. During post-war reconstruction, this part of the façade (with a broken stone doorway) was not reconstructed. A vaulted room (6.2 × 6.3 m) on the ground floor was still intact in 1820, according to a contemporary drawing. Although the ribs, corbels and key stone were discovered during archeological research, the room was not reconstructed. A spiral stairway had connected the room with the missing higher floors.

The remaining part of the Stephen's Castle (with the barrel-vaulted rooms behind) has a simple stone façade with a Gothic doorway. The pointed arch was later restored.

Interior

The interior from the time of Maria Theresa and Franz Joseph was mostly destroyed during World War II and the post-war reconstruction, excluding the Palatinal Crypt, which survived both. Little information exists about the interiors from the medieval and Baroque eras, but the palace built at the turn of the 20th century was meticulously recorded, using detailed descriptions, photographic documentation and grounds plans. Architect Alajos Hauszmann said about the royal apartments: "I created a 200 m [660 ft] long series of

Figure 46: *The lower chapel of the medieval castle*

rooms, longer than any similar royal apartments in continental Europe except Versailles."

A series of rooms from the medieval castle were unearthed and reconstructed during the post-war rebuilding of Buda Castle in 1958–62. They are now part of the permanent exhibition of the Budapest History Museum in "Building E" of Buda Castle.

Medieval period

Architectural context

Only a fragment of the medieval castle survived the destruction of 1686–1715. The surviving rooms are not considered the most important ones; and none of the more famous rooms and buildings mentioned in the medieval sources exist today. The rooms which were unearthed after 1946 were only saved by chance and by their geographical position at a lower level than the newly created Baroque terrace. The Gothic Hall and the Palace Chapel were built by King Sigismund Luxemburg at the beginning of the 15th century. The castle wing is surrounded by a complex system of medieval fortifications.

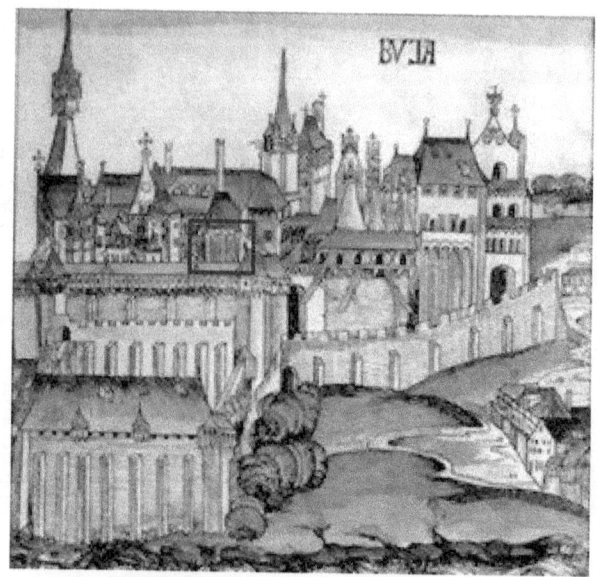

Figure 47: *Buda Castle in the Middle Ages, from the Chronicles of Hartmann Schedel. The castle church, dedicated to St. John the Almoner, is indicated by the blue rectangle.*

Castle chapel

The first chapel in the castle was probably built in the 14th century during the reign of Louis I of Hungary. Eberhard Windecke claimed in his Chronicle that Charles II of Hungary was murdered in 1386 in a room from which the royal chapel could be seen. The chapel was again mentioned in the Chronicle of Lorenzo de Monacis, which was written around 1390.

King Sigismund of Luxemburg thoroughly rebuilt the old Anjou castle during the first decades of the 15th century. He erected a Gothic church in place of the former chapel. The Anjou castle's façade was now facing towards the inner palace courtyard, and the long chancel was projecting from the eastern side of the palace. The chancel was built upon a lower church due to a lack of space on the narrow plateau. The church had a 21-metre-long (69 ft) nave and an 11-metre-long (36 ft) chancel. The flamboyant Royal Church of Buda Castle was similar to the more famous Sainte-Chapelle in Paris.

Archeological research proved the date of the church, because 15th-century strata were discovered under the intact brick floor of the lower church.[318]

In November 1489, Sultan Bayezid II of the Ottoman Empire sent the relics of John the Almoner to King Matthias Corvinus. The King placed the relics in the Royal Chapel, which was re-dedicated and embellished with Renaissance furniture. In 1526, Buda was plundered by the Ottoman Turks after the Battle of Mohács. The relics were rescued in time and carried to Pressburg, where they are still kept currently. A surviving church inventory from 1530 shows a wealth of furnishings. Later, King János Szapolyai converted the lower church into a bastion. The large Gothic windows were walled up; and only the rectangular arrow slits were left open.

In 1541 the Ottoman Turks captured Buda without resistance, and the Royal Church ceased to be a place of Christian worship. The upper church was destroyed in the 1686 siege of Buda, and the ruins were demolished in 1715. The vault of the lower church collapsed, and the interior was filled with rubbish. The remains were then buried under the new Baroque terrace for two centuries.

The ruins of the lower church were discovered by archeologists in 1949–50. The remains were buried in 1953 because of conceptional disputes about the possible reconstruction. The chapel, finally reconstructed by 1963, was re-consecrated in 1990.

Gothic Hall

The Gothic Hall is one of the most important surviving example of secular Gothic architecture in Central Europe. It was built by King Sigismund of Luxemburg in the early 15th century as an extension of the earlier Anjou palace. It was built on the southern edge of the natural rock plateau of Castle Hill. The level difference between the plateau and the southern court was about 2.79 metres (9.2 ft). A vaulted cellar was built under the hall to span this difference.

The Gothic Hall is an irregular rectangle of 20.2 × 11.55 m (66.3 × 37.9 ft), with a closed niche on the eastern side, which is the inside of the balcony tower. It is divided into two naves with Gothic rib vaults. The vaults are supported by two massive pillars which come up through the floor from the cellar beneath the room, and in addition, half-pillars in the corners support the ribs. All six vaults are quadripartite, and the two on the inner side are irregularly shaped.

The hall has four windows, two on the southern side and two on the eastern side, with stone benches in the window niches. The Hall was connected to the palace through a door in the northern wall, supposedly on the place of the original doorway. The northern section of the floor is three steps higher.

All the newly built side walls were plastered and painted white, while the original stone surfaces were left uncovered. The ribs, pillars, arches and window niches were restored by sculptor Ernő Szakál in 1961–62. The ribs have a simple profile, but fragments of a more complicated type were also found in the rubble, together with keystones. These pieces supposedly belonged to another stately hall situated above the room, but they were built into the reconstructed vaults by restorers in the 20th-century.

The northern pillar of the Gothic Hall was already discovered by Alajos Hauszmann at the beginning of the 20th century. The remains were buried under the outbuildings of the Royal Gardens, and Hauszmann protected the medieval pillar by building a brick shaft around it.

Barrel-vaulted rooms

Three interconnected barrel-vaulted rooms belong to the oldest part of the palace, Stephen's Castle, which was built by Prince Stephen, Duke of Slavonia, in the 14th century. The northern room is larger (6.62 × 9.42 m or 21.7 × 30.9 ft) than the southern ones (5 × 4.55 m or 16.4 × 14.9 ft). The northern room is covered by an east-west axial vault while the southern rooms have north-south axial vaults.

The southern room is connected to the inner courtyard by a doorway. There is a small window high on the western wall. The middle room has a similar window. The larger northern room has three slit windows, one facing west and two facing north, all had iron rails. The rooms were connected to each other with carved Gothic corbel doors. The walls were originally plastered. In the southern room, a medieval stairway led to a trapdoor and a medieval toilet hidden in the empty space between the walls of the castle and the keep.

The barrel vaulted rooms were supposedly used as a prison in the Middle Ages. Later the southern vaults collapsed. The intact barrel vault of the northern room was broken by Alajos Hauszmann at the beginning of the 20th century when he filled the cellar with rubble. The barrel-vaulted rooms were restored in 1958–1962.

Albrecht Cellar

A medieval cellar north of the barrel-vaulted rooms, later called *Albrecht pince* (Albrecht Cellar), is covered with a Gothic brick barrel vault. The walls are blackened from burning. The cellar was probably built by King Sigismund of Luxemburg as the *Cisterna Regia*, i.e. the great underground cistern of the palace.

The Cisterna Regia was situated under the former northern zwinger of the palace. This small rectangular courtyard became a private royal garden during the reign of King Matthias Corvinus. The private garden was an early Renaissance *giardino segreto* (hidden garden). It was designed by architect Chimenti Camicia in the 1470s. A well in the middle of the garden was fed by the cistern underneath.

The hidden garden, the well and the cistern survived the 1686 siege of Buda. They were indicated on the plans of the area drawn by military architect Joseph de Haüy in 1687. In 1715–1724 the former Cisterna Regia became the cellar of the new Baroque palace. A section of this room was later used as an ice chamber.

King's Cellar

The King's Cellar (*Király pince*) is not a medieval structure, but a Baroque-era brick cellar under the Danube side of Building E. It was filled with tons of earth and rubble, and the original eastern façade of the medieval royal palace survived under the fill. The inner walls of the Baroque palace were actually built upon the old façade. Only the 7-metre-high (23 ft) basement section of the original façade remained.

This wing was built by King Sigismund of Luxenburg in the early 15th century and was rebuilt by King Matthias Corvinus 50 years later. The surviving eastern façade was built from large, finely carved blocks of stone. It followed the contour of Castle Hill with a break in the middle. A buttress was added and a rectangular tower with two buttresses on its corners. The lower part of a balcony on the tower was reconstructed, with three elegant Gothic corbels decorated with cusps.

It was not possible to demolish the King's Cellar because the whole Baroque palace was resting upon it; the inner fill was removed in 1961. The medieval façade was reconstructed inside the cellar space between 1961–1965. Large windows were cut in the outer wall of the cellar to let in the daylight. Currently, the architectural history of the palace is discernible by viewing the interwoven layers of the past.

On 25 July 2007 Prime Minister Ferenc Gyurcsány chose the King's Cellar as the place to announce the list of the "most important public works projects", financed by European Union funds between 2007–2013.

Baroque and Historicism

Old ceremonial rooms

The old ceremonial rooms were as follows:

"Zenta" Room

The "Zenta" Room (*"Zenta" előterem*) was on the first floor of the Baroque wing, was situated next to the audience antechamber. It opened from the main staircase of the central wing and was the first room of the ceremonial apartments on that side. In the early 1900s, it had a white-golden stucco decoration with one chandelier. The name of the chamber referred to the large painting of the Battle of Zenta contained therein.

Figure 48: *The Zenta Room*

Audience Antechamber

The Audience Antechamber (*Fogadási váróterem*) was situated north of the ballroom on the first floor of the Baroque wing. In the Baroque era it was called *Antichambre Ihrer Majestat der Kaiserin* ("Her Majesty the Empress' Antechamber"). The room gave access to Maria Theresa's private apartments from the ballroom. In the early 1900s, the audience antechamber became part of the ceremonial apartments and had the same white-golden Rococo stucco decoration as the white antechamber on the other side.

Grand Throne Room

The Grand Throne Room (*Nagy trónterem*), formerly known as the ballroom (*Nagyterem*), on the first floor of the Baroque wing had several layers of Baroque decoration from the second half of the 18th and the 19th century. Two surviving drawings record the oldest form of the room. Jakob Schmutzer's drawing from 1777 shows the opening ceremony of the Eötvös Loránd University after it was moved to the palace. The room had a Late Baroque decoration with double grooved Corinthian pilasters between the windows and stucco garlands. The walls were decorated with Vinzenz Fischer's frescoes of the four faculties. József Pollencig's drawing from 1795 shows a ball scene in the "Prunksaal". The pilasters were kept, but the frescoes were already covered, and the whole room was stuccoed. On the vault the coat-of-arms of the

Figure 49: *The Audience Antechamber*

Figure 50: *The Grand Throne Room (c. 1894)*

Figure 51: *The White Antechamber*

Kingdom of Hungary can be seen. After the destruction of the 1849 siege, the room was redecorated in Neo-Baroque style. In 1892 the old ballroom was rebuilt with a new ceiling and a gallery towards the Lions Court; three of its side walls were preserved. It was enlarged again after 1896. The function of the ballroom was given to another new hall and this room was converted into the main throne hall instead. In the early 1900s, the room had a Rococo white-golden stucco decoration with three large chandeliers.

Vinzenz Fischer's frescoes were re-discovered in 1953 during the post-war reconstruction. In spite of this, all the decoration layers were destroyed. Today it houses the Gothic altar collection of the Hungarian National Gallery.

White Antechamber

The White Antechamber (*Fehér előterem*) is on the first floor of the Baroque wing and was situated south of the throne room. In the Baroque era it was called *Zweyten Antichambre* ("second antechamber"). In the early 1900s it had a Rococo white-golden stucco decoration with one chandelier and a white Rococo stove.

Buda Castle

Figure 52: *The Coronation Room*

"Coronation" Room

The "Coronation" Room (*"Koronázás" előterem*), also on the first floor of the Baroque wing, was situated next to the white antechamber. It opened from the main staircase of the southern wing and was the first room of the ceremonial apartments on that side. In the early 1900s it had a white-golden stucco decoration with one chandelier. The name of the chamber referred to the painting of Franz Joseph I's coronation as King of Hungary after the Austro-Hungarian Compromise of 1867.

Old royal apartments

The old royal apartments are as follows:

Small Throne Room

The Small Throne Room (*Kis trónterem*), which was situated next to the Audience Antechamber on the first floor of the Baroque wing. In the Baroque era it was called *Audienz-Zimmer* and was part of the Empress' private apartments. In Hauszmann's time it was converted into the throne room of the palace, with a simple Baroque throne under a baldachin. It had a white-golden stucco decoration with one chandelier and a Rococo tile stove.

Figure 53: *The Small Throne Room*

"Circle" Tearoom

The "Circle" Tearoom (*"Circle" teaszalon*) was on the first floor of the Baroque wing and situated next to the small throne room, in the corner of the southern wing. In the Baroque era it was called *Gesellschaft Zimmer Ihrer Majestat der Kaiserin* ("Her Majesty the Empress' Parlour") and was part of Maria Theresa's private apartments. In the early 1900s, it had a white-golden stucco decoration with one chandelier and a Rococo tile stove. The furniture consisted a Rococo parlour suite.

Antechamber

The Antechamber was on the first floor of the Baroque wing and was situated next to the "circle" tearoom with two windows opening on to the Danube. In the Baroque era it was called *Ankleide-Zimmer Ihrer Majestät der Kaiserin* ("Her Majesty the Empress' Dressing Room") and was part of Maria Theresa's private apartments. It was connected to another small room, the *Frauen Kammer*. In Hauszmann's time the walls were largely clad with wallpaper. The furniture consisted a Rococo tile stove, chairs and paintings. The last small room of the Empress, the former *Schreib cabinet* ("writing room"), with one window opening on to the Danube, later became a simple passageway.

Figure 54: *The "Circle" Tearoom*

Figure 55: *Antechamber, former dressing room of the Queen*

Figure 56: *The Smoking Salon, former bedchamber of Queen Maria Theresa*

Smoking Room

The Smoking Room (*Dohányzó szalon*) was on the first floor of the Baroque wing and was situated in the middle of the Danube side of the old palace. In the Baroque era it was called *Schlafzimmer Ihrer k.k. Majestäten* ("The Imperial Couple's Bedroom"). It was the only common room of Empress Maria Theresa and her husband, Francis I. In the early 1900s, the walls were largely hung with wallpaper. The furniture consisted a Rococo parlour suite and paintings. In the old imperial apartments only the ceilings had the typically white-golden stucco decoration, used in the old ceremonial apartments.

Writing Room

The Writing Room (*Írószoba*) was on the first floor of the Baroque wing, was formerly part of the private apartments of Francis I. One window opened to the Danube. In the Baroque era it was called *Ankleidecabinet S.M. des Kaisers* ("Emperor's Dressing Room"). It was connected to another small room, the second dressing room. Later, the imperial dressing room was divided with a wall; with half being converted into a simple passageway, the other into a small writing room. In the early 1900s the latter's walls were largely clad with a very ornate Rococo wallpaper. It had a white marble mantelpiece with a large Rococo mirror above.

Figure 57: *The Writing Room*

Parlour

The Parlour (*Társalkodó terem*), on the first floor of the Baroque wing, was part of the private apartments of Francis I. It was situated in the corner of the southern wing with 2+3 windows opening on to the Danube. In the Baroque era the room was divided with a wall, one half named *Empfangs Zimmer S.M. des Kaisers* ("Imperial Audience Room"), the other *Arbeits Cabinet* ("Study"). In Hauszmann's time, it was converted to a great parlour with wallpaper clad walls, a Rococo tile stove, a chandelier, paintings, chairs and a mirror.

Antechamber

The Antechamber, on the first floor of the Baroque wing, was the last room of the former private apartments of Francis I. In the Baroque era it was called *Zweyten Audienz Zimmer* ("second audience room"). In Hauszmann's time the walls were mainly clad with wallpaper, and it had a Rococo tile stove, a chandelier, paintings and chairs.

Figure 58: *The Parlour*

Figure 59: *last Antechamber*

Figure 60: *Entrance to the King's Staircase*

South Wing

The rooms of the south wing are as follows:

Baroque Court

The Baroque Court (*Barokk udvar*), a rectangular court, which is the oldest part of the Baroque palace. Here the original 18–19th century façades survived, and in 1997 the court was covered with a glass roof and became the main exhibition hall of the Budapest History Museum.

King's Staircase

The King's Staircase (*Király-lépcső*), the Baroque main staircase of the southern wing gave access to the private apartments of Emperor Francis I. Both the King's Staircase and its northern twin, the Diplomat's Staircase, had ornate gates opening onto Lions Court, decorated with telamons. The kitchens were originally situated on the ground floor of the southern wing, but they were relocated by Hauszmann.

Figure 61: *St Stephen's Chapel*

Central Wing

The central wing had the following rooms:

Diplomat's Staircase

The Diplomat's Staircase (*Diplomata-lépcső*) was the Baroque main staircase of the central (originally northern) wing and gave access to the private apartments of Maria Theresa. In the 18th century there was an officer's dining room and a smaller kitchen on the ground floor and another dining room with a cafe kitchen on the first floor. The southern and northern (later central) wings had the same ground plan: all the rooms opened from a passageway running along the sides of a rectangular central court. The two monumental stairways were rebuilt by Hauszmann in Neo-Baroque style.

St Stephen's Chapel

St Stephen's Chapel, known before as St. Sigismund Chapel, or Castle Church (*Szent Zsigmond-kápolna, Vártemplom*) was the chapel royal in the western end of this wing, which had no façades, only a door opening onto Lions Court (through an antechamber). Construction was finished in 1768 and the church was consecrated in 1769. The ground plan was drawn by Nicolaus Pacassi, with the interior was designed by his follower, Franz Anton Hillebrandt. The ground plan followed a typical "violin" form favoured in the Baroque church architecture of Central Europe at that time. It had a rectangular chancel and a nave with four bays for side altars. On the first and the second floors two oratories opened into the chancel and a two-storey high gallery was situated above the entrance. In 1777–78 a new door was opened in the first side bay to give access to the new chapel of the Holy Right. An engraving from 1771–80 shows the original interior design in its completed form: double pilasters, windows with segmental arches, stucco and false marble decoration, double oratory windows and a doorway with a stucco veil drawn aside by flying putti. The church was slightly rebuilt by Hauszmann, who demolished the Chapel of the Holy Right in 1899 and built a new chapel for the relic behind the chancel (converting a small recess). This chapel was decorated with the golden Venetian mosaics of Károly Lotz. A new Neo-Baroque main altar was built in the church in 1899.

20th-century photos testify that the church survived in its Baroque form until the war. During a siege, the vaults of the church partially collapsed and the furniture was plundered. The Castle Church was left decaying for more than a decade. In 1957 the remaining two vaults collapsed, and the church was totally destroyed and converted to exhibition spaces. The altar table was rescued and re-erected in Pilisvörösvár in 1957. The Lotz mosaics from the Chapel of the Holy Right were also rescued and re-assembled in Balatonalmádi.

Palatinal Crypt

The Palatinal Crypt (*Nádori kripta*) was under the former palace chapel and is the only surviving room of the whole Royal Castle. The underground crypt was first used as a burial place between 1770–1777. In August 1820, Elisabeth Karoline, Palatine Joseph's infant daughter was buried in the crypt. Seventeen years later, the Palatine's 13-year-old son Alexander Leopold followed. Palatine Joseph decided to convert the crypt into a family mausoleum and commissioned Franz Hüppmann with the task. The work was finished in 1838, and other members of the Palatine's family were reburied here. Palatine Joseph himself was interred on 13 January 1847. The crypt was continuously used by the Hungarian branch of the Habsburg family. It was repeatedly restored and enriched with new works of art, frescoes, statues and ornate stone sarcophagi, made by renowned artists of the 19th century. The last member of the family buried there was Archduchess Klotild in 1927. The crypt survived the war unscathed and was spared during the post-war reconstruction.

The crypt was looted in 1966 and 1973 (during the construction works), when some corpses were thrown out of the sarcophagi by the thieves. The human remains were later identified and reburied. The crypt was restored in 1985–1987. Since then the Palatinal Crypt is part of the exhibition of the Hungarian National Gallery.

Figure 62: *Tomb of Archduke Joseph, Palatine of Hungary in the Palatinal Crypt*

North Wing

Lobby

The main lobby (*Előcsarnok*) of the Royal Palace was situated in Hauszmann's Northern Wing on the Danube side. It was a long, rectangular hall divided into four sections with free standing Ionic columns and two square pillars. The section at the southern end was elevated a few steps. Nine arched windows opened towards the Danube. In the middle of the other sidewall, a doorway led to the inner courtyard. The walls and the ceiling were stuccoed. The southern elevation was closed off with a stone balustrade between the pillars and the wall. The ornate lobby was designed for important state ceremonies.

Grand Ballroom

The Grand Ballroom (*Nagy bálterem*), in the middle part of the northern wing, took over the function of the smaller old ballroom in the Baroque wing. Designed by Hauszmann, it was the most splendid room of the palace. The two-storey high, airy room was lavishly decorated with stuccoes, half columns, trabeation, balconies and six crystal chandeliers in Neo-Baroque style. Seven arched windows and doorways opened towards a pillared terrace facing the western forecourt. On the other side, the ballroom was connected to the Buffet Hall through three doors.

Figure 63: *The Grand Ballroom*

Photos made after the war show the room with its vaulted ceiling collapsed. The ballroom was not restored but totally destroyed in the course of the post-war remodelling.

Dining Hall

The Dining Hall (*Buffet-csarnok*), on the Danube side of the northern wing, was a very long hall used for state banquets. It was connected to the Great Ballroom nearby and it was possible to join them together. There was a shorter, passage-like space between the two rooms. This passage was separated from the Buffet Hall by six square pillars, while its other side was a solid wall with three doors. On the eastern side of the Buffet Hall a long row of windows opened towards the Danube and a pillared terrace. The Buffet Hall was divided into three sections with free-standing Ionic columns, holding trabeations. The vaulted ceiling was lavishly decorated with frescoes and stuccoes.

Habsburg Hall

The Habsburg Hall (*Habsburg terem*) was situated in the middle of the long palace complex, under Hauszmann's (false) dome, where the new northern wing and the old palace met. Although this part of the building belonged to the original palace, it was thoroughly rebuilt by Hauszmann–this stately room was totally his own work. It was one of the three historical rooms of the palace representing the important periods of Hungarian history. A free-standing, double

Figure 64: *The Dining Hall*

Figure 65: *The Habsburg Hall*

Buda Castle

Figure 66: *Wing facing the district of Krisztinaváros*

flight of steps, called the Habsburg Steps, connected the room with the Royal Gardens on the Danube terrace. The room had lavish Baroque decorations with half-pillars and gilded stuccoes. The vaulted ceiling was decorated with Károly Lotz's fresco *Apotheosis of the Habsburg Dynasty*. Károly Senyei's four Carrara marble busts stood in front of the sidewalls representing King Charles III, Queen Maria Theresa, King Franz Joseph and Queen Elisabeth.

The Habsburg Hall survived World War II relatively undamaged, but in the 1950s it was demolished for political reasons.

Krisztinaváros wing

The Krisztinaváros wing faces the district of Krisztinaváros, which was named in honour of the daughter of Queen Maria Theresa, Archduchess Maria Christina, Duchess of Teschen.

Entrance hall

The entrance hall (*Előcsarnok*) opened from Lions Court, under an arcaded Neo-Renaissance portico, through ornate wrought-iron doors. This now serves as the entrance of the Hungarian National Library. The hall was a long, oblong-shaped room with 4+4 free standing Ionic columns in front of the walls on the longer sides, holding a trabeation. In the end of the shorter sides two doors

Figure 67: *The Grand Staircase*

opened into antechambers. The three arcaded doorways on the longer side opened into a lobby. The ceiling of the hallway was stuccoed, and the whole design was Italian Renaissance in style.

Lobby

The lobby (*Előcsarnok*) was connected to the hall of the main staircase through pillars. The stuccoed ceiling was held up by two rectangular pillars. The apartments of Archduke József Ágost and his wife, Archduchess Auguszta, were situated on the ground floor of the Krisztinaváros wing and opened from this room. Now it serves as the lobby of the Hungarian National Library in a radically modernised form.

Main Staircase

The monumental main staircase (*Főlépcsőház*), with three flights, led up from the lobby to the first floor in an airy, glass-roofed hall. The side walls of the hall were decorated in Italian Renaissance style with colossal Corinthian half-columns, stuccoes and lunette openings. Ornate wrought-iron chandeliers and intricate balustrades decorated the stairs. On the ground floor, colossal Atlas statues stood beside the side pillars, holding the weight of the upper flights. The marble statues were the works of János Fadrusz from 1897. During the post-war reconstruction the main staircase was radically modernised. Only the

Figure 68: *St Stephen's Room*

two colossal Atlas statues survived. Now they are standing somewhat incongruently near their original places.

St Stephen's Room

St Stephen's Room (*"Szent István" terem*), on the first floor of the Krisztinaváros wing, was one of the "historical rooms" of the palace, created by Hauszmann. Together with the Matthias Room and the Habsburg Room, they represented the three most important periods of Hungarian history. Saint Stephen's Room connected the new Private Royal Apartments and—through a very long passageway—the Old Royal Apartments in the Danube Wing. Its style evoked the age of the Árpáds, the first Hungarian dynasty in the early Middle Ages. The walls were clad with dark carved wood paneling. The most spectacular item was a large stone mantelpiece with Romanesque Revival architectural details and the bust of King Saint Stephen, the first king of Hungary. The room was furnished with medieval-looking metal chandeliers and heavy wooden furniture.

Figure 69: *Matthias Room*

Matthias Room

Matthias Room (*Mátyás terem*) was named after King Matthias Corvinus, who ruled in the late Middle Ages. It was one of the three "historical rooms" of the palace, created by Hauszmann. The room opened from the Royal Bedroom, at the end of the line of private apartments. It had three windows opening towards the hills of Buda. There was a long terrace in front of the room. The style of the Matthias Room was Renaissance, with carved wooden paneling and a coffered ceiling. It was furnished with a mantelpiece in the corner and two chandeliers, the most spectacular item being the equestrian statue of King Matthias, sculpted by János Fadrusz. The statue was a miniature copy of the original standing on the main square of Kolozsvár (now Cluj-Napoca). This copy was saved after the war and put on display in the Hungarian National Gallery.

Strong Room

The Hungarian crown jewels were kept in the specially-designed Strong Room (*Páncélterem*) on the second floor of the Krisztinaváros Wing. The Crown of Saint Stephen was kept here between 1900 and 1944.

Figure 70: *The Entrance Hall*

Queen Elisabeth Memorial Museum

The small Queen Elisabeth Memorial Museum (*Erzsébet Királyné Emlékmúzeum*) on the second floor of the Krisztinaváros Wing was established in remembrance of Queen Elisabeth after her murder in 1898. Memorabilia were collected by Ida Ferenczy, Elisabeth's former lady-in-waiting, Viscountess Pallavicini and Countess Ilona Batthyány. The museum opened on 15 January 1908 as an affiliate of the Hungarian National Museum. The collection contained personal items, letters and clothes. Its most important relic was the costume that Elisabeth had been wearing when she was murdered. One room was meticulously recreated as the Queen's own writing room with her original writing desk and her 219 Hungarian books. The museum was badly damaged during World War II,[319] and the surviving relics were bestowed to other museums.

Private royal apartments

Royal Entrance Hall

The Royal Entrance Hall (*Fejedelmi előterem*), on the first floor of the Krisztinaváros Wing, gave access to the rooms of the Private Royal Apartments of King Franz Joseph I. The private apartments were situated in the southwestern part of the Krisztinaváros wing, their windows opening towards the hills

Figure 71: *Antechamber*

of Buda. The Royal Entrance Hall was connected through a wide passageway to the main staircase hall. The spacious, oblong-shaped hall was divided in three, with two pairs of Ionic marble columns supporting architraves. The central part of the room was much longer than the bays at the ends. Doors connected the hall with the rooms of the private apartments. In the middle of the longer wall stood an ornate stone mantelpiece with the bust of Franz Joseph. On the other side, three windows opened to the inner courtyard of the Krisztinaváros wing. The ceiling was stuccoed and the side walls of the hall were covered with marble.

Antechamber

The antechamber (*Előterem*) of the private apartments opened from the Royal Entrance Hall. It had three windows facing toward the hills. The room had a typical Biedermeier white-golden stucco decoration with floral wallpapers, resembling to the cosy rooms of Schönbrunn Palace. All the rooms of the private apartments followed this Viennese style favoured by the King. The antechamber was furnished with a stone mantelpiece (with a mirror above), an Empire crystal chandelier, a stone flowerpot standing on a fluted column and Neo-Renaissance table with chairs.

Figure 72: *The Audience Room*

Audience Room

The audience room (*Fogadószoba*) of Franz Joseph I was situated in a corner of the private apartments wing, with two windows opening southwards and three windows opening westwards. It had a beautiful stuccoed and frescoed ceiling. The walls were covered with floral wallpapers. The room was furnished with a crystal chandelier, a golden Rococo console table with a large mirror and a parlour suite.

Writing Room

The writing room (*Íroszoba*) of Franz Joseph had two windows opening towards the hills of Buda. It had a white-golden stuccoed ceiling and the walls were covered with floral wallpapers. The room was furnished with a crystal chandelier, an ornate white tile stove, a table and chairs. To the right and left two similar parlours opened from the room.

Royal Bedroom

The bedroom (*Fejedelmi hálószoba*) of the king had two windows opening towards the hills of Buda. It had a white-golden stuccoed ceiling and the walls were covered with floral wallpapers. The room was furnished with a crystal chandelier, the baldachined royal bed and a folding screen. The bedroom was

Figure 73: *Writing room in the royal suite*

Figure 74: *Bedroom of the king*

Figure 75: *The Dining Room*

connected to a dressing room, a private bathroom and smaller rooms belonging to the butler and the servants.

Royal Dining Hall

The Royal Dining Hall (*Fejedelmi ebédlő*) opened from the Royal Entrance Hall, and it was the largest room of the private apartments. The long hall had six windows opening towards Gellért Hill. Three crystal chandeliers gave light to the elegant stuccoed space. In the middle of the longer side wall, between the two doors, stood a marble mantelpiece.

"Circle" Room

The "Circle" Room (*"Circle" terem*) opened from the Royal Dining Hall. It was the last room of the private apartments on the southern side, with three windows opening towards Gellért Hill. It had a white-golden stuccoed ceiling and the walls were covered with floral wallpapers. The room was furnished with a crystal chandelier, an ornate white tile stove and chairs.

Figure 76: *The "Circle" Room*

Dining Room

The small dining room (*Ebédlő*) was situated in the northern part of the Krisztinaváros wing, among the other rooms of the Royal Guest Suite. Four windows opened towards Krisztinaváros. The ceiling was stuccoed, while the walls were covered with carved wooden panelling and wallpaper. A stone mantelpiece and large painting above it (depicting a hunting scene with a deer) gave a homey feeling to the room. It was furnished with a crystal chandelier and a long dining table with 12 chairs.

Archducal Apartments

These apartments, on the ground floor of the Krisztinaváros Wing, were designed in 1902 for Archduke Joseph August of Austria (1872–1962), the head of the Hungarian branch of the Habsburgs and his wife, Archduchess Augusta (1875–1964). They could be reached from the lobby of the Krisztinaváros wing through a long passageway. The most important rooms were (in due course): the *salon*, where guests were entertained; the *great parlour*; *parlour*; *dining room*; the *Archduke's study*; the *Archduke's bedroom*; the *Archduchess' bedroom*; the *Archduchess' study*; and the *breakfast parlour*. All rooms had a relatively simple decoration with white stuccoed ceilings and stucco panels above the doorways. The walls were covered with wallpaper. Crystal chandeliers, stone mantelpieces and typical turn-of-the-century furniture gave the

Figure 77: *The Dining Room in the royal guest suite*

rooms a homey ambiance. The great parlour was decorated with large paintings.

Works of art

The castle and its gardens have been decorated with works of art since their foundation in the 14th century. Only written sources speak about the most important medieval works, but detailed pictorial and written information exists about the 19th-century artistic decoration of the palace, which was mainly created by the most important Hungarian artists of the era. Many of the statues survived the destruction during the siege of Budapest in 1944–45 and were later restored. On the other hand, important works of art were destroyed during the controversial reconstruction of the castle during the 1950s and 1960s.

Sculptural monuments

Matthias Fountain (*Mátyás kútja*)

The spectacular fountain decorates the western forecourt of the palace. It shows a group of hunters led by King Matthias Corvinus together with hounds, a killed deer, Galeotto Marzio with a hawk and Szép Ilonka with a doe. This group of people stands between fallen rocks with water running down into a

Figure 78: *Matthias Fountain*

basin. The fountain was made by sculptor Alajos Stróbl. The dead deer was modelled upon a majestic stag killed in 1896 by poachers in the forest owned by Stróbl. The damaged sculpture was restored after the war. Nowadays it is probably the most photographed object in the palace.

Monument of Prince Eugene of Savoy

The equestrian statue of Prince Eugene of Savoy stands on the Danube terrace, in a prominent position, high above Budapest. The Neo-Baroque statue was made by sculptor József Róna for the town of Zenta, but the town could not afford the price. The monument was bought in 1900 as a temporary solution until the planned equestrian statue of King Franz Joseph was completed. This never happened, so Prince Eugen remained on his plinth. The plinth is decorated with two bronze reliefs showing the capture of the earth-works in Zenta and the decisive cavalry charge in the Battle of Zenta in 1697.

Horseherd (*Csikós*)

The statue of the Hortobágy National Park horseherd taming a wild horse originally stood in front of the Riding School in the former Újvilág terrace. It is the work of György Vastagh from 1901. The statue was displayed in the Exposition Universelle in Paris (1900). The damaged statue was removed during the 1960s, but it was later restored and erected in the western forecourt of the palace in 1983, next to the Matthias Fountain.

Figure 79: *Monument of Prince Eugene of Savoy*

Figure 80: *Statue of the horseherd*

Figure 81: *The mythological Turul bird*

Turulbird (*Turulmadár*)

The mythological Turul, high above the Danube, was made by Gyula Donáth in 1905. The plinth and the ornate Neo-Baroque rail (Gyula Jungfer's work) was seriously damaged during the siege of Buda, but they were restored in 1981, together with the broken coat-of-arms of the Kingdom of Hungary on the plinth.

Fishing Children

The Fountain of the Fishing Children on the Danube terrace is the work of sculptor Károly Senyei from 1912. It depicts two children grappling with a fish. The fine workmanship of the fishing net is remarkable. The fountain was removed in 1955 and re-erected at Rákóczi Square in Pest, but brought back to its original place in 1976. It was restored in 2001.

Csongor and Tünde

The two statues depicting Csongor and Tünde, literary figures from Mihály Vörösmarty's drama, originally decorated the Habsburg Steps in front of the palace. They are the works of sculptor Miklós Ligeti from 1903. The steps were demolished after the war, but the statues were saved and re-erected in 1976 on top of two simple concrete plinths near their original locations.

Figure 82: *Fishing Children by Károly Senyei*

Figure 83: *One of the lions in the inner courtyard*

Lions

Two pairs of lions guard the monumental gate leading into Lions Court. The four statues are the works of János Fadrusz from 1901. The animals standing on the outer side of the gate are calm and dignified, while the inner ones are menacing. One lion was broken in two pieces during the war, but it was recreated in the 1950s.

War and Peace

The monumental allegorical bronze statues of War and Peace stand beside the entrance to the Budapest History Museum. They are the work of Károly Senyei. Both War and Peace are represented by angels, one with a trumpet, the other with an olive branch. Under the angel of Peace is a returning soldier, while under the angel of War there is a dead Ottoman soldier and ancient Hungarian warriors.

There are sepulchral monuments in the Palatinal Crypt decorated with the statues of György Zala, Alajos Stróbl and Károly Senyei.

Lost works of art

Hungaria

The monumental sculpture group decorated the main (northern) façade of the palace, facing Szent György Square. On the top of the attic, crowning the façade, stood the female figure of Hungaria, the allegorical representation of Hungary. Two semi-nude figures sat at her side, one male and one female, representing Industry and Commerce. The group was made by sculptor Gyula Jankovits in 1905. The sculpture was destroyed, together with the whole northern façade, during the 1950s.

Pediment Group

The pediment above the Habsburg Steps was decorated with an allegorical group of Károly Senyei representing the *Apotheosis of the Dual Monarchy*. It was destroyed during the 1950s, together with the great coat-of-arms of the Kingdom of Hungary which originally crowned the façade. The present-day pediment is plain, without any sculptural decoration.

Apotheosis of the Habsburg Dynasty

The ceiling of the Habsburg Room was decorated with a fresco representing the apotheosis of the Habsburg Dynasty. It was the last important work of Károly Lotz, painted in 1903, one year before his death. The artist was already seriously ill when he worked on the fresco. The "Apotheosis" followed the traditions of Baroque court painting, and the work was praised by contemporary critics. The fresco survived the war unscathed, but it was destroyed in the 1950s.

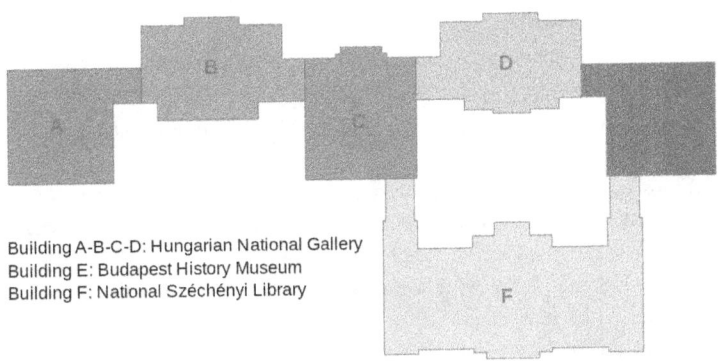

Figure 84: *The ground plan of the castle complex, with the location of the museums*

Museums and institutions

The Budapest History Museum is located in the southern wing of Buda Castle, in Building E, over four floors. It presents the history of Budapest from its beginnings until the modern era. The restored part of the medieval castle, including the Royal Chapel and the rib-vaulted Gothic Hall, belongs to the exhibition. The highlights of the exhibition are the Gothic statues of Buda Castle and a 14th-century silk tapestry decorated with the Angevin coats of arms. Small gardens were recreated in the medieval zwingers around the oldest parts of the building.

The Hungarian National Gallery is located in Building A, B, C and D. The museum presents the history of Hungarian art from the 11th century until the present, with a special exhibition concentrating on Gothic altarpieces (housed in the former Baroque Ballroom). The only surviving interior from the pre-war Royal Palace, the Palatinal Crypt, belongs to the museum.

"Building F" is occupied by the National Széchényi Library, the national library of Hungary. Its collection of rare and antique books, codices and manuscripts contains 35 Corvina pieces from the famous library of King Matthias Corvinus. The original Bibliotheca Corviniana was housed in the medieval Royal Castle of Buda.

References

Notes

- László Prohászka: Szoborhistóriák, Bp, 2004, pp. 145–150.

Further reading

History

- Károly Magyar: The Royal Palace of Buda[320] in the online database The Castle of Buda
- Miklós Horler: Budapest műemlékei I, Bp: 1955, pp. 259–307
- György Kelényi: A királyi udvar építkezései Pest-Budán a XVIII. században, Bp: Akadémiai Kiadó, 2005, pp. 27–34
- György Kelényi: A királyi udvar építkezései Pest-Budán a XVIII. században, Bp: Akadémiai Kiadó, 2005, pp. 34–38
- László Gerő: A helyreállított budai vár, Bp, 1980, pp. 11–60.
- Péter Farbaky: Magyar újkori építészet[321]

External links

- ⚭ Media related to Buda Castle at Wikimedia Commons
- Buda Castle live webcam[322]
- Aerial photographs of the Castle[323]

Interior

- Architectura Hungariae 8(2006), 1[324] – with grounds plan and photos.

Works of art

- (in Hungarian) About Károly Lotz's fresco[325]

Ottoman Hungary

Part of a series on the
History of Hungary
Hungary portal
• v
• t
• e[326]

Ottoman Hungary was the territory of southern Medieval Hungary which was ruled by the Ottoman Empire from 1541 to 1699, roughly two centuries. Ottoman rule was scattered and covered mostly the southern territories of the former medieval Kingdom of Hungary as almost the entire region of the Great Hungarian Plain (except the northeastern parts) and Southern Transdanubia.

History

By the sixteenth century, the power of the Ottoman Empire had increased gradually, as did the territory controlled by them in the Balkans, while the Kingdom of Hungary was weakened by the peasants' uprisings. Under the reign of Louis II Jagiellon (1516–1526), internal dissentions divided the nobility.Wikipedia:Citation needed

Provoked into war by diplomatic insult, Suleyman the Magnificent (1520–1566) attacked the Kingdom of Hungary and captured Belgrade in 1521. He did not hesitate to launch an attack against the weakened kingdom, whose smaller, badly led army (approximately 26,000 Hungarian soldiers compared to 45,000 Ottoman soldiers) was defeated on 29 August 1526 at the Battle of Mohács. Thus he became influential in the Kingdom of Hungary, while his semi-vassal, named John I Zápolya and his enemy Ferdinand I both claimed the throne of the Kingdom. Suleyman went further and tried to

116　　　　　　　　　　　　　　　　　　　　　　　　　　　　　　　　Ottoman Hungary

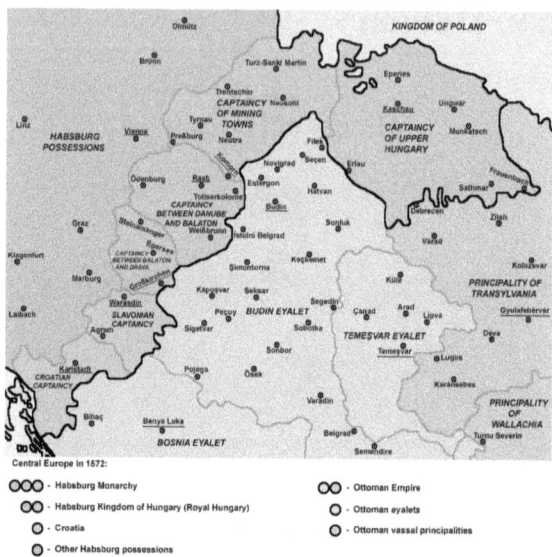

Figure 85: *The political situation around 1572: The Habsburg Kingdom of Hungary (Royal Hungary), Principality of Transylvania, and Ottoman eyalets*

crush Austrian forces, but his siege of Vienna in 1529 failed after the onset of winter forced his retreat. The title of king of Hungary was disputed between Zápolya and Ferdinand until 1540. After the seizure of Buda by the Ottomans in 1541,[327] the West and North recognized a Habsburg as king ("Royal Hungary"), while the central and southern counties were annexed by the Ottoman Sultan and the east was ruled by the son of Zápolya under the name Eastern Hungarian Kingdom which after 1570 became the Principality of Transylvania. Whereas a great many of the 17,000 and 19,000 Ottoman soldiers in service in the Ottoman fortresses in the territory of present-day Hungary were Orthodox and Muslim Balkan Slavs,[328] Southern Slavs were also acting as akıncıs and other light troops intended for pillaging in the territory of present-day Hungary.[329]

In these times, territory of present-day Hungary began to undergo changes due to the Ottoman occupation. Vast lands remained unpopulated and covered with woods. Flood plains became marshes. The life of the inhabitants on the Ottoman side was unsafe. Peasants fled to the woods and marshes, forming guerrilla bands, known as the Hajdú troops. Eventually, the territory of present-day Hungary became a drain on the Ottoman Empire, swallowing much of its revenue into the maintenance of a long chain of border forts. However, some parts of the economy flourished. In the huge unpopulated areas,

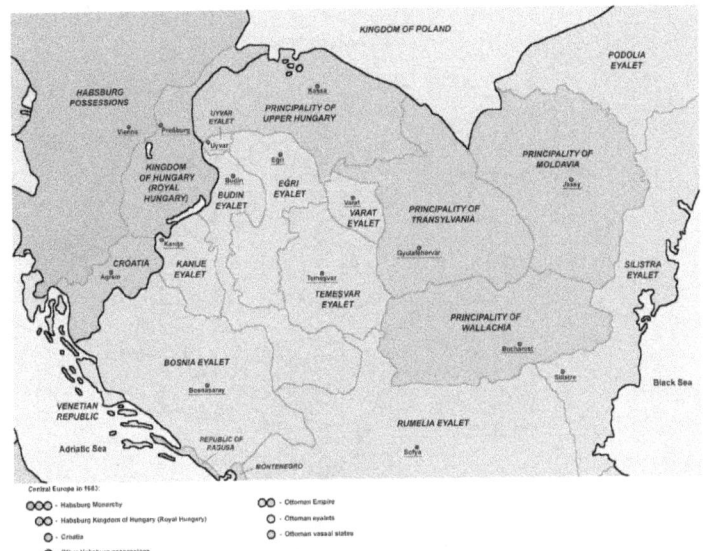

Figure 86: *The political situation around 1683: The Habsburg Kingdom of Hungary (Royal Hungary), Imre Thököly's Principality of Upper Hungary (existed between 1682-1685), Principality of Transylvania, and Ottoman eyalets (Budin Eyalet, Varat Eyalet, Eğri Eyalet, Temeşvar Eyalet)*

townships bred cattle that were herded to south Germany and northern Italy - in some years they exported 500,000 head of cattle. Wine was traded to the Czech lands, Austria and Poland.Wikipedia:Citation needed

The defeat of Ottoman forces led by Grand Vizier Kara Mustafa Pasha at the Second Siege of Vienna in 1683, at the hands of the combined armies of Poland and the Holy Roman Empire under John III Sobieski, was the decisive event that swung the balance of power in the region.Wikipedia:Citation needed Under the terms of the Treaty of Karlowitz, which ended the Great Turkish War in 1699, the Ottomans ceded to Habsburgs much of the territory they had previously taken from the medieval Kingdom of Hungary. Following this treaty, the members of the Habsburg dynasty administered much enlarged Habsburg Kingdom of Hungary (previously they controlled only area known as "Royal Hungary"; see Kingdom of Hungary (1538–1867)).Wikipedia:Citation needed

In the 1540s the total of the four principal fortresses of Buda (2,965), Pest (1,481), Székesfehérvár (2,978) and Esztergom (2,775) were 10,200 troops.[330]

Figure 87: *The 1881 map of Hungary showing the boundaries of the almost completely destroyed Hungarian settlement areas during the Ottoman occupation of Hungary*

Figure 88: *Ottoman soldiers in the territory of present-day Hungary*

Figure 89: *Ottoman soldiers besiege Estolnibelgrad (probably Székesfehérvár) in Hungary.*

The number of Ottoman garrison troops stationed in Ottoman Hungary vary, but during the peak period in the mid-16th century it rose to between 20,000 and 22,000 men. As a force of occupation for a country the size of Hungary, even confined to central portions it was a rather low-profile military presence in much of the country and a relatively large proportion of it was concentrated in a few key fortresses.[331]

In 1640 when the front remained relatively quiet, 8,000 Janissary supported by an undocumented number of local recruits was sufficient to garrison the whole of the Eyalet of Budin.

Administration

The territory was divided into Eyalets (provinces), which were further divided into Sanjaks, with the highest ranking Ottoman official being the Pasha of Budin. At first, Ottoman-controlled territories in present-day Hungary were part of the Budin Eyalet. Later, new eyalets were formed: Temeşvar Eyalet, Zigetvar Eyalet, Kanije Eyalet, Egir Eyalet, and Varat Eyalet. Administrative centers of Budin, Zigetvar, Kanije and Egir eyalets were located in the territory of present-day Hungary, while Temeşvar and Varat eyalets that had their administrative centers in the territory of present-day Romania also included some parts of present-day Hungary. Pashas and Sanjak-Beys were responsible for administration, jurisdiction and defense. The Ottomans' only interest was to secure their hold on the territory.

The Sublime Porte (Ottoman rulers) became the sole landowner and managed about 20 percent of the land for its own benefit, apportioning the rest among soldiers and civil servants. The Ottoman landlords were interested mainly in squeezing as much wealth from the land as quickly as possible. Of major importance to the Sublime Porte was the collection of taxes. Taxation left little for the former landlords to collect; Most of the nobility and large numbers of burghers emigrated into the Habsburg Kingdom of Hungary ("Royal Hungary") province. Wars, slave-taking, and the emigration of nobles who lost their land caused a depopulation of the countryside. However, the Ottomans practiced relative religious tolerance and allowed the various ethnicities living within the empire significant autonomy in internal affairs. Towns maintained some self-government, and a prosperous middle class developed through artisanry and trade.

Ethnic changes during the Ottoman rule

As a consequence of the 150 years of constant warfare between the Christian states and Ottomans, population growth was stunted, and the network of ethnic Hungarian medieval settlements, with their urbanized bourgeois inhabitants, perished. The ethnic composition of the territory that had been part of the medieval Kingdom of Hungary was fundamentally changed through deportations and massacres, so that the number of ethnic Hungarians in existence at the end of the Ottoman period was substantially diminished.Wikipedia:Link rot

The economic decline of Buda the capital city during the Ottoman conquest characterized by the stagnation of population, the population of Buda was not larger in 1686, than the population of the city two centuries earlier in the 15th century. The Ottomans allowed the Hungarian royal place to fall into ruins. The palace was later transformed into a gunpowder storage and magazine by the Ottomans, which caused its detonation during the siege in 1686. The Christian Hungarian population significantly shrank in the next decades, due to their fleeing to the Habsburg ruled Royal Hungary. The number of Jewish and Gypsy immigrants became dominant during the Ottoman rule in Buda.

The Hungarian inhabitants of cities moved to other places when they felt threatened by the Ottoman military presence. Without exception, in the cities that became Ottoman administrative centers the Christian population decreased. The Hungarian population remained only in some cities, where the Ottoman garrisons were not installed.. That area included territories located between

Figure 90: *The Holy League took Buda after a long siege in 1686*

great rivers Sava, Drava, and the Danube–Tisza Interfluve (the territory between the Danube and Tisza rivers).

According to modern estimations, the proportion of Hungarians in the Carpathian Basin was around 80% at the end of the 15th century, while non-Hungarians hardly numbered more than 20% to 25% of the total population.[332,333] The Hungarian population began to decrease at the time of the Ottoman conquest, The decline of the Hungarians was due to the constant wars, Ottoman raids, famines, and plagues during the 150 years of Ottoman rule. The main zones of war were the territories inhabited by the Hungarians, so the death toll depleted them much faster than other nationalities.

The three parts of Hungary; the Habsburg Hungary, Ottoman Hungary and Transylvania, experienced only minor differences in population increase in the 17th century.[334] According to data presented in the most authoritative studies, the collective population of all three regions grew from about 3.5 million inhabitants at the close of the 16th century to about 4 million by the close of the 17th century. This increase was before the immigration to Hungary from other parts of the Habsburg Empire.[335] The Ottoman-Habsburg Wars of the 17th century were fought intermittently and affected populations occupying a much narrower band of territory. Thus wartime dislocations in Hungary do not seem to have seriously affected mortality rates among the general civilian population. The breakdown of social order and other economic links between contiguous regions that is associated with prolonged warfare of the medieval pattern was largely absent in Ottoman warfare of the 17th century. The most severe destructions were experienced during the Hungarian time of troubles, when between 1604 and 1606 the worst effects of the controlled confrontation between Ottoman-Habsburg forces were magnified many times over by Hungary's descent into civil war during the Bocskay rebellion.

Hungary's population in the late 16th century was in Ottoman Hungary 900,000, in Habsburg Hungary 1,800,000 and 'free' (Transylvania) Hungary 800,000, making a total of 3,500,000 inhabitants for the whole of Hungary.

The population growth in Ottoman Hungary during the 17th century was slight: from 900,000 to approximately 1,000,000 inhabitants, a rate similar to that experienced in Royal Hungary and Transylvania.

Culture

Despite the continuous warfare with the Habsburgs, several cultural centres sprang up in this far northern corner of the Empire. Examples of Ottoman architecture of the classical period, seen in the famous centres of Constantinople and Edirne, were also seen in the territory of present-day southern Hungary, where mosques, bridges, fountains, baths and schools were built. After the Habsburg reclamation, most of these works were destroyed and few survive to this day. The introduction of Turkish Baths, with the building of the Rudas Baths, was the beginning of a long tradition in the territory of present-day Hungary. No less than 75 *hammams* (steam baths) were built during the Ottoman age.

Muslim schools

In the seventeenth century, 165 elementary (*mekteb*) and 77 secondary and academic theological schools (*medrese*) were operating in 39 of the major towns of the region.Wikipedia:Citation needed The elementary schools taught writing, basic arithmetics, and the reading of the Koran and of the most important prayers. The *medreses* carried out secondary and academic training within the fields of Muslim religious sciences, church law and natural sciences.Wikipedia:Citation needed Most *medreses* operated in Budin (Buda), where there were twelve. In Peçuy (Pécs) there were five medreses, Eğri had four.Wikipedia:Citation needed The most famous *medrese* in Ottoman-controlled territory of present-day Hungary was that of Budin (Buda), built by the Bosniak-Serb Mehmed-pasha Sokolović during his seventeen years of governing (1566–1578).

In the mosques, people not only prayed, but were taught to read and write, to read the Koran, and prayers. The sermons were the most effective form of political education.Wikipedia:Citation needed There were

Figure 91: *The mosque of Pasha Qasim in Pécs, now used as a Catholic church*

numerous elementary and secondary schools besides the mosques, and the monasteries of the Dervish orders also served as centers of culture and education.Wikipedia:Citation needed The spread of culture was supported by the libraries. The school library of Mehmed-pasha Sokolović in Budin (Buda), contained, besides Muslim religious sciences, other literature, works on oratory, poetry, astronomy, music, architecture, and medical sciences.Wikipedia:Citation needed

Religion

The Ottomans practiced relative religious tolerance, and Christianity was not prohibited. Islam was not spread by force in the areas under the control of the Ottoman Sultan,[336] however, Arnold concludes by quoting a 17th-century author who stated:

> Meanwhile he [the Turk] wins [converts] by craft more than by force, and snatches away Christ by fraud out of the hearts of men. For the Turk, it is true, at the present time compels no country by violence to apostatise; but he uses other means whereby imperceptibly he roots out Christianity...[337]

The relative religious tolerance of the Ottomans enabled Protestantism in Hungary (such as the Reformed Church in Hungary) to survive against the repression of the Catholic Habsburg-ruled Hungarian domains.

Figure 92: *Minaret in Eger*

There were approximately 80,000 Muslim settlers in Ottoman-controlled territory of present-day Hungary; being mainly administrators, soldiers, artisans and merchants of Crimean Tatar origin. The religious life of the Muslims was supervised by the mosques that were either newly built or transformed from older Christian churches. Payment for the servants of the mosques, as well as the maintenance of the churches, was the responsibility of the Ottoman state or charities.

Besides Sunni Islam, a number of dervish communities also flourished including the *bektashis*, the *halvetis*, and the *mevlevis*. The famous Gül Baba monastery of Budin (Buda), sheltering 60 dervishes, belonged to the *bektasi* order. Situated close to the janissaries camp, it was built by Jahjapasazáde Mehmed Pasha, the third *begler bey* (governor) of Budin (Buda). The türbe (mausoleum) in Budapest of the famous dervish and poet Gül Baba is to this day the northernmost site of Islamic conquest.[338]

Another famous monastery of its time was that of the *halveti* dervishes. Built around 1576 next to the türbe of Sultan Süleyman I the Magnificent (1520–1566) in Sigetvar (Szigetvár), it soon became the religious and cultural centre of the area. A famous prior of the zavije (monastery) was the Bosnian Šejh Ali Dede. The monastery of Jakovali Hasan Paša in Peçuy (Pécs) was another famous location. Its most outstanding prior was Mevlevian dervish Peçevi Arifi Ahmed Dede, a Turk and native of Peçuy (Pécs).

By the end of the sixteenth century, around 90% of the inhabitants of Ottoman Hungary were Protestant, most of them being Calvinist.

Gallery

Figure 93: *The Pasha of Budin (Buda) receives the envoy of the Ottoman Sultan.*

Figure 94: *Coffee shop*

Figure 95: *Köçek dancer with castanets. Ottoman miniature by Balázs Szigetvári Csöbör, 1570.*

Figure 96: *Slave woman musician*

References

- ⊛ This article incorporates public domain material from the Library of Congress Country Studies website http://lcweb2.loc.gov/frd/cs/[339].
- *Encyclopaedia Humana Hungarica*: Cross and Crescent: The Turkish Age in Hungary (1526–1699)
- Balázs Sudár: *Baths in Ottoman Hungary* in *"Acta Orientalia Academiae Scientiarum Hungaricae"*, Volume 57, Number 4, 7 December 2004, pp. 391–437(47)

Sources

- Kontler, László (1999). *Millennium in Central Europe: A History of Hungary.* Atlantisz Publishing House. ISBN 963-9165-37-9.
- Fodor, Pál; Dávid, Géza, eds. (2000). *Ottomans, Hungarians, and Habsburgs in Central Europe: The Military Confines in the Era of Ottoman Conquest*[340]. BRILL.

External links

- Cross and Crescent: The Turkish Age in Hungary (1526-1699)[341]

19th century

Hungarian Revolution of 1848

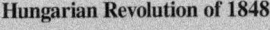 Hungarian Revolution of 1848	
Part of the Revolutions of 1848	
 Artist Mihály Zichy's painting of Sándor Petőfi reciting the National Poem to a crowd on March 15, 1848	
Date	15 March 1848 – 4 October 1849 (1 year, 6 months, and 19 days)
Location	Hungary, Austrian Empire
Result	Austro-Russian victory; revolution suppressed
Belligerents	

- Austrian Empire
  - Kingdom of Croatia
  - Serbian Vojvodina
  - Serbian volunteers
  - Habsburg Hungarians
  - Slovak National Council
  - Transylvanian Romanians
  - Supreme Ruthenian Council
  - Czech volunteers
  - Bohemian and Moravian volunteers
  - Transylvanian Saxons
- Russian Empire

- Kingdom of Hungary
  - Hungarian Slovenes
  - Pro-Hungarian Slovaks
  - Rusyns
  - Zipser Saxons
  - Hungarian Germans
  - Croats from Western Hungary and Međimurje
  - Šokac and Bunjevac people
  - Banat Bulgarians
  - Polish legions
  - German legion
- Viennese legion
  - Italian legion

Commanders and leaders

Franz Joseph I
Ferdinand I (until 1848)
Alfred I, Prince of Windisch-Grätz
Ludwig von Welden
Julius Jacob von Haynau
Josip Jelačić
Stevan Knićanin
Ľudovít Štúr
Avram Iancu
Hryhory Yakhymovych
Nicholas I
Ivan Paskevich

Lajos Kossuth
Lajos Batthyány (POW)
Artúr Görgey (POW)
György Klapka
János Damjanich
Lajos Aulich
Henryk Dembiński
Józef Bem
Józef Wysocki
Peter Giron
Alessandro Monti

Strength

170,000 men from the Austrian Empire, and 200,000 men from the Russian Empire[342]

Beginning of 1849 : 170,000 men[343]

Part of a series on the
History of Hungary

Hungary portal

Hungarian Revolution of 1848

The **Hungarian Revolution of 1848** (Hungarian: *1848–49-es forradalom és szabadságharc*, "1848–49 Revolution and War") was one of the many European Revolutions of 1848 and closely linked to other revolutions of 1848 in the Habsburg areas. The revolution in the Kingdom of Hungary grew into a war for independence from the Austrian Empire, ruled by the Habsburg dynasty.

After a series of serious Austrian defeats in 1849, the Austrian State came close to the brink of collapse. Thus, the new young emperor Franz Joseph I had to call for Russian help in the name of the Holy Alliance.[345] Czar Nicholas I answered, and sent a 200,000 men strong army with 80,000 auxiliary forces. Finally, the joint army of Russian and Austrian forces defeated the Hungarian forces. After the restoration of Habsburg power, Hungary was placed under brutal martial law.[346]

The anniversary of the Revolution's outbreak, 15 March, is one of Hungary's three national holidays.

Hungary before the Revolution

The Kingdom of Hungary had always maintained a separate parliament, the Diet of Hungary, even after the Austrian Empire was created in 1804.[347] The administration and government of the Kingdom of Hungary (until 1848) remained largely untouched by the government structure of the overarching Austrian Empire. Hungary's central government structures remained well separated from the imperial government. The country was governed by the Council of Lieutenancy of Hungary (the Gubernium) - located in Pozsony and later in Pest - and by the Hungarian Royal Court Chancellery in Vienna.[348]

The Hungarian Jacobin Club

After the death of the Holy Roman Emperor, Joseph II, in February 1790, enlightened reforms in Hungary ceased, which outraged many reform-oriented francophone intellectuals who were followers of new radical ideas based on French philosophy and enlightenment. Ignác Martinovics worked as a secret agent for the new Holy Roman Emperor, Leopold II, until 1792. In his Oratio pro Leopoldo II, he explicitly declares that only authority derived from a social contract should be recognized; he saw the aristocracy as the enemy of mankind, because they prevented people from becoming educated. In another

Figure 97: *Photograph of the aged Emperor Ferdinand I dated circa 1870*

of his works, Catechism of People and Citizens, he argued that citizens tend to oppose any repression and that sovereignty resides with the people. He also became a Freemason, and was in favour of the adoption of a federal republic in Hungary. As a member of the Hungarian Jacobins, he was considered an idealistic forerunner of revolutionary thought by some, and an unscrupulous adventurer by others. He was in charge of stirring up a revolt against the nobility among the Hungarian serfs. For these subversive acts, Francis II, the Holy Roman Emperor, dismissed Martinovics and his boss, Ferenc Gotthardi, the former chief of the secret police. He was executed, together with six other prominent Jacobins, in May 1795. More than 42 members of the republican secret society were arrested, including the poet János Batsányi and linguist Ferenc Kazinczy[349,350,351,352,353]

Though the Hungarian Jacobin republican movement did not affect the policy of the Hungarian Parliament and the parliamentary parties, it had strong ideological ties with the extra-parliamentary forces: the radical youths and students like the poet Sándor Petőfi, the philosopher and historian Pál Vasvári and the novel-writer Mór Jókai, who sparked the revolution in the Pilvax coffee house on 15 March 1848.[354]

Origins of the Revolution

The Diet of Hungary had not convened since 1811. The frequent diets held in the earlier part of the reign occupied themselves with little else but war subsidies; after 1811 they ceased to be summoned. In the latter years of Francis I the dark shadow of Metternich's policy of "stability" fell across the kingdom, and the forces of reactionary absolutism were everywhere supreme. But beneath the surface a strong popular current was beginning to run in a contrary direction. Hungarian society, not unaffected by western Liberalism, but without any direct help from abroad, was preparing for the future emancipation. Writers, savants, poets, artists, noble and plebeian, layman and cleric, without any previous concert, or obvious connection, were working towards that ideal of political liberty which was to unite all the Magyars. Mihály Vörösmarty, Ferenc Kölcsey, Ferencz Kazinczy and his associates, to mention but a few of many great names, were, consciously or unconsciously, as the representatives of the renascent national literature, accomplishing a political mission, and their pens proved no less efficacious than the swords of their ancestors.

In 1825 Emperor Francis II convened the Diet in response to growing concerns amongst the Hungarian nobility about taxes and the diminishing economy, after the Napoleonic wars. This – and the reaction to the reforms of Joseph II – started what is known as the Reform Period (Hungarian: *reformkor*).Wikipedia:Citation needed But the Nobles still retained their privileges of paying no taxes and not giving the vote to the masses.

The influential Hungarian politician Count István Széchenyi recognized the need to bring the country the advances of the more developed West European countries, such as England.

It was a direct attack upon the constitution which, to use the words of István Széchenyi, first "startled the nation out of its sickly drowsiness". In 1823, when the reactionary powers were considering joint action to suppress the revolution in Spain, the government, without consulting the diet, imposed a war-tax and called out the recruits. The county assemblies instantly protested against this illegal act, and Francis I was obliged, at the diet of 1823, to repudiate the action of his ministers. But the estates felt that the maintenance of their liberties demanded more substantial guarantees than the dead letter of ancient laws. Széchenyi, who had resided abroad and studied Western institutions, was the recognized leader of all those who wished to create a new Hungary out of the old. For years he and his friends educated public opinion by issuing innumerable pamphlets in which the new Liberalism was eloquently expounded. In particular Széchenyi insisted that the people must not look exclusively to the government, or even to the diet, for the necessary reforms. Society itself must take the initiative by breaking down the barriers of class exclusiveness and reviving a healthy public spirit. The effect of this teaching was manifest at the diet of 1832, when the Liberals in the Lower Chamber had a large majority, prominent among whom were Ferenc Deák and Ödön Beothy. In the Upper House, however, the magnates united with the government to form a conservative party obstinately opposed to any project of reform, which frustrated all the efforts of the Liberals.

The alarm of the government at the power and popularity of the Liberal party induced it, soon after the accession of the new king, the emperor Ferdinand I. (1835-1848), to attempt to crush the reform movement by arresting and imprisoning the most active agitators among them, Louis Kossuth and Miklos Wesselenyi. But the nation was no longer to be cowed. The diet of 1839 refused to proceed to business till the political prisoners had been released, and, while in the Lower Chamber the reforming majority was larger than ever, a Liberal party was now also formed in the Upper House under the leadership of Count Louis Batthyány and Baron Joseph Eotvos. From 1000AD up to 1844, Latin language was the official language of administration, legislation and schooling in Kingdom of Hungary.Wikipedia:Citation needed Two progressive measures of the highest importance were passed by this diet, one making Magyar the official language of Hungary, the other freeing the peasants' holdings from all feudal obligations.

The results of the diet of 1839 did not satisfy the advanced Liberals, while the opposition of the government and of the Upper House still further embittered the general discontent. The chief exponent of this temper was the Pesti Hirlap, Hungary's first political newspaper, founded in 1841 by Kossuth, whose articles, advocating armed reprisals if necessary, inflamed the extremists but alienated Széchenyi, who openly attacked Kossuth's opinions. The polemic on both sides was violent; but, as usual, the extreme views prevailed, and on the assembling of the diet of 1843 Kossuth was more popular than ever, while the influence of Széchenyi had sensibly declined. The tone of this diet was passionate, and the government was fiercely attacked for interfering with the elections. Fresh triumphs were won by the Liberals. Magyar was now declared to be the language of the schools and the law-courts as well as of the legislature; mixed marriages were legalized; and official positions were thrown open to non-nobles.

"Long debate" of reformers in the press (1841-1848)

The interval between the diet of 1843 and that of 1847 saw a complete disintegration and transformation of the various political parties. Széchenyi openly joined the government, while the moderate Liberals separated from the extremists and formed a new party, the Centralists.

Figure 98: *The entrance room of the Pilvax coffee palace at Pest in the 1840s*

Figure 99: *Members of the Batthyány government*

Figure 100: *The recitation of the National Song at the National Museum*

Figure 101: *The crowd captured the Landerer & Heckenast printing house, where they printed the 12 points and the National Song. Thus 15 March became the memorial Day of the Freedom of the Press in Hungary.*

In his 1841 pamphlet *People of the East* (*Kelet Népe*), Count Széchenyi analyzed Kossuth's policy and responded to Kossuth's reform proposals. Széchenyi believed that economic, political and social reforms should proceed slowly and with care, in order to avoid the potentially disastrous prospect of violent interference from the Habsburg dynasty. Széchenyi was aware of the spread of Kossuth's ideas in Hungarian society, which he took to overlook the need for a good relationship with the Habsburg dynasty.

Kossuth, for his part, rejected the role of the aristocracy, and questioned established norms of social status. In contrast to Széchenyi, Kossuth believed that in the process of social reform it would be impossible to restrain civil society in a passive role. He warned against attempting to exclude wider social movements from political life, and supported democracy, rejecting the primacy of elites and the government. In 1885, he labeled Széchenyi a liberal elitist aristocrat, while Széchenyi considered Kossuth to be a democrat.[355]

Széchenyi was an isolationist politician, while Kossuth saw strong relations and collaboration with international liberal and progressive movements as essential for the success of liberty.[356]

Széchenyi based his economic policy on the *laissez-faire* principles practiced by the British Empire, while Kossuth supported protective tariffs due to the comparatively weak Hungarian industrial sector. While Kossuth envisioned the construction of a rapidly industrialized country, Széchenyi wanted to preserve the traditionally strong agricultural sector as the main characteristic of the economy.[357]

"Ten Points" of the reformers

The conservatives - who usually opposed most of the reforms - could maintain a slim majority in the old feudal parliament, the reformer liberals were divided between the ideas of Széchenyi and Kossuth.

Immediately before the elections, however, Deák succeeded in reuniting all the Liberals on the common platform of "The Ten Points".

- (1) Responsible ministries, (All ministries and the government must be elected by the parliament)
- (2) Freedom of the Press (The abolition of censure and the censor's offices)
- (3) Popular representation (by democratic parliamentary elections, the abolition of the old feudal parliament which based on the feudal estates)
- (4) The reincorporation of Transylvania,
- (5) Right of public meeting, (Freedom of assembly and freedom of association)

- (6) Absolute religious liberty, the abolition of the (Catholic) State Religion,
- (7) Universal equality before the law (The abolition of separate laws for the common people and nobility, the abolition of the legal privileges of nobility)
- (8) Universal and equal taxation, (abolition of the tax exemption of the aristocracy)
- (9) The abolition of the Aviticum, (Aviticium was an old feudal origin obsolete and anomalous land-tenure, it declared that only the nobility could own agricultural lands)
- (10) The abolition of serfdom and bondservices, with state financed compensation to the landlords.

The ensuing parliamentary elections resulted in a complete victory of the Progressives. This was also the last election which based on the parliamental system of the old feudal estates. All efforts to bring about an understanding between the government and the opposition were fruitless. Kossuth demanded not merely the redress of actual grievances, but a liberal reform which would make grievances impossible in the future. In the highest circles a dissolution of the diet now seemed to be the sole remedy; but, before it could be carried out, tidings of the February revolution in Paris reached Pressburg on the 1st of March, and on the 3rd of March Kossuth's motion for the appointment of an independent, responsible ministry was accepted by the Lower House. The moderates, alarmed not so much by the motion itself as by its tone, again tried to intervene; but on the 13th of March the Vienna revolution broke out, and the Emperor, yielding to pressure or panic, appointed Count Louis Batthyány premier of the first Hungarian responsible ministry, which included Kossuth, Széchenyi and Deák.

The bloodless revolution in Pest

The crisis came from abroad - as Kossuth expected - and he used it to the full. On 3 March 1848, shortly after the news of the revolution in Paris had arrived, in a speech of surpassing power he demanded parliamentary government for Hungary and constitutional government for the rest of Austria. He appealed to the hope of the Habsburgs, "our beloved Archduke Franz Joseph" (then seventeen years old), to perpetuate the ancient glory of the dynasty by meeting half-way the aspirations of a free people. He at once became the leader of the European revolution; his speech was read aloud in the streets of Vienna to the mob by which Metternich was overthrown (13 March), and when a deputation from the Diet visited Vienna to receive the assent of Emperor Ferdinand to their petition it was Kossuth who received the chief ovation. The arrival of the news of the revolution in Paris, and Kossuth's German speech about freedom

Figure 102: *The Hungarian cockade used in 1848*

and human rights had whipped up the passions of Austrian crowd in Vienna on March 13.[358] While Viennese masses celebrated Kossuth as their hero, revolution broke out in Buda on 15 March; Kossuth traveled home immediately.[359]

The revolution started in the Pilvax coffee palace at Pest, which was a favourite meeting point of the young extra-parliamentary radical liberal intellectuals in the 1840s. On the morning of March 15, 1848, revolutionaries marched around the city of Pest, reading Sándor Petőfi's Nemzeti dal (National Song) and the 12 points (the twelve demands of theirs) to the crowd (which swelled to thousands). Declaring an end to all forms of censorship, they visited the printing presses of Landerer and Heckenast and printed Petőfi's poem together with the demands. A mass demonstration was held in front of the newly built National Museum, after which the group left for the Buda Chancellery (the Office of the Governor-General) on the other bank of the Danube.

The bloodless mass demonstrations in Pest and Buda forced the Imperial governor to accept all twelve of their demands.

Austria had its own problems with the revolution in Vienna that year, and it initially acknowledged Hungary's government. Therefore, the Governor-General's officers, acting in the name of the King appointed Hungary's new parliament with Lajos Batthyány as its first Prime Minister. The Austrian

Figure 103: *A parliamentary election campaign of a candidate*

monarchy also made other concessionsWikipedia:Avoid weasel words to subdue the Vienna masses: on 13 March 1848, Prince Klemens von Metternich was made to resign his position as the Austrian Government's Chancellor. He then fled to London for his own safety.

Parliamentary monarchy, the Batthyány government

On 17 March 1848 the Emperor assented and Batthyány created the first Hungarian Diet. On 23 March 1848, as head of government, Batthyány commended his government to the Diet.

The first responsible government was formed:

Hungarian Revolution of 1848

Figure 104: *5 July 1848: The opening ceremony of the first parliament, which based on popular representation. The members of first responsible government are on the balcony.*

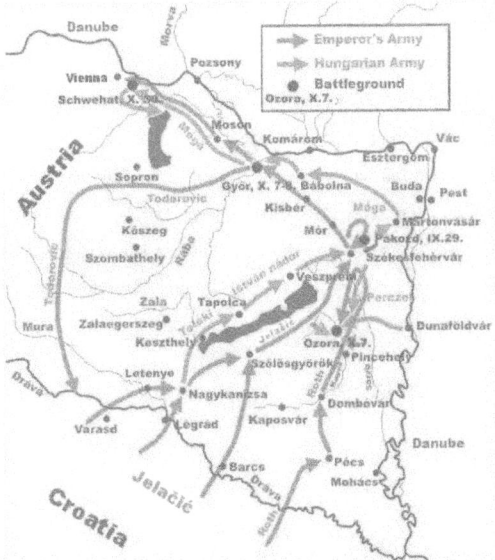

Figure 105: *Jelačić's attacks in the last quarter of 1848*

Figure 106: *Battle of Pákozd was a draw that pushed the loyalist Croatian forces towards Vienna and away from Pest.*

Prime Minister: Lajos Batthyány

Minister of the Interior: Bertalan Szemere,

Finance minister: Lajos Kossuth,

Minister of Justice: Ferenc Deák,

Minister of defense: Lázár Mészáros,

Minister of Agriculture, Industry and Trade: Gábor Klauzál,

Minister of Labour, Infrastructure and Transport: István Széchenyi,

Minister of Education, Science and Culture: József Eötvös,

Minister besides the King (roughly Foreign Minister): Pál Antal Esterházy

With the exception of Lajos Kossuth, all members of the government were the supporters of Széchenyi's ideas.

The Ten Points, or the March Laws as they were now called, were then adopted by the legislature and received royal assent on the 10th of April 10. Hungary had, to all intents and purposes, become an independent state bound to Austria only by the Austrian Archduke as Palatine.[360] The new government approved a sweeping reform package, referred to as the "April laws", which created a democratic political system. The newly established government also demanded that the Habsburg Empire spend all taxes they received from Hungary in Hungary itself, and that the Parliament should have authority over the Hungarian regiments of the Habsburg Army.

The first general parliamentary elections were held in June, which were based on popular representation instead of former feudal parliamentary delegates (Estates General), where the reform oriented political forces won the elections. The electoral system and franchise were similar to the contemporary British system.[361]

At that time the internal affairs and foreign policy of Hungary were not stable, and Batthyány faced many problems. His first and most important act was to organize the armed forces and the local governments. He insisted that the Austrian army, when in Hungary, would come under Hungarian law, and this was conceded by the Austrian Empire. He tried to repatriate conscript soldiers from Hungary. He established the Organisation of Militiamen, whose job was to ensure internal security of the country.

Batthyány was a very capable leader, but he was stuck in the middle of a clash between the Austrian monarchy and the Hungarian separatists. He was devoted to the constitutional monarchy and aimed to keep the constitution, but the Emperor was dissatisfied with his work. On 29 August, with the assent of parliament, he went with Ferenc Deák to the Emperor to ask him to order the Serbs to capitulate and stop Jelačić, who was going to attack Hungary.

In the summer of 1848, Hungarian Government ministers, seeing the civil war ahead, tried to get the Habsburgs' support against the conservative Josip Jelačić. They offered to send troops to northern Italy. By the end of August 1848, the Imperial Government in Vienna officially ordered the Hungarian Government in Pest not to form an Army. Jelačić, being a Count in Croatia and Dalmatia, which were at that time part of Hungary, had a different view. He invaded Hungary to dissolve the Hungarian Government, without any order by the Austrian throne.

Though the Emperor formally relieved Jelačić of his duties, Jelačić and his army invaded Southern Transdanubian parts of Hungary on 11 September 1848.

After the Austrian revolution in Vienna was defeated, the kamarilla orchestrated Franz Joseph I of Austria to replace his uncle Ferdinand I of Austria, who was not of sound mind. The new young monarch Franz Joseph didn't recognise Batthyány's second premiere on 25 September. Franz Joseph was not recognized as "King of Hungary" by the Hungarian parliament, and he was not crowned as "King of Hungary" until 1867. In the end, the final break between Vienna and Pest occurred when Field-Marshal Count Franz Philipp von Lamberg was given control of every army in Hungary (including Jelačić's). He went to Hungary where he was mobbed and viciously murdered; following his murder the Imperial court dissolved the Hungarian Diet and appointed Jelačić as Regent.Wikipedia:Citation needed

Meanwhile, Batthyány travelled again to Vienna to seek a compromise with the new Emperor, however his efforts remained unsuccessful, because Francis Joseph refused to accept the reform laws. This was an unconstitutional deed, because the laws were already signed by his uncle, and the monarch had no right to revoke laws, which were already signed.

Hungarian liberals in Pest saw this as an opportunity. In September 1848, the Diet made concessions to the Pest Uprising, so as not to break up the Austro-Hungarian Union. But the counter-revolutionary forces were gathering. After manyWikipedia:Manual of Style/Dates and numbers local victories, the combined Bohemian and Croatian armies entered Pest on 5 January 1849 to put down the revolt.

So Batthyány and his government resigned, except for Kossuth, Szemere and Mészáros. Later, on Palatine Stephen's request, Batthyány became Prime Minister again. On 13 September Batthyány announced a rebellion and requested that the Palatine lead them. However the Palatine, under the Emperor's orders, resigned and left Hungary.

Hungary now had war raging on three fronts: Jelačić's Croatian troops to the South, Romanians in Banat and in Transylvania to the East, and Austria to the West.

The Hungarian government was in serious military crisis due to the lack of soldiers, therefore they sent Kossuth (a brilliant orator) to recruit volunteers for the new Hungarian army. While Croatian ban Josip Jelačić was marching on Pest, Kossuth went from town to town rousing the people to the defense of the country, and the popular force of the Honvéd was his creation.

With the help of Kossuth's recruiting speech, Batthyány was successful in his hurried effort to arrange the Hungarian Revolutionary Army: the new Hungarian army defeated the Croatians on 29 September at the Battle of Pákozd.

The battle became an icon for the Hungarian army because of it is influence on politics and morale. Kossuth's second letter for the Austrian people and this battle were the causes of the second revolution in Vienna on 6 October.

Pm. Batthyány slowly realised, that he could not reach his main goal, the peaceful compromise with the Habsburg dynasty, so on 2 October he resigned and simultaneously resigned his seat in parliament. Also the ministers of his cabinet resigned on the same day.

The Austrian Stadion Constitution and the renewal of antagonism

Habsburg government in Vienna proclaimed a new constitution, the so-called Stadion Constitution on 4 March 1849. The centralist Stadion Constitution provided very strong power for the monarch, and marked the way of the neo-absolutism. New March Constitution of Austria was drafted by Imperial Diet of Austria, where Kingdom of Hungary had no representation. Austrian legislative bodies like the Imperial parliament traditionally had no power in territory of Hungarian Kingdom. Despite of this, it also tried to abolish the Diet of Hungary (which existed as the legislative power in Hungary since the late 12th century.) Moreover, the Austrian Stadion constitution also went against the historical constitution of Hungary, and tried to nullify it too.

The Hungarian Republic, Regent-President Louis Kossuth

When Batthyány resigned he was appointed with Szemere to carry on the government provisionally, and at the end of September he was made President of the Committee of National Defense. Kossuth was elected by the parliament as the head of state of Hungary. With the exception of Kázmér Batthyány, all members of the new cabinet were formed from Kossuth's supporters.

New government (The Szemere government) was formed on 2 May 1849:[362,363]

Head of state, Lajos Kossuth.

Prime Minister and Minister of the Interior, Bertalan Szemere

Foreign Minister, Minister of Agriculture, Industry and Trade : Kázmér Batthyány

Finance Minister: Ferenc Duschek

Minister of Justice: Sebő Vukovics

Minister of Education, Science and Culture: Mihály Horváth

Minister of Labour, Infrastructure and Transport: László Csány

Minister of Defence: Lázár Mészáros (14 April 1849 - 1 May 1849) Artúr Görgey (7 May 1849 - 7 July 1849) and Lajos Aulich (14 July 1849 - 11 August 1849)

From this time he had increased amounts of power. The direction of the whole government was in his hands. Without military experience, he had to control and direct the movements of armies; he was unable to keep control over the generals or to establish that military co-operation so essential to success. Arthur Görgey in particular, whose abilities Kossuth was the first to recognize, refused obedience; the two men were very different personalities. Twice Kossuth deposed him from the command; twice he had to restore him. It would have been well if Kossuth had had something more of Görgey's calculated ruthlessness, for, as has been truly said, the revolutionary power he had seized could only be held by revolutionary means; but he was by nature soft-hearted and always merciful; though often audacious, he lacked decision in dealing with men. It has been said that he showed a want of personal courage; this is not improbable, the excess of feeling which made him so great an orator could hardly be combined with the coolness in danger required of a soldier; but no one was able, as he was, to infuse courage into others.

During all the terrible winter which followed, his energy and spirit never failed him. It was he who overcame the reluctance of the army to march to the relief of Vienna; after the defeat at the Battle of Schwechat, at which he was present, he sent József Bem to carry on the war in Transylvania. At the end of the year, when the Austrians were approaching Pest, he asked for the mediation of Mr Stiles, the American envoy. Alfred I, Prince of Windisch-Grätz, however, refused all terms, and the Diet and government fled to Debrecen, Kossuth taking with him the Crown of St Stephen, the sacred emblem of the Hungarian nation. In November 1848, Emperor Ferdinand abdicated in favour of Franz Joseph. The new Emperor revoked all the concessions granted in March and outlawed Kossuth and the Hungarian government – set up lawfully on the basis of the April laws. In April 1849, when the Hungarians had won many successes, after sounding the army, Kossuth issued the celebrated Hungarian Declaration of Independence, in which he declared that "the house of Habsburg-Lorraine, perjured in the sight of God and man, had forfeited the Hungarian throne." It was a step characteristic of his love for extreme and dramatic action, but it added to the dissensions between him and those who wished only for autonomy under the old dynasty, and his enemies did not scruple to accuse him of

Hungarian Revolution of 1848

Figure 107: *The Siege of Buda in May 1849*

aiming for Kingship. The dethronement also made any compromise with the Habsburgs practically impossible.

Kossuth played a key role in tying down the Hungarian army for weeks for the siege and recapture of Buda castle, finally successful on 21 May 1849. The hopes of ultimate success were, however, frustrated by the intervention of Russia; all appeals to the western powers were vain, and on 11 August Kossuth abdicated in favor of Görgey, on the ground that in the last extremity the general alone could save the nation. Görgey capitulated at Világos (now Şiria, Romania) to the Russians, who handed over the army to the Austrians.[364]

War of Independence

In 1848 and 1849, the Hungarian people or Magyars, who wanted independence, formed a majority only in the central areas of the country. The Hungarians were surrounded by other nationalities.

In 1848–49, the Austrian monarchy and those advising them manipulated the Croatians, Serbians and Romanians, making promises to the Magyars one day and making conflicting promises to the Serbs and other groups the next.[365] Some of these groups were led to fight against the Hungarian Government

Figure 108: *Battle of Vršac, between army of Serbian Vojvodina and Hungarian army, January 1849*

by their leaders who were striving for their own independence; this triggered numerous brutal incidents between the Magyars and Romanians among others.

In 1848 and 1849, however, the Hungarians were supported by most Slovaks, Germans, Rusyns and Hungarian Slovenes, the Hungarian Jews, and many-Wikipedia:Manual of Style/Dates and numbers Polish, Austrian and Italian volunteers. On 28 July 1849, the Hungarian Revolutionary Parliament proclaimed and enacted the first laws on ethnic and minority rights in Europe, but these were overturned after the Russian and Austrian armies crushed the Hungarian Revolution. Occasionally, the Austrian throne would overplay their hand in their tactics of divide and conquer in Hungary – with some quite unintended results. This happened in the case of the Slovaks who had begun the war as at least indifferent if not positively anti-Magyar, but came to support the Hungarian Government against the Dynasty.[366] But in another case, the Austrians' double-dealing brought some even more surprising new allies to the Hungarian cause during the war in 1849.

Serbs

Between the Tisza river and Transylvania, north of the Danube lies the former region of Hungary called the "Banat". After the Battle of Mohács during the subsequent Ottoman rule the area north of the Danube saw an influx of Southern Slavs along with the invading Ottoman army. In 1804 the semi-independent Principality of Serbia had formed south of the Danube with Belgrade as its capital. So in 1849, the Danube divided Serbia from the Kingdom of Hungary. The Hungarian district on the northern side of the river was called "Vojvodina", and by that time it was home to almost half a million Serbian inhabitants. According to the census of 1840 in Vojvodina Serbs comprised 49% of the total population. The Serbs of Vojvodina had long sought their independence or attachment with the Principality of Serbia on the other side of the Danube. In face of the emerging Hungarian independence movement leading up to the 1848 Revolution the Austrian monarchy had promised an independent status for the Serbs of Vojvodina within the Austrian Empire.Wikipedia:Citation needed

Toward this end, Josif Rajačić was appointed Patriarch of Vojvodina in February 1849.[367] Rajačić was a supporter of the Serbian national movement, although somewhat conservative with pro-Austrian leanings. At a crucial point during the war against the Hungarian Government, in late March 1849 when the Austrians needed more Serbian soldiers to fight the war, the Austrian General Georg Rukavina Baron von Vidovgrad, who commanded the Austrian troops in Hungary, officially re-stated this promise of independence for Vojvodina and conceded to all the demands of the Patriarch regarding Serbian nationhood.[368] Acquiescence to the demands of the Patriarch should have meant a relaxation of the strict military administration of Vojvodina. Under this military administration in the border areas, any male between the ages of 16 years and 60 years of age could be conscripted into the army.[369]

The Serbs of Vojvodina were expecting their requirement for Austrian military conscription to be the first measure to be relaxed. But the new Emperor Franz Joseph had other ideas and this promise was broken not more than two weeks after it had been made to the people of Vojvodina. This caused a split in the population of the Vojvodina and at least part of the Serbs in that province began to support the elected Hungarian Government against the Austrians.[369]

Some Serbs sought to ingratiate the Serb nation with the Austrian Empire to promote the independence of Vojvodina. Followers of the idea of a "Greater Serbia" hoped that an independent Vojvodina would sooner or later attach itself to the Serbian nation. Believers in Greater Serbia already looked forward to acquiring Bosnia (37.1% Serb), Herzegovina (37.9% Serb), and Montenegro (mainly populated by Serbs).[370] But some supporters of Greater Serbia also threw in acquisition of the northern part of Albania (less than 1% Serb) as another desirable goal for Serbian acquisition, not so much because of any ethnic link, but rather so that the Greater Serbia would have "access to the sea".[370]

Figure 109: *Battle at Tápióbicske (4 April 1849) by Mór Than*

With war on three fronts the Hungarian Government should have been squashed immediately-Wikipedia:Manual_of_Style/Words_to_watch#Unsupported_attributions upon the start of hostilities. However, events early in the war worked in favour of the Government. The unity of the Serbs on the southern front was ruined by Austrian perfidy over the legal status of Vojvodina.

Some right-wing participants in the Serbian national movement felt that a "revolution" in Hungary more threatened the prerogatives of landowners, and the nobles in Serbian Vojvodina, than the occupying Austrians.[371]

At the start of the war, the Hungarian Defence Forces (*Honvédség*) won some Wikipedia:Manual of Style/Dates and numbers battles against the Austrians, for example at the Battle of Pákozd in September 1848 and at the Isaszeg in April 1849, at which time they even stated the Hungarian Declaration of Independence from the Habsburg Empire. The same month, Artúr Görgey became the new Commander-in-Chief of all the Hungarian Republic's armies.[372]

Slovaks

The Slovak Uprising was a reactionary movement to the Hungarian Revolution in the Western parts of Upper Hungary (now Western Slovakia). The Slovak nation and people had been poorly defined up to this point, as the Slovak people lacked a definitive border or national identity. However, in the years leading

Figure 110: *Slovak volunteers, 1848/49*

up to the revolution, the Hungarians had taken steps to Magyarize the Slovak region under Hungarian control. The aim of this was to bring the varied ethnic groups around Hungary into a common culture. At the outbreak of the Hungarian Revolution this process was seen as more imminent and threatening to ethnic groups, especially the Slovaks.[373]

The Slovaks made demands that their culture be spared Magyarization and that they be given certain liberties and rights. These demands soon broke out into demonstrations clamouring for the rights of ethnic minorities in Hungary. Arrests were made that further enraged the demonstrators and eventually a Pan-Slavic Congress was held in Vienna. A document was drafted at this congress and sent to the Hungarian government demanding the rights of the Slovak people. The Hungarians responded by imposing martial law on the Slovak region.

The Imperial government recognized that all across the Empire, ethnic minorities were seeking more autonomy, but it was only Hungary that desired a complete break. They used this by supporting the ethnic national movements against the Hungarian government. Slovak volunteer units were commissioned in Vienna to join campaigns against the Hungarians across the theatre. A Slovak regiment then marched to MyjavaWikipedia:Please clarify where a Slovak council openly seceded from Hungary. Tensions rose as the Hungarian army

Figure 111: *Battle of Temesvár in August 1849*

executed a number of Slovak leaders for treason and the fighting became more bloody.

However, the Slovak uprising also wanted its independence from the Empire as well and tensions with the Austrians soon began to rise. Lacking support and with increased Hungarian efforts, the Slovak volunteer corps had little impact for the rest of the war until the Russians marched in. It was used in 'mopping up' resistance in the wake of the Russian advance and then soon after was disbanded, ending Slovak involvement in the Revolution. The conclusion of the uprising is unclear, as the Slovaks fell back under Imperial authority and lacked any autonomy for some time.

Transylvania

On 29 May 1848, at Kolozsvár (now Cluj, Romania), the Transylvanian Diet (formed of 116 Hungarians, 114 Székelys and 35 Saxons) ratified the re-union with Hungary. Romanians and Germans disagreed with the decision.[374]

On 10 June 1848 the newspaper Wiener Zeitung wrote: *In any case, the union of Transylvania, proclaimed against all human rights, is not valid, and the courts of law in the entire world must admit the justness of the Romanian people's protest*

Romanians

On 25 February 1849 the representatives of the Romanian population sent to the Habsburg Emperor *The Memorandum of the Romanian nation from the Great Principality of Transylvania, Banat, from neighbouring territories to Hungary and Bukovina* where they demanded *the union of Bukovina, Transylvania and Banat under a government (...) the union of all Romanians in the Austrian state into one single* independent nation under the rule of Austria as completing part of the Monarchy[375]

Transylvanian Saxons

In the first days of October 1848, Stephan Ludwig Roth considered that there were two options for the Saxons: *The first is to side with the Hungarians, and thus turn against the Romanians and the empire; the second is to side with the Romanians, and thus support the empire against the Hungarians. In this choice, the Romanians and Hungarians are incidental factors. The most important principle is that of a united empire, for it guarantees the extension of Austria's proclaimed constitution.*

The Transylvanian Saxons rejected the incorporation of Transylvania into Hungary.[376]

Russians

Because of the success of revolutionary resistance, Franz Joseph had to ask for help from the *"gendarme of Europe"* Czar Nicholas I of Russia in March 1849. A Russian army, composed of about 8,000 soldiers, invaded Transylvania on 8 April 1849.[377] But as they crossed the Southern Carpathian mountain passes (along the border of Transylvania and Wallachia), they were met by a large Hungarian revolutionary army led by József Bem, a Polish-born General.

Bem had been a participant in the Polish insurrection of 1830 – 1831, had been involved in the uprising in Vienna in 1848 and, finally, became one of the top army commanders for the Hungarian Republic from 1848 – 1849.[378] When he encountered the Russians, Bem defeated them and forced them back out of the towns of Hermannstadt (now Sibiu, Romania) and Kronstadt (now Braşov) in Transylvania, back over the Southern Carpathian Mountains through the Roterturm Pass into Wallachia.[378] Only 2,000 Russian soldiers made it out of Transylvania back into Wallachia, the other 6,000 troops being killed or captured by the Hungarian Army.[379] After securing all of Transylvania, Bem moved his 30,000–40,000-man Hungarian army against Austrian forces in the northern Banat capturing the city of Temesvár (now Timişoara, Romania).[380]

Figure 112: *Artúr Görgey*

Austrians

Laval Nugent von Westmeath was the Austrian Master of Ordnance, but was serving as the general in the field attempting to marshall all the Serbs still loyal to the Austrian throne, for another offensive against the Hungarian Government.[381] Here, even on the southern front the Hungarian Armies were proving successful, initially.

This combat led to the Vienna Uprising of October 1848, when insurgents attacked a garrison on its way to Hungary to support forces. However, the Austrian army was able to quell the rebellion. At the same time, at Schwechat, the Austrians defeated a Hungarian attempt to capture Vienna. After this victory, General Windischgrätz and 70,000 troops were sent to Hungary to crush the Hungarian revolution. the Austrians followed the Danube down from Vienna and crossed over into Hungary to envelope Komorn (now Komárom, Hungary and Komárno, Slovakia). They continued down the Danube to Pest, the capital of the Hungarian Kingdom. After some fierce fighting, the Austrians, led by Alfred I, Prince of Windisch-Grätz, captured Buda and Pest.[382] (the town was known in German as Ofen and later Buda and Pest were united into Budapest).

In April 1849, after these defeats, the Hungarian Government recovered and scored several victories on this western front. They stopped the Austrian advance and retook Buda and Pest.[383] Then, the Hungarian Army relieved the

Figure 113: *Alfred I, Prince of Windisch-Grätz*

siege of Komárom.[384] The spring offensive hence proved to be a great success for the revolution.

Thus, the Hungarian Government was equally successful on its eastern front (Transylvania) against the Russians, and on its western front against the Austrians. But there was a third front – the southern front in the Banat, fighting the troops of the Serbian national movement and the Croatian troops of Jelačić within the province of Vojvodina itself. Mór Perczel, the General of the Hungarian forces in the Banat, was initially successful in battles along the southern front.[385]

In April 1849, Ludwig Baron von Welden replaced Windischgrätz as the new supreme commander of Austrian forces in Hungary.[386] Instead of pursuing the Austrian army, the Hungarians stopped to retake the Fort of Buda and prepared defenses. At the same time, however, victory in Italy had freed many Austrian troops which had hitherto been fighting on this front. In June 1849 Russian and Austrian troops entered Hungary heavily outnumbering the Hungarian army. After all appeals to other European states failed, Kossuth abdicated on August 11, 1849 in favour of Artúr Görgey, who he thought was the only general who was capable of saving the nation.

Figure 114: *Surrender at Világos, 1849*

However, in May 1849, Czar Nicholas I pledged to redouble his efforts against the Hungarian Government. He and Emperor Franz Joseph started to regather and rearm an army to be commanded by Anton Vogl, the Austrian lieutenant-field-marshal who had actively participated in the suppression of the national liberation movement in Galicia in 1848.[387] But even at this stage Vogl was occupied trying to stop another revolutionary uprising in Galicia.[388] The Czar was also preparing to send 30,000 Russian soldiers back over the Eastern Carpathian Mountains from Poland. Austria held Galicia and moved into Hungary, independent of Vogl's forces. At the same time, the able Haynau led an army of 60,000 Austrians from the West and retook the ground lost throughout the spring. On July 18, he finally captured Buda and Pest.[389] The Russians were also successful in the east and the situation of the Hungarians became increasingly desperate.

On August 13, after several bitter defeats, especially the battle of Segesvár against the Russians and the battles of Szöreg and Temesvár against the Austrian army, it was clear that Hungary had lost. In a hopeless situation, Görgey signed a surrender at Világos (now Şiria, Romania) to the Russians (so that the war would be considered a Russian victory and because the rebels considered the Russians more lenient), who handed the army over to the Austrians.

Aftermath

Julius Jacob von Haynau, the leader of the Austrian army, was appointed plenipotentiary to restore order in Hungary after the conflict. He ordered the execution of The 13 Martyrs of Arad (now Arad, Romania) and Prime Minister Batthyány was executed the same day in Pest.

After the failed revolution, in 1849 there was nationwide "passive resistance".[390] In 1851 Archduke Albrecht, Duke of Teschen was appointed as Regent, which lasted until 1860, during which time he implemented a process of Germanisation.

Kossuth went into exile after the revolution. In the US he was warmly received by the general public as well as the then US Secretary of State, Daniel Webster, which made relations between the US and Austria somewhat strained for the following twenty years. Kossuth County, Iowa was named for him. He then also travelled through Constantinople, the Ottoman Empire and to Turin, at the time the capital of Piedmont-Sardinia.

Kossuth thought his biggest mistake was to confront the Hungarian minorities. He set forth the dream of a multi-ethnic confederation of republics along the Danube, which might have prevented the escalation of hostile feelings between the ethnic groups in these areas.[391]

Many of Kossuth's comrades-in-exile joined him in the United States, including the sons of one of his sisters. These "Forty-Eighters" fought on the Union side in the US Civil War. Hungarian lawyer George Lichtenstein, who served as Kossuth's private secretary, fled to Königsberg after the revolution and eventually settled in Edinburgh where he became noted as a musician.

After the Hungarian Army's surrender at Világos in 1849, their revolutionary banners were taken to Russia by the Tsarist troops, and were kept there both under the Tsarist and Communist systems. In 1940 the Soviet Union offered the banners to the Horthy government in exchange for the release of the imprisoned Hungarian Communist leader Mátyás Rákosi – the Horthy government accepted the offer.

Further reading

 Wikimedia Commons has media related to *Hungarian Revolution of 1848*.

- ⓦ This article incorporates text from a publication now in the public domain: Chisholm, Hugh, ed. (1911). "Hungary". *Encyclopædia Britannica* (11th ed.). Cambridge University Press.
- Barany, George. "The awakening of Magyar nationalism before 1848." *Austrian History Yearbook* 2 (1966) pp: 19-50.
- Cavendish, Richard. "Declaration of Hungary's Independence: April 14th, 1849." *History Today* 49#4 (1999) pp: 50-51
- Deák, István. *Lawful Revolution: Louis Kossuth and the Hungarians 1848-1849* (Phoenix, 2001)
- Deme, László. "The Society for Equality in the Hungarian Revolution of 1848." *Slavic Review* (1972): 71-88. in JSTOR[392]
- Gángó, Gábor. "1848-1849 in Hungary," *Hungarian Studies* (2001) 15#1 pp 39–47. online[393]
- Judah, Tim (1997). *The Serbs: History, Myth & the Destruction of Yugoslavia*. New Haven, CT, USA: Yale. ISBN 978-0-300-08507-5.
- Kosáry, Domokos G. *The press during the Hungarian revolution of 1848-1849* (East European Monographs, 1986)
- Szilassy, Sandor. "America and the Hungarian Revolution of 1848-49." *Slavonic and East European Review* (1966): 180-196. in JSTOR[394]

Austria-Hungary

	Austria-Hungary↓
	Österreichisch-Ungarische Monarchie (German) *Osztrák-Magyar Monarchia* (Hungarian)
	1867–1918
	 Civil Ensign  Coat of arms
	Motto *Indivisibiliter ac Inseparabiliter* "Indivisible and Inseparable"
	Anthem *Gott erhalte Franz den Kaiser* "God save Emperor Francis"
	 Austria-Hungary in 1914
Capital	Vienna (main capital) and Budapest
Languages	**Official:** German, Hungarian[395]
Religion	*1910 census*[396] **Majority:** 76.6% Catholics (incl. 64-66% Roman & 10-12% Eastern)
Government	Constitutional monarchy, Liberal autocracy, Personal union (through dual monarchy)

Emperor-King	
• 1867–1916	Franz Joseph I
• 1916–1918	Charles I & IV
Minister-President	
• 1867	Friedrich von Beust (first)
• 1918	Heinrich Lammasch (last)
Prime Minister	
• 1867–1871	Gyula Andrássy (first)
• 1918	János Hadik (last)
Legislature	Imperial Council, Diet of Hungary
• Upper house	Herrenhaus, House of Magnates
• Lower house	Abgeordnetenhaus, House of Representatives
Historical era	New Imperialism/World War I
• 1867 Compromise	1 March 1867
• Czechoslovak indep.	28 October 1918
• State of SCS indep.	29 October 1918
• Vojvodina lost to Serbia	25 November 1918
• Dissolution	11 November 1918
• Dissolution treaties[a]	in 1919 and in 1920
Area	
• 1914	676,615 km^2 (261,243 sq mi)
• 1918	681,727 km^2 (263,216 sq mi)
Population	
• 1914 est.	52,800,000
Density	78/km^2 (202/sq mi)
Currency	• Gulden (to 1892) • Krone (1892–1918)

Austria-Hungary

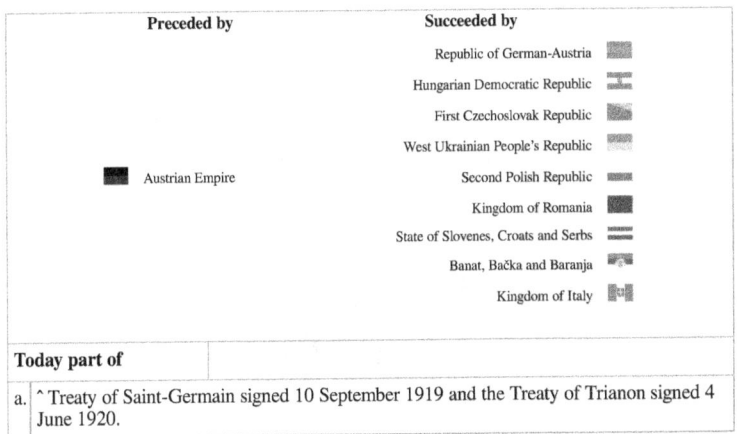

| a. | ^ Treaty of Saint-Germain signed 10 September 1919 and the Treaty of Trianon signed 4 June 1920. |

Austria-Hungary, often referred to as the **Austro-Hungarian Empire** or the **Dual Monarchy** in English-language sources, was a constitutional union of the Austrian Empire (the Kingdoms and Lands Represented in the Imperial Council, or *Cisleithania*) and the Kingdom of Hungary (Lands of the Crown of Saint Stephen or *Transleithania*) that existed from 1867 to 1918, when it collapsed as a result of defeat in World War I. The union was a result of the Austro-Hungarian Compromise of 1867 and came into existence on 30 March 1867. Austria-Hungary consisted of two monarchies (Austria and Hungary), and one autonomous region: the Kingdom of Croatia-Slavonia under the Hungarian crown, which negotiated the Croatian–Hungarian Settlement (*Nagodba*) in 1868. It was ruled by the House of Habsburg, and constituted the last phase in the constitutional evolution of the Habsburg Monarchy. Following the 1867 reforms, the Austrian and the Hungarian states were co-equal. Foreign affairs and the military came under joint oversight, but all other governmental faculties were divided between respective states.

Austria-Hungary was a multinational state and one of the world's great powers at the time. Austria-Hungary was geographically the second-largest country in Europe after the Russian Empire, at 621,538 km² (239,977 sq mi), and the third-most populous (after Russia and the German Empire). The Empire built up the fourth-largest machine building industry of the world, after the United States, Germany, and the United Kingdom.[397] Austria-Hungary also became the world's third largest manufacturer and exporter of electric home appliances, electric industrial appliances and power generation apparatus for power plants, after the United States and the German Empire.

After 1878, Bosnia and Herzegovina was under Austro-Hungarian military and civilian rule[398] until it was fully annexed in 1908, provoking the Bosnian crisis among the other powers. Sandžak/Raška, *de jure* northern part of the Ottoman

Figure 115: *Franz Joseph I. (1885)*

Sanjak of Novi Pazar (in modern-day Montenegro and Serbia), was also under *de facto* joint occupation during that period but the Austro-Hungarian army withdrew as part of their annexation of Bosnia.[399] The annexation of Bosnia also led to Islam being recognized as an official state religion due to Bosnia's Muslim population.

Austria-Hungary was one of the Central Powers in World War I. It was already effectively dissolved by the time the military authorities signed the armistice of Villa Giusti on 3 November 1918. The Kingdom of Hungary and the First Austrian Republic were treated as its successors *de jure*, whereas the independence of the West Slavs and South Slavs of the Empire as the First Czechoslovak Republic, the Second Polish Republic and the Kingdom of Yugoslavia, respectively, and most of the territorial demands of the Kingdom of Romania were also recognized by the victorious powers in 1920.

Structure and name

The realm's full, official name was **The Kingdoms and Lands Represented in the Imperial Council and the Lands of the Holy Hungarian Crown of St. Stephen.**

German: *Die im Reichsrat vertretenen Königreiche und Länder und die Länder der Heiligen Ungarischen Stephanskrone*

Hungarian: *A Birodalmi Tanácsban képviselt királyságok és országok és a Magyar Szent Korona országai*

The Habsburg monarch ruled as Emperor of Austria over the western and northern half of the country that was the Austrian Empire ("Lands Represented in the Imperial Council", or Cisleithania) and as King of Hungary over the Kingdom of Hungary ("Lands of the Crown of Saint Stephen", or Transleithania). Each enjoyed considerable sovereignty with only a few joint affairs (principally foreign relations and defence).

Certain regions, such as Polish Galicia within Cisleithania and Croatia (officially the Kingdom of Croatia-Slavonia-Dalmatia, even Dalmatia was in Cisleithanian part of the *Dual Monarchy*) within Transleithania, enjoyed autonomous status, each with its own unique governmental structures (see: Polish Autonomy in Galicia and Croatian–Hungarian Settlement).

The division between Austria and Hungary was so marked that there was no common citizenship: one was either an Austrian citizen or a Hungarian citizen, never both. This also meant that there were always separate Austrian and Hungarian passports, never a common one. However, neither Austrian nor Hungarian passports were used in the Kingdom of Croatia-Slavonia-Dalmatia. Instead, the Kingdom issued its own passports which were written in Croatian and French and displayed the coat of arms of the Kingdom of Croatia-Slavonia-Dalmatia on them.[400] It is not known what kind of passports were used in Bosnia-Herzegovina, which was under the control of both Austria and Hungary.Wikipedia:Citation needed

The Kingdom of Hungary had always maintained a separate parliament, the Diet of Hungary, even after the Austrian Empire was created in 1804.[401] The administration and government of the Kingdom of Hungary (until 1848-49 Hungarian revolution) remained largely untouched by the government structure of the overarching Austrian Empire. Hungary's central government structures remained well separated from the Austrian imperial government. The country was governed by the Council of Lieutenancy of Hungary (the Gubernium) – located in Pressburg and later in Pest – and by the Hungarian Royal Court Chancellery in Vienna.[402] The Hungarian government and Hungarian parliament were suspended after the Hungarian revolution of 1848, and were reinstated after the Austro-Hungarian Compromise in 1867.

Despite Austria and Hungary sharing a common currency, they were fiscally sovereign and independent entities. Since the beginnings of the personal union (from 1527), the government of the Kingdom of Hungary could preserve its separated and independent budget. After the revolution of 1848–1849, the Hungarian budget was amalgamated with the Austrian, and it was only after the Compromise of 1867 that Hungary obtained a separate budget. From 1527 (the creation of the monarchic personal union) to 1851, the Kingdom of Hungary maintained its own customs controls, which separated her from the other parts of the Habsburg-ruled territories.[403] After 1867, the Austrian and Hungarian customs union agreement had to be renegotiated and stipulated every ten years. The agreements were renewed and signed by Vienna and Budapest at the end of every decade because both countries hoped to derive mutual economic benefit from the customs union. The Austrian Empire and Kingdom of Hungary contracted their foreign commercial treaties independently of each other.

Austria-Hungary was a great power but it contained a large number of ethnic groups that sought their own nation. It was ruled by a coalition of two powerful minorities, the Germans and the Hungarians. Stresses regarding nationalism were building up, and the severe shock of a poorly handled war caused the system to collapse.

Vienna served as the Monarchy's primary capital. The Cisleithanian (Austrian) part contained about 57 percent of the total population and the larger share of its economic resources, compared to the Hungarian part.

Following a decision of Franz Joseph I in 1868, the realm bore the official name **Austro-Hungarian Monarchy/Realm** (German: *Österreichisch-Ungarische Monarchie/Reich*; Hungarian: *Osztrák–Magyar Monarchia/Birodalom*) in its international relations. It was often contracted to the **Dual Monarchy** in English, or simply referred to as **Austria**.

Creation

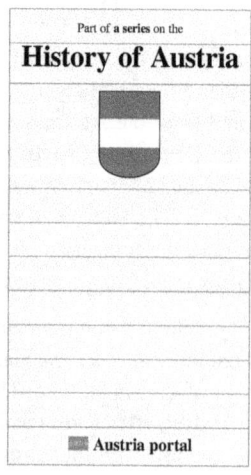

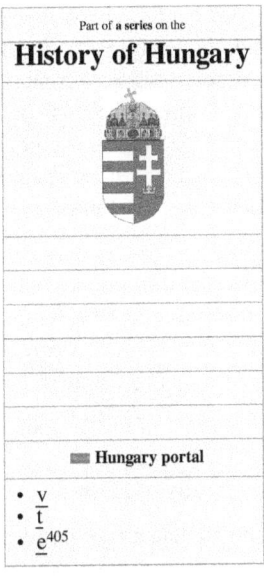

The Austro-Hungarian Compromise of 1867 (called the *Ausgleich* in German and the *Kiegyezés* in Hungarian), which inaugurated the empire's dual structure in place of the former unitary Austrian Empire (1804–67), originated at a time when Austria had declined in strength and in power—both in the Italian Peninsula (as a result of the Second Italian War of Independence of 1859) and among the states of the German Confederation (it had been surpassed by Prussia as the dominant German-speaking power following the Austro-Prussian War of 1866).[406]

Other factors in the constitutional changes were continued Hungarian dissatisfaction with rule from Vienna and increasing national consciousness on the part of other nationalities (or ethnicities) of the Austrian Empire. Hungarian dissatisfaction arose partly from Austria's suppression with Russian support of the Hungarian liberal revolution of 1848–49. However, dissatisfaction with Austrian rule had grown for many years within Hungary and had many other causes.

By the late 1850s, a large number of Hungarians who had supported the 1848–49 revolution were willing to accept the Habsburg monarchy. They argued that while Hungary had the right to full internal independence, under the

Pragmatic Sanction of 1713, foreign affairs and defense were "common" to both Austria and Hungary.

After the Austrian defeat at Königgrätz, the government realized it needed to reconcile with Hungary to regain the status of a great power. The new foreign minister, Count Friedrich Ferdinand von Beust, wanted to conclude the stalemated negotiations with the Hungarians. To secure the monarchy, Emperor Franz Joseph began negotiations for a compromise with the Hungarian nobility, led by Ferenc Deák, to ensure their support. In particular, Hungarian leaders demanded and received the Emperor's coronation as King of Hungary and the re-establishment of a separate parliament at Pest with powers to enact laws for the lands of the Holy Crown of Hungary.

From 1867 onwards, the abbreviations heading the names of official institutions in Austria-Hungary reflected their responsibility: K. u. k. (*kaiserlich und königlich* or Imperial and Royal) was the label for institutions common to both parts of the Monarchy, e.g. the *k.u.k. Kriegsmarine* (War Fleet) and, during the war, the *k.u.k. Armee* (Army). There were three *k.u.k.* or joint ministries:

- The Imperial and Royal Ministry of the Exterior and the Imperial House
- The Imperial and Royal War Ministry
- The Imperial and Royal Ministry of Finance

The last was responsible only for financing the Imperial and Royal household, the diplomatic service, the common army and the common war fleet. All other state functions were to be handled separately by each of the two states.

From 1867 onwards, common expenditures were allocated 70% to Austria and 30% to Hungary. This split had to be negotiated every decade. By 1907, the Hungarian share had risen to 36.4%. The negotiations in 1917 ended with the dissolution of the Dual Monarchy.

The common army changed its label from *k.k.* to *k.u.k.* only in 1889 at the request of the Hungarian government.

- *K. k.* (*kaiserlich-königlich*) or Imperial-Royal was the term for institutions of Cisleithania (Austria); "royal" in this label referred to the Crown of Bohemia.
- *K. u.* (*königlich-ungarisch*) or *M. k.* (*Magyar királyi*) ("Royal Hungarian") referred to Transleithania, the lands of the Hungarian crown. In the Kingdom of Croatia and Slavonia, its autonomous institutions hold *k.* (*kraljevski*) ("Royal") as according to the Croatian-Hungarian Settlement the only official language in Croatia and Slavonia was Croatian and those institutions were "only" Croatian.

Figure 116: *Austrian Parliament building*

Figure 117: *Hungarian Parliament building*

Politics and government

Government

There were three parts to the rule of the Austro-Hungarian Empire:[407]

1. the common foreign, military and a joint financial policy (only for diplomatic, military and naval expenditures) under the monarch
2. the "Austrian" or Cisleithanian government
3. the Hungarian government

Hungary and Austria maintained separate parliaments each with its own prime minister. Linking/co-ordinating the two parliaments fell to a government under the monarch. In this sense Austria-Hungary remained under an authoritarian government, as the Emperor-King appointed both Austrian and Hungarian Prime ministers along with their respective cabinets. This made both Governments responsible to the Emperor-King, as neither half could have a government with a program contrary to the views of the Monarch. The Emperor-King could appoint non-parliamentary governments, for example, or maintain in power a government which does not have a majority in Parliament to block the formation of another which he does not approve. The Monarch had other prerogatives such as the right of Royal Assent before any kind of Bill would be presented to the National Assembly (the common name for the Hungarian Diet), the right to Veto all legislation passed by the National Assembly, and the power to prorogue or dissolve the Assembly and call to new elections (he had the same prerogatives considering the Croatian-Slavonian Diet or Croatian Parliament, the common name for the Croatian-Slavonian Diet). In the Austrian half, however, the Monarchs's power was even greater, as the Emperor had the power to both appoint and dismiss its Prime minister and cabinet members. The monarch's common government, in which its ministers were appointed by the Monarch and responsible to him, had the responsibility for the army, for the navy, for foreign policy, and for the customs union. Due to the lack of common law between Austria and Hungary, to conclude identical texts, each parliament elected 60 of its members to form a delegation that discussed motions of the Imperial and Royal ministries separately and worked towards a compromise.

A common Ministerial Council ruled the common government: it comprised the three ministers for the joint responsibilities (joint finance, military, and foreign policy), the two prime ministers, some Archdukes and the monarch. Two delegations of representatives (60–60 members), one each from the Austrian and Hungarian parliaments, met separately and voted on the expenditures of the Common Ministerial Council giving the two governments influence in the common administration. However, the ministers ultimately answered only to the monarch who had the final decision on matters of foreign and military policy.

Overlapping responsibilities between the joint ministries and the ministries of the two halves caused friction and inefficiencies. The armed forces suffered particularly from overlap. Although the unified government determined the overall military direction, the Austrian and Hungarian governments each remained in charge of recruiting, supplies and training. Each government could have a strong influence over common governmental responsibilities. Each half of the Dual Monarchy proved quite prepared to disrupt common operations to advance its own interests.

Relations during the half-century after 1867 between the two parts of the dual monarchy featured repeated disputes over shared external tariff arrangements and over the financial contribution of each government to the common treasury. Under the terms of the "Austro-Hungarian Compromise of 1867", an agreement renegotiated every ten years, determined these matters. There was political turmoil during the build-up to each renewal of the agreement. The disputes culminated in the early 1900s in a prolonged constitutional crisis. It was triggered by disagreement over which language to use for command in Hungarian army units, and deepened by the advent to power in Budapest in April 1906 of a Hungarian nationalist coalition. Provisional renewals of the common arrangements occurred in October 1907 and in November 1917 on the basis of the *status quo*.

Judicial system

Kingdom of Hungary

The judicial power was independent of the administrative power. After 1868 (Croatian-Hungarian Settlement), Croatia-Slavonia had its own independent judicial system (the Table of Seven was the court of last instance for Croatia-Slavonia with final civil and criminal jurisdiction). The judicial authorities in Hungary were:

1. the district courts with single judges (458 in 1905);
2. the county courts with collegiate judgeships (76 in number); to these were attached 15 jury courts for press offences. These were courts of first instance. In Croatia-Slavonia these were known as the court tables after 1874;
3. Royal Tables (12 in number), which were courts of second instance, established at Budapest, Debrecen, Győr, Kassa, Kolozsvár, Marosvásárhely, Nagyvárad, Pécs, Pressburg, Szeged, Temesvár and Ban's Table at Zagreb.
4. The Royal Supreme Court at Budapest, and the Supreme Court of Justice, or Table of Seven, at Zagreb, which were the highest judicial authorities. There were also a special commercial court at Budapest, a naval court at Fiume, and special army courts.

Figure 118: *Emperor Franz Joseph I visiting Prague and opening the new Emperor Francis I. Bridge in 1901*

Public administration and local governments

Empire of Austria

The organization of the administrative system in the Austrian Empire was complicated by the fact that between the State and the purely local communal administration there intruded yet a third element, grounded in history, the territories (Länder). The State administration comprised all affairs having relation to rights, duties and interests "which are common to all territories"; all other administrative tasks were left to the territories. Finally, the communes had self-government within their own sphere.

To this division of the work of administration corresponded a three-fold organization of the authorities: State, territorial and communal. The State authorities were divided on geographical lines into central, intermediate and local, and side by side with this there was a division of the offices for the transaction of business according to the various branches of the administration. The central authorities, which as early as the 18th century worked together in a common mother cell of the State chancery, became differentiated so soon as the growing tasks of administration called for specialization; in 1869 there were seven departments, and in the concluding decade of the Austrian Empire there were set up Ministries of Labour, Food, Public Health and Social

Figure 119: *Kraków, a historical Polish city in the Austro-Hungarian Empire where in 1870 authorities allowed the use of the Polish language in the Jagiellonian University.*

Care. Under these ministries came the Statthalter, whose administrative area had ordinarily the proportions of a Crown territory (Kronland); but the immense variations in area of the Crown territories made a uniform and consistent intermediate administrative organization practically impossible. The lowest administrative unit was the political sub-district (*Bezirk*) under an official (*Bezirkshauptmann*), who united nearly all the administrative functions which were divided among the various ministries according to their attributions.

Side by side with the State administration certain Crown territory administrations also existed in the 17 Crown territories, carried on by selected honorary officials, having under them a staff of professional officials. Many branches of the territorial administration had great similarities with those of the State, so that their spheres of activity frequently overlapped and came into collision. This administrative "double track", as it was called, led, it is true, in many cases to lively emulation, but was on the whole highly extravagant. The evils of this complicated system are obvious, and easy to condemn. They can be explained, partly by the origin of the State – for the most part through a voluntary union of countries possessed by a strong sense of their own individuality – partly by the influence in Austria of the Germanic spirit, well understood by the Slavs, which has nothing of the Latin tendency to reduce all questions of administration to clear-cut formulae as part of a logically consistent system. Like the English administrative system, the Austrian presented a rich variety, a variety indeed so rich that it clamoured for drastic reform.

Bienerth's last act as premier in May 1911 was the appointment of a commission nominated by the Emperor, to draw up a scheme of administrative reform. So early as 1904 KOrber had declared a complete change in the principles of administration to be essential if the machinery of State were to continue working. After seven years of inaction, however, this imperial rescript was pitched in a far lower key. The continuous progress of society, it said, had made increased demands on the administration, that is to say, it was assumed that reform was not demanded so much by the defects of the administration but by the progress of the times, not because the administration was bad, but because life was better. It was an attempt to reform the administration without first reforming the State on equivalent lines.

A reform commission without a programme naturally first occupied itself with reforms about which there was no controversy. After a year had gone by it drew up "Proposals for the training of State officials". After another two years it had indeed brought to light carefully prepared material for study, which was of great scientific value; but its proposals. though politically of importance, did not provide any basis for reform on a large scale. And so when the World War broke out the commission dispersed without practical results, leaving behind it an imposing array of folio volumes of great scientific value. It was not till March 1918 that the Seidler Government decided upon a programme of national autonomy as a basis for administrative reform, which was, however, never carried into effect.[408]

Kingdom of Hungary

Administrative divisions and the counties of Hungary

Since 1867 the administrative and political divisions of the lands belonging to the Hungarian crown have been in great measure remodelled. In 1868 Transylvania was definitely reunited to Hungary proper, and the town and district of Fiume declared autonomous. In 1873 part of the "Military Frontier" was united with Hungary proper and part with Croatia-Slavonia. Hungary proper, according to ancient usage, was generally divided into four great divisions or circles, and Transylvania up to 1876 was regarded as the fifth. In 1876 a general system of counties was introduced. According to this division Hungary proper is divided into seven circles, of which Transylvania forms one. The whole country is divided into the following counties:

(a) The circle on the left bank of the Danube contains eleven counties: (1) Árva, (2) Bars, (3) Esztergom, (4) Hont, (5) Liptó, (6) Nógrád, (7) Nyitra, (8) Pozsony (9) Trencsén, (10) Túrócz and (11) Zólyom.

(b) The circle on the right bank of the Danube contains eleven counties: Baranya, Fejér, Győr, Komárom, Moson, Somogy, Sopron, Tolna, Vas, Veszprém and Zala.

(c) The circle between the Danube and Tisza contains five counties: Bács-Bodrog, Csongrád, Heves, Jász-Nagykun-Szolnok and Pest-Pilis-Solt-Kiskun.

(d) The circle on the right bank of the Tisza contains eight counties: Abaúj-Torna, Bereg, Borsod, Gömör-es Kis-Hont, Sáros, Szepes, Ung, Zemplén.

(e) The circle on the left bank of the Tisza contains eight counties: Békés, Bihar, Hajdú, Máramaros, Szabolcs, Szatmár, Szilágy and Ugocsa.

(f) The circle between the Tisza and the Maros contains five counties: Arad, Csanád, Krassó-Szörény, Temes and Torontál.

(g) Transylvania contains fifteen counties: Also-Fehér, Besztercze-Naszód, Brassó, Csík, Fogaras, Háromszek, Hunyad, Kis-Küküllő, Kolozs, Maros-Torda, Nagy-Küküllő, Szeben, Szolnok-Doboka, Torda-Aranyos and Udvarhely.

Fiume town and district forms a separate division.

Croatia-Slavonia is divided into eight counties: Bjelovar-Križevci, Lika-Krbava, Modrus-Fiume, Pozega, Srijemska, Varaždin, Virovitica and Zagreb.

Municipal rights of the biggest cities in Hungary

In regard to local government, the country was divided into municipalities or counties, which possessed a certain amount of self-government. Hungary proper was divided into sixty-three rural, and—including Fiume—twenty-six urban municipalities (see section on Administrative Divisions). These urban municipalities were towns which for their local government were independent of the counties in which they were situated, and have, therefore, a larger amount of municipal autonomy than the communes or the other towns. The administration of the municipalities is carried on by an official appointed by the king, aided by a representative body. Since 1876 each municipality had a council of twenty members to exercise control over its administration. According to this division Hungary proper is divided into seven circles.

Besides these sixty-three rural counties for Hungary, and eight for Croatia-Slavonia, Hungary had twenty-six urban counties or towns with municipal rights. These were: Arad, Baja, Debreczen, Győr, Hódmezővásárhely, Kassa, Kecskemét, Kolozsvár, Komárom, Marosvásárhely, Nagyvárad, Pancsova, Pécs, Pozsony, Selmecz- és Bélabanya, Sopron, Szabadka, Szatmárnémeti, Szeged, Székesfehervár, Temesvár, Újvidék, Versecz, Zombor, the town of Fiume and Budapest, the capital of the country.

In Croatia-Slavonia there are four urban counties or towns with municipal rights namely: Osijek, Varaždin and Zagreb and Zemun.

Politics

The first prime minister of Hungary after the Compromise was Count Gyula Andrássy (1867–1871). The old Hungarian Constitution was restored, and Franz Joseph was crowned as King of Hungary. Andrássy next served as the Foreign Minister of Austria-Hungary (1871–1879).

The Empire relied increasingly on a cosmopolitan bureaucracy—in which Czechs played an important role—backed by loyal elements, including a large part of the German, Hungarian, Polish and Croat aristocracy.

Political struggles in the Empire

The traditional aristocracy and land-based gentry class gradually faced increasingly wealthy men of the cities, who achieved wealth through trade and industrialization. The urban middle and upper class tended to seek their own power and supported progressive movements in the aftermath of revolutions in Europe. They were described as "leftist liberals" and their representatives began to be elected to the parliaments of Vienna and Budapest. These leftist liberal parliamentary parties were backed by the big industrialists, bankers, businessmen, and the predominant majority of newspaper publishers.

As in the German Empire, the Austro-Hungarian Empire frequently used liberal economic policies and practices. From the 1860s, businessmen succeeded in industrializing parts of the Empire. Newly prosperous members of the bourgeoisie erected large homes, and began to take prominent roles in urban life that rivaled the aristocracy's. In the early period, they encouraged the government to seek foreign investment to build up infrastructure, such as railroads, in aid of industrialization, transportation and communications, and development.

The influence of liberals in Austria, most of them ethnic Germans, weakened under the leadership of Count Eduard von Taaffe, the Austrian prime minister from 1879 to 1893. Taaffe used a coalition of clergy, conservatives and Slavic parties to weaken the liberals. In Bohemia, for example, he authorized Czech as an official language of the bureaucracy and school system, thus breaking the German speakers' monopoly on holding office. Such reforms encouraged other ethnic groups to push for greater autonomy as well. By playing nationalities off one another, the government ensured the monarchy's central role in holding together competing interest groups in an era of rapid change.

During the First World War, rising national sentiments and labour movements contributed to strikes, protests and civil unrest in the Empire. After the war, republican, national parties contributed to the disintegration and collapse of the monarchy in Austria and Hungary. Republics were established in Vienna and Budapest.

Figure 120: *Ethno-linguistic map of Austria-Hungary, 1910*

Ethnic relations

In July 1849, the Hungarian Revolutionary Parliament proclaimed and enacted ethnic and minority rights. (The next such laws were in Switzerland), but these were overturned after the Russian and Austrian armies crushed the Hungarian Revolution. After the Kingdom of Hungary reached the Compromise with the Habsburg Dynasty in 1867, one of the first acts of its restored Parliament was to pass a Law on Nationalities (Act Number XLIV of 1868). It was a liberal piece of legislation, and offered extensive language and cultural rights. It did not recognize non-Hungarians to have rights to form states with any territorial autonomy.

The "Austro-Hungarian Compromise of 1867" created the semi-independent states of Hungary and Austria linked by personal union under a common monarch. The Hungarian majority asserted more of their identity within the Kingdom of Hungary. The nationalism of German-speakers prevalent in the Empire of Austria created tension between ethnic Germans and ethnic Czechs. In addition, the emergence of national identity in the newly independent Romania and Serbia also contributed to ethnic issues in the empire.

Article 19 of the 1867 "Basic State Act" (*Staatsgrundgesetz*), valid only for the Cisleithanian (Austrian) part of Austria-Hungary, said:

Figure 121: *Meyers Konversations-Lexikon map of Austria-Hungary, 1885*

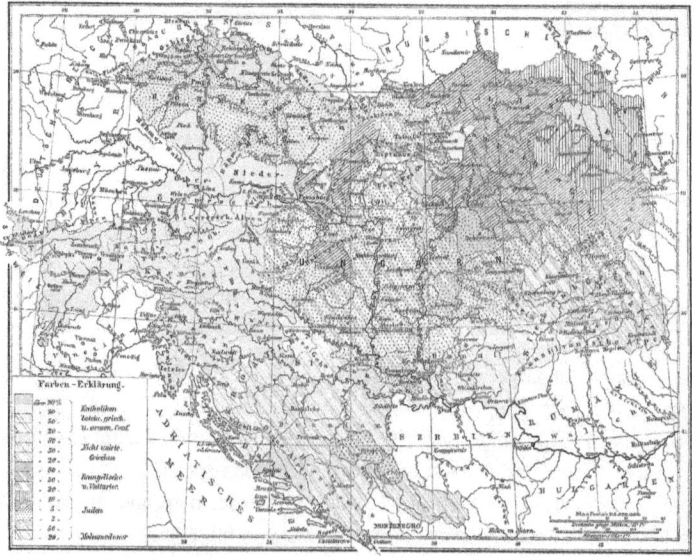

Figure 122: *Religions in Austria-Hungary, from the 1881 edition of Andrees Allgemeiner Handatlas. Catholics (both Roman and Uniate) are blue, Protestants purple, Eastern Orthodox yellow, and Muslims green.*

Austria-Hungary

Figure 123: *Literacy in Austria-Hungary (census 1880)*

Figure 124: *Austria-Hungary 1914, physical*

*All races of the empire have equal rights, and every race has an inviolable right to the preservation and use of its own nationality and language. The equality of all customary languages ("*landesübliche Sprachen*") in school, office and public life, is recognized by the state. In those territories in which several races dwell, the public and educational institutions are to be so arranged that, without applying compulsion to learn a second country language ("Landessprache"), each of the races receives the necessary means of education in its own language.*[409]

The implementation of this principle led to several disputes, as it was not clear which languages could be regarded as "customary". The Germans, the traditional bureaucratic, capitalist and cultural elite, demanded the recognition of their language as a customary language in every part of the empire. Italian was regarded as an old "culture language" (*Kultursprache*) by German intellectuals and had always been granted equal rights as an official language of the Empire, but the Germans had difficulty in accepting the Slavic languages as equal to their own. On one occasion Count A. Auersperg (Anastasius Grün) entered the Diet of Carniola carrying what he claimed to be the whole corpus of Slovene literature under his arm; this was to demonstrate that the Slovene language could not be substituted for German as the language of higher education.

The following years saw official recognition of several languages, at least in Austria. From 1867, laws awarded Croatian equal status with Italian in Dalmatia. From 1882, there was a Slovene majority in the Diet of Carniola and in the capital Laibach (Ljubljana); they ruled to replace German with Slovene as their primary official language. Galicia designated Polish instead of German in 1869 as the customary language of government. The Poles systematically disregarded the large Ukrainian minority in their territory, and did not grant Ukrainian the status of an official language.

The language disputes were most fiercely fought in Bohemia, where the Czech speakers formed a majority and sought equal status for their language to German. The Czechs had lived primarily in Bohemia since the 6th century and German immigrants had begun settling the Bohemian periphery since the 13th century. The constitution of 1627 made the German language a second official language and equal to Czech. German speakers lost their majority in the Bohemian Diet in 1880 and became a minority to Czech speakers in the cities of Prague and Pilsen (while retaining a slight numerical majority in the city of Brno (Brünn)). The old Charles University in Prague, hitherto dominated by German speakers, was divided into German and Czech-speaking faculties in 1882.

At the same time, Hungarian dominance faced challenges from the local majorities of Romanians in Transylvania and in the eastern Banat, Slovaks in today's Slovakia, and Croats and Serbs in the crown lands of Croatia and of Dalmatia (today's Croatia), in Bosnia and Herzegovina, and in the provinces known as the Vojvodina (today's northern Serbia). The Romanians and the Serbs began to agitate for union with their fellow nationalists and language speakers in the newly founded states of Romania (1859–78) and Serbia.

Hungary's leaders were generally less willing than their Austrian counterparts to share power with their subject minorities, but they granted a large measure of autonomy to Croatia in 1868. To some extent, they modelled their relation to that kingdom on their own compromise with Austria of the previous year. In spite of nominal autonomy, the Croatian government was an economic and administrative part of Hungary, which the Croatians resented. In the Triune Kingdom of Croatia and Bosnia and Herzegovina many advocated the idea of a trialist Austro-Hungaro-Croatian monarchy among the supporters of the idea where Archduke Leopold Salvator, Archduke Franz Ferdinand and emperor and king Charles I. (IV.) who during his short reign supported the trialist idea only to be vetoed by the Hungarian government and Count Istvan Tisza. The count finally signed the trialist proclamation after heavy pressure from the king on 23 October 1918. one day after the king.[410]

Language was one of the most contentious issues in Austro-Hungarian politics. All governments faced difficult and divisive hurdles in deciding on the languages of government and of instruction. The minorities sought the widest opportunities for education in their own languages, as well as in the "dominant" languages—Hungarian and German. By the "Ordinance of 5 April 1897", the Austrian Prime Minister Count Kasimir Felix Badeni gave Czech equal standing with German in the internal government of Bohemia; this led to a crisis because of nationalist German agitation throughout the empire. The Crown dismissed Badeni.

The Hungarian Minority Act of 1868 gave the minorities (Slovaks, Romanians, Serbs, et al.) individual (but not also communal) rights to use their language in offices, schools (although in practice often only in those founded by them and not by the state), courts and municipalities (if 20% of the deputies demanded it). From June 1907, all public and private schools in Hungary were obliged to ensure that after the fourth grade, the pupils could express themselves fluently in Hungarian. This led to the closing of several minority schools, devoted mostly to the Slovak and Rusyn languages.

The two kingdoms sometimes divided their spheres of influence. According to Misha Glenny in his book, *The Balkans, 1804–1999*, the Austrians responded to Hungarian support of Czechs by supporting the Croatian national movement in Zagreb.

In recognition that he reigned in a multi-ethnic country, Emperor Franz Joseph spoke (and used) German, Hungarian and Czech fluently, and Croatian, Serbian, Polish and Italian to some degree.

In 1914, Jews in the empire numbered about two million;Wikipedia:Citation needed their position was ambiguous. Antisemitic parties and movements existed, but the governments of Vienna and Budapest did not initiate pogroms or implement official antisemitic policies.Wikipedia:Citation needed They feared that such ethnic violence could ignite other ethnic minorities and escalate out of control. The antisemitic parties remained on the periphery of the political sphere due to their low popularity among voters in the parliamentary elections.Wikipedia:Citation needed

In that period, the majority of Jews in Austria-Hungary lived in small towns (*shtetls*) in Galicia and rural areas in Hungary and Bohemia, although there were large communities in Vienna, Budapest, Prague and other large cities. Of the pre-World War military forces of the major European powers, the Austro-Hungarian army was almost alone in its regular promotion of Jews to positions of command.[411] While the Jewish population of the lands of the Dual Monarchy was about five percent, Jews made up nearly eighteen percent of the reserve officer corps.[412] Thanks to the constitution's modern laws and to the benevolence of emperor Franz Joseph, the Austrian Jews came to regard the era of Austria-Hungary as a golden era of their history.[413] By 1910 about 900,000 Jews made up approximately 5 percent of the population of Hungary and about 23 percent of Budapest's citizenry. Jews accounted for 54 percent of commercial business owners, 85 percent of financial institution directors and owners, and 62 percent of all employees in commerce

Foreign policy

The minister of foreign affairs conducted the foreign relations of the Dual Monarchy, and negotiated treaties.[414]

The Dual Monarchy was created in the wake of a losing war in 1866 with Prussia and Italy. To rebuild Habsburg prestige and gain revenge against Prussia, Count Friedrich Ferdinand von Beust became foreign secretary. He hated Prussia's diplomat, Otto von Bismarck, who had repeatedly outmaneuvered him. Beust looked to France and negotiated with Emperor Napoleon III and Italy for an anti-Prussian alliance. No terms could be reached. The decisive victory of Prusso-German armies in the war of 1870 with France and the founding of the German Empire ended all hope of revenge and Beust retired.[415]

After being forced out of Germany and Italy, the Dual Monarchy turned to the Balkans, which were in tumult as nationalistic efforts were trying to end

Figure 125: *Muslim Bosniak resistance during the battle of Sarajevo in 1878 against the Austro-Hungarian occupation.*

the rule of the Ottomans. Both Russia and Austria-Hungary saw an opportunity to expand in this region. Russia in particular took on the role of protector of the Slavs and the orthodox Christians. Austria envisioned a multi-ethnic, religiously diverse empire under Vienna's control. Count Gyula Andrássy, a Hungarian who was Foreign Minister (1871 to 1879), made the centerpiece of his policy one of opposition to Russian expansion in the Balkans and blocking Serbian ambitions to dominate a new South Slav federation. He wanted Germany to ally with Austria, not Russia.[416]

When Russia defeated Turkey in a war the resulting Treaty of San Stefano was seen in Austria as much too favourable for Russia and its Orthodox-Slavic goals. The Congress of Berlin in 1878 let Austria occupy (but not annex) the province of Bosnia and Herzegovina, a predominantly Slavic area. In 1914, Slavic militants in Bosnia rejected Austria's plan to fully absorb the area; they assassinated the Austrian heir and precipitated World War I.[417]

Economy

The Austro-Hungarian economy changed dramatically during the Dual Monarchy. The capitalist way of production spread throughout the Empire during its 50-year existence, replacing medievalWikipedia:Citation needed institutions.

Figure 126: *A 20-crown banknote of the Dual Monarchy, using all official and recognized languages*

Technological change accelerated industrialization and urbanization. The first Austrian stock exchange (the Wiener Börse) was opened in 1771 in Vienna, the first stock exchange of the Kingdom of Hungary (the Budapest Stock Exchange) was opened in Budapest in 1864. The central bank (Bank of issue) was founded as Austrian National Bank in 1816. In 1878, it transformed into Austro-Hungarian National Bank with principal offices in both Vienna and Budapest. The central bank was governed by alternating Austrian or Hungarian governors and vice-governors.[418]

The gross national product per capita grew roughly 1.76% per year from 1870 to 1913. That level of growth compared very favorably to that of other European nations such as Britain (1%), France (1.06%), and Germany (1.51%). However, in a comparison with Germany and Britain, the Austro-Hungarian economy as a whole still lagged considerably, as sustained modernization had begun much later. Like the German Empire, that of Austria-Hungary frequently employed liberal economic policies and practices. In 1873, the old Hungarian capital Buda and Óbuda (Ancient Buda) were officially merged with the third city, Pest, thus creating the new metropolis of Budapest. The dynamic Pest grew into Hungary's administrative, political, economic, trade and cultural hub. Many of the state institutions and the modern administrative system of Hungary were established during this period. Economic growth centered on Vienna and Budapest, the Austrian lands (areas of modern Austria), the Alpine region and the Bohemian lands. In the later years of the 19th century, rapid economic growth spread to the central Hungarian plain and to the

Carpathian lands. As a result, wide disparities of development existed within the empire. In general, the western areas became more developed than the eastern. The Kingdom of Hungary became the world's second largest flour exporter after the United States. The large Hungarian food exports were not limited to neighbouring Germany and Italy: Hungary became the most important foreign food supplier of the large cities and industrial centres of the United Kingdom.[419]

However, by the end of the 19th century, economic differences gradually began to even out as economic growth in the eastern parts of the monarchy consistently surpassed that in the western. The strong agriculture and food industry of the Kingdom of Hungary with the centre of Budapest became predominant within the empire and made up a large proportion of the export to the rest of Europe. Meanwhile, western areas, concentrated mainly around Prague and Vienna, excelled in various manufacturing industries. This division of labour between the east and west, besides the existing economic and monetary union, led to an even more rapid economic growth throughout Austria-Hungary by the early 20th century. However, since the turn of the twentieth century, the Austrian half of the Monarchy could preserve its dominance within the empire in the sectors of the first industrial revolution, but Hungary had a better position in the industries of the second industrial revolution, in these modern sectors of the second industrial revolution the Austrian competition could not become dominant.

The empire's heavy industry had mostly focused on machine building, especially for the electric power industry, locomotive industry and automotive industry, while in light industry the precision mechanics industry was the most dominant. Through the years leading up to World War I the country became the 4th biggest machine manufacturer in the world.

The two most important trading partners were traditionally Germany (1910: 48% of all exports, 39% of all imports), and Great Britain (1910: almost 10% of all exports, 8% of all imports), the third most important partner was the United States, it followed by Russia, France, Switzerland, Romania, the Balkan states and South America. Trade with the geographically neighbouring Russia, however, had a relatively low weight (1910: 3% of all exports /mainly machinery for Russia, 7% of all imports /mainly raw materials from Russia).

Automotive industry

Austrian Empire

Prior to World War I, the Austrian Empire had five car manufacturer companies. These were: Austro-Daimler in Wiener-Neustadt (cars trucks, buses),[420] Gräf & Stift in Vienna (cars),[421] Laurin & Klement in Mladá Boleslav (motorcycles, cars), Nesselsdorfer in Nesselsdorf (Kopřivnice), Moravia (automobiles), and Lohner-Werke in Vienna (cars).[422] Austrian car production started in 1897.

Kingdom of Hungary

Prior to World War I, the Kingdom of Hungary had four car manufacturer companies. These were: the Ganz company[423,424] in Budapest, RÁBA Automobile[425] in Győr, MÁG (later Magomobil)[426] in Budapest, and MARTA (Hungarian Automobile Joint-stock Company Arad)[427] in Arad. Hungarian car production started in 1900. Automotive factories in the Kingdom of Hungary manufactured motorcycles, cars, taxicabs, trucks and buses.Wikipedia:Citation needed

Aeronautic industry

Austrian Empire

The first airplane in Austria was Edvard Rusjan's design, the Eda I, which had its maiden flight in the vicinity of Gorizia on 25 November 1909.

Kingdom of Hungary

The first Hungarian hydrogen filled experimental ballons were built by István Szabik and József Domin in 1784. The first Hungarian designed and produced airplane (powered by Hungarian built inline engine) was flown at Rákosmező on 4 November[428] 1909.[429] The earliest Hungarian radial engine powered airplane was built in 1913. Between 1913 and 1918, the Hungarian aircraft industry began developing. The three greatest: UFAG Hungarian Aircraft Factory (1914), Hungarian General Aircraft Factory (1916), Hungarian Lloyd Aircraft, Engine Factory at Aszód (1916),[430] and Marta in Arad (1914). During the First World War, fighter planes, bombers and reconnaissance planes were produced in these factories. The most important aeroengine factories were Weiss Manfred Works, GANZ Works, and Hungarian Automobile Joint-stock Company Arad.

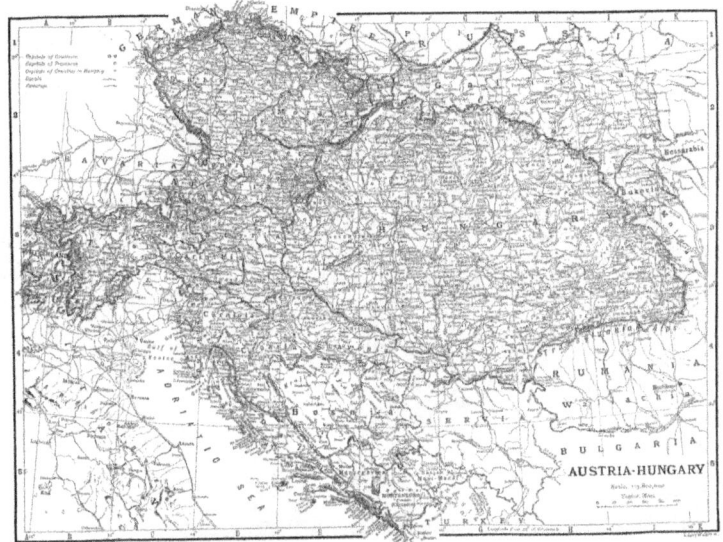

Figure 127: *Detailed railway and canal map of the Austro-Hungarian Empire in 1910.*

Locomotive engine and railway vehicle manufacturers

Austrian Empire

The locomotive (steam engines and wagons, bridge and iron structures) factories were installed in Vienna (Locomotive Factory of the State Railway Company, founded in 1839), in Wiener Neustadt (New Vienna Locomotive Factory, founded in 1841), and in Floridsdorf (Floridsdorf Locomotive Factory, founded in 1869).Wikipedia:Citation needed

Kingdom of Hungary

The Hungarian Locomotive (engines and wagons bridge and iron structures) factories were the MÁVAG company in Budapest (steam engines and wagons) and the Ganz company in Budapest (steam engines, wagons, the production of electric locomotives and electric trams started from 1894). and the RÁBA Company in Győr.

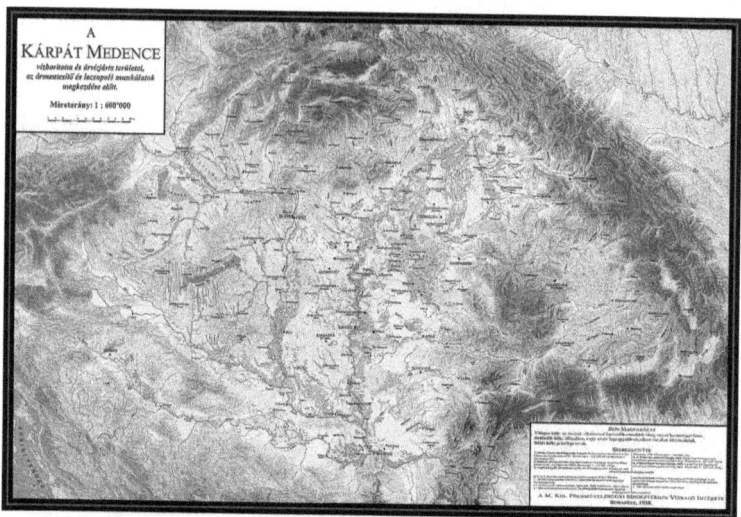

Figure 128: *Hydrography of the Pannonian basin before the Hungarian river and lake regulations in the 19th century.*

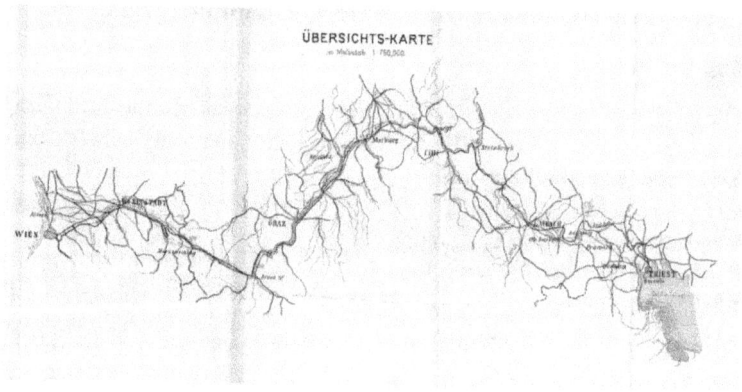

Figure 129: *Plan (1900) to link the Danube and the Adriatic Sea by a canal.*

Figure 130: *The start of construction of the underground in Budapest (1894–1896)*

Figure 131: *The SS Kaiser Franz Joseph I (12.567 t) of the Austro-Americana company was the largest passenger ship ever built in Austria. Because of its control over the Littorals and much of the Balkans, Austria-Hungary had access to several seaports.*

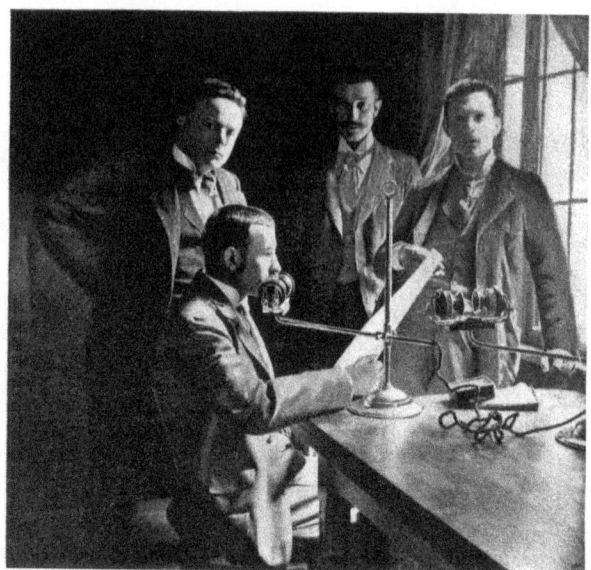

Figure 132: *A stentor reading the day's news in the Telefonhírmondó of Budapest*

Figure 133: *An Austrian public telephone in a rural post office, 1890*

Infrastructure

Transport

Railways

By 1913, the combined length of the railway tracks of the Austrian Empire and Kingdom of Hungary reached 43,280 kilometres (26,890 miles). In Western Europe only Germany had more extended railway network (63,378 km, 39,381 mi); the Austro-Hungarian Empire was followed by France (40,770 km, 25,330 mi), the United Kingdom (32,623 km, 20,271 mi), Italy (18,873 km, 11,727 mi) and Spain (15,088 km, 9,375 mi).

Railway network of the Austrian Empire

Rail transport expanded rapidly in the Austro-Hungarian Empire. Its predecessor state, the Habsburg Empire, had built a substantial core of railways in the west, originating from Vienna, by 1841. Austria's first steam railway from Vienna to Moravia with its terminus in Galicia (Bochnie) was opened in 1839. The first train travelled from Vienna to Lundenburg (Břeclav) on 6 June 1839 and one month later between the imperial capital in Vienna and the capital of Moravia Brünn (Brno) on 7 July. At that point, the government realized the military possibilities of rail and began to invest heavily in construction. Pozsony (Bratislava), Budapest, Prague, Kraków, Graz, Laibach (Ljubljana) and Venedig (Venice) became linked to the main network. By 1854, the empire had almost 2,000 km (1,200 mi) of track, about 60–70% of it in state hands. The government then began to sell off large portions of track to private investors to recoup some of its investments and because of the financial strains of the 1848 Revolution and of the Crimean War.

From 1854 to 1879, private interests conducted almost all rail construction. What would become Cisleithania gained 7,952 km (4,941 mi) of track, and Hungary built 5,839 km (3,628 mi) of track. During this time, many new areas joined the railway system and the existing rail networks gained connections and interconnections. This period marked the beginning of widespread rail transportation in Austria-Hungary, and also the integration of transportation systems in the area. Railways allowed the empire to integrate its economy far more than previously possible, when transportation depended on rivers.

After 1879, the Austrian and the Hungarian governments slowly began to renationalize their rail networks, largely because of the sluggish pace of development during the worldwide depression of the 1870s. Between 1879 and 1900, more than 25,000 km (16,000 mi) of railways were built in Cisleithania and Hungary. Most of this constituted "filling in" of the existing network, although some areas, primarily in the far east, gained rail connections for the first time.

The railway reduced transportation costs throughout the empire, opening new markets for products from other lands of the Dual Monarchy. In 1914, of a total of 22,981 km (14,279.73 mi) of railway tracks in Austria, 18,859 km (11,718 mi) (82%) were state owned.

Railway network in the Kingdom of Hungary

The first Hungarian steam locomotive railway line was opened on 15 July 1846 between Pest and Vác.[431] In 1890 most large Hungarian private railway companies were nationalized as a consequence of the poor management of private companies, except the strong Austrian-owned Kaschau-Oderberg Railway (KsOd) and the Austrian-Hungarian Southern Railway (SB/DV). They also joined the zone tariff system of the MÁV (Hungarian State Railways). By 1910, the total length of the rail networks of Hungarian Kingdom reached 22,869 kilometres (14,210 miles), the Hungarian network linked more than 1,490 settlements. Nearly half (52%) of the empire's railways were built in Hungary, thus the railroad density there became higher than that of Cisleithania. This has ranked Hungarian railways the 6th most dense in the world (ahead of countries as Germany or France).

Metropolitan transit systems

Tramway lines in the cities

Horse-drawn tramways appeared in the first half of the 19th century. Between the 1850s and 1880s many were built. Vienna (1865), Budapest (1866), Brno (1869). Steam trams appeared in the late 1860s. The electrification of tramways started from the late 1880s. The first electrified tramway in Austria-Hungary was built in Budapest in 1887.

Electric tramway lines in the Austrian Empire:

- Austria: Gmunden (1894); Linz, Vienna (1897); Graz (1898); Ljubljana (1901); Innsbruck (1905); Unterlach, Ybbs an der Donau (1907); Salzburg (1909); Klagenfurt, Sankt Pölten (1911); Piran (1912)
- Bohemia: Prague (1891); Teplice (1895); Liberec (1897); Ústí nad Labem, Plzeň, Olomouc (1899); Moravia, Brno, Jablonec nad Nisou (1900); Ostrava (1901); Mariánské Lázně (1902); Opava (1905); Budějovice, České Budějovice, Jihlava (1909); Český Těšín/Cieszyn (1911)
- Galicia: Bielsko-Biała (1895); Kraków (1901); Tarnów, Cieszyn (1911)[432,433,434]

Electric tramway lines in the Kingdom of Hungary:

- Hungary: Budapest (1887); Pressburg/Pozsony/Bratislava (1895); Szabadka/Subotica, Szombathely (1897), Miskolc (1897); Temesvár/Timişoara (1899); Sopron (1900); Szatmárnémeti/Satu Mare (1900); Nyíregyháza (1905); Nagyszeben/Sibiu (1905); Nagyvárad/Oradea (1906); Szeged (1908); Debrecen (1911); Újvidék/Novi Sad (1911); Kassa/Košice (1913); Pécs (1913)
- Croatia: Fiume (1899); Pula (1904); Opatija – Lovran (1908); Zagreb (1910); Dubrovnik (1910).[435,436,437]

Electrified commuter railway lines

- Budapest (See: BHÉV): Ráckeve line (1887), Szentendre line (1888), Gödöllő line (1888), Csepel line (1912)[438]

Underground

The Budapest metro Line 1 (originally the "Franz Joseph Underground Electric Railway Company") is the second oldest underground railway in the world[439] (the first being the London Underground's Metropolitan Line), and the first on the European mainland. It was built from 1894 to 1896 and opened on 2 May 1896. In 2002, it was listed as a UNESCO World Heritage Site.

Canals and river regulations

In 1900 the engineer C. Wagenführer drew up plans to link the Danube and the Adriatic Sea by a canal from Vienna to Trieste. It was born from the desire of Austria-Hungary to have a direct link to the Adriatic Sea but was never constructed.

Regulation of the lower Danube and the Iron Gates

In 1831 a plan had already been drafted to make the passage navigable, at the initiative of the Hungarian politician István Széchenyi. Finally Gábor Baross, Hungary's "Iron Minister", succeeded in financing this project. The riverbed rocks and the associated rapids made the gorge valley an infamous passage for shipping. In German, the passage is still known as the Kataraktenstrecke, even though the cataracts are gone. Near the actual "Iron Gates" strait the Prigrada rock was the most important obstacle until 1896: the river widened considerably here and the water level was consequently low. Upstream, the Greben rock near the "Kazan" gorge was notorious.

Regulation of the Tisza River

The length of the Tisza in Hungary used to be 1,419 kilometres (882 miles). It flowed through the Great Hungarian Plain, which is one of the largest flat areas in central Europe. Since plains can cause a river to flow very slowly, the Tisza used to follow a path with many curves and turns, which led to many large floods in the area.

After several small-scale attempts, István Széchenyi organised the "regulation of the Tisza" (Hungarian: a Tisza szabályozása) which started on August 27, 1846, and substantially ended in 1880. The new length of the river in Hungary was 966 km (600 mi) (1,358 km (844 mi) total), with 589 km (366 mi) of "dead channels" and 136 km (85 mi) of new riverbed. The resultant length of the flood-protected river comprises 2,940 km (1,830 mi) (out of 4,220 km (2,620 mi) of all Hungarian protected rivers).

Shipping and ports

The first Hungarian steamship was built by Antal Bernhard in 1817, called S.S. *Carolina*. It was also the first steamship in Habsburg ruled states.[440] However it was Count István Széchenyi (with the help of Austrian ship's company Erste Donaudampfschiffahrtsgesellschaft (DDSG)), who established the Óbuda Shipyard on the Hungarian Hajógyári Island in 1835, which was the first industrial scale steamship building company in the Habsburg Empire.[441]

The most significant seaport was Trieste (today part of Italy), where the Austrian merchant marine was based. In addition, the two major shipping companies (Austrian Lloyd and Austro-Americana) and several shipyards were located there. The k.u.k. navy used the port's shipyards to construct new naval ships. This port grew as Venice declined. From 1815 to 1866, Venice was included within the monarchy and was prevented from competing with Austrian-ruled ports. The merchant marine did not develop until Venice's shipping interest declined. The navy became significant during the time of the k.u.k. monarchy, as industrialization and development provided sufficient revenues to develop it.

The most important seaport for the Hungarian part of the k.u.k. was Fiume (Rijeka, today part of Croatia), where the Hungarian shipping companies, such as the Adria, operated. The largest Hungarian shipbuilding company was the Ganz-Danubius. Another significant seaport was Pola (Pula, today part of Croatia) – especially for the navy. In 1889, the Austrian merchant marine consisted of 10,022 ships, with 7,992 fishing vessels. The coast and sea trade had a total of 1,859 sailboats with crews of 6,489 men and a load capacity of 140,838 tons; and 171 steamers with a load capacity of 96,323 tons and a crew of 3,199 men.

The first Danubian steamer company, Donau-Dampfschiffahrt-Gesellschaft (DDSG), was the largest inland shipping company in the world until the collapse of the k.u.k. The Austrian Lloyd was one of the biggest ocean shipping companies of the time. Prior to the beginning of World War I, the company owned 65 middle-sized and large steamers. The Austro-Americana owned one third of them, including the biggest Austrian passenger ship, the SS *Kaiser Franz Joseph I*. In comparison to the Austrian Lloyd, the Austro-American concentrated on destinations in North and South America.

Telecommunication

Telegraph

In 1847, the first telegraph connection (Vienna – Brno – Prague) started operation.[442] The first telegraph station on Hungarian territory was opened in December 1847 in Pressburg/ Pozsony /Bratislava/. In 1848, during the Hungarian Revolution, another telegraph centre was built in Buda to connect the most important governmental centres. The first telegraph connection between Vienna and Pest–Buda (later Budapest) was constructed in 1850, and Vienna–Zagreb (capital of the Triune Kingdom of Croatia) in 1850. Austria joined a telegraph union with German states.[443]

Kingdom of Hungary

In 1884, 2,406 telegraph post offices operated in the Kingdom of Hungary. By 1914 the number of telegraph offices reached 3,000 in post offices and further 2,400 were installed in the railway stations of the Kingdom of Hungary.[444]

Telephone

The first telephone exchange was opened in Zagreb (8 January 1881),[445,446] the second was in Budapest (1 May 1881),[447] and the third was opened in Vienna (3 June 1881).[448] Initially telephony was available in the homes of individual subscribers, companies and offices. Public telephone stations appeared in the 1890s, and they quickly became widespread in post offices and railway stations. Austria-Hungary had 568 million telephone calls in 1913; only two Western European countries had more phone calls: the German Empire and the United Kingdom. The Austro-Hungarian Empire was followed by France with 396 million telephone calls and Italy with 230 million phone calls.[449]

Austrian Empire

In 1916, there were 366 million telephone calls in the Austrian half of the monarchy, among them 8.4 million long distant calls.[450]

Kingdom of Hungary

All telephone exchanges of the cities, towns and larger villages in Kingdom of Hungary were linked until 1893. By 1914, more than 2000 settlements had telephone exchange in Kingdom of Hungary.

Electronic broadcasting

The Telefon Hírmondó (Telephone Herald) news and entertainment service was introduced in Budapest in 1893. Two decades before the introduction of radio broadcasting, people could listen to political, economic and sport news, cabaret, music and opera in Budapest daily. It operated over a special type of telephone exchange system.

Demographics

The following data is based on the official Austro-Hungarian census conducted in 1910.

Population and area

Area	Territory [km^2]	Population
Empire of Austria	300,005 (~48% of Austria-Hungary)	28,571,934 (~57.8% of Austria-Hungary)
Kingdom of Hungary	325,411 (~52% of Austria-Hungary)	20,886,487 (~42.2% of Austria-Hungary)
Bosnia & Herzegovina	51,027	1,931,802
Sandžak (occupied until 1909)	8,403	135,000

Languages

The census of 1910 recorded *Umgangssprache*, everyday language. Jews and those using German in offices often stated German as their *Umgangssprache*, even when having a different *Muttersprache*. In "Hungary proper", 5% of the population were Jews, who were included in speakers of the Hungarian language.[451]

Language	Number	%
German	12,006,521	23.36
Hungarian	10,056,315	19.57
Czech	6,442,133	12.54
Serbo-Croatian	5,621,797	10.94
Polish	4,976,804	9.68
Ruthenian (Ukrainian)	3,997,831	7.78
Romanian	3,224,147	6.27
Slovak	1,967,970	3.83
Slovene	1,255,620	2.44
Italian	768,422	1.50
Other	1,072,663	2.09
Total	51,390,223	100.00

In the Austrian Empire, 36.8% of the total population spoke German as their native language, and more than 71% of the inhabitants spoke some German. In the Kingdom of Hungary, 54.4% of the total population spoke Hungarian as their native language. Not counting autonomous Croatia, more than 64% of the inhabitants of the Hungarian Kingdom spoke Hungarian.

Linguistic distribution of Austria-Hungary as a whole	
German	24%
Hungarian	20%
Czech	13%
Polish	10%
Ruthenian	8%
Romanian	6%
Croat	5%
Slovak	4%
Serbian	4%
Slovene	3%
Italian	3%

Mother tongues in Cisleithania (1910 census)

Land	Most common language		Other languages (more than 2%)					
Bohemia	63.2%	Czech	36.8%	German				
Dalmatia	96.2%	Croatian	2.8%	Italian				
Galicia	58.6%	Polish	40.2%	Ukrainian				
Lower Austria	95.9%	German	3.8%	Czech				
Upper Austria	99.7%	German						
Bukovina	38.4%	Ukrainian	34.4%	Romanian	21.2%	German	4.6%	Polish
Carinthia	78.6%	German	21.2%	Slovene				
Carniola	94.4%	Slovene	5.4%	German				
Salzburg	99.7%	German						
Silesia	43.9%	German	31.7%	Polish	24.3%	Czech		
Styria	70.5%	German	29.4%	Slovene				
Moravia	71.8%	Czech	27.6%	German				
Tyrol	57.3%	German	42.1%	Italian				
Littoral	37.3%	Slovene	34.5%	Italian	24.4%	Croatian	2.5%	German
Vorarlberg	95.4%	German	4.4%	Italian				

Mother tongues in Hungary (1910 census)

Language	Hungary proper		Croatia-Slavonia	
	speakers	% of population	speakers	% of population
Hungarian	9,944,627	54.5%	105,948	4.1%
Romanian	2,948,186	16.0%	846	<0.1%
Slovak	1,946,357	10.7%	21,613	0.8%
German	1,903,657	10.4%	134,078	5.1%
Serbian	461,516	2.5%	644,955	24.6%
Ruthenian	464,270	2.3%	8,317	0.3%
Croatian	194,808	1.1%	1,638,354	62.5%
Others and unspecified	401,412	2.2%	65,843	2.6%
Total	18,264,533	100%	2,621,954	100%

Note that some languages are considered dialects of more widely spoken languages. For example, Rusyn and Ukrainian were both counted as "Ruthenian" in the census, and Rhaeto-Romance languages were counted as "Italian".

Historical regions:

Region	Main spoken language	Hungarian language	Other languages
Transylvania	Romanian – 2,819,467 (54%)	1,658,045 (31.7%)	German – 550,964 (10.5%)
Upper Hungary	Slovak – 1,688,413 (55.6%)	881,320 (32.3%)	German – 198,405 (6.8%)
Vojvodina	Serbo-Croatian – 601,770 (39.8%)	425,672 (28.1%)	German – 324,017 (21.4%)
Transcarpathia	Ruthenian – 330,010 (54.5%)	185,433 (30.6%)	German – 64,257 (10.6%)
Fiume	Italian – 24,212 (48.6%)	6,493 (13%)	Croatian and Serbian – 13,351 (26.8%) Slovene - 2,336 (4.7%) German - 2,315 (4.6%)
Burgenland	German – 217,072 (74.4%)	26,225 (9%)	Croatian – 43,633 (15%)
Prekmurje	Slovene – 74,199 (80.4%) – in 1921	14,065 (15.2%) – in 1921	German – 2,540 (2.8%) – in 1921

Religion

Religion in Austria-Hungary 1910[452]

Religion	Austria-Hungary	Austria/-Cisleithania	Hungary/-Transleithania	Bosnia and Herzegovina
Catholics (both Roman and Eastern)	76,6 %	90,9 %	61,8 %	22,9 %
Protestants	8,9 %	2,1 %	19,0 %	0 %
Serbian Orthodox	8,7 %	2,3 %	14,3 %	43,5 %
Jews	4,4 %	4,7 %	4,9 %	0,6 %
Muslims	1,3 %	0 %	0 %	32,7 %

Solely in the Empire of Austria:

Religion	Austria
Latin Catholic	79.1% (20,661,000)
Eastern Catholic	12% (3,134,000)
Jewish	4.7% (1,225,000)
Eastern Orthodox	2.3% (607,000)

Lutheran	1.9% (491,000)
Other or no religion	14,000

Solely in the Kingdom of Hungary:[453]

Religion	Hungary proper & Fiume	Croatia & Slavonia
Latin Catholic	49.3% (9,010,305)	71.6% (1,877,833)
Calvinist	14.3% (2,603,381)	0.7% (17,948)
Eastern Orthodox	12.8% (2,333,979)	24.9% (653,184)
Eastern Catholic	11.0% (2,007,916)	0.7% (17,592)
Lutheran	7.1% (1,306,384)	1.3% (33,759)
Jewish	5.0% (911,227)	0.8% (21,231)
Unitarian	0.4% (74,275)	0.0% (21)
Other or no religion	0.1% (17,066)	0.0 (386)

Largest cities

Data: census in 1910[454]

Austrian Empire

Rank	Current English name	Contemporary official name	Other	Present-day country	Population in 1910	Present-day Population
1.	Vienna	Wien	Bécs, Beč, Dunaj	Austria	2,083,630 (city without the suburb 1,481,970)	1,840,573 (Metro: 2,600,000)
2.	Prague	Prag, Praha	Praga	Czech Republic	668,000 (city without the suburb 223,741)	1,267,449 (Metro: 2,156,097)
3.	Trieste	Triest	Trst	Italy	229,510	204,420
4.	Lviv	Lemberg, Lwów	Львів, Lvov	Ukraine	206,113	728,545
5.	Kraków	Krakau, Kraków	Krakov	Poland	151,886	762,508
6.	Graz		Gradec	Austria	151,781	280,020
7.	Brno	Brünn, Brno		Czech Republic	125,737	377,028
8.	Chernivtsi	Czernowitz	Cernăuți, Чернівці	Ukraine	87,100	242,300
9.	Plzeň	Pilsen, Plzeň		Czech Republic	80,343	169,858
10.	Linz		Linec	Austria	67,817	200,841

Figure 134: *Funeral in Galicia by Teodor Axentowicz, 1882*

Kingdom of Hungary

Rank	Current English name	Contemporary official name	Other	Present-day country	Population in 1910	Present-day Population
1.	Budapest		Budimpešta	Hungary	1,232,026 (city without the suburb 880,371)	1,735,711 (Metro: 3,303,786)
2.	Szeged		Szegedin, Segedin	Hungary	118,328	170,285
3.	Subotica	Szabadka	Суботица	Serbia	94,610	105,681
4.	Debrecen			Hungary	92,729	208,016
5.	Zagreb		Zágráb, Agram	Croatia	79,038	790,017
6.	Bratislava	Pozsony	Pressburg, Prešporok	Slovakia	78,223	425,167
7.	Timişoara	Temesvár	Temeswar	Romania	72,555	319,279
8.	Oradea	Nagyvárad	Großwardein	Romania	64,169	196,367

9.	Arad	Arad		▮ Romania	63,166	159,074
10.	Cluj-Napoca	Kolozsvár	Klausenburg	▮ Romania	60,808	324,576

Education

Austrian Empire

Primary and secondary schools

The organization of the Austrian elementary schools was based on the principle of compulsory school attendance, free education, and the imparting of public instruction in the child's own language. Side by side with these existed private schools. The proportion of children attending private schools to those attending the public elementary schools in 1912 was 144,000 to 4.5 millions, i.e. a thirtieth part. Hence the accusation of denationalizing children through the Schulvereine must be accepted with caution. The expenses of education were distributed as follows: the communes built the schoolhouses, the political sub-districts (Bezirke) paid the teachers, the Crown territory gave a grant, and the State appointed the inspectors. Since the State supervised the schools without maintaining them, it was able to increase its demands without being hampered by financial considerations. It is remarkable that the difference between the State educational estimates in Austria and in Hungary was one of 9.3 millions in the former as opposed to 67.6 in the latter. Under Austria, since everywhere that 40 scholars of one nationality were to be found within a radius of 5 km. a school had to be set up in which their language was used, national schools were assured even to linguistic minorities. It is true that this mostly happened at the expense of the German industrial communities, since the Slav labourers as immigrants acquired schools in their own language. The number of elementary schools increased from 19,016 in two to 24,713 in 1913; the number of scholars from 3,49 0, 000 in 1900 to 4,630,000 in 1913.[455]

Universities in Austrian Empire

The first University in the Austrian half of the Empire (Charles University) was founded by H.R. Emperor Charles IV in Prague in 1347. The second oldest university (University of Vienna) was founded by Duke Rudolph IV in 1365.

The higher educational establishments, which in the middle of the 19th century had had a predominantly German character, underwent in Galicia a conversion into Polish national institutions, in Bohemia and Moravia a separation into German and Czech ones. Thus Germans, Czechs and Poles were provided for. But now the smaller nations also made their voices heard: the Ruthenians, Slovenes and Italians. The Ruthenians demanded at first, in view of the predominantly Ruthenian character of East Galicia, a national partition of the Polish university existing there. Since the Poles were at first unyielding, Ruthenian demonstrations and strikes of students arose, and the Ruthenians were no longer content with the reversion of a few separate professorial chairs, and with parallel courses of lectures. By a pact concluded on Jan. 28 1914 the Poles promised a Ruthenian university; but owing to the war the question lapsed. The Italians could hardly claim a university of their own on grounds of population (in 19to they numbered 783,000), but they claimed it all the more on grounds of their ancient culture. All parties were agreed that an Italian faculty of laws should be created; the difficulty lay in the choice of the place. The Italians demanded Trieste; but the Government was afraid to let this Adriatic port become the centre of an irredenta; moreover the Southern Sla y s of the city wished it kept free from an Italian educational establishment. Bienerth in 1910 brought about a compromise; namely, that it should be founded at once, the situation to be provisionally in Vienna, and to be transferred within four years to Italian national territory. The German National Union (Nationalverband) agreed to extend temporary hospitality to the Italian university in Vienna, but the Southern Slav Hochschule Club demanded a guarantee that a later transfer to the coast provinces should not be contemplated, together with the simultaneous foundation of Slovene professorial chairs in Prague and Cracow, and preliminary steps towards the foundation of a Southern Slav university in Laibach. But in spite of the constant renewal of negotiations for a compromise it was impossible to arrive at any agreement, until the outbreak of war left all the projects for a Ruthenian university at Lemberg, a Slovene one in Laibach, and a second Czech one in Moravia, unrealized.

Kingdom of Hungary

Primary and secondary schools

One of the first measures of newly established Hungarian government was to provide supplementary schools of a non-denominational character. By a law passed in 1868 attendance at school is obligatory on all children between the ages of 6 and 12 years. The communes or parishes are bound to maintain elementary schools, and they are entitled to levy an additional tax of 5% on the state taxes for their maintenance. But the number of state-aided elementary schools is continually increasing, as the spread of the Magyar language to the other races through the medium of the elementary schools is one of the principal concerns of the Hungarian government, and is vigorously pursued.' In 1902 there were in Hungary 18,729 elementary schools with 32,020 teachers, attended by 2,573,377 pupils, figures which compare favourably with those of 1877, when there were 15,486 schools with 20,717 teachers, attended by 1,559,636 pupils. In about 61% of these schools the language used was exclusively Magyar, in about 6 20% it was mixed, and in the remainder some non-Magyar language was used. In 1902, 80.56% of the children of school age actually attended school. Since 1891 infant schools, for children between the ages of 3 and 6 years, have been maintained either by the communes or by the state.

The public instruction of Hungary contains three other groups of educational institutions: middle or secondary schools, " high schools " and technical schools. The middle schools comprise classical schools (gymnasia) which are preparatory for the universities and other " high schools," and modern schools (Realschulen) preparatory for the technical schools. Their course of study is generally eight years, and they are maintained mostly by the state. The state-maintained gymnasia are mostly of recent foundation, but some schools maintained by the various churches have been in existence for three, or sometimes four, centuries. The number of middle schools in 1902 was 243 with 4705 teachers, attended by 71,788 pupils; in 1880 their number was 185, attended by 40,747 pupils.

Universities in Kingdom of Hungary

In the year 1276, the university of Veszprém was destroyed by the troops of Péter Csák and it was never rebuilt. A university was established by Louis I of Hungary in Pécs in 1367. Sigismund established a university at Óbuda in 1395. Another, Universitas Istropolitana, was established 1465 in Pozsony (now Bratislava in Slovakia) by Mattias Corvinus. None of these medieval universities survived the Ottoman wars. Nagyszombat University was founded in 1635 and moved to Buda in 1777 and it is called Eötvös Loránd University today. The world's first institute of technology was founded in Selmecbánya, Kingdom of Hungary (since 1920 Banská Štiavnica, now Slovakia) in 1735. Its legal successor is the University of Miskolc in Hungary. The Budapest University of Technology and Economics (BME) is considered the oldest institute of technology in the world with university rank and structure. Its legal predecessor the Institutum Geometrico-Hydrotechnicum was founded in 1782 by Emperor Joseph II.

The high schools include the universities, of which Hungary possesses Five, all maintained by the state: at Budapest (founded in 1635), at Kolozsvár (founded in 1872), and at Zagreb (founded in 1874). Newer universities were established in Debrecen in 1912, and Pozsony university was reestablished after a half millennium in 1912. They have four faculties: of theology, law, philosophy and medicine (the university at Zagreb was without a faculty of medicine). There are besides ten high schools of law, called academies, which in 1900 were attended by 1569 pupils. The Polytechnicum in Budapest, founded in 1844, which contains four faculties and was attended in 1900 by 1772 pupils, is also considered a high school. There were in Hungary in 1900 forty-nine high theological colleges, twenty-nine Roman Catholic; five Greek Uniat, four

Austria-Hungary

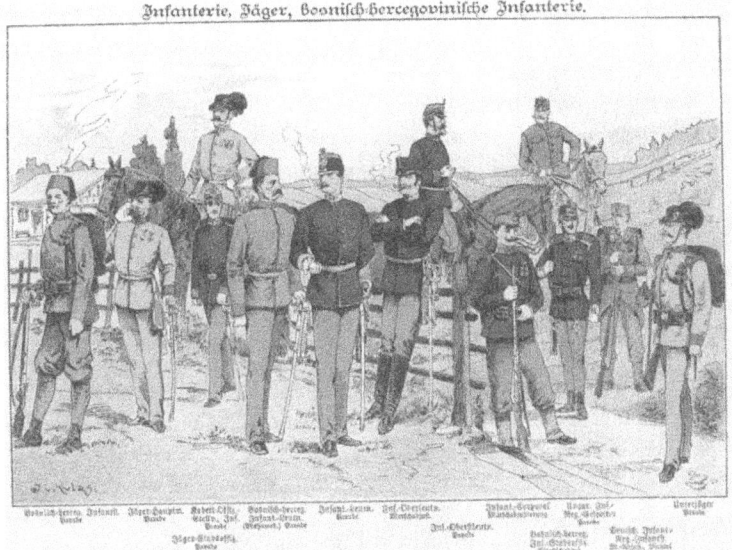

Figure 135: *k.u.k. Infantry 1898*

Greek Orthodox, ten Protestant and one Jewish. Among special schools the principal mining schools are at Selmeczbánya, Nagyág and Felsőbánya; the principal agricultural colleges at Debreczen and Kolozsvár; and there are a school of forestry at Selmeczbánya, military colleges at Budapest, Kassa, Déva and Zagreb, and a naval school at Fiume. There are besides an adequate number of training institutes for teachers, a great number of schools of commerce, several art schools - for design, painting, sculpture, music.

Military

The military system of the Austro-Hungarian monarchy was similar in both states, and rested since 1868 upon the principle of the universal and personal obligation of the citizen to bear arms. Its military force was composed of the common army; the special armies, namely the Austrian Landwehr, and the Hungarian Honved, which were separate national institutions, and the Landsturm or levy-en masse. As stated above, the common army stood under the administration of the joint minister of war, while the special armies were under the administration of the respective ministries of national defence. The yearly contingent of recruits for the army was fixed by the military bills voted on by the Austrian and Hungarian parliaments, and was generally determined on the basis of the population, according to the last census returns. It amounted in

1905 to 103,100 men, of which Austria furnished 59,211 men, and Hungary 43,889. Besides 10,000 men were annually allotted to the Austrian Landwehr, and 12,500 to the Hungarian Honved. The term of service was two years (three years in the cavalry) with the colours, seven or eight in the reserve and two in the Landwehr; in the case of men not drafted to the active army the same total period of service was spent in various special reserves.

The common minister of war was the head for the administration of all military affairs, except those of the Austrian Landwehr and of the Hungarian Honved, which were committed to the ministries for national defence of the two respective states. But the supreme command of the army was vested in the monarch, who had the power to take all measures regarding the whole army.

The Austro-Hungarian navy was mainly a coast defence force, and also included a flotilla of monitors for the Danube. It was administered by the naval department of the ministry of war.[456]

World War I

Preludes: Bosnia and Herzegovina

Russian Pan-Slavic organizations sent aid to the Balkan rebels and so pressured the tsar's government to declare war on the Ottoman Empire in 1877 in the name of protecting Orthodox Christians. Unable to mediate between the Ottoman Empire and Russia over the control of Serbia, Austria-Hungary declared neutrality when the conflict between the two powers escalated into a war. With help from Romania and Greece, Russia defeated the Ottomans and with the Treaty of San Stefano tried to create a large pro-Russian Bulgaria. This treaty sparked an international uproar that almost resulted in a general European war. Austria-Hungary and Britain feared that a large Bulgaria would become a Russian satellite that would enable the tsar to dominate the Balkans. British prime minister Benjamin Disraeli moved warships into position against Russia to halt the advance of Russian influence in the eastern Mediterranean so close to Britain's route through the Suez Canal.[457]

The Congress of Berlin rolled back the Russian victory by partitioning the large Bulgarian state that Russia had carved out of Ottoman territory and denying any part of Bulgaria full independence from the Ottomans. Austria occupied Bosnia and Herzegovina as a way of gaining clout in the Balkans. Serbia, Montenegro and Romania became fully independent. Nonetheless the Balkans remained a site of political unrest with teeming ambition for independence and great power rivalries. At the Congress of Berlin in 1878 Gyula Andrássy (Minister of Foreign Affairs) managed to force Russia to retreat from further demands in the Balkans. As a result, Greater Bulgaria was broken up and

Austria-Hungary 205

Figure 136: *Recruits from Bosnia-Herzegovina, including Muslim Bosniaks (31%), were drafted into special units of the Austro-Hungarian Army as early as 1879 and were commended for their bravery in service of the Austrian emperor, winning more medals than any other unit. The jaunty military march Die Bosniaken Kommen was composed in their honor by Eduard Wagnes.*

Serbian independence was guaranteed. In that year, with Britain's support, Austria-Hungary stationed troops in Bosnia to prevent the Russians from expanding into nearby Serbia. In another measure to keep the Russians out of the Balkans Austria-Hungary formed an alliance, the Mediterranean Entente, with Britain and Italy in 1887 and concluded mutual defence pacts with Germany in 1879 and Romania in 1883 against a possible Russian attack. Following the Congress of Berlin the European powers attempted to guarantee stability through a complex series of alliances and treaties.

File:1913 Austro-Hungarian order banning Serb cultural societies in Bosnia.jpg

Excerpt from a 1913 Austro-Hungarian order, that banned numerous social-democratic and ethnic Serb cultural societies in Bosnia-Herzegovina.

Anxious about Balkan instability and Russian aggression, and to counter French interests in Europe, Austria-Hungary forged a defensive alliance with Germany in October 1879 and in May 1882. In October 1882 Italy joined this partnership in the Triple Alliance largely because of Italy's imperial rivalries with France. Tensions between Russia and Austria-Hungary remained high, so Bismarck replaced the League of the Three Emperors with the Reinsurance Treaty with Russia to keep the Habsburgs from recklessly starting a war over Pan-Slavism.[458] The Sandžak-Raška / Novibazar region was under Austro-Hungarian occupation between 1878 and 1909, when it was returned to the Ottoman Empire, before being ultimately divided between kingdoms of Montenegro and Serbia.

On the heels of the Great Balkan Crisis, Austro-Hungarian forces occupied Bosnia and Herzegovina in August 1878 and the monarchy eventually annexed Bosnia and Herzegovina in October 1908 as a common holding of Cis- and Transleithania under the control of the Imperial & Royal finance ministry rather than attaching it to either territorial government. The annexation in 1908 led some in Vienna to contemplate combining Bosnia and Herzegovina with Croatia to form a third Slavic component of the monarchy. The deaths of Franz Joseph's brother, Maximilian (1867), and his only son, Rudolf made the Emperor's nephew, Franz Ferdinand, heir to the throne. The Archduke was rumoured to have been an advocate for this trialism as a means to limit the power of the Hungarian aristocracy.[459]

Status of Bosnia-Herzegovina

A proclamation issued on the occasion of its annexation to the Habsburg Monarchy in 1908 promised these lands constitutional institutions, which should secure to their inhabitants full civil rights and a share in the management of their own affairs by means of a local representative assembly. In performance of this promise a constitution was promulgated in 1910. This included a Territorial Statute (Landesstatut) with the setting up of a Territorial Diet, regulations for the election and procedure of the Diet, a law of associations, a law of public meetings, and a law dealing with the district councils. According to this statute Bosnia-Herzegovina formed a single administrative territory under the responsible direction and supervision of the Ministry of Finance of the Dual Monarchy in Vienna. The administration of the country, together with the carrying out of the laws, devolved upon the Territorial Government in Sarajevo, which was subordinate and responsible to the Common Ministry of Finance. The existing judicial and administrative authorities of the Territory retained their previous organization and functions. That statute introduced the modern rights and laws in Bosnia – Herzegovina, and it guaranteed generally the civil rights of the inhabitants of the Territory, namely citizenship, personal liberty, protection by the competent judicial authorities, liberty of creed and conscience, preservation of the national individuality and language, freedom of speech, freedom of learning and education, inviolability of the domicile, secrecy of posts and telegraphs, inviolability of property, the right of petition, and finally the right of holding meetings.[460]

The Diet (Sabor) of Bosnia-Herzegovina set up consisted of a single Chamber, elected on the principle of the representation of interests. It numbered 92 members. Of these 20 consisted of representatives of all the religious confessions, the president of the Supreme Court, the president of the Chamber of Advocates, the president of the Chamber of Commerce, and the mayor of Sarajevo. In addition to these were 72 deputies, elected by three curiae or electoral groups. The first curia included the large landowners, the highest taxpayers, and people who had reached a certain standard of education without regard to the amount they paid in taxes. To the second curia belonged inhabitants of the towns not qualified to vote in the first; to the third, country dwellers disqualified in the same way. With this curial system was combined the grouping of the mandates and of the electors according to the three dominant creeds (Catholic, Serbian Orthodox, Muslim). To the adherents of other creeds the right was conceded of voting with one or other of the religious electoral bodies within the curia to which they belonged.

Figure 137: *This picture is usually associated with the arrest of Gavrilo Princip, although some believe it depicts Ferdinand Behr, a bystander.*

Sarajevo assassination

On 28 June 1914, Archduke Franz Ferdinand visited the Bosnian capital, Sarajevo. A group of six assassins (Cvjetko Popović, Gavrilo Princip, Muhamed Mehmedbašić, Nedeljko Čabrinović, Trifko Grabež, Vaso Čubrilović) from the nationalist group Mlada Bosna, supplied by the Black Hand, had gathered on the street where the Archduke's motorcade would pass. Čabrinović threw a grenade at the car, but missed. It injured some people nearby, and Franz Ferdinand's convoy could carry on. The other assassins failed to act as the cars drove past them quickly. About an hour later, when Franz Ferdinand was returning from a visit at the Sarajevo Hospital, the convoy took a wrong turn into a street where Gavrilo Princip by coincidence stood. With a pistol, Princip shot and killed Franz Ferdinand and his wife Sophie. The reaction among the Austrian people was mild, almost indifferent. As historian Z.A.B. Zeman later wrote, "the event almost failed to make any impression whatsoever. On Sunday and Monday [June 28 and 29], the crowds in Vienna listened to music and drank wine, as if nothing had happened."

Escalation of violence in Bosnia

The assassination excessively intensified the existing traditional religion-based ethnic hostilities in Bosnia. However, in Sarajevo itself, Austrian authorities encouraged violence against the Serb residents, which resulted in the Anti-Serb riots of Sarajevo, in which Catholic Croats and Bosnian Muslims killed

Austria-Hungary

Figure 138: *Crowds on the streets in the aftermath of the Anti-Serb riots in Sarajevo, 29 June 1914.*

two and damaged numerous Serb-owned buildings. Writer Ivo Andrić referred to the violence as the "Sarajevo frenzy of hate." Violent actions against ethnic Serbs were organized not only in Sarajevo but also in many other larger Austro-Hungarian cities in modern-day Croatia and Bosnia and Herzegovina. Austro-Hungarian authorities in Bosnia and Herzegovina imprisoned and extradited approximately 5,500 prominent Serbs, 700 to 2,200 of whom died in prison. 460 Serbs were sentenced to death and a predominantly Muslim special militia known as the *Schutzkorps* was established and carried out the persecution of Serbs.

Decision for war

While the empire's military spending had not even doubled since the 1878 Congress of Berlin, Germany's spending had risen fivefold, and the British, Russian, and French expenditures threefold. The empire had lost ethnic Italian areas to Piedmont because of nationalist movements that had swept through Italy, and many Austro-Hungarians perceived as imminent the threat of losing to Serbia the southern territories inhabited by Slavs. Serbia had recently gained considerable territory in the Second Balkan War of 1913, causing much distress in government circles in Vienna and Budapest. Former ambassador and foreign

Figure 139: *MÁVAG armoured train in 1914*

minister Count Alois Aehrenthal had assumed that any future war would be in the Balkan region.

Hungarian prime minister and political scientist István Tisza opposed the expansion of the monarchy on the Balkan (see Bosnian crisis in 1908), because "the Dual Monarchy already had too many Slavs", which would further threaten the integrity of the Dual Monarchy.[461]

In March 1914, Tisza wrote a memorandum to Emperor Franz Joseph. His letter had strongly apocalyptic predictive and embittered tone. He used exactly the hitherto unknown word "Weltkrieg" (means World War) phrase in his letter. "It is my firm conviction that Germany's two neighbors [Russia and France] are carefully proceeding with military preparations, but will not start the war so long as they have not attained a grouping of the Balkan states against us that confronts the monarchy with an attack from three sides and pins down the majority of our forces on our eastern and southern front."[462]

On the day of the assassination of Archduke Franz Ferdinand, Tisza immediately traveled to Vienna where he met Minister of Foreign Affairs Count Leopold Berchtold and Army Commander Count Franz Conrad von Hötzendorf. They proposed to solve the dispute with arms, attacking Serbia. Tisza proposed to give the government of Serbia time to take a stand as to whether it was involved in the organisation of the murder and proposed a peaceful resolution, arguing that the international situation would settle soon. Returning to Budapest, he wrote to Emperor Franz Joseph saying he would not take any responsibility for the armed conflict because there was no proof that Serbia had plotted the assassination. Tisza opposed a war with Serbia, stating (correctly, as it turned out) that any war with the Serbs was bound to trigger a war with Russia and hence a general European war.[463] He did not trust in the Italian alliance, due to the political aftermath of the Second Italian War of Independence. He thought that even a successful Austro-Hungarian war would be disastrous for the integrity of Kingdom of Hungary, where Hungary would be the next victim of Austrian politics. After a successful war against Serbia, Tisza foresaw a possible Austrian military attack against the Kingdom of Hungary, where the Austrians want to break up the territory of Hungary.

Some members of the government, such as Count Franz Conrad von Hötzendorf, had wanted to confront the resurgent Serbian nation for some years in a preventive war, but the Emperor, 84 years old and an enemy of all adventures, disapproved.

The foreign ministry of Austro-Hungarian Empire sent ambassador László Szőgyény to Potsdam, where he inquired about the standpoint of the German Emperor on 5 July. Szőgyény described what happened in a secret report to Vienna later that day:

"I presented His Majesty [Wilhelm] with [Franz Joseph's] letter and the attached memorandum. The Kaiser read both papers quite carefully in my presence. First, His Majesty assured me that he had expected us to take firm action against Serbia, but he had to concede that, as a result of the conflicts facing [Franz Joseph], he needed to take into account a serious complication in Europe, which is why he did not wish to give any definite answer prior to consultations with the chancellor....

When, after our déjeuner, I once again emphasized the gravity of the situation, His Majesty authorized me to report to [Franz Joseph] that in this case, too, we could count on Germany's full support. As mentioned, he first had to consult with the Chancellor, but he did not have the slightest doubt that Herr von Bethmann Hollweg would fully agree with him, particularly with regard to action on our part against Serbia. In his [Wilhelm's] opinion, though, there was no need to wait patiently before taking action. The Kaiser said that Russia's stance would always be a hostile one, but he had been prepared for this for many years, and even if war broke out between Austria-Hungary and Russia, we could rest assured that Germany would take our side, in line with its customary loyalty. According to the Kaiser, as things stood now, Russia was not at all ready for war. It would certainly have to think hard before making a call to arms."[464]

But now the leaders of Austria-Hungary, especially General Count Leopold von Berchtold, backed by its ally Germany, decided to confront Serbia militarily before it could incite a revolt; using the assassination as an excuse, they presented a list of ten demands called the July Ultimatum, expecting Serbia would never accept. When Serbia accepted nine of the ten demands but only partially accepted the remaining one, Austria-Hungary declared war. Franz Joseph I finally followed the urgent counsel of his top advisers.

Over the course of July and August 1914, these events caused the start of World War I, as Russia mobilized in support of Serbia, setting off a series of counter-mobilizations. In support of his German ally, on Thursday, August 6, 1914, the Emperor Franz Joseph signed the declaration of war on Russia. Italy initially remained neutral, although it had an alliance with Austria-Hungary. In 1915, it switched to the side of the Entente powers, hoping to gain territory from its former ally.[465]

Wartime foreign policy

The Austro-Hungarian Empire played a relatively passive diplomatic role in the war, as it was increasingly dominated and controlled by Germany.[466,467] The only goal was to punish Serbia and try to stop the ethnic breakup of the Empire, and it completely failed. Instead as the war went on the ethnic unity declined; the Allies encouraged breakaway demands from minorities and the Empire faced disintegration. Starting in late 1916 the new Emperor Karl removed the pro-German officials and opened peace overtures to the Allies, whereby the entire war could be ended by compromise, or perhaps Austria would make a separate peace from Germany.[468] The main effort was vetoed by Italy, which had been promised large slices of Austria for joining the Allies in 1915. Austria was only willing to turn over the Trentino region but nothing more.[469] Karl was seen as a defeatist, which weakened his standing at home and with both the Allies and Germany.[470]

As the Imperial economy collapsed into severe hardship and even starvation, its multi-ethnic army lost its morale and was increasingly hard pressed to hold its line. In the capital cities of Vienna and Budapest, the leftist and liberal movements and opposition parties strengthened and supported the separatism of ethnic minorities. As it became apparent that the Allies would win the war, nationalist movements, which had previously been calling for a greater degree of autonomy for their majority areas, started demanding full independence. The Emperor had lost much of his power to rule, as his realm disintegrated.[471]

Homefront

The heavily rural Empire did have a small industrial base, but its major contribution was manpower and food.[472,473] Nevertheless, Austria-Hungary was more urbanized (25%) than its actual opponents in the First World War, like the Russian Empire (13.4%), Serbia (13.2%) or Romania (18.8%). Furthermore, the Austro-Hungarian Empire had also more industrialized economy and higher GDP per capita than the Kingdom of Italy, which was the economically most developed actual opponent of the Empire.

On the home front, food grew scarcer and scarcer, as did heating fuel. The hog population fell 90 percent, as the dwindling supplies of ham and bacon percent of the Army. Hungary, with its heavy agricultural base, was somewhat better fed. The Army conquered productive agricultural areas in Romania and elsewhere, but refused to allow food shipments to civilians back home. Morale fell every year, and the diverse nationalities gave up on the Empire and looked for ways to establish their own nation states.[474]

Inflation soared, from an index of 129 in 1914 to 1589 in 1918, wiping out the cash savings of the middle-class. In terms of war damage to the economy, the war used up about 20 percent of the GDP. The dead soldiers amounted to about four percent of the 1914 labor force, and the wounded ones to another six percent. Compared all the major countries in the war, Austria's death and casualty rate was toward the high-end.[475]

By summer 1918, "Green Cadres" of army deserters formed armed bands in the hills of Croatia-Slavonia and civil authority disintegrated. By late October violence and massive looting erupted and there were efforts to form peasant republics. However The Croatian political leadership was focused on creating a new state (Yugoslavia) and worked with the advancing Serbian army to impose control and end the uprisings.[476]

Military events

The Austro-Hungarian Empire conscripted 7.8 million soldiers during the WW1. General von Hötzendorf was the Chief of the Austro-Hungarian General Staff. Franz Joseph I, who was much too old to command the army, appointed Archduke Friedrich von Österreich-Teschen as Supreme Army Commander (Armeeoberkommandant), but asked him to give Von Hötzendorf freedom to take any decisions. The latter remained in effective command of the military forces until Emperor Karl I took the supreme command himself in late 1916 and dismissed Conrad von Hötzendorf in 1917. Meanwhile, economic conditions on the homefront deteriorated rapidly. The Empire depended on agriculture, and agriculture depended on the heavy labor of millions of men who are now in the Army. Food production fell, the transportation system became overcrowded, and industrial production could not successfully handle the overwhelming need for munitions. Germany provided a great deal of help, but it was not enough. Furthermore, the political instability of the multiple ethnic groups of Empire now ripped apart any hope for national consensus in support of the war. Increasingly there was a demand for breaking up the Empire and setting up autonomous national states based on historic language-based cultures. The new Emperor sought peace terms from the Allies, but his initiatives were vetoed by Italy.[477]

Serbian front 1914–1916

At the start of the war, the army was divided in two: the smaller part attacked Serbia while the larger part fought against the formidable Imperial Russian Army. The invasion of Serbia in 1914 was a disaster: by the end of the year, the Austro-Hungarian Army had taken no territory, but had lost 227,000 out of a total force of 450,000 men. However, in the autumn of 1915, the Serbian Army was defeated by the Central Powers, which led to the occupation of Serbia. Near the end of 1915, in a massive rescue operation involving more than 1,000 trips made by Italian, French and British steamers, 260,000 Serb soldiers were transported to Corfu, where they waited for the chance of the victory of Allied Powers to reclaim their country. Corfu hosted the Serbian government in exile after the collapse of Serbia, and served as a supply base to the Greek front. In April 1916 a large number of Serbian troops were transported in British and French naval vessels from Corfu to mainland Greece. The contingent numbering over 120,000 relieved a much smaller army at the Macedonian Front and fought alongside British and French troops.

Russian front 1914–1917

On the Eastern front, the war started out equally poorly. The Austro-Hungarian Army was defeated at the Battle of Lemberg and the great fortress city of Przemyśl was besieged and fell in March 1915. The Gorlice–Tarnów Offensive started as a minor German offensive to relieve the pressure of the Russian numerical superiority on the Austro-Hungarians, but the cooperation of the Central Powers resulted in huge Russian losses and the total collapse of the Russian lines, and their 100 km (62 mi) long retreat into Russia. The Russian Third Army perished. In summer 1915, the Austro-Hungarian Army, under a unified command with the Germans, participated in the successful Gorlice–Tarnów Offensive. From June 1916, the Russians focused their attacks on the Austro-Hungarian army in the Brusilov Offensive, recognizing the numerical inferiority of the Austro-Hungarian army. By the end of September 1916, Austria-Hungary mobilized and concentrated new divisions, and the successful Russian advance was halted and slowly repelled; but the Austrian armies took heavy losses (about 1 million men) and never recovered. The Battle of Zborov

Figure 140: *Siege of Przemyśl in 1915*

(1917) was the first significant action of the Czechoslovak Legions, who fought for the independence of Czechoslovakia against the Austro-Hungarian army. However the huge losses in men and material inflicted on the Russians during the offensive contributed greatly to the revolutions of 1917, and it caused an economic crash in the Russian Empire.

Italian front 1915–1918

In May 1915, Italy attacked Austria-Hungary. Italy was the only military opponent of Austria-Hungary which had a similar degree of industrialization and economic level; moreover, her army was numerous (~1,000,000 men were immediately fielded), but suffered poor leadership, training and organization. Chief of Staff Luigi Cadorna marched his army towards the Isonzo river, hoping to seize Ljubljana, and to eventually threaten Vienna. However, the Royal Italian Army were halted on the river, where four battles took place over five months (23 June – 2 December 1915). The fight was extremely bloody and exhausting for both the contenders.[478] On 15 May 1916, the Austrian Chief of Staff Conrad von Hötzendorf launched the *Strafexpedition* ("punitive expedition"): the Austrians broke through the opposing front and occupied the Asiago plateau. The Italians managed to resist and in a counteroffensive, seized Gorizia on 9 August. Nonetheless, they had to stop on the Carso, a few kilometres away from the border. At this point, several months of indecisive trench warfare (analogous to the Western front one) ensued. As the Russian Empire collapsed as a result of the Bolshevik Revolution and Russians ended their

Figure 141: *The military cemetery of Redipuglia (Italy), the resting place of approximately 100,000 Italian soldiers dead in battles of the First World War.*

involvement in the war, Germans and Austrians were able to move on the Western and Southern fronts much manpower from the erstwhile Eastern fighting. On 24 October 1917, Austrians (now enjoying decisive German support) attacked at Caporetto using new infiltration tactics; although they advanced more than 100 km (62.14 mi) in the direction of Venice and gained considerable supplies, they were halted and could not cross the Piave river. Italy, although suffering massive casualties, recovered from the blow: a coalition government under Vittorio Emanuele Orlando was formed. Italy also enjoyed support by the Entente powers: by 1918, large amounts of war materials and a few auxiliary American, British, and French divisions arrived in the Italian battle zone.[479] Cadorna was replaced by General Armando Diaz; under his command, the Italians retook the initiative and won the decisive Battle of the Piave river (15–23 June 1918), in which some 60,000 Austrian and 43,000 Italian soldiers were killed. The multiethnic Austro-Hungarian Empire started to disintegrate, leaving its army alone on the battlefields. The final battle was at Vittorio Veneto; after 4 days of stiff resistance, Italian troops crossed the Piave River, and after losing 90,000 men the defeated Austrian troops retreated in disarray pursued by the Italians. The Italians captured 428,000 Austrian-Hungarian soldiers,Wikipedia:Citation needed 24 of whom were generals,[480] 5,600 cannons and mortars, 4,000 machine guns.[481] The military breakdown also marked the start of the rebellion for the numerous ethnicities who made up the multiethnic Empire, as they refused to keep on fighting for a cause which now appeared senseless. These events marked the end of Austria-Hungary, which collapsed on 31 October 1918. The armistice was signed at Villa Giusti on 3 November.

Romanian front 1916

On 27 August 1916, Romania declared war against Austria-Hungary. The Romanian Army crossed the borders of Eastern Hungary (Transylvania). By November 1916, the Central Powers had defeated the Romanian Army and occupied the southern and eastern parts of Romania. On 6 December the Central Powers captured Bucharest, the Romanian capital city.[482]

Whereas the German army realized it needed close cooperation from the homefront, Habsburg officers saw themselves as entirely separate from the civilian world, and superior to it. When they occupied productive areas, such as RomaniaWikipedia:Citation needed, they seized food stocks and other supplies for their own purposes, and blocked any shipments intended for civilians back in the Austro-Hungarian Empire. The result was that the officers lived well, as the civilians began to starve. Vienna even transferred training units to Serbia and Poland for the sole purpose of feeding them. In all, the Army obtained about 15 percent of its cereal needs from occupied territories.[483]

Role of Hungary

Despite of Kingdom of Hungary consisted only 42% of the Austro-Hungarian population,[484] the thin majority - more than 3.8 million soldiers – of the Austro-Hungarian armed forces were conscripted from Kingdom of Hungary during the WW1. Roughly 600,000 soldiers were killed in action, and 700,000 soldiers were wounded in the war.

Austria-Hungary held on for years, as the Hungarian half provided sufficient supplies for the military to continue to wage war. This was shown in a transition of power after which the Hungarian prime minister, Count István Tisza, and foreign minister, Count István Burián, had decisive influence over the internal and external affairs of the monarchy. By late 1916, food supply from Hungary became intermittent and the government sought an armistice with the Entente powers. However, this failed as Britain and France no longer had any regard for the integrity of the monarchy because of Austro-Hungarian support for Germany.

Figure 142: *War memorial in Păuleni-Ciuc, Romania.*

Analysis of defeat

The setbacks that the Austrian army suffered in 1914 and 1915 can be attributed to a large extent to Austria-Hungary becoming a military satellite of Imperial Germany from the first day of the war. They were made worse by the incompetence of the Austrian high command. After attacking Serbia, its forces soon had to be withdrawn to protect its eastern frontier against Russia's invasion, while German units were engaged in fighting on the Western Front. This resulted in a greater than expected loss of men in the invasion of Serbia. Furthermore, it became evident that the Austrian high command had had no plans for a possible continental war and that the army and navy were also ill-equipped to handle such a conflict.

From 1916, the Austro-Hungarian war effort became more and more subordinated to the direction of German planners. The Austrians viewed the German army favorably, on the other hand by 1916 the general belief in Germany was that Germany, in its alliance with Austria-Hungary, was "shackled to a corpse". The operational capability of the Austro-Hungarian army was seriously affected by supply shortages, low morale and a high casualty rate, and by the army's composition of multiple ethnicities with different languages and customs.

The last two successes for the Austrians, the Romanian Offensive and the Caporetto Offensive, were German-assisted operations. As the Dual Monarchy became more politically unstable, it became more and more dependent on German assistance. The majority of its people, other than Hungarians and German Austrians, became increasingly restless.

In 1917, the Eastern front of the Entente Powers completely collapsed. The Austro-Hungarian Empire then withdrew from all defeated countries. By 1918, the economic situation had deteriorated. Leftist and pacifist political movements organized strikes in factories, and uprisings in the army had become commonplace. During the Italian battles, the Czechoslovaks and Southern Slavs declared their independence. On 31 October Hungary ended the personal union officially dissolving the Austro-Hungarian state. At the last Italian offensive, the Austro-Hungarian Army took to the field without any food and munition supply, and fought without any political supports for a *de facto* non-existent empire. On the end of the decisive joint Italian, British and French offensive at Vittorio Veneto, the disintegrated Austria-Hungary signed the Armistice of Villa Giusti on 3 November 1918.

The government had failed badly on the homefront. Historian Alexander Watson reports:

> across central Europe... The majority lived in a state of advanced misery by the spring of 1918 and conditions would worsen, for the summer of 1918 saw both the drop in food supplied to the levels of the 'turnip winter' and the onset of an influenza pandemic that would kill at least 20 million worldwide. Society was relieved, exhausted and yearned for peace.[485]

Dissolution

The Austro-Hungarian Monarchy collapsed with dramatic speed in the autumn of 1918. In the capital cities of Vienna and Budapest, the leftist and liberal movements and politicians (the opposition parties) strengthened and supported the separatism of ethnic minorities. These leftist or left-liberal pro-Entente maverick parties opposed the monarchy as a form of government and considered themselves internationalist rather than patriotic. Eventually, the German defeat and the minor revolutions in Vienna and Budapest gave political power to the left/liberal political parties. As it became apparent that the Allied powers would win World War I, nationalist movements, which had previously been calling for a greater degree of autonomy for various areas, started pressing for full independence. The Emperor had lost much of his power to rule, as his realm disintegrated.[486]

Alexander Watson argues that, "The Habsburg regime's doom was sealed when Wilson's response to the note sent two and a half weeks earlier arrived

Figure 143: *The revolt of ethnic Czech units in Austria in May 1918 was brutally suppressed. It was considered as mutiny by the code of military justice*

on 20 October." Wilson rejected the continuation of the dual monarchy as a negotiable possibility.[487] As one of his Fourteen Points, President Woodrow Wilson demanded that the nationalities of Austria-Hungary have the "freest opportunity to autonomous development". In response, Emperor Karl I agreed to reconvene the Imperial Parliament in 1917 and allow the creation of a confederation with each national group exercising self-governance. However the leaders of these national groups rejected the idea; they deeply distrusted Vienna and were now determined to get independence.

On 14 October 1918, Foreign Minister Baron István Burián von Rajecz asked for an armistice based on the Fourteen Points. In an apparent attempt to demonstrate good faith, Emperor Karl issued a proclamation ("Imperial Manifesto of 16 October 1918") two days later which would have significantly altered the structure of the Austrian half of the monarchy. The Polish majority regions of Galicia and Lodomeria were to be granted the option of seceding from the empire, and it was understood that they would join their ethnic brethren in Russia and Germany in resurrecting a Polish state. The rest of Cisleithania was transformed into a federal union composed of four parts—German, Czech, South Slav and Ukrainian. Each of these was to be governed by a national council that would negotiate the future of the empire with Vienna. Trieste was to receive a special status. No such proclamation could be issued in Hungary, where Hungarian aristocrats still believed they could subdue other nationalities and maintain the "Holy Kingdom of St. Stephen".

It was a dead letter. Four days later, on 18 October United States Secretary of State Robert Lansing replied that the Allies were now committed to the causes of the Czechs, Slovaks and South Slavs. Therefore, Lansing said, autonomy for the nationalities – the tenth of the Fourteen Points – was no longer enough and Washington could not deal on the basis of the Fourteen Points any more. In fact, a Czechoslovak provisional government had joined the Allies on 14 October. The South Slavs in both halves of the monarchy had already declared in favor of uniting with Serbia in a large South Slav state by way of the 1917 Corfu Declaration signed by members of the Yugoslav Committee. Indeed, the Croatians had begun disregarding orders from Budapest earlier in October.

The Lansing note was, in effect, the death certificate of Austria-Hungary. The national councils had already begun acting more or less as provisional governments of independent countries. With defeat in the war imminent after the Italian offensive in the Battle of Vittorio Veneto on 24 October, Czech politicians peacefully took over command in Prague on 28 October (later declared the birthday of Czechoslovakia) and followed up in other major cities in the next few days. On 30 October, the Slovaks followed in Martin. On the 29th of October, the Slavs in both portions of what remained of Austria-Hungary proclaimed the State of Slovenes, Croats and Serbs. They also declared their ultimate intention was to unite with Serbia and Montenegro in a large South Slav state. On the same day, the Czechs and Slovaks formally proclaimed the establishment of Czechoslovakia as an independent state.

In Hungary, the most prominent opponent of continued union with Austria, Count Mihály Károlyi, seized power in the Aster Revolution on 31 October. Charles was all but forced to appoint Károlyi as his Hungarian prime minister. One of Károlyi's first acts was to cancel the Compromise agreement, officially dissolving the Austro-Hungarian state.

By the end of October, there was nothing left of the Habsburg realm but its majority-German Danubian and Alpine provinces, and Karl's authority was being challenged even there by the German-Austrian state council.[488] Karl's last Austrian prime minister, Heinrich Lammasch, concluded that Karl was in an impossible situation, and persuaded Karl that the best course was to relinquish, at least temporarily, his right to exercise sovereign authority.

Consequences

On 11 November, Karl issued a carefully worded proclamation in which he recognized the Austrian people's right to determine the form of the state. He also renounced the right to participate in Austrian affairs of state. He also dismissed Lammasch and his government from office and released the officials in the Austrian half of the empire from their oath of loyalty to him. Two days later, he issued a similar proclamation for Hungary. However, he did not abdicate, remaining available in the event the people of either state should recall him. For all intents and purposes, this was the end of Habsburg rule.

Karl's refusal to abdicate was ultimately irrelevant. On the day after he announced his withdrawal from Austria's politics, the German-Austrian National Council proclaimed the Republic of German Austria. Károlyi followed suit on 16 November, proclaiming the Hungarian Democratic Republic.

The Treaty of Saint-Germain-en-Laye (between the victors of World War I and Austria) and the Treaty of Trianon (between the victors and Hungary) regulated the new borders of Austria and Hungary, leaving both as small landlocked states. The Allies assumed without question that the minority nationalities wanted to leave Austria and Hungary, and also allowed them to annex significant blocks of German- and Hungarian-speaking territory. As a result, the Republic of Austria lost roughly 60% of the old Austrian Empire's territory. It also had to drop its plans for union with Germany, as it was not allowed to unite with Germany without League approval. The restored Kingdom of Hungary, which had replaced the republican government in 1920, lost roughly 72% of the pre-war territory of the Kingdom of Hungary.

The decisions of the nations of the former Austria-Hungary and of the victors of the Great War, contained in the heavily one-sided treaties, had devastating political and economic effects. The previously rapid economic growth of the Dual Monarchy ground to a halt because the new borders became major economic barriers. All the formerly well established industries, as well as the infrastructure supporting them, were designed to satisfy the needs of an extensive realm. As a result, the emerging countries were forced to make considerable sacrifices to transform their economies. The treaties created major political unease. As a result of these economic difficulties, extremist movements gained strength; and there was no regional superpower in central Europe.

The new Austrian state was, at least on paper, on shakier ground than Hungary. While what was left of Austria had been a single unit for over 700 years, it was united only by loyalty to the Habsburgs. With the loss of 60% of the Austrian Empire's prewar territory, Vienna was now an imperial capital without an empire to support it. By comparison, Hungary had been a nation and a state for over 900 years. However, after a brief period of upheaval and the

Allies' foreclosure of union with Germany, Austria established itself as a federal republic. Despite the temporary *Anschluss* with Nazi Germany, it still survives today. Adolf Hitler cited that all "Germans", such as he and the other Austrians should be united with Germany, as all other Germans should.

Hungary, however, was severely disrupted by the loss of 72% of its territory, 64% of its population and most of its natural resources. The Hungarian Democratic Republic was short-lived and was temporarily replaced by the communist Hungarian Soviet Republic. Romanian troops ousted Béla Kun and his communist government during the Hungarian-Romanian War of 1919.

In the summer of 1919, a Habsburg, Archduke Joseph August, became regent, but was forced to stand down after only two weeks when it became apparent the Allies would not recognise him. Finally, in March 1920, royal powers were entrusted to a regent, Miklós Horthy, who had been the last commanding admiral of the Austro-Hungarian Navy and had helped organize the counter-revolutionary forces. It was this government that signed the Treaty of Trianon under protest on 4 June 1920 at the Grand Trianon Palace in Versailles, France.

In March and again in October 1921, ill-prepared attempts by Karl to regain the throne in Budapest collapsed. The initially wavering Horthy, after receiving threats of intervention from the Allied Powers and neighboring countries, refused his cooperation. Soon afterward, the Hungarian government nullified the Pragmatic Sanction, effectively dethroning the Habsburgs. Two years later, Austria had passed the "Habsburg Law," which not only dethroned the Habsburgs, but banned Karl from ever returning to Austria again.

Subsequently, the British took custody of Karl and removed him and his family to the Portuguese island of Madeira, where he died the following year.

Successor states

The following successor states were formed (entirely or in part) on the territory of the former Austria-Hungary:

- German Austria and First Austrian Republic
- Hungarian Democratic Republic, Hungarian Soviet Republic, and Kingdom of Hungary
- Czecho-Slovakia ("Czechoslovakia" from 1920 to 1938)
- State of Slovenes, Croats and Serbs (joined on 1 December 1918 with the Kingdom of Serbia to form the Kingdom of Serbs, Croats and Slovenes, later Kingdom of Yugoslavia)
- Second Polish Republic
- West Ukrainian People's Republic (united with the Ukrainian People's Republic through Act Zluky, while its territory was fully overran by the Second Polish Republic)

- Duchy of Bukovina and Transylvania were joined to the Kingdom of Romania

Austro-Hungarian lands were also ceded to the Kingdom of Romania and the Kingdom of Italy. The Principality of Liechtenstein, which had formerly looked to Vienna for protection, formed a customs and defense union with Switzerland, and adopted the Swiss currency instead of the Austrian. In April 1919, Vorarlberg – the westernmost province of Austria – voted by a large majority to join Switzerland; however, both the Swiss and the Allies disregarded this result.

Figure 144: *New hand-drawn borders of Austria-Hungary in the Treaty of Trianon and Saint Germain. (1919–1920)*

Figure 145:
*New borders of Austria-Hungary after the Treaty of Trianon and Saint Germain.
Border of Austria-Hungary in 1914
Borders in 1914
Borders in 1920
Empire of Austria in 1914
Kingdom of Hungary in 1914
Bosnia and Herzegovina in 1914*

Figure 146: *After-WWI borders on an ethnic map)*

Territorial legacy

Austria-Hungary

Austria-Hungary

Kingdoms and countries of Austria-Hungary:
Cisleithania (Empire of Austria): 1. Bohemia, 2. Bukovina, 3. Carinthia, 4. Carniola, 5. Dalmatia, 6. Galicia, 7. Küstenland, 8. Lower Austria, 9. Moravia, 10. Salzburg, 11. Silesia, 12. Styria, 13. Tyrol, 14. Upper Austria, 15. Vorarlberg;
Transleithania (Kingdom of Hungary): 16. Hungary proper 17. Croatia-Slavonia; 18. Bosnia and Herzegovina (Austro-Hungarian condominium)

The following present-day countries and parts of countries were located within the boundaries of Austria-Hungary when the empire was dissolved:

Empire of Austria (Cisleithania):

- Austria (with the exception of Burgenland)
- Czech Republic (with the exception of the Hlučínsko area)
- Slovenia (with the exception of Prekmurje)
- Italy (Trentino, South Tyrol, parts of the province of Belluno and small portions of Friuli-Venezia Giulia)
- Croatia (Dalmatia, Istria)
- Poland (voivodeships of Lesser Poland, Subcarpathia, southernmost part of Silesia (Bielsko and Cieszyn))
- Ukraine (oblasts of Lviv, Ivano-Frankivsk, Ternopil (except its northern corner) and most of the oblast of Chernivtsi)
- Romania (county of Suceava)
- Montenegro (bay of Boka Kotorska, the coast and the immediate hinterland around the cities of Budva, Petrovac and Sutomore)

Kingdom of Hungary (Transleithania):

- Hungary;
- Slovakia
- Austria (Burgenland)
- Slovenia (Prekmurje)
- Croatia (Slavonia, Central Croatia, southern parts of the pre-1918 Baranya and Zala counties – today's Croatian part of Baranja and Međimurje county)
- Ukraine (oblast of Zakarpattia)
- Romania (region of Transylvania and Partium)
- Serbia (autonomous province of Vojvodina and northern Belgrade region)

- Poland (Polish parts of Orava and Spiš)
- Bosnia and Herzegovina (the villages of Zavalje, Mali skočaj and Veliki skočaj including the immediate surrounding area west of the city of Bihać)

Austro-Hungarian Condominium

- Bosnia and Herzegovina
- Montenegro (Sutorina – western part of the Municipality of Herceg–Novi between present borders with Croatia (SW) and Bosnia and Herzegovina (NW), Adriatic coast (E) and the township of Igalo (NE))
- Sandžak- Raška region, Austro-Hungarian occupied 1878 until withdrawal in 1908 whilst formally part of the Ottoman Empire

Possessions of the Austro-Hungarian Monarchy

- The empire was unable to gain and maintain large colonies owing to its geographical position. Its only possession outside of Europe was its concession in Tianjin, China, which it was granted in return for supporting the Eight-Nation Alliance in suppressing the Boxer Rebellion. However although the city was only an Austro-Hungarian possession for 16 years, the Austro-Hungarians left their mark on that area of the city, in the form of architecture that still stands in the city.

Other parts of Europe had been part of the Habsburg monarchy once but had left it before its dissolution in 1918. Prominent examples are the regions of Lombardy and Veneto in Italy, Silesia in Poland, most of Belgium and Serbia, and parts of northern Switzerland and southwestern Germany. They persuaded the government to search out foreign investment to build up infrastructure such as railroads. Despite these measures, Austria-Hungary remained resolutely monarchist and authoritarian.

Flags and heraldry

Flags

Although Austria-Hungary did not have a common flag (a "national flag" could not exist since both halves of the Dual Monarchy consisted of inhabitants of various nationalities), a common civil ensign (introduced in 1869) did exist. Until 1918, the k.u.k. War Fleet continued to carry the Austrian ensign it had used since 1786; and the regiments of the k.u.k. Army carried the double-eagle flags they had used before 1867, as they had a long history in many cases. New ensigns created in 1915 had not been implemented until 1918 due to the war. At state functions, the Austrian black-yellow and the Hungarian red-white-green tricolor were used.

Austria-Hungary

Figure 147: *Naval ensign 1786-1918 and civil ensign 1786-1869*

Figure 148: *Civil ensign 1869-1918*

Figure 149: *Naval ensign of 1915 (not implemented)*

Figure 150: *War ensign (not implemented)*

Figure 151: *Royal Hungarian maritime ensign*

Austria was represented by the black-yellow flag. The Hungarian half of the state, on the other hand, legally had no flag of its own.[489] According to the Croatian–Hungarian Settlement (art. 62 and 63), in all joint Croatian and Hungarian affairs symbols of both Croatia and Hungary respectively had to be used. For instance, whenever the joint Hungarian-Croatian Parliament held its session in Budapest, both the Croatian and Hungarian flags were hoisted on the parliament building in Budapest.[490,491] In Vienna, in front of Schönbrunn Palace, the black and yellow flag was flown for Cisleithania, while both Croatian and Hungarian flags were flown for Transleithania. Hungary proper used a red-white-green tricolor defaced with the Hungarian coat of arms, sometimes used to represent the entirety of the Lands of the Hungarian Crown.

Figure 152: *Flag of Imperial Austria (Cisleithania) and of the House of Habsburg*

Figure 153: *Flag of Royal Hungary*

Figure 154: *Flag of the Kingdom of Croatia-Slavonia*

Coat of arms

The double-headed eagle of the House of Habsburg was used as the coat of arms of the common institutions of Austria-Hungary between 1867 and 1915. In 1915, a new one was introduced, which combined the coat of arms of the two halves of the Dual Monarchy and that of the dynasty.

Figure 155: *Common small coat of arms (until 1915)*

Figure 156: *Common small coat of arms (1915–1918)*

Figure 157: *Common medium coat of arms (until 1915)*

Figure 158: *Common medium coat of arms (1915–1918)*

Additionally, each of the two parts of Austria-Hungary had its own coat of arms.

Figure 159: *Small coat of arms of the Austrian part (1915–1918)*

Figure 160: *Medium coat of arms of the Austrian part (1915–1918)*

Figure 161: *Small coat of arms of the Hungarian part (1915-1918)*

Figure 162: *Medium coat of arms of the Hungarian part (1915–1918)*

References

Further reading

Surveys

- Cornwall, Mark, ed. *The Last Years of Austria-Hungary* University of Exeter Press, 2002. ISBN 0-85989-563-7
- *Encyclopædia Britannica* (12th ed. 1922) comprises the 11th edition plus three new volumes 30–31–32 that cover events since 1911 with very thorough coverage of the war as well as every country and colony. partly online
    - Full text of vol 30 ABBE to ENGLISH HISTORY online free[492]; the article "Austrian Empire" is vol 30 pp 313–343
- Evans, R.J.W. *Austria, Hungary, and the Habsburgs: Central Europe c.1683-1867* (2008) doi:10.1093/acprof:oso/9780199541621.001.0001[493] online
- Herman, Arthur. *What Life Was Like: At Empire's End : Austro-Hungarian Empire 1848–1918* (Time Life, 2000); heavily illustrated
- Judson, Pieter M. *The Habsburg Empire: A New History* (2016) excerpt[494]
- Kann, Robert A. *A History of the Habsburg Empire: 1526–1918* (U of California Press, 1974); highly detailed history; emphasis on ethnicity

- Macartney, Carlile Aylmer *The Habsburg Empire, 1790–1918*, New York, Macmillan 1969.
- Oakes, Elizabeth and Eric Roman. *Austria-Hungary and the Successor States: A Reference Guide from the Renaissance to the Present* (2003)
- Palmer, Alan. *Twilight of the Habsburgs: The Life and Times of Emperor Francis Joseph.* New York: Weidenfeld & Nicolson, 1995. ISBN 0871136651
- Redlich, Joseph. *Emperor Francis Joseph Of Austria.*[495] New York: Macmillan, 1929. online free[496]
- Sked Alan *The Decline and Fall of the Habsburg Empire, 1815–1918*, London: Longman, 1989.
- Steed, Henry Wickham; et al. (1914). *A short history of Austria-Hungary and Poland*[497].
- Sugar, Peter F. et al. eds. *A History of Hungary* (1990), coverage by experts
- Taylor, A.J.P. *The Habsburg monarchy, 1809–1918: a history of the Austrian Empire and Austria-Hungary*, (London: Penguin Books. 2nd ed. 1964); politics and diplomacy

World war

- Boyer, John W. "Silent war and bitter peace: the revolution of 1918 in Austria." *Austrian History Yearbook* 34 (2003): 1–56.
- Cornwall, Mark. "News, Rumour and the Control of Information in Austria-Hungary, 1914–1918." *History* 77#249 (1992): 50–64.
- Cornwall, Mark. *The undermining of Austria-Hungary: the battle for hearts and minds* (London: Macmillan, 2000)
- Craig, Gordon A. "The World War I alliance of the Central Powers in retrospect: the military cohesion of the alliance." *Journal of Modern History* (1965): 336–344. in JSTOR[498]
- Healy, Maureen. *Vienna and the Fall of the Habsburg Empire: Total War and Everyday Life in World War I* (2007)
- Herweg, Holger H. *The First World War: Germany and Austria-Hungary 1914–1918* (2009)
- Jászi, Oszkár *The Dissolution of the Habsburg Monarchy*, (University of Chicago Press, 1966)
- Kann, Robert A. et al., eds. *The Habsburg Empire in World War I: Essays on the Intellectual, Military, Political and Economic Aspects of the Habsburg War Effort* (1977) online borrowing copy[499]
- Kapp, Richard W. "Divided Loyalties: The German Reich and Austria-Hungary in Austro-German Discussions of War Aims, 1914–1916." *Central European History* 17#2–3 (1984): 120–139.

- Schulze, Max-Stephan. "Austria-Hungary's economy in World War I," in Stephen Broadberry and Mark Harrison, eds. *The Economics of World War I* (2005) ch 3 online[500]
- Watson, Alexander. *Ring of Steel: Germany and Austria-Hungary in World War I* (2014)
- Wawro, Geoffrey. *A Mad Catastrophe: The Outbreak of World War I and the Collapse of the Habsburg Empire* (2014)
- Williamson, Samuel R. *Austria-Hungary and the Origins of the First World War* (1991)

Specialty topics

- Agnew, Hugh LeCaine. *Origins of the Czech National Renascence* (University of Pittsburgh Press, 1993)
- Bassett, Richard. *For God and Kaiser: The Imperial Austrian Army, 1619-1918* (2016).
- Boyer, John W. *Culture and political crisis in Vienna: Christian socialism in power, 1897–1918* (1995)
- Bridge, F.R. *From Sadowa to Sarajevo: The Foreign Policy of Austria-Hungary 1866-1914* (1972; reprint 2016) online review[501]; excerpt[502]
- Good, David. *The Economic Rise of the Habsburg Empire: 1750–1914* (1984)
- Kieval, Hillel. *The Making of Czech Jewry: National Conflict and Jewish Society in Bohemia, 1870–1918* (Oxford University Press, 1988)
- King, Jeremy. *Budweisers into Czechs and Germans: A Local History of Bohemian Politics, 1848–1948* (Princeton University Press, 2002)
- Langer, William L. (1956). *European Alliances and Alignments* (2nd ed.). detailed coverage of major diplomatic moves
- McCagg, Jr., William O. *A History of the Habsburg Jews, 1670–1918* (Indiana University Press, 1989)
- Milward, Alan S. and S. B. Saul. *The Development of the Economies of Continental Europe: 1850–1914* (1977) pp 271–331
- Milward, Alan S. and S. B. Saul. *The Economic Development of Continental Europe 1780–1870* (2nd ed. 1979), 552pp
- Phelps, Nicole M. *U.S.-Habsburg Relations from 1815 to the Paris Peace Conference* (2013) online review[503]
- Rothenberg, Gunther E. (1976), *The Army of Francis Joseph*, Purdue University Press
- Rothenberg, E. Gunther. "Nobility and Military Careers: The Habsburg Officer Corps, 1740–1914," *Military Affairs* (1976) 40#4 pp. 182–186 in JSTOR[504]
- Rothenberg, E. Gunther. "The Austrian Army in the Age of Metternich," *Journal of Modern History* (1968) 40#2 pp. 155–165 in JSTOR[505]

- Rothenberg, E. Gunther. "Toward a National Hungarian Army: The Military Compromise of 1868 and Its Consequences," *Slavic Review*, (1972) 31#4 pp. 805–816 in JSTOR[506]
- Stauter-Halsted, Keely. *The Nation in the Village: The Genesis of Peasant National Identity in Austrian Poland, 1848–1914* (Cornell University Press, 2001)
- Sugar, Peter F. (1994). *A History of Hungary*. et al. (2nd ed.). Indiana University Press.

Primary sources

- Baedeker, Karl. *Austria-Hungary: Including Dalmatia and Bosnia; Handbook for Travellers* (1905) online[507]
- Gooch, G. P. *Recent Revelations Of European Diplomacy* (1940), pp 103–59 summarizes memoirs of major participants

Historiography and memory

- Boyd, Kelly, ed. *Encyclopedia of Historians and Historical Writers* (Rutledge, 1999) 1:60–63, historiography
- Kozuchowski, Adam. *The Afterlife of Austria-Hungary: The Image of the Habsburg Monarchy in Interwar Europe* (University of Pittsburgh Press; 2013) 208 pages; Translation of a Polish study of cultural memories of A-H as seen in histories, journalism, and literature.
- Kwan, Jonathan. "Review Article: Nationalism and all that: Reassessing the Habsburg Monarchy and its legacy." *European History Quarterly* 41#1 (2011): 88–108.

In German

- *Geographischer Atlas zur Vaterlandskunde an der österreichischen Mittelschulen*. (ed.: Rudolf Rothaug), K. u. k. Hof-Kartographische Anstalt G. Freytag & Berndt, Vienna, 1911.

External links

 Wikivoyage has a travel guide for *Austro-Hungarian Empire*.

Wikimedia Commons has media related to *Austria-Hungary*.

- Habsburg Empire Austrian line[508]
- Microsoft Encarta: The height of the dual monarchy[509] (Archived[510] 31 October 2009)
- The Austro-Hungarian Military[511]
- Heraldry of the Austro-Hungarian Empire[512]
- Austria-Hungary[513] at the Wayback Machine (archived 12 January 2008) - extensive list of heads of state, ministers, and ambassadors
- History of Austro-Hungarian currency[514]
- Austria-Hungary, Dual Monarchy[515]
- The Austro-Hungarian Army in the Italian Dolomites (in Italian)[516]
- Map of Europe[517] and the collapse of Austria-Hungary at omniatlas.com
- Mangham, Arthur Neal. The Social Bases of Austrian Politics: The German Electoral Districts of Cisleithania, 1900–1914. Ph.D. thesis 1974[518]
- Austro-Hungarian Land Forces 1848–1918[519]
- HABSBURG is a email discussion list dealing with the culture and history of the Habsburg Monarchy and its successor states in central Europe since 1500[520], with discussions, syllabi, book reviews, queries, conferences; edited daily by scholars since 1994

Coordinates: 48°12′N 16°21′E[521]

20th century

Hungary in World War II

During World War II, the Kingdom of Hungary was a member of the Axis powers.[522] In the 1930s, the Kingdom of Hungary relied on increased trade with Fascist Italy and Nazi Germany to pull itself out of the Great Depression. By 1938, Hungarian politics and foreign policy had become more stridently nationalistic, and Hungary adopted an irredentist policy similar to Germany's, attempting to incorporate ethnic Hungarian areas in neighboring countries into Hungary. Hungary benefited territorially from its relationship with the Axis. Settlements were negotiated regarding territorial disputes with the Czechoslovak Republic, the Slovak Republic, and the Kingdom of Romania. In 1940, under pressure from Germany, Hungary joined the Axis. In 1941, Hungarian forces participated in the invasion of Yugoslavia and the invasion of the Soviet Union.

While waging war against the Soviet Union, Hungary engaged in armistice negotiations with the United States and the United Kingdom. Hitler discovered this betrayal and, in March 1944, German forces occupied Hungary. When Soviet forces began threatening Hungary, an armistice was signed between Hungary and the USSR by Regent Miklós Horthy. Soon after, Horthy's son was kidnapped by German commandos and Horthy was forced to revoke the armistice. The Regent was then deposed from power, while Hungarian fascist leader Ferenc Szálasi established a new government, with German backing. In 1945, Hungarian and German forces in Hungary were defeated by invading Soviet armies.

Approximately 300,000 Hungarian soldiers and more than 600,000 civilians died during World War II, including among them at least 450,000 Jews and 28,000 Roma. Many cities were damaged, most notably the capital of Budapest. Most Jews in Hungary were protected from deportation to German extermination camps for the first few years of the war, although they were

Figure 163: *Hungarian leader Miklós Horthy and German leader Adolf Hitler in 1938*

subject to a series of anti-Jewish laws which imposed limits on Jewish participation in Hungary's public and economic life.[523] From the start of the German occupation of Hungary in 1944, Jews and Roma were deported to the Auschwitz concentration camp. By the end of the war, the death toll was between 450,000 and 606,000 Hungarian Jews[524] and an estimated 28,000 Hungarian Roma.[525] Hungary's borders were returned to their pre-1938 status after its surrender.

Movement to the right

In Hungary, the joint effect of the Great Depression and the Treaty of Trianon resulted in shifting the political mood of the country towards the right. In 1932, the regent Miklós Horthy appointed a new Prime Minister, Gyula Gömbös. Gömbös was identified with the Hungarian National Defence Association (*Magyar Országos Véderő Egylet*, or MOVE). He led Hungarian international policy towards closer cooperation with Germany and started an effort to assimilate minorities in Hungary. Gömbös signed a trade agreement with Germany (21 February 1934[526]) that led to fast expansion of the economy, drawing Hungary out of the Great Depression but making Hungary dependent on the German economy for both raw materials and export revenues.

Hungary in World War II 241

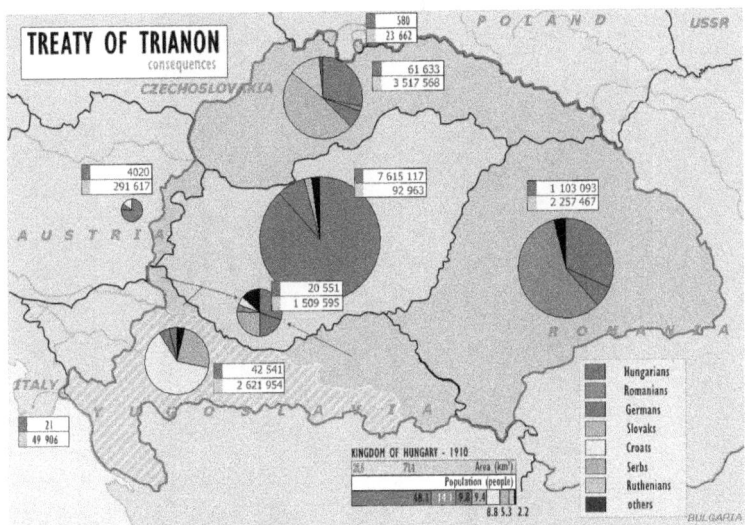

Figure 164: *The partition of Hungary in accordance with the Treaty of Trianon. This unwelcome political division dominated the political life of Hungary during the period between World War I and World War II*

Gömbös advocated a number of social reforms, one-party governmentWikipedia:Citation needed, revision of the Treaty of Trianon, and Hungary's withdrawal from the League of Nations. Although he assembled a strong political machine, his efforts to achieve his vision and reforms were frustrated by a parliament composed mostly of István Bethlen's supporters and by Hungary's creditors, who forced Gömbös to follow conventional policies in dealing with the economic and financial crisis. The result of the 1935 elections gave Gömbös more solid support in parliament. He succeeded in gaining control of the ministries of finance, industry, and defense and in replacing several key military officers with his supporters. In October 1936, he died due to kidney problems without realizing his goals.

Hungary used its relationship with Germany to attempt to revise the Treaty of Trianon. In 1938, Hungary openly repudiated the treaty's restrictions on its armed forces. Adolf Hitler gave promises to return lost territories and threats of military intervention and economic pressure to encourage the Hungarian Government to support the policies and goals of Nazi Germany. In 1935, a Hungarian fascist party, the Arrow Cross Party, led by Ferenc Szálasi was founded. Gömbös' successor, Kálmán Darányi, attempted to appease both Nazis and Hungarian antisemites by passing the First Jewish Law, which set

Figure 165: *Pál Teleki, prime minister of the Kingdom of Hungary (1920–1921 and 1939–1941)*

quotas limiting Jews to 20% of positions in several professions. The law satisfied neither the Nazis nor Hungary's own radicals, and when Darányi resigned in May 1938 Béla Imrédy was appointed Prime Minister.

Imrédy's attempts to improve Hungary's diplomatic relations with the United Kingdom initially made him very unpopular with Germany and Italy. Aware of Germany's Anschluss with Austria in March, he realized that he could not afford to alienate Germany and Italy on a long term basis: in the autumn of 1938 his foreign policy became very much pro-German and pro-Italian. Intent on amassing a powerbase in Hungarian right wing politics, Imrédy started to suppress political rivals, so the increasingly influential Arrow Cross Party was harassed, and eventually banned by Imrédy's administration. As Imrédy drifted further to the right, he proposed that the government be reorganized along totalitarian lines and drafted a harsher Second Jewish Law. Imrédy's political opponents, however, forced his resignation in February 1939 by presenting documents showing that his grandfather was a Jew. Nevertheless, the new government of Count Pál Teleki approved the Second Jewish Law, which cut the quotas on Jews permitted in the professions and in business. Furthermore, the new law defined Jews by race instead of just religion, thus altering the status of those who had formerly converted from Judaism to Christianity.

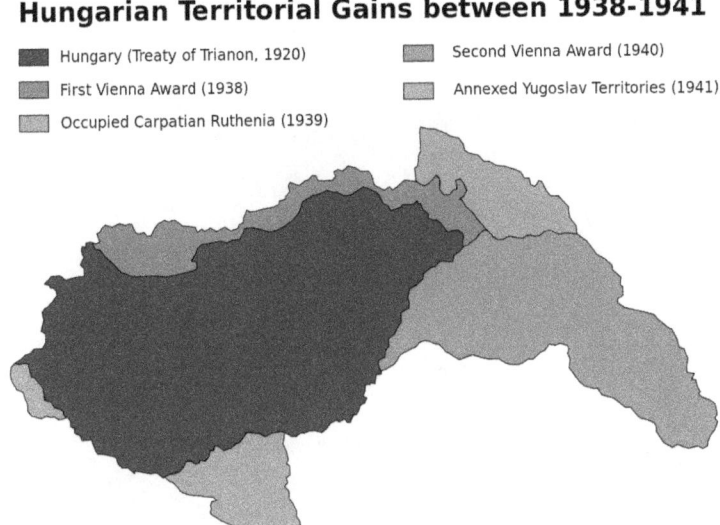

Figure 166: *Territories that Hungary gained back with the Vienna Awards and military occupation (1938-1941)*

Territorial expansion

Nazi Germany and Fascist Italy sought to peacefully enforce the claims of Hungarians on territories Hungary had lost with the signing of the 1920 Treaty of Trianon. Two significant territorial awards were made. These awards were known as the First Vienna Award and the Second Vienna Award.

In October 1938, the Munich Agreement caused the dissolution of the Czechoslovak Republic and the creation of the Czecho-Slovak Republic (also known as the "Second Czechoslovak Republic"). Some autonomy was granted to Slovakia and to Carpathian Ruthenia in the new republic. On 5 October, about 500 members of the Hungarian Ragged Guard infiltrated Slovakia and Ruthenia as "guerrillas". On 9 October, the Kingdom of Hungary started talks with the Czecho-Slovak Republic over Magyar-populated regions of southern Slovakia and southern Ruthenia. On 11 October, the Hungarian guards were defeated by Czecho-Slovak troops at Berehovo and Borzsava in Ruthenia. The Hungarians suffered approximately 350 casualties and, by 29 October, the talks were deadlocked.[527]

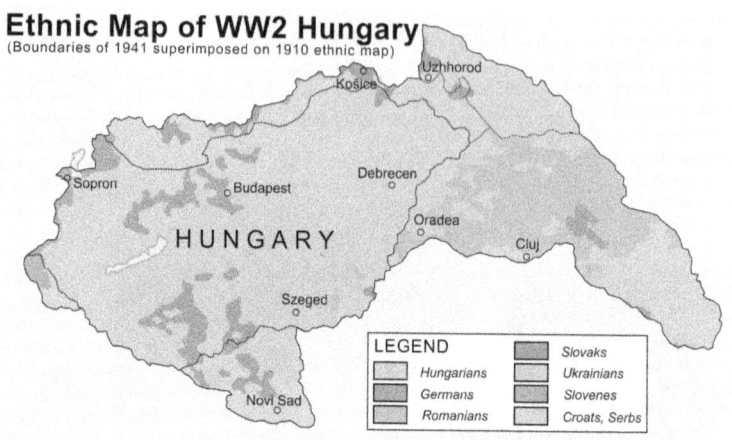

Figure 167: *Ethnic make-up of post-1941 Hungary*

First Vienna Award

On 2 November 1938, the First Vienna Award transferred to Hungary parts of Southern Slovakia and Carpathian Ruthenia, an area amounting to 11,927 km² and a population of 869,299 (46.5% of which were Hungarians according to a 1941 census). Between 5 November and 10 November, Hungarian armed forces peacefully occupied the newly transferred territories. Hitler later promised to transfer all of Slovakia to Hungary in exchange for a military alliance, but his offer was rejected. Instead, Horthy chose to pursue a territorial revision to be decided along ethnic lines.Wikipedia:Accuracy dispute#Disputed statement

Occupation of Carpatho-Ukraine

In March 1939, the Czecho-Slovak Republic was dissolved, Germany invaded it, and the Protectorate of Bohemia and Moravia was established. On 14 March, Slovakia declared itself to be an independent state. On 15 March, Carpatho-Ukraine declared itself to be an independent state. Hungary rejected the independence of Carpatho-Ukraine and, between 14 March and 18 March, Hungarian armed forces occupied the rest of Carpathian Ruthenia and ousted the government of Avgustyn Voloshyn. By contrast, Hungary recognized the German puppet state of Slovakia led by the Clerical Fascist Jozef Tiso. But on 23 March 1939, Hungarian attacks on the eastern borders of Slovakia, led to a localized armed conflict between the two countries. The Slovak–Hungarian War, also known as the "Little War", ended with Hungary gaining only the easternmost strip of Slovakia.

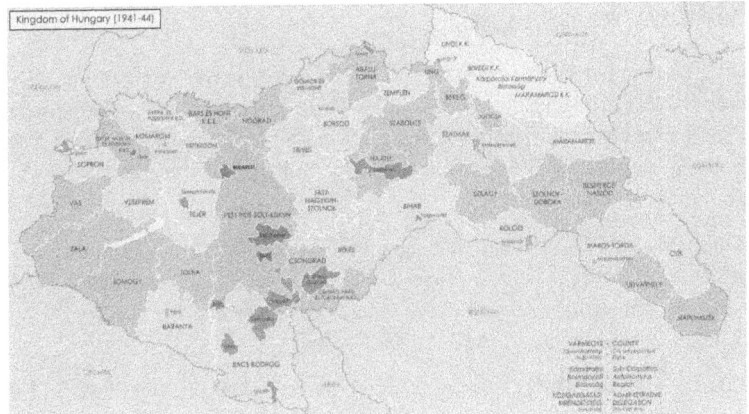

Figure 168: *Kingdom of Hungary 1941-44*

Second Vienna Award

In September 1940, with troops massing on both sides of the Hungarian-Romanian border, war was averted by the Second Vienna Award. This award transferred to Hungary the northern half of Transylvania, with a total area of 43,492 km² and a total population of 2,578,100 divided more or less evenly between Hungarians and Romanians (depending on the census, cf. Second Vienna Award). By dividing Transylvania between Romania and Hungary, Hitler was able to ease tensions in Hungary.

Occupation of Yugoslav territories

After invading Yugoslavia on 11 April 1941, Hungary forcibly annexed sections of Baranja, Bačka, Međimurje, and Prekmurje.[528]

Greater Hungary

Following the two Vienna awards, a number of counties that had been lost in whole or part by the Treaty of Trianon were restored to Hungarian rule. As a result, some previously *merged counties* - in Hungarian *közigazgatásilag egyelőre egyesített vármegye* (k.e.e. vm.) - were de-merged and restored to their pre-1920 boundaries.

The region of Sub-Carpathia was given special autonomous status with the intention that (eventually) it would be self-governed by the Ruthenian minority.

Military campaigns

On 20 November 1940, under pressure from Germany, Hungarian prime Minister Pál Teleki signed the Tripartite Pact. In December 1940, Teleki also signed an ephemeral "Treaty of Eternal Friendship" with the Kingdom of Yugoslavia. At that time, Yugoslavia was under a Regent, Prince Paul who was also under German pressure.

On 25 March 1941, Prince Paul signed the Tripartite Pact on behalf of Yugoslavia. Two days later, a Yugoslavian *coup d'état* removed Prince Paul, replaced him with pro-British King Peter, and threatened the success of the planned German invasion of the Soviet Union.

Hitler asked the Hungarians to support his invasion of Yugoslavia. He promised to return some territory to Hungary in exchange for military cooperation. On 3 April 1941, unable to prevent Hungary's participation in the war alongside Germany, Teleki committed suicide. The right-wing radical László Bárdossy succeeded him as Prime Minister.

Invasion of Yugoslavia

Three days after Teleki's death, the Luftwaffe bombed Belgrade without warning. The German Army invaded Yugoslavia and quickly crushed Yugoslavian armed resistance. Horthy dispatched the Hungarian Third Army to occupy Vojvodina.

Invasion of the Soviet Union

Hungary did not immediately participate in the invasion of the Soviet Union. The invasion began on 22 June 1941, but Hitler did not directly ask for Hungarian assistance. Nonetheless, many Hungarian officials argued for participation in the war in order to encourage Hitler not to favour Romania in the event of border revisions in Transylvania. On 26 June 1941, the Soviet air force bombed Košice (Kassa). Some speculation exists that this was a "false-flag" attack instigated by Germany (possibly in cooperation with Romania) to give Hungary a *casus belli* for joining Operation Barbarossa and the war. Hungary declared war against the Soviets on 27 June 1941.

On 1 July 1941, under German instruction, the Hungarian "Carpathian Group" (*Karpat Group*) attacked the 12th Soviet Army. Attached to the German 17th Army, the Karpat Group advanced far into Soviet Ukraine, and, later, southern Russia. At the Battle of Uman, fought between 3 and 8 August, the Karpat Group's mechanized corps acted as one half of a pincer that encircled the 6th Soviet Army and the 12th Soviet Army. Twenty Soviet divisions were captured or destroyed in this action.

Figure 169: *Hungarian Toldi I tank used during the 1941 invasion of the Soviet Union.*

In July 1941, the Hungarian government transferred responsibility for 18,000 Jews from Carpato-Ruthenian Hungary to the German armed forces. These Jews, without Hungarian citizenship, were sent to a location near Kamenets-Podolski, where in one of the first acts of mass killing of Jews during World War II, all but two thousand of these individuals were shot by Nazi mobile killing units.[529] Bardossy then passed the "Third Jewish Law" in August 1941, prohibiting marriage and sexual intercourse of Hungarians with Jews.

Six months after the mass murder at Kamianets-Podilskyi, Hungarian troops killed 3,000 Serbian and Jewish hostages near Novi Sad, Yugoslavia, in reprisal for resistance activities.

Worried about Hungary's increasing reliance on Germany, Admiral Horthy forced Bárdossy to resign and replaced him with Miklós Kállay, a veteran conservative of Bethlen's government. Kállay continued Bárdossy's policy of supporting Germany against the Red Army while also initiating negotiations with the Western Allies. Hungarian participation in Operation Barbarossa during 1941 was limited in part because the country had no real army before 1939, and time to train and equip troops had been short. But by 1942, tens of thousands of Hungarians were fighting on the eastern front in the Royal Hungarian Army.

During the Battle of Stalingrad, the Hungarian Second Army suffered terrible losses. The Soviet breakthrough at the Don River sliced directly through the Hungarian units. Shortly after the fall of Stalingrad in January 1943, the Hungarian 2nd Army was crushed by the Soviets at the Battle of Voronezh.

Figure 170: *Hungarian Arrow Cross militia and a German Tiger II tank in Budapest, October 1944.*

Ignoring German orders to stand and fight to the death, the bewildered Hungarian troops, fighting without antitank weaponry or armored support, turned and fled. Harassed by partisan groups and Soviet air attacks, and having to endure the Russian winter weather, they tried in vain to retreat. Most of the survivors were taken prisoner by the Soviet army, and total casualties numbered more than 100,000 men. The Hungarian army ceased to exist as an effective fighting force, and the Germans pulled them from the front.

While Kállay was Prime Minister, the Jews endured increased economic and political repression, although many, particularly those in Budapest, were temporarily protected from the final solution. For most of the war, the Hungarian Jews lived an uneasy existence. They were deprived of most freedoms, but were not subjected to physical harm, and Horthy tried to contain anti-Semitic groups like the Arrow Cross. Secret negotiations with the British and Americans continued. As per the request of the Western Allies, there were no connections made with the Soviets.

German occupation of Hungary

Aware of Kállay's deceit and fearing that Hungary might conclude a separate peace, in March 1944, Hitler launched Operation Margarethe and ordered Nazi troops to occupy Hungary. Horthy was confined to a castle, in essence, placed under house arrest. Döme Sztójay, an avid supporter of the National

Figure 171: *German occupying forces - Budapest, 1944.03.19*

Socialists, became the new Prime Minister. Sztójay governed with the aid of a National Socialist military governor, Edmund Veesenmayer. The Hungarian populace was not happy with their nation being reduced in effect to a German protectorate, but Berlin threatened to occupy Hungary with Slovak, Croat, and Romanian troops if they did not comply. The thought of these ancestral enemies on Hungarian soil was seen as far worse than German control. Ironically, Hungary still kept whole divisions on the border with Romania even as the troops of both nations were fighting and dying together in the Russian winter.

As the Soviets pushed westward, Sztojay's government proceeded to muster new armies. The Hungarian troops again suffered terrible losses, but now had a motive to protect their homeland from Soviet occupation.

In August 1944, Horthy replaced Sztójay with the anti-Fascist General Géza Lakatos. Under the Lakatos regime, acting Interior Minister Béla Horváth ordered Hungarian gendarmes to prevent any Hungarian citizens from being deported. The Germans were unhappy with the situation, but could not do a great deal about it. Horthy's actions thus bought the Jews of Budapest a few months of time.

Soviet occupation of Hungary

In September 1944, Soviet forces crossed the Hungarian border. On 15 October, Horthy announced that Hungary had signed an armistice with the Soviet Union. The Hungarian army ignored the armistice, fighting desperately to keep the Soviets out. The Germans launched Operation Panzerfaust and, by kidnapping his son Miklós Horthy, Jr., forced Horthy to abrogate the armistice, depose the Lakatos government, and name the leader of the Arrow Cross Party,

Figure 172: *Hungarian soldiers in the Carpathian Mountains in 1944.*

Ferenc Szálasi, as Prime Minister. Horthy resigned and Szálasi became Prime Minister of a new "Government of National Unity" (*Nemzeti Összefogás Kormánya*) controlled by the Germans. Horthy himself was taken to Germany as a prisoner. He ultimately survived the war and spent his last years exiled in Portugal, dying in 1957.

In cooperation with the Nazis, Szálasi attempted to resume deportations of Jews, but Germany's fast-disintegrating communications largely prevented this from happening. Nonetheless, the Arrow Cross launched a reign of terror against the Jews of Budapest. Thousands were tortured, raped and murdered in the last months of the war, and their property looted or destroyed. Swedish diplomat Raoul Wallenberg saved thousands of Budapest Jews using Swedish protective passports. He was ultimately taken prisoner by the Soviets and died some years later in a labor camp. Other foreign diplomats like Nuncio Angelo Rotta, Giorgio Perlasca, Carl Lutz, Friedrich Born, Harald Feller, Angel Sanz Briz and George Mandel-Mantello also organized false papers and safe houses for Jews in Budapest. Of the approximately 800,000 Jews residing within Hungary's expanded borders of 1941, only 200,000 (about 25%) survived the Holocaust.[530] An estimated 28,000 Hungarian Roma were also killed as part of the Porajmos.

Soon Hungary itself became a battlefield. Szálasi promised a Greater Hungary and prosperity for the peasants, but in reality Hungary was crumbling and its armies were slowly being destroyed. As an integral part of German General

Maximilian Fretter-Pico's *Armeegruppe Fretter-Pico*, the re-formed Hungarian Second Army enjoyed a modest level of combat success. From 6 October to 29 October 1944, during the Battle of Debrecen, *Armeegruppe Fretter-Pico* managed to achieve a major win on the battlefield. Avoiding encirclement itself, *Armeegruppe Fretter-Pico* encircled and severely mauled three Soviet tank corps serving under the Mobile Group of Issa Pliyev. Earlier in the same battle, Mobile Group Pliyev had sliced through the Hungarian Third Army. But success was costly and, unable to replace lost armor and heavy artillery munitions, the Hungarian Second Army was defeated on 1 December 1944. The remnants of the Second Army were incorporated into the Third Army.

In October 1944, the Hungarian First Army was attached to the German 1st Panzer Army, participating defensively against the Red Army's advance towards Budapest. On 28 December 1944, a provisional government was formed in Hungary under acting Prime Minister Béla Miklós. Miklós and Szálasi each claimed to be the legitimate Head of government. The Germans and pro-German Hungarians loyal to Szálasi fought on.

The Soviets and Romanians completed the encirclement of Budapest on 29 December 1944. The battle for the city turned into the Siege of Budapest. During the fight, most of what remained of the Hungarian First Army was destroyed about 200 kilometres (120 mi) north of Budapest in a running battle from 1 January to 16 February 1945. On 20 January 1945, representatives of the Miklós provisional government signed an armistice in Moscow. In January 1945, 32,000 ethnic Germans from within Hungary were arrested and transported to the Soviet Union as forced laborers. In some villages, the entire adult population were taken to labor camps in the Donets Basin.[21] Many died there as a result of hardships and ill-treatment. Overall, between 100,000 and 170,000 Hungarian ethnic Germans were transported to the Soviet Union.[38]

The remaining German and Hungarian units within Budapest surrendered on 13 February 1945. Although the German forces in Hungary were generally defeated, the Germans had one more surprise for the Soviets. On 6 March 1945, the Germans launched the Lake Balaton Offensive, attempting to hold on to the Axis' last source of oil. It was their final operation of the war and it quickly failed. By 19 March 1945, Soviet troops had recaptured all the territory lost during the 13-day German offensive.[531:182]

After the failed offensive, the Germans in Hungary were eliminated. Most of what remained of the Hungarian Third Army was destroyed about 50 kilometres (31 mi) west of Budapest between 16 March and 25 March 1945. From 26 March and 15 April, the Soviets and Bulgarians launched the

Figure 173: *Hungarian soldiers in Denmark, April 1945.*

Nagykanizsa–Körmend Offensive and more Hungarian remnants were destroyed as part of Army Group South fighting alongside the 2nd Panzer Army. By the start of April, the Germans, with the Arrow Cross in tow, had completely vacated Hungarian soil.

Retreat into Germany

Officially, Soviet operations in Hungary ended on 4 April 1945, when the last German troops were expelled. Some pro-Fascist Hungarians like Szálasi escaped—for a time—with the Germans. A few pro-German Hungarian units fought on until the end of the war. Units like the Szent László Infantry Division ended the war in southern Austria.

On 8 May 1945, at 4:10 p.m. Major General Stanley Eric Reinhart's 259th Infantry Regiment was authorized to accept the surrender of the 1st Hungarian Cavalry Division and of the 1st Hungarian Panzer Division. Surrender and movement across the Enns River had to be completed prior to midnight.

In the town of Landsberg in Bavaria, a Hungarian garrison stood in parade formation to surrender as the Americans advanced through the area very late in the war.[532] A few Hungarian soldiers ended the war in Denmark in some of the last Nazi territory not yet occupied.

Major engagements

This is a list of battles and other combat operations in World War II in which Hungarian forces took part.

Battle	Date	Location	Hungary and its allies	Enemies	Issue
Invasion of Yugoslavia	6 – 18 April 1941	Yugoslavia	Germany Hungary Italy	Yugoslavia	Victory
Operation Barbarossa	22 June – 5 December 1941	Soviet Union	Germany Romania Finland Italy Hungary Slovakia Croatia	Soviet Union	Defeat
Kozara Offensive	10 June – August 1942	Yugoslavia	Germany Hungary Croatia	Yugoslav Partisans Chetniks	Victory
Battle of Uman	15 July – 8 August 1941	Soviet Union	Germany Romania Hungary Slovakia Croatia	Soviet Union	Victory
Case Blue	28 June – 24 November 1942	Soviet Union	Germany Italy Romania Hungary Slovakia Croatia	Soviet Union	Defeat
First Battle of Voronezh	28 June – 24 July 1942	Soviet Union	Germany Hungary	Soviet Union	Victory
Battle of Stalingrad	23 August 1942 – 2 February 1943	Soviet Union	Germany Italy Romania Hungary Croatia	Soviet Union	Defeat
Battle of Nikolayevka	13 – 26 January 1943	Soviet Union	Italy Germany Hungary	Soviet Union	Victory
Ostrogozhsk–Rossosh Offensive	13 January – 3 March 1943	Soviet Union	Hungary Italy	Soviet Union	Defeat
Second Battle of Voronezh	24 January – 17 February 1943	Soviet Union	Germany Hungary	Soviet Union	Defeat

Battle	Date	Location	Axis	Allies	Result
Lvov–Sandomierz Offensive	13 July – 29 August 1944	Ukraine/-Poland	Germany Hungary	Soviet Union Polish Underground State	Defeat
Battle of Turda	5 September – 8 October 1944	Romania	Germany Hungary	Soviet Union Romania	Defeat
Battle of the Dukla Pass	8 September – 28 October 1944	Poland/-Slovakia	Germany Hungary	Soviet Union Czechoslovakia	Indecisive
Battle of Păuliș	14 – 19 September 1944	Romania	Hungary	Romania	Defeat
Battle of Debrecen	6 – 29 October 1944	Hungary	Germany Hungary	Soviet Union Romania	Defeat
Budapest Offensive	29 October 1944 – 13 February 1945	Hungary	Germany Hungary	Soviet Union Romania	Defeat
Siege of Budapest	29 December 1944 – 13 February 1945	Hungary	Germany Hungary	Soviet Union Romania	Defeat
Battle of Poznań	24 January – 23 February 1945	Poland	Germany Hungary	Soviet Union Poland	Defeat
Operation Spring Awakening	6 – 16 March 1945	Hungary	Germany Hungary	Soviet Union Bulgaria Yugoslav Partisans	Defeat
Western Allied invasion of Germany	22 March – 8 May 1945	Germany	Germany Hungary	United States United Kingdom Canada France Poland Norway Denmark Netherlands Belgium	Defeat
Nagykanizsa–Körmend Offensive	26 March – 15 April 1945	Hungary	Germany Hungary Croatia	Soviet Union Bulgaria Yugoslav Partisans	Defeat

Vienna Offensive	2 – 13 April 1945	Austria	Germany Hungary	Soviet Union Bulgaria Austrian resistance	Defeat
Prague Offensive	6 – 11 May 1945	Czechoslovakia	Germany Hungary Slovakia	Soviet Union Poland Czechoslovakia Romania ✗ Russian Liberation Army	Defeat

Oppression at home

The Holocaust

On March 19, 1944 German troops occupied Hungary, prime minister Miklós Kállay was deposed and soon mass deportations of Jews to German death camps in occupied Poland began. SS-Obersturmbannführer Adolf Eichmann went to Hungary to oversee the large-scale deportations. Between 15 May and 9 July, Hungarian authorities deported 437,402 Jews. All but 15,000 of these Jews were sent to Auschwitz-Birkenau, and 90% of those were immediately killed. One in three of all Jews killed at Auschwitz were Hungarian citizens. Sztojay, unlike previous prime ministers, answered mostly to Berlin and was thus able to act independently of Horthy. However, reports of the conditions in the concentration camps led the admiral to resist his policies.

In early July 1944, Horthy stopped the deportations, and after the failed attempt on Hitler's life, the Germans backed off from pressing Horthy's regime to continue further, large-scale deportations, although some smaller groups continued to be deported by train. In late August, Horthy refused Eichmann's request to restart the deportations. Himmler ordered Eichmann to leave Budapest.

Forced labor

The forced labor service system was introduced in Hungary in 1939. The system affected primarily the Jewish population, but many people belonging to minorities, sectarians, leftists and Roma were also inducted.

Thirty-five thousand to 40,000 forced laborers, mostly Jews or of Jewish origin, served in the Hungarian Second Army, which fought in the USSR (see below). Eighty percent of them—28,000 to 32,000 people—never returned; they died either on the battlefield or in captivity.

Approximately half of the 6,000 Jewish forced laborers working in the copper mines in Bor, Yugoslavia (now Serbia) were executed by the Germans during

Figure 174: *Hungarian Jewish Women and children from Carpatho-Ruthenia after their arrival at the Auschwitz death-camp (May/June 1944). Photo from the Auschwitz Album.*

the death march from Bor to Győr in August–October 1944, including the 35-year-old poet Miklós Radnóti, shot at the Hungarian village of Abda for being too weak to continue after a savage beating.

Resistance movement

In autumn of 1941 anti-German demonstrations took place in Hungary. On 15 March 1942, the anniversary of the outbreak of the 1848-49 War of Independence, a crowd of 8,000 people gathered at the Sándor Petőfi monument in Budapest to demand an "independent democratic Hungary". The underground Hungarian Communist Party published newspaper and leaflets, 500 communist activists were arrested and the party's leaders Ferenc Ryzsa and Zytan Schunherz were executed.

The Hungarian underground opposition contributed little to the military defeat of National Socialism. In July 1943 the Smallholders Party adopted Endre Bajcsy-Zsilinszky's policy of working more closely with Hungarian Social Democratic Party and the Communists and on 31 July demanded from the government an end to hostilities and joining the Allies even at the price of armed conflict with Germany. At the beginning of August 1943 a programme of action was formally concluded with the Social Democrats and on 11 September they issued a joint declaration against the war on the side of Germany.

Various opposition groups deprived of their leaders most of whom had been arrested by the Gestapo after the German occupation in March 1944 joined forces in May 1944 in the Communist-inspired Hungarian Front (Magyar Front). They demanded a "new struggle of liberation" against the German occupation forces and their collaborators and called for the creation of a new democratic Hungary after the war. The representatives of the Hungarian Front, being informed by Horthy of plans for an armistice on 11 October, founded the Committee of Liberation of the Hungarian National Uprising on 11 November 1944. Although immediately weakened by the arrest and execution of its leaders, it called for an armed uprising against the German forces which took the form of limited isolated partisan actions and attacks on German military installations.

Peace treaty

By 2 May 1945, Hitler was dead and Berlin surrendered. On 7 May, General Alfred Jodl, the German Chief of Staff, signed the surrender of Germany. On 23 May, the "Flensburg Government" was dissolved. On 11 June, the Allies agreed to make 8 May 1945 the official "Victory in Europe" day.:298

The Treaty of Peace with Hungary[533] signed on 10 February 1947 declared that "The decisions of the Vienna Award of 2 November 1938 are declared null and void" and Hungarian boundaries were fixed along the former frontiers as they existed on 1 January 1938, except a minor loss of territory on the Czechoslovakian border. Two thirds of the ethnic German minority (202,000 people) was deported to Germany in 1946-48, and there was a forced "population exchange" between Hungary and Czechoslovakia.

On February 1, 1946, the Kingdom of Hungary was formally abolished and replaced by the Second Republic of Hungary. Post-war Hungary was eventually taken over by a Soviet-allied government and became part of the Eastern Bloc. The People's Republic of Hungary was declared in 1949 and lasted until the Revolutions of 1989 and the End of Communism in Hungary.

References

- Dollinger, Hans. *The Decline and Fall of Nazi Germany and Imperial Japan.* Library of Congress Catalogue Card Number 67-27047
- Braham, Randolph (1981). *The Politics of Genocide: The Holocaust in Hungary.* Columbia University Press.

- Fenyö, Mario D. (1969). "Some Aspects of Hungary's Participation in World War II". *East European Quarterly.* **3** (2): 219–29.
- Stafford, David. *Endgame, 1945: The Missing Final Chapter of World War II.* Little, Brown and Company, New York, 2007. ISBN 978-0-31610-980-2
- Szabo, Laszlo Pal; Thomas, Nigel (2008). *The Royal Hungarian Army in World war II.* New York: Osprey Publishing. p. 48. ISBN 978-1-84603-324-7.

External links

- Axis History Factbook — Hungary[534]
- WW2 bunkers, fortifications, maps and museums (in English and Hungarian)[535]
- Map[536]
- Map[537]

Hungarian Revolution

Hungarian Revolution of 1956

Hungarian Revolution of 1956	
Part of the Cold War	
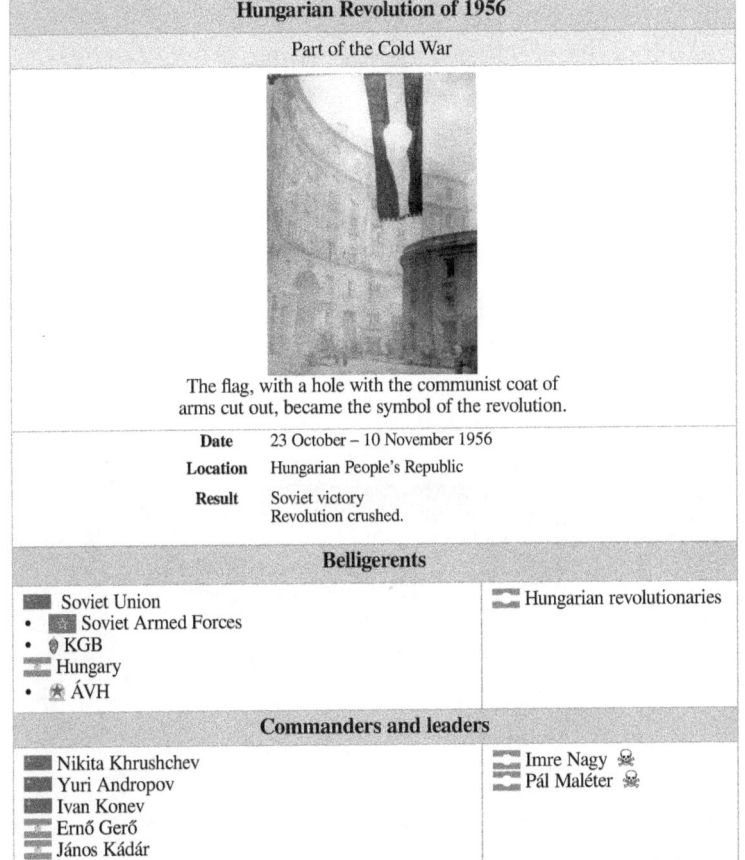 The flag, with a hole with the communist coat of arms cut out, became the symbol of the revolution.	
Date	23 October – 10 November 1956
Location	Hungarian People's Republic
Result	Soviet victory Revolution crushed.
Belligerents	
Soviet Union • Soviet Armed Forces • KGB Hungary • ÁVH	Hungarian revolutionaries
Commanders and leaders	
Nikita Khrushchev Yuri Andropov Ivan Konev Ernő Gerő János Kádár	Imre Nagy ☠ Pál Maléter ☠

Strength	
31,550 troops 1,130 tanks[538] Unknown number of government loyalists	Unknown number of soldiers, militia, and armed civilians
Casualties and losses	
Soviet casualties: 722 killed or missing 1,540 wounded	2,500–3,000 killed (est.) 13,000 wounded (est.)[539]
3,000 civilians killed[540]	

Part of a series on the
History of Hungary

Hungary portal

- v
- t
- e[541]

Eastern Bloc

Hungarian Revolution of 1956

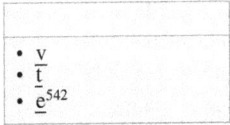

- $\underline{v}$
- $\underline{t}$
- $\underline{e}$[542]

The **Hungarian Revolution of 1956** or the **Hungarian Uprising of 1956**[543] (Hungarian: *1956-os forradalom* or *1956-os felkelés*) was a nationwide revolt against the government of the Hungarian People's Republic and its Soviet-imposed policies, lasting from 23 October until 10 November 1956. Though leaderless when it first began, it was the first major threat to Soviet control since the USSR's forces drove Nazi Germany from its territory at the end of World War II.

The revolt began as a student demonstration, which attracted thousands as they marched through central Budapest to the Parliament building, calling out on the streets using a van with loudspeakers. A student delegation, entering the radio building to try to broadcast the students' demands, was detained. When the delegation's release was demanded by the demonstrators outside, they were fired upon by the State Security Police (ÁVH) from within the building. One student died and was wrapped in a flag and held above the crowd. This was the start of the revolution. As the news spread, disorder and violence erupted throughout the capital.

The revolt spread quickly across Hungary and the government collapsed. Thousands organised into militias, battling the ÁVH and Soviet troops. Pro-Soviet communists and ÁVH members were often executed or imprisoned and former political prisoners were released and armed. Radical impromptu workers' councils wrested municipal control from the ruling Hungarian Working People's Party and demanded political changes. A new government formally disbanded the ÁVH, declared its intention to withdraw from the Warsaw Pact, and pledged to re-establish free elections. By the end of October, fighting had almost stopped and a sense of normality began to return.

After announcing a willingness to negotiate a withdrawal of Soviet forces, the Politburo changed its mind and moved to crush the revolution. On 4 November, a large Soviet force invaded Budapest and other regions of the country. The Hungarian resistance continued until 10 November. Over 2,500 Hungarians and 700 Soviet troops were killed in the conflict, and 200,000 Hungarians fled as refugees. Mass arrests and denunciations continued for months thereafter. By January 1957, the new Soviet-installed government had suppressed all public opposition. These Soviet actions, while strengthening control over the Eastern Bloc, alienated many Western Marxists, leading to splits and/or considerable losses of membership for communist parties in capitalist states.

Public discussion about this revolution was suppressed in Hungary for more than 30 years. Since the thaw of the 1980s, it has been a subject of intense study and debate. At the inauguration of the Third Hungarian Republic in 1989, 23 October was declared a national holiday.

Prelude

During World War II Hungary was a member of the Axis powers, allied with the forces of Nazi Germany, Fascist Italy, Romania, and Bulgaria. In 1941, the Hungarian military participated in the occupation of Yugoslavia and the invasion of the Soviet Union. The Red Army was able to force back the Hungarian and other Axis invaders, and by 1944 was advancing towards Hungary.

Fearing invasion, the Hungarian government began armistice negotiations with the Allies. These ended when Nazi Germany invaded and occupied the country and set up the pro-Axis Government of National Unity.

Both Hungarian and German forces stationed in Hungary were subsequently defeated when the Soviet Union invaded the country in 1945.

Postwar occupation

Towards the end of World War II, the Soviet Army occupied Hungary, with the country coming under the Soviet Union's sphere of influence. Immediately after World War II, Hungary was a multiparty democracy, and elections in 1945 produced a coalition government under Prime Minister Zoltán Tildy. However, the Hungarian Communist Party, a Marxist–Leninist group who shared the Soviet government's ideological beliefs, constantly wrested small concessions in a process named salami tactics, which sliced away the elected government's influence, despite the fact that it had received only 17% of the vote.[544,545]

After the elections of 1945, the portfolio of the Interior Ministry, which oversaw the Hungarian State Security Police (*Államvédelmi Hatóság*, later known as the ÁVH), was transferred from the Independent Smallholders Party to a nominee of the Communist Party.[546] The ÁVH employed methods of intimidation, falsified accusations, imprisonment, and torture to suppress political opposition.[547] The brief period of multi-party democracy came to an end when the Communist Party merged with the Social Democratic Party to become the Hungarian Working People's Party, which stood its candidate list unopposed in 1949. The People's Republic of Hungary was then declared.

The Hungarian Working People's Party set about to modify the economy into socialism by undertaking radical nationalization based on the Soviet model.

Figure 175: *Mátyás Rákosi speaks in Budapest, 1948*

This forced method of economic socialisation during infrastructural recovery from the war initially resulted in economic stagnation, lower standards of living, and a deep malaise.Wikipedia:Citation needed Writers and journalists were the first to voice open criticism of the government and its policies, publishing critical articles in 1955.[548] By 22 October 1956, Technical University students had resurrected the banned MEFESZ student union,[549] and staged a demonstration on 23 October that set off a chain of events leading directly to the revolution.

Political repression and economic decline

Hungary became a communist state under the authoritarian leadership of Mátyás Rákosi.[550] Under Rákosi's reign, the Security Police (ÁVH) began a series of purges, first within the Communist Party to end opposition to Rákosi's reign. The victims were labeled as "Titoists," "western agents," or "Trotskyists" for as insignificant a crime as spending time in the West to participate in the Spanish Civil War. In total, about half of all the middle and lower level party officials—at least 7,000 people—were purged.[551]

From 1950 to 1952, the Security Police forcibly relocated thousands of people to obtain property and housing for the Working People's Party members, and to remove the threat of the intellectual and 'bourgeois' class. Thousands were arrested, tortured, tried, and imprisoned in concentration camps, deported to the east, or were executed, including ÁVH founder László Rajk.[552] In a single year, more than 26,000 people were forcibly relocated from Budapest. As a consequence, jobs and housing were very difficult to obtain. The deportees generally experienced terrible living conditions and were interned as slave labor on collective farms. Many died as a result of poor living conditions and malnutrition.

The Rákosi government thoroughly politicised Hungary's educational system to supplant the educated classes with a "toiling intelligentsia". Russian language study and Communist political instruction were made mandatory in schools and universities nationwide. Religious schools were nationalized and church leaders were replaced by those loyal to the government.[553] In 1949 the leader of the Hungarian Catholic Church, Cardinal József Mindszenty, was arrested and sentenced to life imprisonment for treason.[554] Under Rákosi, Hungary's government was among the most repressive in Europe.

The post-war Hungarian economy suffered from multiple challenges. Hungary agreed to pay war reparations approximating US$300 million to the Soviet Union, Czechoslovakia, and Yugoslavia and to support Soviet garrisons.[555] The Hungarian National Bank in 1946 estimated the cost of reparations as "between 19 and 22 per cent of the annual national income." In 1946, the Hungarian currency experienced marked depreciation, resulting in the highest historic rates of hyperinflation known.[556] Hungary's participation in the Soviet-sponsored COMECON (Council Of Mutual Economic Assistance) prevented it from trading with the West or receiving Marshall Plan aid.

In addition, Rákosi began his first Five-Year Plan in 1950-based on Joseph Stalin's industrial program of the same name that sought to raise industrial output by 380 percent. Like its Soviet counterpart, the Five-Year Plan never achieved these outlandish goals due in part to the crippling effect of the exportation of most of Hungary's raw resources and technology to the Soviet Union as well as Rákosi's purges of much of the former professional class. In fact, the Five-Year Plan weakened Hungary's existing industrial structure and caused real industrial wages to fall by 18 percent between 1949 and 1952. Rákosi's agricultural programs met with the same lack of success, with attempted collectivization of the peasantry causing a marked fall in agricultural output and a rise in food shortages.Wikipedia:Citation needed

Although national income per capita rose in the first third of the 1950s, the standard of living fell. Huge income deductions to finance industrial investment reduced disposable personal income; mismanagement created chronic shortages in basic foodstuffs resulting in rationing of bread, sugar, flour, and meat.[557] Compulsory subscriptions to state bonds further reduced personal

Figure 176: *Imre Nagy (center) in October 1956*

income. The net result was that disposable real income of workers and employees in 1952 was only two-thirds of what it had been in 1938, whereas in 1949, the proportion had been 90%.[558] These policies had a cumulative negative effect and fueled discontent as foreign debt grew and the population experienced shortages of goods.[559]

International events

On 5 March 1953, Joseph Stalin died, ushering in a period of moderate liberalization, when most European communist parties developed a reform wing. In Hungary, the reformist Imre Nagy replaced Rákosi, "Stalin's Best Hungarian Disciple", as Prime Minister. However, Rákosi remained General Secretary of the Party, and was able to undermine most of Nagy's reforms. By April 1955, he had Nagy discredited and removed from office. After Khrushchev's "secret speech" of February 1956, which denounced Stalin and his protégés, Rákosi was deposed as General Secretary of the Party and replaced by Ernő Gerő on 18 July 1956.[560] Radio Free Europe would broadcast the "secret speech" to Eastern Europe on the advice of Ray S. Cline, who saw it as a way to "as I think I told [Allen Dulles] to say, 'indict the whole Soviet system'."[561]

On 14 May 1955, the Soviet Union created the Warsaw Pact, binding Hungary to the Soviet Union and its satellite states in Central and Eastern Europe.

Among the principles of this alliance were "respect for the independence and sovereignty of states" and "non-interference in their internal affairs".

In 1955, the Austrian State Treaty and ensuing declaration of neutrality established Austria as a demilitarised and neutral country.[562] This raised Hungarian hopes of also becoming neutral and in 1955 Nagy had considered "... the possibility of Hungary adopting a neutral status on the Austrian pattern".[563]

In June 1956, a violent uprising by Polish workers in Poznań was put down by the government, with scores of protesters killed and wounded. Responding to popular demand, in October 1956, the government appointed the recently rehabilitated reformist communist Władysław Gomułka as First Secretary of the Polish United Workers' Party, with a mandate to negotiate trade concessions and troop reductions with the Soviet government. After a few tense days of negotiations, on 19 October the Soviets finally gave in to Gomułka's reformist demands. News of the concessions won by the Poles, known as Polish October, emboldened many Hungarians to hope for similar concessions for Hungary and these sentiments contributed significantly to the highly charged political climate that prevailed in Hungary in the second half of October 1956.

Within the Cold War context of the time, by 1956, a fundamental tension had appeared in US policy towards Hungary and the Eastern Bloc generally. The United States hoped to encourage European countries to break away from the bloc through their own efforts but wanted to avoid a US-Soviet military confrontation, as escalation might lead to nuclear war. For these reasons, US policy makers had to consider other means of diminishing Soviet influence in Eastern Europe, short of a rollback policy. This led to the development of containment policies such as economic and psychological warfare, covert operations, and, later, negotiation with the Soviet Union regarding the status of the Eastern states. Vice President Richard Nixon had also argued to the National Security Council that it would serve US interests if the Soviet Union would turn on another uprising as they had in Poland, providing a source of anti-Communist propaganda.[564] However, while CIA director Allen Dulles had claimed he was creating an extensive network in Hungary, at the time the agency had no Hungarian station, almost no agents who spoke the language, and unreliable, corrupt local assets. The agency's own secret history would admit "at no time did we have anything that could or should have been mistaken for an intelligence operation".[565]

In the summer of 1956, relations between Hungary and the US began to improve. At that time, the US responded very favourably to Hungary's overtures about a possible expansion of bilateral trade relations. Hungary's desire for better relations was partly attributable to the country's catastrophic economic situation. Before any results could be achieved, however, the pace of negotiations was slowed by the Hungarian Ministry of Internal Affairs, which feared that better relations with the West might weaken Communist rule in Hungary.

Social unrest builds

Rákosi's resignation in July 1956 emboldened students, writers, and journalists to be more active and critical in politics. Students and journalists started a series of intellectual forums examining the problems facing Hungary. These forums, called Petőfi circles, became very popular and attracted thousands of participants.[566] On 6 October 1956, László Rajk, who had been executed by the Rákosi government, was reburied in a moving ceremony that strengthened the party opposition.

On 16 October 1956, university students in Szeged snubbed the official communist student union, the DISZ, by re-establishing the MEFESZ (Union of Hungarian University and Academy Students), a democratic student organization, previously banned under the Rákosi dictatorship. Within days, the student bodies of Pécs, Miskolc, and Sopron followed suit. On 22 October, students of the Technical University compiled a list of sixteen points containing several national policy demands.[567] After the students heard that the Hungarian Writers' Union planned on the following day to express solidarity with pro-reform movements in Poland by laying a wreath at the statue of Polish-born General Bem, a hero of the Hungarian Revolution of 1848 (1848–49), the students decided to organize a parallel demonstration of sympathy.[568]

Revolution

Politics portal
• v
• t
• e[569]

First shots

On the afternoon of 23 October 1956, approximately 20,000 protesters convened next to the statue of József Bem—a national hero of Poland and Hungary.[570] Péter Veres, President of the Writers' Union, read a manifesto to the crowd, which included: The desire for Hungary to be independent from all foreign powers; a political system based on democratic socialism (land reform and public ownership of businesses); Hungary joining the United Nations; and citizens of Hungary should have all the rights of free men. After the students read their proclamation, the crowd chanted a censored patriotic poem the "National Song", with the refrain: "This we swear, this we swear, that we will no longer be slaves." Someone in the crowd cut out the Communist coat of arms from the Hungarian flag, leaving a distinctive hole, and others quickly followed suit. Afterwards, most of the crowd crossed the River Danube to join demonstrators outside the Parliament Building. By 18:00, the multitude had swollen to more than 200,000 people;[571] the demonstration was spirited, but peaceful.[572]

At 20:00, First Secretary Ernő Gerő broadcast a speech condemning the writers' and students' demands. Angered by Gerő's hard-line rejection, some demonstrators decided to carry out one of their demands, the removal of Stalin's 30-foot-high (9.1 m) bronze statue that was erected in 1951 on the site of a church, which was demolished to make room for the monument. By 21:30, the statue was toppled and crowds celebrated by placing Hungarian flags in Stalin's boots, which was all that was left of the statue.

At about the same time, a large crowd gathered at the Radio Budapest building, which was heavily guarded by the ÁVH. The flash point was reached as a delegation attempting to broadcast their demands was detained and the crowd grew increasingly unruly as rumours spread that the protesters had been shot. Tear gas was thrown from the upper windows and the ÁVH opened fire on the crowd, killing many.[573] The ÁVH tried to re-supply itself by hiding arms inside an ambulance, but the crowd detected the ruse and intercepted it. Hungarian soldiers sent to relieve the ÁVH hesitated and then, tearing the red stars from their caps, sided with the crowd. Provoked by the ÁVH attack, protesters reacted violently. Police cars were set ablaze, guns were seized from military depots and distributed to the masses and symbols of the Communist regime were vandalised.[574]

Figure 177: *Placing of Hungarian flag into remains of dismantled Stalin statue*

Fighting spreads, government falls

During the night of 23 October, Hungarian Working People's Party Secretary Ernő Gerő requested Soviet military intervention "to suppress a demonstration that was reaching an ever greater and unprecedented scale." The Soviet leadership had formulated contingency plans for intervention in Hungary several months before.[575] By 02:00 on 24 October, acting in accordance with orders of Georgy Zhukov, the Soviet defence minister, Soviet tanks entered Budapest.[576]

By noon, on 24 October, Soviet tanks were stationed outside the Parliament, and Soviet soldiers guarded key bridges and crossroads. Armed revolutionaries quickly set up barricades to defend Budapest, and were reported to have already captured some Soviet tanks by mid-morning. That day, Imre Nagy replaced András Hegedüs as Prime Minister.[577] On the radio, Nagy called for an end to violence and promised to initiate political reforms that had been shelved three years earlier. The population continued to arm itself as sporadic violence erupted.[578]

Armed protesters seized the radio building. At the offices of the Communist newspaper *Szabad Nép* unarmed demonstrators were fired upon by ÁVH guards who were then driven out as armed demonstrators arrived. At this point, the revolutionaries' wrath focused on the ÁVH;[579] Soviet military units were not yet fully engaged, and there were reports of some Soviet troops showing open sympathy for the demonstrators.[580]

Figure 178: *March of protesters on 25 October*

On 25 October, a mass of protesters gathered in front of the Parliament Building. ÁVH units began shooting into the crowd from the rooftops of neighbouring buildings.[581] Some Soviet soldiers returned fire on the ÁVH, mistakenly believing that they were the targets of the shooting.[582] Supplied by arms taken from the ÁVH or given by Hungarian soldiers who joined the uprising, some in the crowd started shooting back.

During this time, the Hungarian Army was divided as the central command structure disintegrated with the rising pressures from the protests on the government. The majority of Hungarian military units in Budapest and the countryside remained uninvolved, as the local commanders generally avoided using force against the protesters and revolutionaries. From 24 to 29 October, however, there were 71 cases of armed clashes between the army and the populace in fifty communities, ranging from the defence of attacks on civilian and military objectives to fighting with insurgents depending on the commanding officer.

One example is in the town of Kecskemét on 26 October, where demonstrations in front of the office of State Security and the local jail led to military action by the Third Corps under the orders of Major General Lajos Gyurkó, in which seven protesters were shot and several of the organizers were arrested. In another case, a fighter jet strafed a protest in the town of Tiszakécske, killing 17 people and wounding 117.

The attacks at the Parliament forced the collapse of the government.[583] Communist First Secretary Ernő Gerő and former Prime Minister András Hegedüs

Figure 179: *Body of executed Party member at Central Committee of the Communist Party*

fled to the Soviet Union; Imre Nagy became Prime Minister and János Kádár First Secretary of the Communist Party.[584] Revolutionaries began an aggressive offensive against Soviet troops and the remnants of the ÁVH.

Units led by Béla Király, after attacking the building of the Central Committee of the Communist Party, executed dozens of suspected communists, state security members, and military personnel. Photographs showed victims with signs of torture. On 30 October, Király's forces attacked the Central Committee of the Communist Party building.[585] Hungarian politician János Berecz referred to how rebels detained thousands of people, and that thousands more had their names on death lists. In the city of Kaposvár, 64 persons including 13 army officers were detained on 31 October.[586]

In Budapest and other areas, the Hungarian Communist committees organised defence. At the Csepel neighbourhood of Budapest, some 250 Communists defended the Csepel Iron and Steel Works. On 27 October, army units were brought in to secure Csepel and restore order. They later withdrew on 29 October, after which the rebels seized control of the area. Communists of Budapest neighbourhood Angyalföld led more than 350 armed workers and 380 servicemen from the Láng Factory. Anti-fascist resistance veterans from World War II participated in the offensive by which the *Szabad Nép* newspaper's building was recaptured. In the countryside, defence measures were taken by pro-Communist forces. In Békés County, in and around the town of

Szarvas, the armed guards of the Communist Party were in control throughout.[587]

As the Hungarian resistance fought Soviet tanks using Molotov cocktails in the narrow streets of Budapest, revolutionary councils arose nationwide, assumed local governmental authority, and called for general strikes. Public Communist symbols such as red stars and Soviet war memorials were removed, and Communist books were burned. Spontaneous revolutionary militias arose, such as the 400-man group loosely led by József Dudás, which attacked or murdered Soviet sympathisers and ÁVH members.[588] Soviet units fought primarily in Budapest; elsewhere the countryside was largely quiet. One armoured division stationed in Budapest, commanded by Pál Maléter, instead opted to join the insurgents. Soviet commanders often negotiated local cease-fires with the revolutionaries.[589]

In some regions, Soviet forces managed to quell revolutionary activity. In Budapest, the Soviets were eventually fought to a stand-still and hostilities began to wane. Hungarian general Béla Király, freed from a life sentence for political offences and acting with the support of the Nagy government, sought to restore order by unifying elements of the police, army and insurgent groups into a National Guard.[590] A ceasefire was arranged on 28 October, and by 30 October most Soviet troops had withdrawn from Budapest to garrisons in the Hungarian countryside.[591]

Interlude

Fighting ceased between 28 October and 4 November, as many Hungarians believed that Soviet military units were withdrawing from Hungary.[592] There were approximately 213 Hungarian Working People's Party members lynched or executed during this period.[593]

New Government

The rapid spread of the uprising in the streets of Budapest and the abrupt fall of the Gerő-Hegedüs government left the new national leadership surprised, and at first disorganised. Nagy, a loyal party reformer described as possessing "only modest political skills", initially appealed to the public for calm and a return to the old order. Yet Nagy, the only remaining Hungarian leader with credibility in both the eyes of the public and the Soviets, "at long last concluded that a popular uprising rather than a counter-revolution was taking place". At 13:20 on 28 October, Nagy announced an immediate and general cease-fire over the radio and, on behalf of the new national government, declared the following:

Hungarian Revolution of 1956

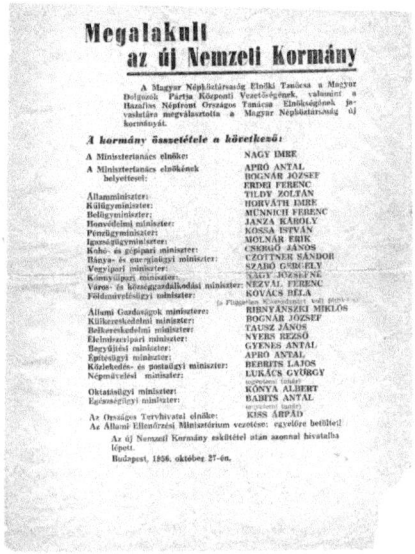

Figure 180: *Flyer. Imre Nagy, Head of government – 1956.10.27*

- that the government would assess the uprising not as counter-revolutionary but as a "great, national and democratic event"
- an unconditional general ceasefire and amnesty for those who participated in the uprising; negotiations with the insurgents
- the dissolution of the ÁVH
- the establishment of a national guard
- the immediate withdrawal of Soviet troops from Budapest and negotiations for the withdrawal of all Soviet forces from Hungary

On 1 November, in a radio address to the Hungarian people, Nagy formally declared Hungary's withdrawal from the Warsaw Pact as well as Hungary's stance of neutrality.[594] Because it held office only ten days, the National Government had little chance to clarify its policies in detail. However, newspaper editorials at the time stressed that Hungary should be a neutral, multi-party social democracy.[595] Many political prisoners were released, most notably Cardinal József Mindszenty.[596] Political parties that were previously banned, such as the Independent Smallholders and the National Peasant Party (under the name "Petőfi Party"),[597] reappeared to join the coalition.[598]

During this time, in 1,170 communities across Hungary there were 348 cases in which revolutionary councils and protesters dismissed employees of the local administrative councils, 312 cases in which they sacked the persons in charge,

Figure 181: *Crowd cheers Hungarian troops in Budapest*

and 215 cases in which they burned the local administrative files and records. In addition, in 681 communities demonstrators damaged symbols of Soviet authority such as red stars, Stalin or Lenin statues; 393 in which they damaged Soviet war memorials, and 122 communities in which book burnings took place.

Local revolutionary councils formed throughout Hungary,[599,600,601,602] generally without involvement from the preoccupied National Government in Budapest, and assumed various responsibilities of local government from the defunct Communist party.[603] By 30 October, these councils had been officially sanctioned by the Hungarian Working People's Party, and the Nagy government asked for their support as "autonomous, democratic local organs formed during the Revolution". Likewise, workers' councils were established at industrial plants and mines, and many unpopular regulations such as production norms were eliminated. The workers' councils strove to manage the enterprise while protecting workers' interests, thus establishing a socialist economy free of rigid party control.[604] Local control by the councils was not always bloodless; in Debrecen, Győr, Sopron, Mosonmagyaróvár and other cities, crowds of demonstrators were fired upon by the ÁVH, with many lives lost. The ÁVH were disarmed, often by force, in many cases assisted by the local police.

In total there were approximately 2,100 local revolutionary and workers councils with over 28,000 members. These councils held a combined conference in Budapest, deciding to end the nationwide labour strikes and resume work on 5 November, with the more important councils sending delegates to the Parliament to assure the Nagy government of their support.

Soviet perspective

On 24 October, the Presidium of the Central Committee of the Communist Party of the Soviet Union (the Politburo) discussed the political upheavals in Poland and Hungary. A hard-line faction led by Molotov was pushing for intervention, but Khrushchev and Marshal Zhukov were initially opposed. A delegation in Budapest reported that the situation was not as dire as had been portrayed. Khrushchev stated that he believed that Party Secretary Ernő Gerő's request for intervention on 23 October indicated that the Hungarian Party still held the confidence of the Hungarian public. In addition, he saw the protests not as an ideological struggle, but as popular discontent over unresolved basic economic and social issues. The concurrent Suez Crisis was another reason to not intervene; as Khrushchev said on 28 October, it would be a mistake to imitate the "real mess" of the French and British.

After some debate,[605] the Presidium on 30 October decided not to remove the new Hungarian government. Even Marshal Georgy Zhukov said: "We should withdraw troops from Budapest, and if necessary withdraw from Hungary as a whole. This is a lesson for us in the military-political sphere." They adopted a *Declaration of the Government of the USSR on the Principles of Development and Further Strengthening of Friendship and Cooperation between the Soviet Union and other Socialist States*, which was issued the next day. This document proclaimed: "The Soviet Government is prepared to enter into the appropriate negotiations with the government of the Hungarian People's Republic and other members of the Warsaw Treaty on the question of the presence of Soviet troops on the territory of Hungary."[606] Thus for a brief moment it looked like there could be a peaceful solution.

On 30 October, armed protesters attacked the ÁVH detachment guarding the Budapest Hungarian Working People's Party headquarters on Köztársaság tér (Republic Square), incited by rumours of prisoners held there and the earlier shootings of demonstrators by the ÁVH in the city of Mosonmagyaróvár.[607,608] Over 20 ÁVH officers were killed, some of them lynched by the mob. Hungarian army tanks sent to rescue the party headquarters mistakenly bombarded the building. The head of the Budapest party committee, Imre Mező, was wounded and later died. Scenes from Republic Square were shown on Soviet newsreels a few hours later.[609] Revolutionary leaders in Hungary condemned the incident and appealed for calm, and the mob violence soon died down, but images of the victims were nevertheless used as propaganda by various Communist organs.

Figure 182: *Damaged Party headquarters on Köztársaság tér*

On 31 October the Soviet leaders decided to reverse their decision from the previous day. There is disagreement among historians whether Hungary's declaration to exit the Warsaw Pact caused the second Soviet intervention. Minutes of 31 October meeting of the Presidium record that the decision to intervene militarily was taken one day before Hungary declared its neutrality and withdrawal from the Warsaw Pact. Historians who deny that Hungarian neutrality—or other factors such as Western inaction in Hungary or perceived Western weakness due to the Suez crisis—caused the intervention state that the Soviet decision was based solely on the rapid loss of Communist control in Hungary. However, some Russian historians who are not advocates of the Communist era maintain that the Hungarian declaration of neutrality caused the Kremlin to intervene a second time.[610]

Two days earlier, on 30 October, when Soviet Politburo representatives Anastas Mikoyan and Mikhail Suslov were in Budapest, Nagy had hinted that neutrality was a long-term objective for Hungary, and that he was hoping to discuss this matter with the leaders in the Kremlin. This information was passed on to Moscow by Mikoyan and Suslov.[611,612] At that time, Khrushchev was in Stalin's dacha, considering his options regarding Hungary. One of his speech writers later said that the declaration of neutrality was an important factor in his subsequent decision to support intervention.[613] In addition, some Hungarian leaders of the revolution as well as students had called for their country's withdrawal from the Warsaw Pact much earlier, and this may have influenced Soviet decision making.[614]

Several other key events alarmed the Presidium and cemented the interventionists' position:[615]

- Simultaneous movements towards multi-party parliamentary democracy, and a democratic national council of workers, which could "lead towards a capitalist state." Both movements challenged the pre-eminence of the Soviet Communist Party in Eastern Europe and perhaps Soviet hegemony itself. Hannah Arendt considered the councils "the only free and acting soviets (councils) in existence anywhere in the world".
- Khrushchev stated that many in the Communist Party would not understand a failure to respond with force in Hungary. Destalinisation had alienated the more conservative elements of the Party, who were alarmed at threats to Soviet influence in Eastern Europe. On 17 June 1953, workers in East Berlin had staged an uprising, demanding the resignation of the government of the German Democratic Republic. This was quickly and violently put down with the help of the Soviet military, with 84 killed and wounded and 700 arrested.[616] In June 1956, in Poznań, Poland, an anti-government workers' revolt had been suppressed by the Polish security forces with between 57[617] and 78[618,619] deaths and led to the installation of a less Soviet-controlled government. Additionally, by late October, unrest was noticed in some regional areas of the Soviet Union: while this unrest was minor, it was intolerable.
- Hungarian neutrality and withdrawal from the Warsaw Pact represented a breach in the Soviet defensive buffer zone of satellite nations. Soviet fear of invasion from the West made a defensive buffer of allied states in Eastern Europe an essential security objective.

In the light of what was taking place in China and the news from Budapest, these militants arrived at the conclusion that "the Party is the incarnation of bureaucratic despotism" and that "socialism can develop only on the foundations of direct democracy". For them the struggle of the Hungarian workers was a struggle "for the principle of direct democracy" and "all power should be transferred to the Workers Committees of Hungary". The Presidium decided to break the *de facto* ceasefire and crush the Hungarian revolution. The plan was to declare a "Provisional Revolutionary Government" under János Kádár, who would appeal for Soviet assistance to restore order. According to witnesses, Kádár was in Moscow in early November,[620] and he was in contact with the Soviet embassy while still a member of the Nagy government.[621] Delegations were sent to other Communist governments in Eastern Europe and China, seeking to avoid a regional conflict, and propaganda messages prepared for broadcast when the second Soviet intervention had begun. To disguise these intentions, Soviet diplomats were to engage the Nagy government in talks discussing the withdrawal of Soviet forces.

Figure 183: *Soviet T-54 tanks in Budapest on 31 October*

According to some sources, the Chinese leader Mao Zedong played an important role in Khrushchev's decision to suppress the Hungarian uprising. Chinese Communist Party Deputy Chairman Liu Shaoqi pressured Khrushchev to send in troops to put down the revolt by force.[622,623] Although the relations between China and the Soviet Union had deteriorated during the recent years, Mao's words still carried great weight in the Kremlin, and they were frequently in contact during the crisis. Initially, Mao opposed a second intervention, and this information was passed on to Khrushchev on 30 October, before the Presidium met and decided against intervention.[624] Mao then changed his mind in favour of intervention but, according to William Taubman, it remains unclear when and how Khrushchev learned of this and thus if it influenced his decision on 31 October.[625]

From 1 to 3 November, Khrushchev left Moscow to meet with his European allies and inform them of the decision to intervene. At the first such meeting, he met with Władysław Gomułka in Brest. Then, he had talks with the Romanian, Czechoslovak, and Bulgarian leaders in Bucharest. Finally Khrushchev flew with Malenkov to Yugoslavia, where they met with Josip Broz Tito, who was on holiday on his island Brioni in the Adriatic. The Yugoslavs also persuaded Khrushchev to choose János Kádár instead of Ferenc Münnich as the new leader of Hungary.[626,627] Two months after the Soviet crackdown, Tito confided in Nikolai Firiubin, the Soviet ambassador to Yugoslavia, that "the reaction raised its head, especially in Croatia, where the reactionary elements openly incited the employees of the Yugoslav security organs to violence."[628]

International reaction

Although John Foster Dulles, the United States Secretary of State recommended on 24 October for the United Nations Security Council to convene to discuss the situation in Hungary, little immediate action was taken to introduce a resolution, in part because other world events unfolded the day after the peaceful interlude started, when allied collusion started the Suez Crisis. The problem was not that Suez distracted US attention from Hungary but that it made the condemnation of Soviet actions very difficult. As Vice President Richard Nixon later explained, "We couldn't on one hand, complain about the Soviets intervening in Hungary and, on the other hand, approve of the British and the French picking that particular time to intervene against [Gamel Abdel] Nasser".

The US response was reliant on the CIA to covertly effect change, with both covert agents and Radio Free Europe. However, their Hungarian operations collapsed rapidly and they could not locate any of the weapon caches hidden across Europe, nor be sure who they'd send arms too. The agency's main source of information were the newspapers and a State Department employee in Budapest called Geza Katona. By 28 October, on the same night that the new Nagy government came to power, RFE was ramping up its broadcasts—encouraging armed struggle, advising on how to combat tanks and signing off with "Freedom or Death!"—on the orders of Frank Wisner. When Nagy did come to power, CIA director Allen Dulles advised the White House that Cardinal Mindszenty would be a better leader (due to Nagy's communist past); he had CIA radio broadcasts run propaganda against Nagy, calling him a traitor who'd invited Soviet troops in. Broadcasts continued to broadcast armed response while the CIA mistakenly believed that the Hungarian army was switching sides and the rebels were gaining arms.[629] (Wisner was recorded as having a "nervous breakdown" by William Colby as the uprising was crushed[630])

Responding to the plea by Nagy at the time of the second massive Soviet intervention on 4 November, the Security Council resolution critical of Soviet actions was vetoed by the Soviet Union; instead resolution 120 was adopted to pass the matter onto the General Assembly. The General Assembly, by a vote of 50 in favour, 8 against and 15 abstentions, called on the Soviet Union to end its Hungarian intervention, but the newly constituted Kádár government rejected UN observers.[631]

US President Dwight D. Eisenhower was aware of a detailed study of Hungarian resistance that recommended against US military intervention, and of

Figure 184: *March to support Hungary in Eindhoven, the Netherlands, 5 November 1956*

earlier policy discussions within the National Security Council that focused upon encouraging discontent in Soviet satellite nations only by economic policies and political rhetoric. In a 1998 interview, Hungarian Ambassador Géza Jeszenszky was critical of Western inaction in 1956, citing the influence of the United Nations at that time and giving the example of UN intervention in Korea from 1950 to 1953.[632]

However, a Department of Defense study recently declassified by the National Security Archive suggests that one of the main reasons the United States did not intervene was the risk of inadvertently starting a nuclear war with the Soviet Union. These concerns made the Eisenhower Administration take a more cautious approach to the situation.

During the uprising, the Radio Free Europe (RFE) Hungarian-language programs broadcast news of the political and military situation, as well as appealing to Hungarians to fight the Soviet forces, including tactical advice on resistance methods. After the Soviet suppression of the revolution, RFE was criticised for having misled the Hungarian people that NATO or United Nations would intervene if citizens continued to resist. Allen Dulles lied to Eisenhower that RFE had not promised US aid; Eisenhower believed him, as the transcripts of the broadcasts were kept secret.

Figure 185: *1 November newsreel about the situation in Hungary*

Soviet intervention of 4 November

On 1 November, Imre Nagy received reports that Soviet forces had entered Hungary from the east and were moving towards Budapest.[633] Nagy sought and received assurances (which proved false) from Soviet ambassador Yuri Andropov that the Soviet Union would not invade. The Cabinet, with János Kádár in agreement, declared Hungary's neutrality, withdrew from the Warsaw Pact, and requested assistance from the diplomatic corps in Budapest and the UN Secretary-General to defend Hungary's neutrality.[634] Ambassador Andropov was asked to inform his government that Hungary would begin negotiations on the removal of Soviet forces immediately.

On 3 November, a Hungarian delegation led by the Minister of Defense Pál Maléter were invited to attend negotiations on Soviet withdrawal at the Soviet Military Command at Tököl, near Budapest. At around midnight that evening, General Ivan Serov, Chief of the Soviet Security Police (KGB) ordered the arrest of the Hungarian delegation,[635] and the next day, the Soviet army again attacked Budapest.[636]

During the early morning hours of 4 November, Ferenc Münnich announced on Radio Szolnok the establishment of the "Revolutionary Workers'-Peasants' Government of Hungary".

Figure 186: *A Soviet built armored car burns on a street in Budapest in November*

The second Soviet intervention, codenamed "Operation Whirlwind", was launched by Marshal Ivan Konev.[637] The five Soviet divisions stationed in Hungary before 23 October were augmented to a total strength of 17 divisions. The 8th Mechanized Army under command of Lieutenant General Hamazasp Babadzhanian and the 38th Army under Lieutenant General Hadzhi-Umar Mamsurovs from the nearby Carpathian Military District were deployed to Hungary for the operation. Some rank-and-file Soviet soldiers reportedly believed they were being sent to Berlin to fight German fascists. By 21:30 on 3 November, the Soviet Army had completely encircled Budapest.[638]

At 03:00 on 4 November, Soviet tanks penetrated Budapest along the Pest side of the Danube in two thrusts: one up the Soroksári road from the south and the other down the Váci road from the north. Thus before a single shot was fired, the Soviets had effectively split the city in half, controlled all bridgeheads, and were shielded to the rear by the wide Danube river. Armoured units crossed into Buda and at 04:25 fired the first shots at the army barracks on Budaörsi Road. Soon after, Soviet artillery and tank fire was heard in all districts of Budapest. Operation Whirlwind combined air strikes, artillery, and the coordinated tank-infantry action of 17 divisions.

Between 4 and 9 November, the Hungarian Army put up sporadic and disorganised resistance, with Marshal Zhukov reporting the disarming of twelve divisions, two armoured regiments, and the entire Hungarian Air Force. The Hungarian Army continued its most formidable resistance in various districts

Figure 187: *Two Soviet ISU-152 assault guns positioned in a street in Budapest 8th District. An abandoned T-34/85 stands behind them*

of Budapest and in and around the city of Pécs in the Mecsek Mountains, and in the industrial centre of Dunaújváros (then called Stalintown). Fighting in Budapest consisted of between ten and fifteen thousand resistance fighters, with the heaviest fighting occurring in the working-class stronghold of Csepel on the Danube River. Although some very senior officers were openly pro-Soviet, the rank and file soldiers were overwhelmingly loyal to the revolution and either fought against the invasion or deserted. The United Nations reported that there were no recorded incidents of Hungarian Army units fighting on the side of the Soviets.[639]

At 05:20 on 4 November, Imre Nagy broadcast his final plea to the nation and the world, announcing that Soviet Forces were attacking Budapest and that the Government remained at its post.[640] The radio station, Free Kossuth Rádió, stopped broadcasting at 08:07.[641] An emergency Cabinet meeting was held in the Parliament but was attended by only three ministers. As Soviet troops arrived to occupy the building, a negotiated evacuation ensued, leaving Minister of State István Bibó as the last representative of the National Government remaining at his post. He wrote For Freedom and Truth, a stirring proclamation to the nation and the world.

At 06:00, on 4 November,[642] in the town of Szolnok, János Kádár proclaimed the "Hungarian Revolutionary Worker-Peasant Government". His statement

Figure 188: *Ruszkik haza! (Russians go home!) slogan in Budapest*

declared "We must put an end to the excesses of the counter-revolutionary elements. The hour for action has sounded. We are going to defend the interest of the workers and peasants and the achievements of the people's democracy."[643] Later that evening, Kádár called upon "the faithful fighters of the true cause of socialism" to come out of hiding and take up arms. However, Hungarian support did not materialise; the fighting did not take on the character of an internally divisive civil war, but rather, in the words of a United Nations report, that of "a well-equipped foreign army crushing by overwhelming force a national movement and eliminating the Government."[644]

By 08:00 organised defence of the city evaporated after the radio station was seized, and many defenders fell back to fortified positions.[645] During the same hour, the parliamentary guard laid down their arms, and forces under Major General K. Grebennik captured Parliament and liberated captured ministers of the Rákosi-Hegedüs government. Among the liberated were István Dobi and Sándor Rónai, both of whom became members of the re-established socialist Hungarian government. As they came under attack even in civilian quarters, Soviet troops were unable to differentiate military from civilian targets.[646] For this reason, Soviet tanks often crept along main roads firing indiscriminately into buildings. Hungarian resistance was strongest in the industrial areas of Budapest, with Csepel heavily targeted by Soviet artillery and air strikes.[647]

The longest holdouts against the Soviet assault occurred in Csepel and in Dunaújváros, where fighting lasted until 11 November before the insurgents

Figure 189: *Rubble after end of fighting in Budapest 8th District*

finally succumbed to the Soviets. At the end of the fighting, Hungarian casualties totalled at around 2,500 dead with an additional 20,000 wounded. Budapest bore the brunt of the bloodshed, with 1,569 civilians killed. Approximately 53 percent of the dead were workers, and about half of all the casualties were people younger than thirty. On the Soviet side, 699 men were killed, 1,450 men were wounded, and 51 men were missing in action. Estimates place around 80 percent of all casualties occurring in fighting with the insurgents in the eighth and ninth districts of Budapest.[648,649]

Soviet version of the events

Soviet reports of the events surrounding, during, and after the disturbance were remarkably consistent in their accounts, more so after the Second Soviet intervention cemented support for the Soviet position among international Communist Parties. Pravda published an account 36 hours after the outbreak of violence, which set the tone for all further reports and subsequent Soviet historiography:

1. On 23 October, the honest socialist Hungarians demonstrated against mistakes made by the Rákosi and Gerő governments.
2. Fascist, Hitlerite, reactionary, counter-revolutionary hooligans financed by the imperialist West took advantage of the unrest to stage a counter-revolution.

3. The honest Hungarian people under Nagy appealed to Soviet (Warsaw Pact) forces stationed in Hungary to assist in restoring order.
4. The Nagy government was ineffective, allowing itself to be penetrated by counter-revolutionary influences, weakening then disintegrating, as proven by Nagy's culminating denouncement of the Warsaw Pact.
5. Hungarian patriots under Kádár broke with the Nagy government and formed a government of honest Hungarian revolutionary workers and peasants; this genuinely popular government petitioned the Soviet command to help put down the counter-revolution.
6. Hungarian patriots, with Soviet assistance, smashed the counter-revolution.

The first Soviet report came out 24 hours after the first Western report. Nagy's appeal to the United Nations was not reported. After Nagy was arrested outside the Yugoslav embassy, his arrest was not reported. Nor did accounts explain how Nagy went from patriot to traitor.[650] The Soviet press reported calm in Budapest while the Western press reported a revolutionary crisis was breaking out. According to the Soviet account, Hungarians never wanted a revolution at all.[651]

In January 1957, representatives of the Soviet Union, Bulgaria, Hungary, and Romania met in Budapest to review internal developments in Hungary since the establishment of the Soviet-imposed government. A communiqué on the meeting "unanimously concluded" that Hungarian workers, with the leadership of the Kádár government and support of the Soviet army, defeated attempts "to eliminate the socialist achievements of the Hungarian people".[652]

Soviet, Chinese, and other Warsaw Pact governments urged Kádár to proceed with interrogation and trial of former Nagy government ministers, and asked for punitive measures against the "counter-revolutionists".[653] In addition the Kádár government published an extensive series of "white books" (*The Counter-Revolutionary Forces in the October Events in Hungary*) documenting real incidents of violence against Communist Party and ÁVH members, and the confessions of Nagy supporters. These white books were widely distributed in several languages in most of the socialist countries and, while based in fact, present factual evidence with a colouring and narrative not generally supported by non-Soviet aligned historians.[654]

Aftermath

Hungary

In the immediate aftermath, many thousands of Hungarians were arrested. Eventually, 26,000 of these were brought before the Hungarian courts, 22,000 were sentenced and imprisoned, 13,000 interned, and 229 executed. Hundreds were also deported to the Soviet Union, many without evidence.Wikipedia:Citation needed Approximately 200,000[655] fled Hungary as refugees. Former Hungarian Foreign Minister Géza Jeszenszky estimated 350 were executed. Sporadic resistance and strikes by workers' councils continued until mid-1957, causing economic disruption. By 1963, most political prisoners from the 1956 Hungarian revolution had been released.[656]

With most of Budapest under Soviet control by 8 November, Kádár became Prime Minister of the "Revolutionary Worker-Peasant Government" and General Secretary of the Hungarian Communist Party. Few Hungarians rejoined the reorganised Party, its leadership having been purged under the supervision of the Soviet Praesidium, led by Georgy Malenkov and Mikhail Suslov. Although Party membership declined from 800,000 before the uprising to 100,000 by December 1956, Kádár steadily increased his control over Hungary and neutralised dissenters. The new government attempted to enlist support by espousing popular principles of Hungarian self-determination voiced during the uprising, but Soviet troops remained.[657] After 1956 the Soviet Union severely purged the Hungarian Army and reinstituted political indoctrination in the units that remained. In May 1957, the Soviet Union increased its troop levels in Hungary and by treaty Hungary accepted the Soviet presence on a permanent basis.[658]

The Red Cross and the Austrian Army established refugee camps in Traiskirchen and Graz.[659] Imre Nagy along with Georg Lukács, Géza Losonczy, and László Rajk's widow, Júlia, took refuge in the Embassy of Yugoslavia as Soviet forces overran Budapest. Despite assurances of safe passage out of Hungary by the Soviets and the Kádár government, Nagy and his group were arrested when attempting to leave the embassy on 22 November and taken to Romania. Losonczy died while on a hunger strike in prison awaiting trial when his jailers "carelessly pushed a feeding tube down his windpipe."[660]

The remainder of the group was returned to Budapest in 1958. Nagy was executed, along with Pál Maléter and Miklós Gimes, after secret trials in June 1958. Their bodies were placed in unmarked graves in the Municipal Cemetery outside Budapest.[661]

During the November 1956 Soviet assault on Budapest, Cardinal Mindszenty was granted political asylum at the United States embassy, where he lived for

Figure 190: *Eleanor Roosevelt meets exiled Hungarian revolutionaries at Camp Roeder in Salzburg, 10 May 1957*

the next 15 years, refusing to leave Hungary unless the government reversed his 1949 conviction for treason. Because of poor health and a request from the Vatican, he finally left the embassy for Austria in September 1971.

International

Despite Cold War rhetoric by western countries espousing a roll-back of the domination of Europe by the USSR and Soviet promises of the imminent triumph of socialism, national leaders of this period as well as later historians saw the failure of the uprising in Hungary as evidence that the Cold War in Europe had become a stalemate.[662]

The Foreign Minister of West Germany recommended that the people of Eastern Europe be discouraged from "taking dramatic action which might have disastrous consequences for themselves." The Secretary-General of NATO called the Hungarian revolt "the collective suicide of a whole people". In a newspaper interview in 1957, Khrushchev commented "support by United States ... is rather in the nature of the support that the rope gives to a hanged man."

In January 1957, United Nations Secretary-General Dag Hammarskjöld, acting in response to UN General Assembly resolutions requesting investigation and observation of the events in Soviet-occupied Hungary, established the Special Committee on the Problem of Hungary. The Committee, with representatives from Australia, Ceylon (Sri Lanka), Denmark, Tunisia, and Uruguay, conducted hearings in New York, Geneva, Rome, Vienna, and London. Over five months, 111 refugees were interviewed including ministers, military commanders and other officials of the Nagy government, workers, revolutionary council members, factory managers and technicians, Communists and non-Communists, students, writers, teachers, medical personnel, and Hungarian soldiers. Documents, newspapers, radio transcripts, photos, film footage, and other records from Hungary were also reviewed, as well as written testimony of 200 other Hungarians.[663]

The governments of Hungary and Romania refused the UN officials of the Committee entry, and the government of the Soviet Union did not respond to requests for information.[664] The 268-page Committee Report[665] was presented to the General Assembly in June 1957, documenting the course of the uprising and Soviet intervention, and concluding that "the Kádár government and Soviet occupation were in violation of the human rights of the Hungarian people."[666] A General Assembly resolution was approved, deploring "the repression of the Hungarian people and the Soviet occupation" but no other action was taken.[667] The chairman of the Committee was Alsing Andersen, a Danish politician and leading figure of Denmark's Social Democratic Party. He served in the Buhl government in 1942 during the Nazi German occupation of Denmark. He defended collaboration with the occupation forces and denounced the Resistance. He was appointed Interior Minister in 1947, but resigned because of scrutiny of his role in 1940 as Defence Minister. He then entered Denmark's UN delegation in 1948.[668,669]

The Committee Report and the motives of its authors were criticised by delegations to the United Nations. The Hungarian representative disagreed with the report's conclusions, accusing it of falsifying the events, and argued that the establishment of the Committee was illegal. The Committee was accused of being hostile to Hungary and its social system.[670] An article in the Russian journal "International Affairs", published by the Foreign Affairs Ministry, carried an article in 1957 in which it denounced the report as a "collection of falsehoods and distortions".[671]

Time magazine named the Hungarian Freedom Fighter its Man of the Year for 1956. The accompanying *Time* article comments that this choice could not have been anticipated until the explosive events of the revolution, almost at the end of 1956. The magazine cover and accompanying text displayed an artist's depiction of a Hungarian freedom fighter, and used pseudonyms for the three participants whose stories are the subject of the article.[672]

In 2006, Hungarian Prime Minister Ferenc Gyurcsány referred to this famous *Time* Man of the Year cover as "the faces of free Hungary" in a speech to mark the 50th anniversary of the 1956 uprising.[673] Prime Minister Gyurcsány, in a joint appearance with British Prime Minister Tony Blair, commented specifically on the Time cover itself, that "It is an idealised image but the faces of the figures are really the face of the revolutionaries"[674]

At the Melbourne Olympics in 1956, the Soviet handling of the Hungarian uprising led to a boycott by Spain, the Netherlands, and Switzerland.[675] At the Olympic Village, the Hungarian delegation tore down the Communist Hungarian flag and raised the flag of Free Hungary in its place. A confrontation between Soviet and Hungarian teams occurred in the semi-final match of the water polo tournament on 6 December. The match was extremely violent, and was halted in the final minute to quell fighting among spectators. This match, now known as the "blood in the water match", became the subject of several films.[676,677] The Hungarian team won the game 4–0 and later was awarded the Olympic gold medal. Norway declined an invitation to the inaugural Bandy World Championship in 1957, citing the presence of a team from the Soviet Union as the reason.

On Sunday, 28 October 1956, as some 55 million Americans watched Ed Sullivan's popular television variety show, with the then 21-year-old Elvis Presley headlining for the second time, Sullivan asked viewers to send aid to Hungarian refugees fleeing from the effects of the Soviet invasion. Presley himself made another request for donations during his third and last appearance on Sullivan's show on 6 January 1957. Presley then dedicated a song for the finale, which he thought fit the mood of the time, namely the gospel song "Peace in the Valley". By the end of 1957, these contributions, distributed by the Geneva-based International Red Cross as food rations, clothing, and other essentials, had amounted to some SFR 26 million (US$6 million in 1957 dollars), the equivalent of $51,200,000 in today's dollars.[678] On 1 March 2011, István Tarlós, the Mayor of Budapest, made Presley an honorary citizen, posthumously, and a plaza located at the intersection of two of the city's most important avenues was named after Presley, as a gesture of gratitude.

Meanwhile, as the 1950s drew to a close the events in Hungary produced fractures within the Communist political parties of Western European countries. The Italian Communist Party (PCI) suffered a split. According to the official newspaper of the PCI, *l'Unità*, most ordinary members and the Party leadership, including Palmiro Togliatti and Giorgio Napolitano, supported the actions of the Soviet Union in suppressing the uprising.[679] However Giuseppe Di Vittorio, chief of the Communist trade union CGIL, spoke out against the leadership's position, as did prominent party members Antonio Giolitti, Loris Fortuna, and many others influential in the Communist party. Pietro Nenni of

Figure 191: *2016 Hungarian stamp dedicated to the 60th anniversary of the 1956 Revolution, featuring Erika Kornélia Szeles (1941–1956) in the center*

the Italian Socialist Party, a close ally of the PCI, opposed the Soviet intervention as well. Napolitano, elected in 2006 as President of the Italian Republic, wrote in his 2005 political autobiography that he regretted his justification of Soviet action in Hungary, stating at the time he believed Party unity and the leadership of Soviet communism was more important.

The Communist Party of Great Britain, (CPGB), suffered the loss of thousands of party members following the events in Hungary. Though Peter Fryer, correspondent for the CPGB newspaper *The Daily Worker*, reported on the violent suppression of the uprising, his dispatches were heavily censored by the party leadership. Upon his return from Hungary Fryer resigned from the paper. He was later expelled by the Communist Party.

In France, moderate Communists, such as historian Emmanuel Le Roy Ladurie, resigned, questioning the French Communist Party's policy of supporting Soviet actions. The French philosopher and writer Albert Camus wrote an open letter, *The Blood of the Hungarians*, criticising the West's lack of action. Even Jean-Paul Sartre, still a determined Communist, criticised the Soviets in his article *Le Fantôme de Staline*, in *Situations VII*.[680] Left Communists were particularly supportive of the revolution.

Figure 192: *Memorial plaque at the Embassy of Serbia, Budapest in memory of Imre Nagy who took sanctuary there during the Hungarian Revolution of 1956*

Commemoration

In December 1991, the preamble of the treaties with the dismembered Soviet Union, under Mikhail Gorbachev, and Russia, represented by Boris Yeltsin, apologised officially for the 1956 Soviet actions in Hungary. This apology was repeated by Yeltsin in 1992 during a speech to the Hungarian parliament.

On 13 February 2006, the US State Department commemorated the fiftieth anniversary of the 1956 Hungarian Revolution. US Secretary of State Condoleezza Rice commented on the contributions made by 1956 Hungarian refugees to the United States and other host countries, as well as the role of Hungary in providing refuge to East Germans during the 1989 protests against Communist rule. US President George W. Bush also visited Hungary on 22 June 2006, to commemorate the fiftieth anniversary.

On 16 June 1989, the 31st anniversary of his execution, Imre Nagy's body was reburied with full honours. The Republic of Hungary was declared in 1989 on the 33rd anniversary of the Revolution, and 23 October is now a Hungarian national holiday.

In the north-west corner of MacArthur Park in Los Angeles, California, the Hungarian-American community built a commemorative statue to honour the Hungarian freedom fighters. Built in the late 1960s, the obelisk statue stands with an American eagle watching over the city of Los Angeles.

There are several monuments dedicated to the Commemoration of the Hungarian Revolution throughout the United States. One such monument may be found here in Cleveland, Ohio at the Cardinal Mindszenty Plaza.

Further reading

- Arendt, Hannah (1951). *Origins of Totalitarianism*. New York: Harcourt. pp. 480–510. ISBN 0-15-670153-7.
- Bekes, Csaba; Byrne, Malcolm; Rainer, Janos (Editor), eds. (2003). *The 1956 Hungarian Revolution: A History in Documents (National Security Archive Cold War Readers)*. Central European University Press. p. 600. ISBN 963-9241-66-0.
- Bibó, István (1991). *Democracy, Revolution, Self-Determination*. New York: Columbia University Press. pp. 331–54. ISBN 0-88033-214-X.
- Gadney, Reg (October 1986). *Cry Hungary: Uprising 1956*. Macmillan Pub Co. pp. 169 pages. ISBN 0-689-11838-4.
- Gati, Charles (2006). *Failed Illusions: Moscow, Washington, Budapest, and the 1956 Hungarian Revolt (Cold War International History Project Series)*. Stanford University Press. p. 264. ISBN 0-8047-5606-6.
- Granville, Johanna (2004). *The First Domino: International Decision Making during the Hungarian Crisis of 1956*. Texas A&M University Press. p. 323. ISBN 1-58544-298-4.
- Granville, Johanna (1999) In the Line of Fire: New Archival Evidence on the Soviet Intervention in Hungary, 1956[681], *Carl Beck Paper*, no. 1307 (1999).
- Györkei, Jenő; Kirov, Alexandr; Horvath, Miklos (1999). *Soviet Military Intervention in Hungary, 1956*. New York: Central European University Press. p. 350. ISBN 963-9116-36-X.
- Kertesz, Stephen D. (1953). *Diplomacy in a Whirlpool: Hungary between Nazi Germany and Soviet Russia*[682]. University of Notre Dame Press, Notre Dame, Indiana. ISBN 0-8371-7540-2. Archived from the original[683] on 3 September 2007.
- Korda, Michael. *Journey to a Revolution: A Personal Memoir and History of the Hungarian Revolution of 1956*. Harper Perrenial (2006). ISBN 978-0-06-077262-8
- Michener, James A. (1985). *The Bridge at Andau* (reissue ed.). New York: Fawcett. ISBN 0-449-21050-2.
- Morris, William E. (August 2001). Lettis, Richard, ed. *The Hungarian Revolt: 23 October–4 November 1956* (Reprint ed.). Simon Publications. ISBN 1-931313-79-2.
- Napolitano, Giorgio (2005). *Dal Pci al socialismo europeo. Un'autobiografia politica (From the Communist Party to European*

Socialism. A political autobiography) (in Italian). Laterza. ISBN 88-420-7715-1.
- Péter, László (2008). *Resistance, Rebellion and Revolution in Hungary and Central Europe: Commemorating 1956.* London: UCL SSEES. p. 361. ISBN 978-0-903425-79-7.
- Schmidl, Erwin A. & Ritter, László. (2006) *The Hungarian Revolution, 1956*; Osprey Elite series #148. ISBN 1-84603-079-X ISBN 978-1-84603-079-6
- Sebestyen, Victor (2006). *Twelve Days: The Story of the 1956 Hungarian Revolution.* New York: Pantheon. p. 340. ISBN 0-375-42458-X.
- Sugar, Peter F. (1994). Hanak, Peter, Frank, Tibor, eds. *A History of Hungary: From Liberation to Revolution (pp. 368–83).* Bloomington: Indiana University Press. p. 448. ISBN 0-253-20867-X.
- United Nations: *Report of the Special Committee on the Problem of Hungary*, General Assembly, Official Records, Eleventh Session, Supplement No. 18 (A/3592), New York, 1957 "(268 pages)"[684] (PDF). (1.47 MB)
- Ürményházi, Attila J.(2006) "The Hungarian Revolution-Uprising, Budapest 1956"[685], National Library of Australia ISBN 0-646-45885-X, Record Id: 40312920
- Zinner, Paul E. (1962). *Revolution in Hungary.* Books for Libraries Press. p. 380. ISBN 0-8369-6817-4.
- Lendvai, Paul (2008). *One Day That Shook the Communist World: The 1956 Hungarian Uprising and Its Legacy.* Princeton UP. p. 254. ISBN 978-0-691-13282-2.
- Litván, György (1996). *The Hungarian Revolution of 1956: Reform, Revolt and Repression, 1953–1963.* Longman. p. 221. ISBN 0-582-21505-6.
- Cox, Terry. Hungary 1956 – forty Years on. London: F. Cass, 1997. Print.
- Matthews, John P. C. Explosion: The Hungarian Revolution of 1956. New York, NY: Hippocrene, 2007. Print.
- Watry, David M. *Diplomacy at the Brink: Eisenhower, Churchill, and Eden in the Cold War.* Baton Rouge: Louisiana State University Press, 2014.

External links

 Wikimedia Commons has media related to *Hungarian Revolution of 1956*.

Historical collections

- 1956 Hungarian Revolution Collection[686] of the Woodrow Wilson International Center for Scholars, Cold War International History Project, containing documents and other source materials relating to the 1956 Revolution.
- Institute of Revolutionary History, Hungary[687] A Hungarian language site providing historical photos and documents, books and reviews, and links to English language sites.
- OSA Digital Archive[688] Videos of the 1956 Hungarian Revolution
- Universal Pictures and Warner Pathé newsreels regarding the revolution[689]
- "On this day 4 November 1956: Soviet troops overrun Hungary"[690] (Accessed 12 October 2006) – BBC reports on the first day of the second Soviet intervention and the fall of the Nagy government.
- Hungary '56[691] Andy Anderson's pamphlet, written in 1964 and originally published by Solidarity (UK), about events of the Hungarian uprising of 1956, focusing on Hungarian demands for economic and political self-management. (AK Press 2002, ISBN 0-934868-01-8)
- The short film *Big Picture: Operation Mercy*[692] is available for free download at the Internet Archive
- The short film *Hungarian Revolution Aftermath (1956)*[693] is available for free download at the Internet Archive
- The short film *Hungarian Revolution (1956)*[694] is available for free download at the Internet Archive

Other academic sources

- The 1956 Hungarian revolution and the Soviet bloc countries: reactions and repercussions[695] (MEK)
- Hungary, 1956: Reviving the Debate over U.S. (In)action during the Revolution[696], published by the National Security Archive

Feature films

- *Freedom's Fury*[697] The 2005 documentary film depicting events surrounding the Hungarian-Soviet confrontation in the Olympic water polo tournament, now known as the "blood in the water match". Narrated by Mark Spitz, produced by Lucy Liu and Quentin Tarantino.

- *Torn from the flag*[698] Documentary film 2007. The significant global effects of the Hungarian revolution of 1956.

Commemorations

- The 1956 Portal[699] A resource for Hungarian-American organizations to highlight and promote their 1956 Hungarian Revolution commemoration activities, including 1956 photos, videos, resources, and events across the US.
- Freedom Fighter 56[700] Personal stories of survival and escape from participants in the revolution
- 1956 Hungarian Memorial Oral History Project[701] Multicultural Canada oral history collection of revolution refugees in Canada
- From the noon bell to the lads of Pest[702]

<indicator name="featured-star"> ⭐ </indicator>

Timeline

Timeline of Budapest

The following is a timeline of the history of the city of Budapest, Hungary.

Prior to 19th century

See also: Pest, Buda and Óbuda

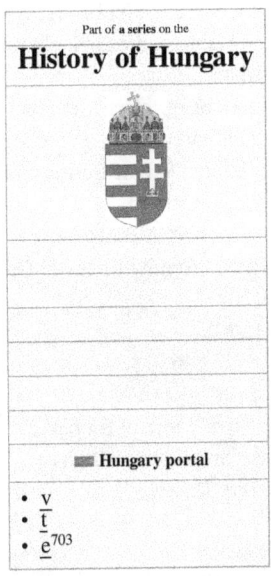

- B.C. - Neolithic, Chalcolithic-, bronze and iron age cultures, Celtic and Eravisci settlements on present day Budapest.

- 1st century CE - Romans found the settlements known as Aquincum, Contra-Aquincum and Campona. Aquincum becomes the largest town of the Danubian region and one of the capitals of Pannonia.[704]
- 5th century - The Age of Huns.[704] King Attila builds a city for himself here according to later chronicles. After his death, the sons of his brother Mundzuk (Hungarian: Bendegúz, Turkish: Boncuk), Attila and Bleda (Hungariahn:Buda), in control of the united Hun tribes.
- 896 - Following the foundation of Hungary, Árpád, leader of the Hungarians, settles in the "Town of Attila", usually identified as Aquincum.
- 10th century - Out of the seven to ten Hungarian tribes, four have settlements in the territory of modern Budapest: Megyer, Keszi, Jenő and Nyék.Wikipedia:Citation needed
- 1015 - Saint Stephen church established (approximate date).Wikipedia:Citation needed
- 1046 - Bishop Gerard of Csanád dies at the hands of pagans on present-day Gellért Hill.
- 1241 - Mongol invasions destroy both towns.[704]
- 1248 - King Béla IV builds the first royal castle on Castle Hill, Buda.[704] The new town adopts the name of Buda from the earlier one (present day Óbuda). Pest is surrounded by city walls.
- 1255 - Matthias Church reconstruction begins.Wikipedia:Citation needed
- 1270 - Saint Margaret of Hungary dies in a cloister on the Isle of Rabbits (present day Margaret Island).
- 1458 - The noblemen of Hungary elect Matthias Corvinus (in Latin) or Hunyadi Mátyás (in Hungarian) as king on the ice of the Danube. Under his reign Buda becomes a main hub of European Renaissance. He dies in 1490, after capturing Vienna in 1485.
- 1472 - Printing press established in Buda.
- 1526 - 26 November: Buda taken by forces of Ottman Suleyman.[704,705]
- 1530 - Siege of Buda (1530).
- 1540 - Siege of Buda (1540).
- 1541
  - Siege of Buda (1541).
  - Buda becomes part of the Ottoman Empire.[705,706] The Turkish Pashas build multiple mosques and baths in Buda.
  - Budin Eyalet established.[704]
- 1542 - Siege of Pest.[704]
- 1550 - Rudas Baths built.
- 1566 - Sokollu Mustafa Pasha becomes Pasha of Buda.[704]
- 1602 - An unsuccessful assault on Budapest under Feldmarschall Christof Hermann Graf von Rußworm (2 October - 15 November 1602).Wikipedia:Citation needed

- 1686 - Battle of Buda (1686).[704] Buda and Pest are reconquered from the Turks with Habsburg leadership. Both towns are destroyed completely in the battles.[705]
- 1690s - Resettlement, initially only a few hundred German settlers.
- 1771 - Citadel built in Buda.[707]
- 1773 - Election of the first Mayor of Pest.Wikipedia:Citation needed
- 1777 - Maria Theresa of Austria moves Nagyszombat University to Castle Hill in Buda.[707]
- 1783 - Joseph II places the acting government (Helytartótanács) and Magyar Kamara on Buda.
- 1795 - 20 May - Ignác Martinovics and other Jacobin leaders are executed on Vérmező or 'The Field of Blood'.

19th century

- 1810 - A fire in the Tabán district.
- 1811 - City Park laid out in Pest.
- 1823 - Fasori Gimnázium (school) founded.
- 1825 - Commencement of the Reform Era. Pest becomes the cultural and economic centre of the country. The first National Theatre is built, along with the Hungarian National Museum.
- 1830 - Steamboat to Vienna begins operating.
- 1833 - Vigadó Concert Hall opens in Pest.
- 1836 - Pest-Buda Musical Association founded.
- 1838 - 1838 Pest flood.[708] The biggest flood in recent memory in March completely inundates Pest.
- 1839 - Industrial flour mill begins operating.
- 1844 - Ganz Works iron foundry in business in Buda.
- 1846
  - Vác-Budapest railway begins operating.
  - Railway station built.[709]
- 1848 - 15 March - Start of the Revolution and War of Independence of 1848-49. Pest replaces Pozsony/Pressburg (Bratislava) as the new capital of Hungary and seat of the Batthyány government and the Parliament.
- 1849
  - 5 January: Austrians occupy the city.
  - April: Hungarian Honvédsereg (Army of National Defense) reclaims city, taking the fortress of Buda on May 21 after an 18-day Battle of Buda (1849).
  - July: Habsburg army again captures the two towns.
  - 6 October - Lajos Batthyány, the first Hungarian Prime Minister is executed on the present-day Szabadság tér.

- Széchenyi Lánchíd, or Széchenyi Chain Bridge, the first permanent bridge across the Danube in Budapest was opened linking Buda (West bank) and Pest (East bank).[707]
- 1853 - Budapest Philharmonic Orchestra founded.
- 1857 - Pest Academy of Commerce founded.
- 1859 - Dohány Street Synagogue consecrated in Pest.[710]
- 1860 - Raitzenbad (bath) rebuilt.[711,712]
- 1864 - Vigadó Concert Hall built.[709]
- 1865
  - Esterhazy Gallery of art established.[708]
  - Hungarian Academy of Sciences building constructed in Pest.[707]
- 1867
  - 8 June: Coronation of Franz Joseph as King of Hungary.[705]
  - Austro-Hungarian Compromise of 1867, followed by unprecedented civic development, resulting in the style of present-day Budapest.[709]
  - *Budapesti Közlöny* government newspaper headquartered in Pest.
- 1868
  - Municipal council established in Pest.[713]
  - *Borsszem Jankó* humor magazine headquartered in Pest.
  - Leopold Basilica built in Pest.[707]
- 1869
  - János Gundel restaurant in busienss.[714]
  - Margaret Island park opens.[715]
- 1870
  - Közmunkatanács (metro planning entity) established.[714]
  - Zagreb-Budapest railway begins operating.
  - Café Gerbeaud moves to Régi Színház Square.
- 1872
  - Military academy built in Pest.[707]
  - Rumbach Street Synagogue built.

1873–1900

- 1873
  - 17 November: The former cities: **Pest, Buda and Óbuda are united**, and with that the Hungarian capital is established with the name of **Budapest**.
  - Ráth Károly becomes Mayor of Budapest
  - Coat of arms of Budapest design adopted.[716]
  - *Budapesti Szemle* scholarly journal headquartered in city.
- 1874
  - Budapest Cog-wheel Railway service is inaugurated.
  - Customhouse built.[707]

- *Egyetértés* newspaper headquartered in city.
- 1875
  - 26 June: Storm.[705]
  - Liszt Academy of Music founded.
- 1876
  - Andrássy Avenue opens.
  - Margaret Bridge built.[707]
- 1877
  - Budapest-Nyugati Railway Terminal opens.[709]
  - Országos Pedagógiai Könyvtár és Múzeum founded.
- 1878
  - Electric public lighting installed in the city centre.
  - *Pesti Hírlap* newspaper in publication.
  - *Bolond Istók* humor magazine begins publication.
- 1881
  - *Budapesti Hírlap* newspaper begins publication.
  - Population: 370,767 (75,794 in Buda + 294,973 in Pest).[707]
- 1884
  - Budapest Keleti railway station built.[709]
  - Hungarian Royal Opera House opens.[714]
- 1885 - Dobos torte (cake) introduced.
- 1886
  - Budapest Opera Ball begins.
  - Manfred Weiss Ammunition Factory begins operating near city.
- 1888 - Electric tram begins operating.
- 1891 - Population: 491,938.[707]
- 1892 - Cholera epidemic.[713]
- 1893
  - Electric power plant built.
  - Electrification of Budapest finished.Wikipedia:Citation needed
- 1894
  - March: Funeral of Lajos Kossuth.[714]
  - Aquincum Museum[717] and New York Café open.
  - Nemzeti Szalon (art society) founded.
  - Wampetics (later Gundel) restaurant in business.
- 1895 - Hall of Art, Budapest built.
- 1896
  - Budapest Metro begins operating.[714]
  - Hungary Millennium Celebrations.[705]
  - Franz Joseph Bridge, Grand Boulevard, and Museum of Applied Arts[709] built.
- 1899

- Hungarian Transportation Museum opens.
- Uránia Hungarian Scientific Theatre active.
- Institute of Geology built.[709]
- 1900
  - Heroes' Square constructed, with its Millennium Memorial.
  - Population: 732,222.[705]

20th century

1901–1945

- 1901
  - 21 December: Economic unrest.[705]
  - Postal Savings Bank built.[709]
  - Gödöllö artists' colony founded near city.
- 1902
  - Hungarian Parliament Building constructed.[709]
  - Fortuna cinema opens.
- 1903
  - Cifrapalota built.
  - Elisabeth Bridge[709] and Varosliget Picture House open.
- 1904 - Thalia Theatre opens.
- 1905 - Museum of Fine Arts (Budapest) built.[711]
- 1906
  - István Bárczy becomes mayor.[709]
  - Gresham Palace built.
- 1908 - *Nyugat* literary magazine begins publication.[718]
- 1909
  - Athletic Club of Kispest established.
  - Endre Nagy cabaret active.[718]
- 1909–1910 - Electric public lighting expanded to the suburbs, the nearby towns villages had Electric public lighting.
- 1910
  - Population: The census finds 880,000 people in Budapest and 55,000 in the largest suburb of Újpest (now part of Budapest). The religious make-up was 60.9% Catholic, 23.1% Jewish, 9.9% Calvinist and 5.0% Lutheran. Újpest was 65.9% Catholic, 18.4% Jewish, 9.7% Calvinist and 4.5% Lutheran. The percentage of ethnic Germans was 9.0% in Budapest and 5.7% in Újpest, while 2.3% of the population claimed to be Slovak.[719]
- 1913 - Bozsik Stadion (stadium) built.
- 1915 - *A Tett* cultural magazine begins publication.

- 1916 - Helios cinema and Magyar Zsidó Museum open.
- 1918
  - 31 October: Socialist Aster Revolution begins.[720] Revolution and the 133 days of the Hungarian Republic of Councils (March–August 1919) under the leadership of Béla Kun. It is the first Communist government to be formed in Europe after the October Revolution in Russia.
- 1919
  - 21 March: City becomes capital of the Hungarian Soviet Republic.[720]
  - 6 August: French-supported Romanian forces enter city. The Communist government collapsed and its leaders fled. In retaliation for the Red Terror, reactionary crews now exacted revenge in a two-year wave of violent repression known today as the White Terror.
  - 1 November: Budapest becomes capital of the Hungarian Democratic Republic, established by Mihály Károlyi.
  - 14 November: Romanian occupation ends.
  - 16 November: Miklós Horthy and National Army enter Budapest;[721] regency government established in 1920.
- 1921 - *Magyar Írás* newspaper begins publication.
- 1924 - Hungarian National Bank is founded.
- 1925 - Hungarian Radio commences broadcasting.
- 1926
  - Corvin Áruház (shop) in business on Blaha Lujza tér.
  - Forum Cinema active.
- 1930 - Population: 1,442,869.
- 1933
  - Disassembly of the Tabán commences.
  - April: National Socialist demonstrations.
- 1937 - Petőfi Bridge built.
- 1938
  - Magyar Optical Works active.
  - Barlang cinema opens.
- 1944
  - 19 March - German forces occupy Budapest. At the time of the occupation, there were 184,000 Jews and between 65,000 and 80,000 Christians of Jewish descent in the town. The Arrow Cross collaborated with the Germans in murdering Jews. Fewer than half of Budapest's Jews (approximately 119,000) survived the following 11 months.
  - 3 November: Budapest Offensive by Soviet forces begins.
  - 26 December: Siege of Budapest begins.
- 1945
  - 15–18 January: Soviet and Romanian troops besiege Budapest. The

retreating Germans destroy all Danube bridges. On 18 January, the soviets complete the occupation of Pest.
- 13 February: The Buda castle falls; Siege of Budapest ends. World War II took the lives of close to 200,000 Budapest residents and caused widespread damage to the buildings of the city.

1946–1990s

- 1946
  - Kossuth Bridge built.
  - Széll Kálmán Square renamed "Moscow Square."[722]
- 1947 - Liberty Statue (Budapest) erected.
- 1949 - City becomes capital of the Hungarian People's Republic.
- 1950 - Árpád Bridge opens.
- 1952 - *Esti Budapest* newspaper begins publication.
- 1956
  - 23 October - 4 November - The Hungarian Revolution of 1956 breaks out, ending in the invasion of a large Soviet force.
  - *Népszabadság* newspaper headquartered in city.
- 1959 - Béla Balázs Studio of film established.
- 1960s - Wartime damage is largely repaired.
- 1963 - Rákosi bunker built.
- 1964 - Elizabeth Bridge rebuilt, the final bridge to be repaired postwar.
- 1968
  - Budapest Transport established.
  - Iparterv art group active.
- 1969 - Marriott hotel built.[715]
- 1970 - The first phase of the East-Western Metro begin operating.
- 1972 - Moszkva tér (Budapest Metro) opens at Moscow Square.[723]
- 1974
  - Rubik's Cube invented.
  - Population: 2,051,354.
- 1975 - Budapest-Déli Railway Terminal built.
- 1976
  - The first phase of the North-Southern Metro begins.
  - Hilton hotel built.[715]
- 1979 - Artpool founded.
- 1983 - Budapest Festival Orchestra founded.
- 1985 - Petőfi Csarnok youth center opens.
- 1987
  - Budapest designated an UNESCO World Heritage Site.
  - Dimitrov Square renamed "Church Square."
- 1989 - City becomes part of the Third Hungarian Republic.

- 1990
  - Gábor Demszky becomes mayor.
  - Budapest Stock Exchange re-established.
  - Population: The city is home to 2,016,100 residents.
  - Gyöngyösi utca (Budapest Metro) opens.
- 1992 - Kempinski Hotel Corvinus in business.[723]
- 1995 - Rákóczi Bridge opens.
- 1996
  - European Roma Rights Center established.
  - Polus Center (shopping mall), Duna Plaza shopping mall,[715] and Corvin cinema[723] established.
- 1997 - Budapest Pride event begins.
- 1999 - WestEnd City Center shopping mall in business.
- 2000 - Buda Health Center established.

21st century

- 2001 - December: International academics meet in Budapest, formulate "Open Access" statement.
- 2002
  - August: Flood.
  - National Theatre (Budapest) rebuilt.
  - Andrássy Avenue is added to the list of World heritage Sites, along with the Millennium Underground railway and Heroes' Square.
- 2004
  - 1 May: Hungary joins the European Union.
  - Budapest City Archives new building opens.
- 2006
  - September–October: Anti-government protests in Kossuth Lajos square.
  - Budapest Fringe Festival begins.
  - 200 km of the 1000 km road in capital level local government handling is reconstructed after 80 km in the former year. The world's longest trams, Siemens Combino Supras start service on Grand Boulevard, by the end of the year 150 Volvo 7700 buses take part in replacing the aging BKV fleet. Reconstruction of metro line 2 finishes.
- 2008
  - The Eastern part of the M0 motorway around the city with Megyeri Bridge is finished and given to public. The new Northern Railway Bridge is finished and is opened to public.

- By this year 400 km road have been reconstructed due to the road reconstruction program paired with pipe (heating and water) replacements to modern, narrow and heat-conserving ones, and where needed sewer system expansion or replacement.
- 2009 - The 2007-2009 complete reconstruction of Liberty Bridge finishes.
- 2010
  - István Tarlós becomes mayor.
  - The Central Wastewater Treatment Plant starts its normal operation. This increases biologically treated sewage from 51% to 100%.
- 2011
  - The 2009-2011 complete and historical reconstruction of Margaret Bridge finishes.
  - Population: 1,729,040 city; 3,284,110 metro.
- 2012 - Protest related to new Constitution of Hungary.
- 2014
  - First phase of Line 4 (Budapest Metro) opens for use by the public.
  - 2014 Hungarian Internet tax protests.
- 2015 - September: Demonstration by migrants.
- 2016 - March: Share of modern, air conditioned low-floor buses increases over 80%.

References

This article incorporates information from the Hungarian Wikipedia and German Wikipedia.

Bibliography

in English

- William Henry Overall, ed. (1870). "Buda"[724]. *Dictionary of Chronology*. London: William Tegg – via HathiTrust.
- Albert Shaw (1897). "Budapest"[725]. *Municipal government in continental Europe*. New York: Century Co.
- "Pesth"[726], *Chambers's Encyclopaedia*, London: W. & R. Chambers, 1901
- Alexander Büchler (1907), "Budapest"[727], *Jewish Encyclopedia*, **3**, New York
- "Budapest"[728], *Encyclopædia Britannica* (11th ed.), New York, 1910, OCLC 14782424[729]
- Benjamin Vincent (1910), "Buda"[730], *Haydn's Dictionary of Dates* (25th ed.), London: Ward, Lock & Co.

- New York Public Library (1913). "Budapest"[731]. *List of Works Relating to City Charters, Ordinances, and Collected Documents.*
- István Deák (1968). "Budapest and the Hungarian Revolutions of 1918-1919". *Slavonic and East European Review.* **46**. JSTOR 4205930[732].
- Mario D. Fenyo (1987). "Literature and Political Change: Budapest, 1908-1918". *Transactions of the American Philosophical Society.* **77**. JSTOR 1006574[733].
- Judit Bodnár (1998). "Assembling the Square: Social Transformation in Public Space and the Broken Mirage of the Second Economy in Postsocialist Budapest". *Slavic Review.* **57**. JSTOR 2500709[734].
- Judit Bodnaŕ (2001). *Fin de Millénaire Budapest: Metamorphoses of Urban Life*[735]. University of Minnesota Press. ISBN 978-1-4529-0477-1.
- Zsuzsa L. Nagy (2002). Chris Wrigley, ed. *Budapest and the revolutions of 1918 and 1919*[736]. *Challenges of Labour: Central and Western Europe 1917-1920.* Routledge. p. 72+. ISBN 978-1-134-90143-2.
- Geza David (2009). "Buda"[737]. In Gabor Agoston; Bruce Alan Masters. *Encyclopedia of the Ottoman Empire.* Facts on File. ISBN 978-1-4381-1025-7.
- Robert Nemes (2009). "Budapest"[738]. In Emily Gunzburger Makas; Tanja Damljanovic Conley. *Capital Cities in the Aftermath of Empires: Planning in Central and Southeastern Europe.* Routledge. p. 141+. ISBN 978-1-135-16725-7.
- Colum Hourihane, ed. (2012). "Budapest"[739]. *Grove Encyclopedia of Medieval Art and Architecture.* Oxford University Press. ISBN 978-0-19-539536-5.
- John Lukacs (2012). *Budapest 1900: A Historical Portrait of a City and Its Culture*[740]. Grove Press. ISBN 978-0-8021-9421-3.
- Michelle M. Metro-Roland (2012). *Tourists, Signs and the City: The Semiotics of Culture in an Urban Landscape*[741]. Ashgate. ISBN 978-1-4094-9025-8. (about Budapest)

in other languages

- *Neuer und vollständiger Führer durch Pest-Ofen*[742] [*New and Complete Guide to Pest-Ofen*] (in German) (2nd ed.). Pest: Eggenberger'sche Buchhandlung (Hoffmann & Molnár). 1870.
- Alexander Franz Heksch (1895). *Illustrirter Führer durch Budapest*[743] [*Illustrated Guide to Budapest*] (in German). Vienna: A. Hartleben.

External links

 Wikimedia Commons has media related to *Budapest*.

Appendix

References

[1] //en.wikipedia.org/w/index.php?title=Template:History_of_Hungary&action=edit
[2] Langó 2005, p. 175.
[3] Langó 2005, p. 296.
[4] Türk 2012, pp. 2–3.
[5] Langó 2005, p. 299.
[6] Curta 2006, p. 124.
[7] Kovács 2005, p. 354.
[8] Kovács 2005, p. 353.
[9] Türk 2012, p. 3.
[10] Róna-Tas 1999, pp. 32, 92.
[11] Berend, Urbańczyk & Wiszewski 2013, p. 63.
[12] Róna-Tas 1999, pp. 33–34, 93–94.
[13] Róna-Tas 1999, pp. 93–95.
[14] Berend, Urbańczyk & Wiszewski 2013, p. 64.
[15] Róna-Tas 1999, pp. 109–112.
[16] Kristó 1996, p. 7.
[17] Róna-Tas 1999, p. 45.
[18] Harmatta 1997, pp. 120, 123.
[19] Harmatta 1997, pp. 122–123.
[20] Berend, Urbańczyk & Wiszewski 2013, p. 61.
[21] Kristó 1996, p. 8.
[22] Kristó 1996, pp. 7–8.
[23] Róna-Tas 1999, pp. 297–298.
[24] Kristó 1996, p. 15.
[25] Róna-Tas 1999, p. 54.
[26] Tóth 2005, p. 47.
[27] Róna-Tas 1999, p. 53.
[28] Tóth 1998, p. 10.
[29] Kristó 1996, p. 103.
[30] Róna-Tas 1999, p. 69.
[31] Zimonyi 2005, p. 88.
[32] Tóth 2005, p. 49.
[33] Róna-Tas 1999, p. 57.
[34] Róna-Tas 1999, pp. 60–61.
[35] Róna-Tas 1999, p. 62.
[36] Berend, Urbańczyk & Wiszewski 2013, p. 489.
[37] Róna-Tas 1999, p. 58.
[38] Berend, Urbańczyk & Wiszewski 2013, p. 490.
[39] Róna-Tas 1999, p. 59.
[40] Macartney 1953, p. 59.
[41] Spinei 2003, p. 13.
[42] Kristó 1996, p. 57.
[43] Kristó 1996, p. 59.
[44] Gulya 1997, p. 92.
[45] Gulya 1997, pp. 89, 91.
[46] Róna-Tas 1999, p. 303.
[47] Ertl 2008, p. 358.
[48] Róna-Tas 1999, p. 286.
[49] Kristó 1996, p. 119.
[50] Róna-Tas 1999, p. 328.

[51] Kristó 1996, pp. 119–120.
[52] Kristó 1996, p. 120.
[53] Kristó 1996, pp. 120–121.
[54] Macartney 1953, p. 100.
[55] *Simon of Kéza: The Deeds of the Hungarians* (ch. 1.4–5), pp. 13–17.
[56] Engel 2001, p. 10.
[57] *The Annals of St-Bertin* (year 862), p. 102
[58] Kristó 1996, p. 78.
[59] *The Chronicle of Regino of Prüm* (year 889), p. 202.
[60] Fodor 1975, pp. 36–37.
[61] Fodor 1975, pp. 37–38.
[62] *The Taktika of Leo VI* (18.41), p. 453.
[63] Kristó 1996, p. 79.
[64] Fodor 1975, p. 37.
[65] *Anonymus, Notary of King Béla: The Deeds of the Hungarians* (ch. 5), p. 17.
[66] Kristó 1996, p. 81.
[67] Engel 2001, p. 121.
[68] Kontler 1999, pp. 100–101.
[69] Szíj 2005, p. 118.
[70] Fodor 1975, p. 38.
[71] Szíj 2005, p. 119.
[72] Tóth 2005, p. 54.
[73] Fodor 1975, p. 39.
[74] Berend, Urbańczyk & Wiszewski 2013, p. 62.
[75] Kontler 1999, p. 34.
[76] Szíj 2005, p. 150.
[77] Tóth 2005, pp. 77–79.
[78] Tóth 2005, p. 77.
[79] Tóth 2005, p. 78.
[80] Róna-Tas 1999, p. 173.
[81] Molnár 2001, pp. 4–5.
[82] Róna-Tas 1999, pp. 93–94.
[83] Klima 2004, p. 20.
[84] Fodor 1975, p. 51.
[85] Róna-Tas 1999, p. 317.
[86] Fodor 1975, p. 54.
[87] Fodor 1975, p. 75.
[88] Kontler 1999, p. 36.
[89] Veres 2004, p. 34.
[90] Róna-Tas 1999, p. 318.
[91] Csorba 1997, p. 19.
[92] Csorba 1997, pp. 23–24.
[93] Veres 2004, p. 35.
[94] Kristó 1996, p. 31.
[95] Kontler 1999, pp. 36–37.
[96] Kontler 1999, p. 37.
[97] Csorba 1997, p. 32.
[98] Fodor 1975, pp. 193–194.
[99] Róna-Tas 1999, p. 195.
[100] Fodor 1975, p. 180.
[101] Kristó 1996, p. 32.
[102] Róna-Tas 1999, p. 319.
[103] Fodor 1975, p. 201.
[104] Fodor 1975, pp. 180–181.
[105] Macartney 1953, pp. 85–86.
[106] Fodor 1975, p. 197.

[107] Fodor 1975, p. 198, 201.
[108] Róna-Tas 1999, p. 429.
[109] Tóth 1998, p. 15.
[110] Kristó 1996, p. 87.
[111] Kristó 1996, p. 68.
[112] Kristó 1996, pp. 67–68.
[113] Fodor 1975, pp. 122–123.
[114] Róna-Tas 1999, pp. 121, 429.
[115] Fodor 1975, p. 202.
[116] Fodor 1975, p. 203.
[117] Róna-Tas 1999, p. 209.
[118] Róna-Tas 1999, pp. 209–213, 230–231.
[119] Róna-Tas 1999, p. 105.
[120] Engel 2001, pp. 9–10.
[121] Kristó 1996, p. 35.
[122] Róna-Tas 1999, p. 323.
[123] Kristó 1996, pp. 49–50.
[124] Spinei 2003, p. 40.
[125] Róna-Tas 1999, p. 230.
[126] Kristó 1996, p. 125.
[127] Spinei 2003, p. 41.
[128] Róna-Tas 1999, pp. 139–140.
[129] *Constantine Porphyrogenitus: De Administrando Imperio* (ch. 38), p. 171.
[130] Fodor 1975, p. 213.
[131] Róna-Tas 1999, p. 418.
[132] Kristó 1996, p. 108.
[133] Kristó 1996, p. 110.
[134] Kristó 1996, pp. 87, 132.
[135] Fodor 1975, p. 210.
[136] Róna-Tas 1999, p. 288.
[137] Kristó 1996, pp. 139–140.
[138] Spinei 2003, p. 43.
[139] Kristó 1996, p. 131.
[140] Róna-Tas 1999, pp. 230, 417.
[141] Szabados 2011, p. 96.
[142] Berend, Urbańczyk & Wiszewski 2013, p. 72.
[143] Curta 2006, pp. 156–157.
[144] Curta 2006, p. 157.
[145] Kristó 1996, pp. 15–17.
[146] *The Annals of St-Bertin* (year 839), p. 44.
[147] Curta 2006, p. 123.
[148] Kristó 1996, p. 86.
[149] *Ibn Rusta on the Magyars*, p. 122.
[150] Brook 2006, p. 31.
[151] Kristó 1996, p. 16.
[152] Kristó 1996, p. 116.
[153] Spinei 2003, pp. 30–31.
[154] Berend, Urbańczyk & Wiszewski 2013, p. 105.
[155] *Anonymus, Notary of King Béla: The Deeds of the Hungarians* (Prologue), p. 3.
[156] *The Hungarian Illuminated Chronicle* (ch. 27), p. 98.
[157] Kristó 1996, p. 117.
[158] *Constantine Porphyrogenitus: De Administrando Imperio* (ch. 40), p. 179.
[159] Berend, Urbańczyk & Wiszewski 2013, pp. 105–106.
[160] Engel 2001, p. 19.
[161] Róna-Tas 1999, p. 340.
[162] Brook 2006, p. 142.

[163] Kristó 1996, p. 107.
[164] Kristó 1996, p. 145.
[165] Spinei 2003, pp. 42–43.
[166] Kristó 1996, pp. 144, 147.
[167] Kristó 1996, p. 144.
[168] *Constantine Porphyrogenitus: De Administrando Imperio* (ch. 38), pp. 171–173.
[169] *Constantine Porphyrogenitus: De Administrando Imperio* (ch. 38), p. 175.
[170] Spinei 2003, p. 44.
[171] Kristó 1996, p. 156.
[172] Kristó 1996, p. 157.
[173] Fodor 1975, p. 248.
[174] *Anonymus, Notary of King Béla: The Deeds of the Hungarians* (ch. 1), p. 5.
[175] Spinei 2003, pp. 52–53.
[176] Róna-Tas 1999, p. 416.
[177] Kristó 1996, p. 159.
[178] Spinei 2003, p. 33.
[179] Kristó 1996, pp. 164–165.
[180] Róna-Tas 1999, p. 417.
[181] Fodor 1975, p. 250.
[182] Fodor 1975, p. 236.
[183] Kristó 1996, p. 136.
[184] Engel 2001, p. 18.
[185] Cartledge 2011, p. 55.
[186] Engel 2001, p. 22.
[187] Kristó 1996, p. 148.
[188] Spinei 2003, p. 51.
[189] Kristó 1996, pp. 152–153.
[190] *Constantine Porphyrogenitus: De Administrando Imperio* (ch. 39), p. 175.
[191] Kristó 1996, p. 153.
[192] Fodor 1975, p. 251.
[193] *The Life of Constantine* (ch.8), p. 45.
[194] Curta 2006, pp. 124, 185.
[195] Molnár 2001, p. 11.
[196] Spinei 2003, p. 50.
[197] Róna-Tas 1999, p. 331.
[198] Kristó 1996, p. 150.
[199] Brook 2006, p. 143.
[200] László 1996, p. 43.
[201] Kristó 1996, pp. 175, 219.
[202] Spinei 2003, p. 36.
[203] Fodor 1975, p. 261.
[204] *The Life of Methodius* (ch.16), p. 125.
[205] Fodor 1975, p. 278.
[206] Róna-Tas 1999, p. 92.
[207] Kristó 1996, p. 175.
[208] *The Annals of Fulda* (year 894), p. 129.
[209] Kristó 1996, p. 178.
[210] Fodor 1975, p. 280.
[211] Spinei 2003, p. 53.
[212] Cartledge 2011, pp. 5–6.
[213] Cartledge 2011, p. 6.
[214] Molnár 2001, p. 13.
[215] Curta 2006, p. 188.
[216] Engel 2001, pp. 12–13.
[217] Cartledge 2011, p. 8.
[218] Spinei 2003, pp. 69–70.

[219] Fodor 1975, p. 61.
[220] Fodor 1975, pp. 62–65.
[221] Fodor 1975, pp. 66–71.
[222] Fodor 1975, pp. 66–69.
[223] Kontler 1999, pp. 34–36.
[224] Fodor 1975, p. 78.
[225] Fodor 1975, pp. 76–77.
[226] Fodor 1975, p. 80.
[227] Fodor 1975, pp. 80–81.
[228] Fodor 1975, p. 81.
[229] Fodor 1975, p. 92.
[230] Róna-Tas 1999, p. 99.
[231] Fodor 1975, pp. 103–105, 121, 126.
[232] Fodor 1975, p. 105.
[233] Fodor 1975, p. 104.
[234] Fodor 1975, pp. 106, 126.
[235] Fodor 1975, p. 184.
[236] Róna-Tas 1999, p. 110.
[237] Kristó 1996, pp. 44, 46.
[238] Spinei 2003, p. 22.
[239] Spinei 2003, p. 19.
[240] Fodor 1975, p. 249.
[241] Fodor 1975, pp. 261–262.
[242] László 1996, p. 195.
[243] Kovács 2005, p. 355.
[244] Spinei 2003, p. 24.
[245] Fodor 1975, pp. 298–299.
[246] Fodor 1975, pp. 299–308.
[247] László 1996, pp. 110–111.
[248] László 1996, p. 117.
[249] László 1996, p. 118.
[250] László 1996, p. 122.
[251] László 1996, pp. 123–124.
[252] László 1996, pp. 135–136.
[253] László 1996, p. 135.
[254] Csorba 1997, p. 46.
[255] László 1996, p. 127.
[256] Engel 2001, p. 15.
[257] Engel 2001, p. 16.
[258] Fodor 1975, p. 263.
[259] *The* Chronicle *of Regino of Prüm* (year 889), p. 205.
[260] László 1996, pp. 128–129.
[261] László 1996, p. 129.
[262] Fodor 1975, p. 299.
[263] Berend, Urbańczyk & Wiszewski 2013, p. 127.
[264] *The Taktika of Leo VI* (18.53–56), p. 457.
[265] Berend, Urbańczyk & Wiszewski 2013, p. 133.
[266] Engel 2001, p. 47.
[267] Spinei 2003, p. 35.
[268] Berend, Urbańczyk & Wiszewski 2013, pp. 132–133.
[269] László 1996, p. 148.
[270] László 1996, pp. 147–148.
[271] Róna-Tas 1999, p. 366.
[272] Spinei 2003, p. 37.
[273] Róna-Tas 1999, p. 368.
[274] Spinei 2003, pp. 37–39.

[275] Spinei 2003, p. 39.
[276] Berend, Urbańczyk & Wiszewski 2013, p. 134.
[277] László 1996, pp. 140–141.
[278] Róna-Tas 1999, pp. 364, 366.
[279] Róna-Tas 1999, pp. 366–367.
[280] László 1996, pp. 133–134.
[281] László 1996, p. 134.
[282] http://www.hungarianarchaeology.hu/wp-content/uploads/2012/08/eng_turk_12Ny_0827.pdf
[283] http://www.c3.hu/scripta/books/96/03/02hofer.htm
[284] //tools.wmflabs.org/geohack/geohack.php?pagename=Aquincum&params=47_33_51_N_19_2_58_E_type:landmark
[285] Lovely Budapest http://lovelybudapest.com/en/about-budapest/budapest-attractions.html
[286] http://www.aquincum.hu
[287] http://www.civertan.hu/legifoto/legifoto.php?page_level=875
[288] https://web.archive.org/web/20071011115749/http://tube108.com/travel/ruins-from-the-roman-empire/
[289] https://www.panoramio.com/user/510240/tags/ruins
[290] Adeleye, Gabriel G. (1999). *World Dictionary of Foreign Expressions*. Ed. Thomas J. Sienkewicz and James T. McDonough, Jr. Wauconda, IL: Bolchazy-Carducci Publishers, Inc.
[291] //en.wikipedia.org/w/index.php?title=Template:History_of_Hungary&action=edit
[292] //en.wikipedia.org/w/index.php?title=Template:History_of_Slovakia&action=edit
[293] Katalin Péter, Beloved Children: History of Aristocratic Childhood in Hungary in the Early Modern Age https://books.google.com/books?id=cqNEYfZI0kUC&pg=PA22, Central European University Press, 2001, p. 22
[294] Howell A. Lloyd, Glenn Burgess, European political thought 1450–1700: religion, law and philosophy https://books.google.com/books?id=8AsNAQAAMAAJ&pg=PA177, Yale University Press, 2007, pp. 177–189
[295] Július Bartl, Slovak History: Chronology & Lexicon https://books.google.com/books?id=3orG2yZ9mBkC&pg=PA60, Bolchazy-Carducci Publishers, 2002, p. 60
[296] Lajos Besenyei, Géza Érszegi, Maurizio Pedrazza Gorlero, De bulla aurea Andreae II regis Hungariae, 1222 https://books.google.com/books?id=cOVnAAAAMAAJ&pg=PA222, Valdonega, 1999, p. 222
[297] Hajdú, Zoltán, DISCUSSION PAPERS No. 44, Carpathian Basin and the Development of the Hungarian Landscape Theory Until 1948 http://webdoc.sub.gwdg.de/ebook/serien/qg/rkk/44.pdf, CENTRE FOR REGIONAL STUDIES OF HUNGARIAN ACADEMY OF SCIENCES, p. 10
[298] Raphael Patai The Jews of Hungary: History, Culture, Psychology https://books.google.com/books?id=LLuPS1yVDf8C&pg=PA153, Wayne State University Press, 1996, p. 153
[299] Peter F. Sugar, Péter Hanák, A History of Hungary https://books.google.com/books?id=SKwmGQCT0MAC, Indiana University Press, 1994, p. 91
[300] István Keul, Early Modern Religious Communities in East-Central Europe: Ethnic Diversity, Denominational Plurality, and Corporative Politics in the Principality of Transylvania (1526-1691) https://books.google.com/books?id=5J09mqMWiogC&pg=PA253, Brill, 2009, p. 253
[301] Giambattista Vico, Statecraft: The Deeds of Antonio Carafa https://books.google.com/books?id=6vRnP8jXZjMC&pg=PA400, Peter Lang, 2004, p. 400
[302] "... the Estates of the realm have submitted themselves not only to His Majesty's, but also his heirs' power and rule for ever ..." (Section 5 of Article V of 1547).
[303] István Keul, Early modern religious communities in East-Central Europe: ethnic diversity, denominational plurality, and corporative politics in the principality of Transylvania (1526–1691) https://books.google.com/books?id=5J09mqMWiogC&pg=PA40, BRILL, 2009, p. 40
[304] István Keul, *Early modern religious communities in East-Central Europe: ethnic diversity, denominational plurality, and corporative politics in the principality of Transylvania (1526–1691)* 2009, pp. 61-255 https://books.google.com/books?id=5J09mqMWiogC&pg=PA40
[305] Dennis P. Hupchick, Conflict and chaos in Eastern Europe https://books.google.com/books?id=ycNApODqgRUC, Palgrave Macmillan, 1995, p. 62

306 http://www.britannica.com/EBchecked/topic/603323/Transylvania
307 Richard C. Frucht, Eastern Europe: an introduction to the people, lands, and culture / edited by Richard Frucht, Volume 1, ABC-CLIO, 2005, p. 348 https://books.google.com/books?id= lVBB1a0rC70C&pg=PA348
308 Posse, Otto, ed. (1909–13). "Bey der Niederlegung der kaiserlichen Reichs-Regierung. Dekret vom 6. August 1806". Die Siegel der deutschen Kaiser und Könige von 751 bis 1806 (in German). Band 5, Beilage 3. p 256ff
309 " From the perspective of the Court since 1723, regnum Hungariae had been a hereditary province of the dynasty's three main branches on both lines. From the perspective of the ország, Hungary was regnum independens, a separate Land as Article X of 1790 stipulated .... In 1804 Emperor Franz assumed the title of Emperor of Austria for all the Erblande of the dynasty and for the other Lands, including Hungary. Thus Hungary formally became part of the Empire of Austria. The Court reassured the diet , however, that the assumption of the monarch's new title did not in any sense affect the laws and the constitution of Hungary"
310 "Vor dem Jahr 1848 is das Kaisertum Österreich verfassungsrechtlich als ein monarchischer Einheitsstaat auf differenziert föderalistischer Grundlage zu sehen, wobei die besondere Stelung Ungarns im Rahmen dieses Gesamtstaates stets offenkundig war. Eine weitere Differenzierung der föderalistischen Grundlage erfolgte ab 1815 durch die Zugehörigkeit eines teiles des Kaisertums zum Deutschen Bund."
311 József Zachar, Austerlitz, 1805. december 2. A három császár csatája – magyar szemmel http: //tortenelemszak.elte.hu/data/23763/ZacharJozsef.pdf, In: Eszmék, forradalmak, háborúk. Vadász Sándor 80 éves, ELTE, Budapest, 2010 p. 557
312 //tools.wmflabs.org/geohack/geohack.php?pagename=Buda_Castle&params=47_29_46_N_ 19_02_23_E_region:HU_type:landmark
313 http://whc.unesco.org/en/list/400
314 Ungarische Revue, Volume 11, S.53, Magyar Tudományos Akadémia, Franklin-Verein, 1891.
315 Briefe an ihre Kinder und Freunde; Verfasser/in: Maria Theresa, Empress of Austria; Alfred Ritter von Arneth, Verlag: Braumüller, Wien 1881.
316 Europe's centre around AD 1000, Volume 1, page 7, Council of Europe, Art Exhibition, Alfried Wieczorek, Hans-Martin Hinz, Theiss, 2000.
317 Ruđer Bošković, page 54, Željko Brnetić, Školska knjiga, 1990.
318 László Zolnay: A budai vár, Bp: 1981, p. 60
319 "Budapest including the Banks of the Danube, the Buda Castle", UNESCO.hu, 2010.
320 http://budavar.btk.mta.hu/en/art-monuments/the-royal-palace-of-buda.html
321 https://web.archive.org/web/20070706132444/http://szabadbolcseszet.elte.hu/index.php? option=com_tanelem&tip=0&id_tanelem=593
322 https://web.archive.org/web/20120513202500/http://www.citylive.hu/budai-var
323 http://www.legifoto.com/magyar/galeria/varnegyed/
324 http://arch.et.bme.hu/arch_old/korabbi_folyam/29/29fekete.html
325 http://mek.oszk.hu/04000/04094/html/eletrajz.htm
326 //en.wikipedia.org/w/index.php?title=Template:History_of_Hungary&action=edit
327 Melvin E. Page, Colonialism: an international social, cultural, and political encyclopedia, ABC-CLIO, 2003, p. 648 https//books.google.com
328 Kontler 1999, p. 145.
329 Inalcik Halil: "The Ottoman Empire"
330 Ottoman Warfare 1500-1700, Rhoads Murphey, 1999, p.227
331 Ottoman Warfare 1500-1700, Rhoads Murphey, 1999, p.56
332 Hungary. (2009). In Encyclopædia Britannica. Retrieved May 11, 2009, from Encyclopædia Britannica Online http://www.britannica.com/EBchecked/topic/276730/Hungary
333 *Historical World Atlas. With the commendation of the Royal Geographical Society.* Carthographia, Budapest, Hungary, 2005. CM
334 Ottoman Warfare 1500-1700, Rhoads Murphey, 1999, p.173-174
335 Ottoman Warfare 1500-1700, Rhoads Murphey, 1999, p.254
336 The preaching of Islam: a history of the propagation of the Muslim faith By Sir Thomas Walker Arnold, pg. 135-144

[337] The preaching of Islam: a history of the propagation of the Muslim faith By Sir Thomas Walker Arnold, pg. 136

[338] Christina Shea, Joseph S. Lieber, Erzsébet Barát, Frommer's Budapest & the Best of Hungary, John Wiley and Sons, 2004, p 122-123 https//books.google.com

[339] http://lcweb2.loc.gov/frd/cs/

[340] https://books.google.com/books?id=V9vom-ZAElcC

[341] http://mek.oszk.hu/01900/01911/html/

[342] Dr Zachary C Shirkey: Joining the Fray: Outside Military Intervention in Civil Wars Military Strategy and Operational Art -PAGE: 1944- , 9781409470915 https//books.google.hu

[343] A Global Chronology of Conflict: From the Ancient World to the Modern Middle ..., by Spencer C. Tucker, 2009 p. 1188

[344] //en.wikipedia.org/w/index.php?title=Template:History_of_Hungary&action=edit

[345] Eric Roman: Austria-Hungary & the Successor States: A Reference Guide from the Renaissance to the Present -PAGE: 67, Publisher: Infobase Publishing, 2003

[346] The Making of the West: Volume C, Lynn Hunt, Pages 683–684

[347] ". In 1804 Emperor Franz assumed the title of Emperor of Austria for all the Erblande of the dynasty and for the other Lands, including Hungary. Thus Hungary formally became part of the Empire of Austria. The Court reassured the diet, however, that the assumption of the monarch's new title did not in any sense affect the laws and the constitution of Hungary

[348] Éva H. Balázs: Hungary and the Habsburgs, 1765–1800: An Experiment in Enlightened Absolutism. p. 320.

[349] Charles W. Ingrao : The Habsburg Monarchy, 1618–1815, Volume 21 of New Approaches to European History, Publisher: Cambridge University Press, 2000

[350] Jean Berenger, C.A. Simpson: The Habsburg Empire 1700-1918 , Publisher: Routledge, 2014,

[351] Tomasz Kamusella: The Politics of Language and Nationalism in Modern Central Europe, Publisher: Palgrave Macmillan, 2009,

[352] Paschalis M. Kitromilides: Enlightenment and Revolution, Publisher: Harvard University Press, 2013,

[353] Peter McPhee: A Companion to the French Revolution -PAGE: 391 , Publisher: John Wiley & Sons, 2014,

[354] Ödön Beöthy and Tibor Vágvölgyi: A Magyar Jakobinusok Köztársasági Mozgalma, -PAGE: 103 Budapest 1968, English: The Hungarian jacobin republican movement.

[355] Mihály Lackó: *Széchenyi és Kossuth vitája*, Gondolat, 1977.

[356] See: Lacko p. 47

[357] *Gróf Széchenyi István írói és hírlapi vitája Kossuth Lajossal* [Count Stephen Széchenyi,s Literary and Publicistic Debate with Louis Kossuth], ed. Gyula Viszota, 2 vols. (Budapest: Magyar Történelmi Társulat, 1927–1930).

[358] Charles Frederick Henningsen: Kossuth and 'The Times', by the author of 'The revelations of Russia'. 1851 -PAGE: 10

[359] Peter F. Sugar, Péter Hanák, Tibor Frank: A History of Hungary (Indiana University Press, Jan 1, 1994) -PAGE: 213

[360] Encyclopædia Britannica 1911, "Hungary" article

[361] Steven A. Seidman and Peter Lang: Posters, Propaganda, and Persuasion in Election Campaigns Around the World -PAGE: 201

[362] Romsics, Béla K. Király: Geopolitics in the Danube Region: Hungarian Reconciliation Efforts 1848-1998 -PAGE: 413 , Publisher: Central European University Press, 1999,

[363] Greger-Delacroix: The Reliable Book of Facts: Hungary '98 -PAGE: 32

[364] Encyclopædia Britannica 1911

[365] Marx & Engels, p. 229.

[366] Marx & Engels, p. 390, 3 May 1848.

[367] Marx & Engels, p. 613.

[368] Marx & Engels, p. 250, The War in Hungary.

[369] Marx & Engels, 8 April 1848.

[370] Judah 1997, p. 58.

[371] Judah 1997, p. 60.

[372] Marx & Engels, p. 603.

[373] Špiesz, Anton (2006), Illustrated Slovak History, Wauconda, Illinois: Bolchazy-Carducci Publishers,
[374] Pál Hatos and Attila Novák (editors). *Between Minority and Majority. Hungarian and Jewish/Israeli Ethnical and Cultural Experiences in Recent Centuries* https//books.google.com
[375] http://www.brukenthalmuseum.ro/pdf/BAM/BRUKENTHALIA_1.pdf
[376] Miklós Molnár. *A Concise History of Hungary"* https//books.google.com
[377] Marx & Engels, pp. 242, 262, 8 April 1849.
[378] Marx & Engels, p. 319, 22 April 1848.
[379] Marx & Engels, p. 242, 22 April 1848.
[380] Marx & Engels, p. 334.
[381] Marx & Engels, p. 611.
[382] Marx & Engels, p. 343.
[383] Marx & Engels, p. 304.
[384] Marx & Engels, p. 346.
[385] Marx & Engels, p. 331.
[386] Marx & Engels, p. 293, 19 April 1849.
[387] Marx & Engels, p. 618.
[388] Marx & Engels, p. 303.
[389] The Cambridge modern history; Leathes, Prothero and Vard
[390] Tamás Csapody: *Deák Ferenc és a passzív rezisztencia* http://www.matud.iif.hu/05mar/06.html
[391] "Encyclopædia Britannica: Kossuth article"
[392] http://www.jstor.org/stable/2494145
[393] http://epa.niif.hu/01400/01462/00025/pdf/039-047.pdf
[394] http://www.jstor.org/stable/4205719
[395] Fisher, Gilman. *The Essentials of Geography for School Year 1888–1889*, p. 47 https://books.google.com/?id=TLkUAAAAYAAJ&pg=PA47. New England Publishing Company (Boston), 1888. Retrieved 20 August 2014.
[396] Geographischer Atlas zur Vaterlandskunde, 1911, Tabelle 3.
[397] Schulze, Max-Stephan. *Engineering and Economic Growth: The Development of Austria-Hungary's Machine-Building Industry in the Late Nineteenth Century*, p. 295. Peter Lang (Frankfurt), 1996.
[398] Minahan, James. *Miniature Empires: A Historical Dictionary of the Newly Independent States*, p. 48 https://books.google.com/?id=RSxt-JB-PDkC&pg=PA48.
[399] Anderson, Frank Maloy and Amos Shartle Hershey, *Handbook for the Diplomatic History of Europe, Asia, and Africa 1870–1914.- The Austrian occupation of Novibazar, 1878–1909* https://www.mtholyoke.edu/acad/intrel/boshtml/bos128.htm
[400] Antun Radić, "Hrvatski pašuši (putnice)" Dom, 15 January 1903, page 11)
[401] "In 1804 Emperor Franz assumed the title of Emperor of Austria for all the Erblande of the dynasty and for the other Lands, including Hungary. Thus Hungary formally became part of the Empire of Austria. The Court reassured the diet, however, that the assumption of the monarch's new title did not in any sense affect the laws and the constitution of Hungary."
[402] Éva H. Balázs: Hungary and the Habsburgs, 1765–1800: An Experiment in Enlightened Absolutism. p. 320.
[403] Richard L. Rudolph: Banking and Industrialization in Austria-Hungary: The Role of Banks in the Industrialization of the Czech Crownlands, 1873–1914, Cambridge University Press, 2008 (page 17)
[404] //en.wikipedia.org/w/index.php?title=Template:History_of_Austria&action=edit
[405] //en.wikipedia.org/w/index.php?title=Template:History_of_Hungary&action=edit
[406] Kann (1974); Sked (1989); Taylor (1964)
[407] Kann, *A History of the Habsburg Empire: 1526–1918* (1974)
[408] "Austrian Empire" article of *Encyclopedia Britannica* 1911
[409] Headlam 1911, p. 39.
[410] Budisavljević, Srđan, *Stvaranje-Države-SHS, Creation of the state of SHS*, Zagreb, 1958, p. 132.-133.
[411] Rothenberg 1976, p. 118.
[412] Rothenberg 1976, p. 128.

[413] David S. Wyman, Charles H. Rosenzveig: *The World Reacts to the Holocaust.* (page: 474)
[414] F.R. Bridge, *From Sadowa to Sarajevo: The Foreign Policy of Austria-Hungary 1866–1914* (1972)
[415] Hans A. Schmitt, "Count Beust and Germany, 1866–1870: Reconquest, Realignment, or Resignation?" *Central European History* (1968) 1#1 p. 20–34 in JSTOR https://www.jstor.org/stable/4545476
[416] William L. Langer, *European Alliances and Alignments: 1871–1890* (2nd ed. 1950) p. 20
[417] Langer, *European Alliances and Alignments: 1871–1890* pp. 138, 155–6, 163
[418] Peter F. Sugar, Péter Hanák: A History of Hungary (Publisher: Indiana University Press) Page: 262
[419] Commercial Relations of the United States: Reports from the Consuls of the United States on the Commerce, Manufactures, Etc., of Their Consular Districts. Publisher: U.S. Government Printing Office, 1881 (page: 371)
[420] Erik Eckermann: World History of the Automobile – Page 325
[421] Hans Seper: Die Brüder Gräf: Geschichte der Gräf & Stift-Automobile
[422] Kurt Bauer (2003), Faszination des Fahrens: unterwegs mit Fahrrad, Motorrad und Automobil (in German), Böhlau Verlag Wien, Kleine Enzyklopädie des Fahrens, "Lohner", pp. 250–1
[423] Iván Boldizsár: NHQ; the New Hungarian Quarterly – Volume 16, Issue 2; Volume 16, Issues 59–60 – Page 128
[424] Hungarian Technical Abstracts: Magyar Műszaki Lapszemle – Volumes 10–13 – Page 41
[425] Joseph H. Wherry: Automobiles of the World: The Story of the Development of the Automobile, with Many Rare Illustrations from a Score of Nations (Page:443)
[426] Commerce Reports Volume 4, page 223 (printed in 1927)
[427] G.N. Georgano: The New Encyclopedia of Motorcars, 1885 to the Present. S. 59.
[428] http://mek.oszk.hu/02100/02185/html/812.html
[429] The American Institute of Aeronautics and Astronautics (AIAA): History of Flight from Around the World http://www.aiaa.org/Secondary.aspx?id=356: Hungary article.
[430] Mária Kovács: Short History Of Hungarian Aviation http://www.hungarianhistory.com/pics/aviation.pdf
[431] Mikulas Teich, Roy Porter: The Industrial Revolution in National Context: Europe and the USA (page: 266.)
[432] Tramways in Austria: Book: Buckley, Richard (2000). Tramways and Light Railways of Switzerland and Austria (2nd edition), pp. 129–135 .
[433] Tramways in Czech Republic: Book: Jan Vinař : Historické krovy (page 351)
[434] Tramways in Poland (including Galicia), Book: Arkadiusz Kołoś, Uniwersytet Jagielloński. Instytut Geografii i Gospodarki Przestrzennej: Rozwój przestrzenny a współczesne funkcjonowanie miejskiego transportu szynowego w Polsce (page: 19)
[435] History of Public Transport in Hungary. Book: Zsuzsa Frisnyák: A magyarországi közlekedés krónikája, 1750–2000
[436] Tramways in Croatia: Book: Vlado Puljiz, Gojko Bežovan, Teo Matković, dr. Zoran Šućur, Siniša Zrinščak: Socijalna politika Hrvatske
[437] Tramways in Slovakia: Book: Július Bartl: Slovak History: Chronology & Lexicon – p. 112
[438] István Tisza and László Kovács: A magyar állami, magán- és helyiérdekű vasúttársaságok fejlődése 1876–1900 között, Magyar Vasúttörténet 2. kötet. Budapest: Közlekedési Dokumentációs Kft., 58–59, 83–84. o. (1996)(English: The development of Hungarian private and state owned commuter railway companies between 1876 – 1900, Hungarian railway History Volume II.
[439] Kogan Page: *Europe Review 2003/2004*, fifth edition, Wolden Publishing Ltd, 2003, page 174 https://books.google.com/?id=Hwi0s3I5jLEC&pg=PA174&dq=%22The+world%27s+second-oldest+undergound%2Fmetro+system+after+London+is+identified+by+large%22
[440] Iván Wisnovszky, Study trip to the Danube Bend https://books.google.com/?id=iqpTAAAAYAAJ&q=Study+trip+to+the+Danube+Bend, Hydraulic Documentation and Information Centre, 1971, p. 13
[441] Victor-L. Tapie, *The Rise and Fall of the Habsburg Monarchy* p. 267
[442] Paula Sutter Fichtner: Historical Dictionary of Austria (p. 69)

[443] Kiesewetter, Herbert: *Industrielle Revolution in Deutschland. Regionen als Wachstumsmotoren.* Stuttgart, Franz Steiner 2004, , p. 246.
[444] Dániel Szabó, Zoltán Fónagy, István Szathmári, Tünde Császtvay: Kettős kötődés : Az Osztrák–Magyar Monarchia (1867–1918)|http://mek.oszk.hu/01900/01905/html/index7.html
[445] Museum of Moslavina Kutina, Jasmina Uroda Kutlić: 'Telefon - čudo Novoga vijeka' (Telephone the miracle of Modern era)
[446] HT Muzej (Croatian Telecom Museum): '125 godina telefonije u Hrvatskoj' (125 years of Telephony in Croatia), Zagreb 2006., P.-2,
[447] Telephone History Institute: Telecom History – Issue 1 – Page 14
[448] Thomas Derdak, Adéle Hast: International Directory of Company Histories – Volume 5 – Page 315
[449] See the above cited book: Stephen Broadberry and Kevin H. O'Rourke: The Cambridge Economic History of Modern Europe: Volume 2, 1870 to the Present, page: 80
[450] Brousek; Karl M.: *Die Großindustrie Böhmens 1848–1918*, München: Oldenbourg 1987, , p. 31.
[451] A. J. P. Taylor, The Habsburg Monarchy 1809–1918, 1948.
[452] Geographischer Atlas zur Vaterlandskunde, 1911, Tabelle 3.
[453] 1910. évi népszámlálás adatai. (Magyar Statisztikai Közlemények, Budapest, 1912. pp 30–33)
[454] Kogutowicz Károly, Hermann Győző: *Zsebatlasz: Naptárral és statisztikai adatokkal az 1914. évre.* Magyar Földrajzi Intézet R. T., Budapest 1913, S. 69, 105.
[455] Austrian Empire article of E. Britannica 1911
[456] Headlam 1911b, p. 4.
[457] Rene Albrecht-Carrie, *A Diplomatic History of Europe Since the Congress of Vienna* (1973) CH 6
[458] Rene Albrecht-Carrie, *A Diplomatic History of Europe Since the Congress of Vienna* (1973) pp 201–14
[459] Rene Albrecht-Carrie, *A Diplomatic History of Europe Since the Congress of Vienna* (1973) ch 8
[460] Rene Albrecht-Carrie, *A Diplomatic History of Europe Since the Congress of Vienna* (1973) pp 259–72
[461] William Jannen: Lions of July: Prelude to War, 1914 – PAGE:456
[462] David G. Herrmann: The Arming of Europe and the Making of the First World War, p. 211, Princeton University Press, (1997)
[463] Fischer, Fritz: Germany's Aims in the First World War, New York, W.W. Norton, 1967, , p. 52
[464] Source: Ladislaus Count von Szögyény-Marich (Berlin) to Leopold Count von Berchtold (July 5, 1914), in Ludwig Bittner, et. al., eds., Österreich-Ungarns Aussenpolitik von der Bosnischen Krise 1908 bis zum Kriegsausbruch 1914 [Austria-Hungary's Foreign Policy prior to the Bosnian Crisis of 1908 up to the Outbreak of War in 1914]. 8 vols, Vienna, 1930, vol. 8, no. 10,058.
[465] Christopher Clark, *The Sleepwalkers: How Europe Went to War in 1914* pp. 420–30 (2013)
[466] A. F. Pribram, *Austrian Foreign Policy, 1908-18* (1923) pp 68-128.
[467] Z.A.B. Zeman, *A diplomatic history of the First World War* (1971) pp 121-61.
[468] Stevenson, *The First World War and International Politics* (1988) pp 139-48.
[469] David Stevenson, "The failure of peace by negotiation in 1917." *Historical Journal* 34#1 (1991): 65-86.
[470] Edward P. Keleher, "Emperor Karl and the Sixtus Affair: Politico-Nationalist Repercussions in the Reich German and Austro-German Camps, and the Disintegration of Habsburg Austria, 1916-1918." *East European Quarterly* 26.2 (1992): 163+.
[471] Alexander Watson, *Ring of Steel: Germany and Austria-Hungary at War, 1914-1918* (2014). pp 536–40.
[472] Max-Stephan Schulze, "Austria-Hungary's economy in World War I," in Stephen Broadberry and Mark Harrison, eds. *The Economics of World War I* (2005) ch 3 online https://www.library6.com/books/523600.pdf#page=95
[473] Robert A. Kann, et al. eds. *The Habsburg Empire in World War I: Essays on the Intellectual, Military, Political and Economic Aspects of the Habsburg War Effort* (1977)

[474] Maureen Healy, *Vienna and the Fall of the Habsburg Empire: Total War and Everyday Life in World War I* (2007)
[475] Schulze, "Austria-Hungary's economy in World War I,"
[476] Ivo Banac, "'Emperor Karl Has Become a Comitadji': The Croatian Disturbances of Autumn 1918." *Slavonic and East European Review* 70#2 (1992): 284-305.
[477] Alexander Watson, *Ring of Steel: Germany and Austria-Hungary in World War I* (2014), excerpt https://www.amazon.com/Ring-Steel-Germany-Austria-Hungary-World-ebook/dp/B00JZBA9MO/
[478] John R. Schindler, *Isonzo: The Forgotten Sacrifice of the Great War* (2001)
[479] Gaetano V. Cavallaro (2010). The Beginning of Futility: Diplomatic, Political, Military and Naval Events on the Austro-Italian Front in the First World War 1914–1917 I. p. 339.
[480] Pier Paolo Cervone, *Vittorio Veneto, l'ultima battaglia*, Milano, Mursia, 1993.
[481] Indro Montanelli; Mario Cervi, *Due secoli di guerre*, VII, Novara, Editoriale Nuova, 1981.
[482] Glenn E. Torrey, *Romania and World War I* (Histria Books, 1998)
[483] Watson, *Ring of Steel* p 396-97
[484] See: 1910 census
[485] Alexander Watson, *Ring of Steel: Germany and Austria-Hungary in World War I* (2014), p 536
[486] Watson, *Ring of Steel* pp 536–40
[487] Watson, *Ring of Steel* pp 541–2
[488] Watson, *Ring of Steel* pp 542–56
[489] Croatian-Hungarian Settlement https://www.h-net.org/~habsweb/sourcetexts/nagodba2.htm
[490] Croatian-Hungarian Settlement https://www.h-net.org/~habsweb/sourcetexts/nagodba2.htm
[491] , p. 50
[492] https://books.google.com/?id=CMYUAAAAQAAJ
[493] https://doi.org/10.1093%2Facprof%3Aoso%2F9780199541621.001.0001
[494] https://www.amazon.com/Habsburg-Empire-New-History/dp/0674047761/
[495] https://archive.org/details/emperorfrancisjo002603mbp
[496] https://archive.org/details/in.ernet.dli.2015.176378
[497] https://books.google.com/?id=dAJDAAAAIAAJ&pg=PA145
[498] https://www.jstor.org/stable/1875406
[499] https://archive.org/details/habsburgempirein00kann
[500] https://www.library6.com/books/523600.pdf#page=95
[501] https//www.cambridge.org
[502] https://books.google.com/books?id=vdqCCwAAQBAJ
[503] http://www.history.ac.uk/reviews/review/1556
[504] https://www.jstor.org/stable/1986702
[505] https://www.jstor.org/stable/1876727
[506] https://www.jstor.org/stable/2493764
[507] https://www.questia.com/read/100089084/austria-hungary-including-dalmatia-and-bosnia-handbook
[508] http://www.zum.de/whkmla/histatlas/germany/haxhabsbdaust.html
[509] http://encarta.msn.com/encyclopedia_761579967_1____7/austria-hungary.html#s7
[510] https://www.webcitation.org/5kwKqzJwX?url=http://encarta.msn.com/encyclopedia_761579967_1____7/austria-hungary.html
[511] http://www.austro-hungarian-army.co.uk/
[512] http://www.ngw.nl/int/oos/ooshong/ooshong.htm
[513] https://web.archive.org/web/20080112124023/http://www.geocities.com/CapitolHill/Rotunda/2209/Austria_Hungary.html
[514] http://www.geldschein.at/
[515] http://www.aeiou.at/aeiou.encyclop.o/o818181.htm;internal&action=_setlanguage.action?LANGUAGE=en
[516] http://www.frontedolomitico.it/
[517] http://maps.omniatlas.com/europe/19181025/
[518] http://hdl.handle.net/1911/15059
[519] http://www.austro-hungarian-army.co.uk/index.htm
[520] http://www.h-net.org/~habsweb/

[521] //tools.wmflabs.org/geohack/geohack.php?pagename=Austria-Hungary&params=48_12_N_16_21_E_source:kowiki

[522] *Hungary: The Unwilling Satellite* http://historicaltextarchive.com/books.php?op=viewbook&bookid=7&pre=1 John F. Montgomery, *Hungary: The Unwilling Satellite*. Devin-Adair Company, New York, 1947. Reprint: Simon Publications, 2002.

[523] Pogany, Istvan, *Righting Wrongs in Eastern Europe*, Manchester University Press, 1997, pp.26-39, 80-94.

[524] Dawidowicz, Lucy. *The War Against the Jews*, Bantam, 1986, p. 403; Randolph Braham, *A Magyarországi Holokauszt Földrajzi Enciklopediája* (*The Geographic Encyclopedia of the Holocaust in Hungary*), Park Publishing, 2006, Vol 1, p. 91.

[525] Crowe, David. "The Roma Holocaust," in Barnard Schwartz and Frederick DeCoste, eds., *The Holocaust's Ghost: Writings on Art, Politics, Law and Education*, University of Alberta Press, 2000, pp. 178–210.

[526] '2. Zusatzvertrag zum deutsch-ungarischen Wirtschaftsabkommen von 1931 (Details https://books.google.de/books?id=lefKBgAAQBAJ&pg=PA155)

[527] Thomas, *The Royal Hungarian Army in World War II*, pg. 11

[528] Hungary http://www.usc.edu/libraries/archives/arc/libraries/sfa/hungary.html - Shoah Foundation Institute Visual History Archive

[529] Holocaust in Hungary http://www.hdke.hu/index.php?menu=070101&mgroup=1&app=info&page=main&artid=b39689db307eea957accaa1d04e4c330The Holocaust Memorial Centre.

[530] Victims of Holocaust http://www.hdke.hu/index.php?menu=070102&mgroup=1&app=info&page=main&artid=41e4d6b481e6ac01d487afa1b38b615c - Holocaust Memorial Centre.

[531] *The Decline and Fall of Nazi Germany and Imperial Japan*, Hans Dollinger, Library of Congress Catalogue Card Number 67-27047

[532] Stafford, *Endgame, 1945*, p. 242.

[533] Treaty of Peace with Hungary http://www.law.fsu.edu/library/collection/LimitsnSeas/IBS076.pdf

[534] http://www.axishistory.com/index.php?id=36

[535] http://www.bunkermuzeum.hu/

[536] https://web.archive.org/web/20070701005927/http://www.terra.es/personal7/jqvaraderey/194145fc.gif

[537] http://terkepek.adatbank.transindex.ro/kepek/netre/224.gif

[538] Sources vary widely on numbers of Soviet forces involved in the intervention. The UN General Assembly *Special Committee on the Problem of Hungary* (1957) estimated 75,000–200,000 troops and 1,600–4,000 tanks OSZK.hu http://mek.oszk.hu/01200/01274/01274.pdf (p. 56, para. 183), but recently released Soviet archives (available in Lib.ru, Maksim Moshkow's Library) list the troop strength of the Soviet forces as 31,550, with 1,130 tanks and self-propelled artillery pieces. Lib.ru http://fan.lib.ru/c/chekmarew_w_a/text_0200.shtml

[539] UN General Assembly *Special Committee on the Problem of Hungary* (1957)

[540] "B&J": Jacob Bercovitch and Richard Jackson, International Conflict : A Chronological Encyclopedia of Conflicts and Their Management 1945–1995 (1997)

[541] //en.wikipedia.org/w/index.php?title=Template:History_of_Hungary&action=edit

[542] //en.wikipedia.org/w/index.php?title=Template:Eastern_Bloc_sidebar&action=edit

[543] Alternate references are "Hungarian Revolt" and "Hungarian Uprising". In Hungarian, first the term "felkelés" (uprising) was used, then in the 1957–1988 period, the term "ellenforradalom" (counter-revolution) was mandated by the government, while the new official name after 1990 has become "forradalom és szabadságharc" (revolution and freedom fight) to imitate the old expression for the 1848–1849 revolution. Another explanation of the terms is that "Revolution" conforms to both English (see US Department of State background on Hungary) https://www.state.gov/r/pa/ei/bgn/26566.htm and Hungarian ("forradalom") conventions. There is a distinction between the "complete overthrow" of a revolution and an uprising or revolt that may or may not be successful (Oxford English Dictionary). The 1956 Hungarian event, although short-lived, is a true "revolution" in that the sitting government was deposed.

Unlike the terms "coup d'état" and "putsch" that imply action of a few, the 1956 revolution was initiated by the masses.

[544] Retrieved 8 October 2006
[545] UN General Assembly *Special Committee on the Problem of Hungary* (1957)
[546] UN General Assembly *Special Committee on the Problem of Hungary* (1957)
[547] UN General Assembly *Special Committee on the Problem of Hungary* (1957)
[548] UN General Assembly *Special Committee on the Problem of Hungary* (1957)
[549] Crampton, R. J. (2003). *Eastern Europe in the Twentieth Century–and After*, p. 295. Routledge: London.
[550] **Video**: Hungary in Flames CEU.hu http://files.osa.ceu.hu/holdings/selection/rip/4/av/1956-43.html producer: CBS (1958) – Fonds 306, Audiovisual Materials Relating to the 1956 Hungarian Revolution, OSA Archivum, Budapest, Hungary ID number: HU OSA 306–0–1:40
[551] Tőkés, Rudolf L. (1998). *Hungary's Negotiated Revolution: Economic Reform, Social Change and Political Succession*, p. 317. Cambridge University Press: Cambridge.
[552] Gati describes "the most gruesome forms of psychological and physical torture ... The reign of terror (by the Rákosi government) turned out to be harsher and more extensive than it was in any of the other Soviet satellites in Central and Eastern Europe." He further references a report prepared after the collapse of communism, the Fact Finding Commission *Törvénytelen szocializmus* (Lawless Socialism): "Between 1950 and early 1953, the courts dealt with 650,000 cases (of political crimes), of whom 387,000 or 4 percent of the population were found guilty. (Budapest, Zrínyi Kiadó/Új Magyarország, 1991, 154).
[553] , Chapter 2 (The Society and Its Environment) "Religion and Religious Organizations"
[554] Douglas, J. D. and Philip Comfort (eds.) (1992). *Who's Who in Christian History*, p. 478. Tyndale House: Carol Stream, Illinois.
[555] The Avalon Project at Yale Law School: Armistice Agreement with Hungary; 20 January 1945 http://www.yale.edu/lawweb/avalon/wwii/hungary.htm#art12 . Retrieved 27 August 2006.
[556] Magyar Nemzeti Bank – English Site: History http://english.mnb.hu/Engine.aspx?page=mnben_1_jegybankrol&ContentID=2326 Retrieved 27 August 2006 According to Wikipedia Hyperinflation article, 4.19×10^{16} percent per month (prices doubled every 15 hours).
[557] pp. 214, 217
[558] Transformation of the Hungarian economy http://www.rev.hu/history_of_45/tanulm_gazd/gazd_e.htm The Institute for the History of the 1956 Hungarian Revolution (2003). Retrieved 27 August 2006.
[559] Library of Congress: Country Studies: Hungary, Chapter 3 Economic Policy and Performance, 1945–85 http://lcweb2.loc.gov/frd/cs/hutoc.html#hu0138. Retrieved 27 August 2006.
[560] UN General Assembly *Special Committee on the Problem of Hungary* (1957)
[561] *Legacy of Ashes: The History of the CIA* by Tim Weiner, p. 144 (2008 Penguin Books edition)
[562] **Video** (in German): Berichte aus Budapest: Der Ungarn Aufstand 1956 {{ CEU.hu http://files.osa.ceu.hu/holdings/selection/rip/4/av/1956-29.html Director: Helmut Dotterweich, (1986) – Fonds 306, Audiovisual Materials Relating to the 1956 Hungarian Revolution, OSA Archivum, Budapest, Hungary ID number: HU OSA 306-0-1:27}}
[563] UN General Assembly *Special Committee on the Problem of Hungary* (1957)
[564] *Legacy of Ashes: The History of the CIA* by Tim Weiner, page 145 (2008 Penguin Books edition)
[565] *Legacy of Ashes: The History of the CIA* by Tim Weiner, p. 149 (2008 Penguin Books edition)
[566] UN General Assembly *Special Committee on the Problem of Hungary* (1957)
[567] Internet Modern History Sourcebook: Resolution by students of the Building Industry Technological University: Sixteen Political, Economic, and Ideological Points, Budapest, 22 October 1956 http://www.fordham.edu/halsall/mod/1956hungary-16points.html. Retrieved 22 October 2006.
[568] United Nations Report of the Special Committee on the Problem of Hungary http://mek.oszk.hu/01200/01274/01274.pdf. p. 145, para 441. Retrieved 11 April 2007.
[569] //en.wikipedia.org/w/index.php?title=Template:Revolution_sidebar&action=edit
[570] **Video** (in Hungarian): The First Hours of the Revolution {{http://files.osa.ceu.hu/holdings/selection/rip/4/av/1956-42.html director: György Ordódy, producer: Duna Televízió – Fonds

306, Audiovisual Materials Relating to the 1956 Hungarian Revolution, OSA Archivum, Budapest, Hungary ID number: HU OSA 306-0-1:40}}

[571] UN General Assembly *Special Committee on the Problem of Hungary* (1957)

[572] UN General Assembly *Special Committee on the Problem of Hungary* (1957)

[573] UN General Assembly *Special Committee on the Problem of Hungary* (1957)

[574] UN General Assembly *Special Committee on the Problem of Hungary* (1957)

[575] Gati states: "discovered in declassified documents, the Soviet Ministry of Defense had begun to prepare for large-scale turmoil in Hungary as early as July 1956. Codenamed "Wave", the plan called for restoration of order in less than six hours ... the Soviet Army was ready. More than 30,000 troops were dispatched to—and 6,000 reached—Budapest by the 24th, that is, in less than a day."

[576] UN General Assembly *Special Committee on the Problem of Hungary* (1957)

[577] UN General Assembly *Special Committee on the Problem of Hungary* (1957)

[578] UN General Assembly *Special Committee on the Problem of Hungary* (1957)

[579] UN General Assembly *Special Committee on the Problem of Hungary* (1957)

[580] UN General Assembly *Special Committee on the Problem of Hungary* (1957)

[581] UN General Assembly *Special Committee on the Problem of Hungary* (1957)

[582] UN General Assembly *Special Committee on the Problem of Hungary* (1957)

[583] UN General Assembly *Special Committee on the Problem of Hungary* (1957)

[584] UN General Assembly *Special Committee on the Problem of Hungary* (1957)

[585] Олег Филимонов: Мифы о восстании – ПОЛИТ.РУ http://www.polit.ru/article/2006/10/30/mify_vengr/. Polit.ru (30 October 2006). Retrieved on 28 October 2016.

[586] János Berecz. *1956 Counter-Revolution in Hungary*. Akadémiai Kiadó. 1986. p. 116

[587] Berecz, 117

[588] Cold War International History Project (CWIHP), KGB Chief Serov's report, 29 October 1956 http://digitalarchive.wilsoncenter.org/document/111091, (by permission of the Woodrow Wilson International Center for Scholars) Retrieved 8 October 2006

[589] UN General Assembly *Special Committee on the Problem of Hungary* (1957)

[590] (pp. 176–77)

[591] UN General Assembly *Special Committee on the Problem of Hungary* (1957)

[592] **Video**:

[593] *Ellenforradalmi erők a magyar októberi eseményekben 1–5*, Budapest: a Magyar Népköztársaság Minisztertanácsa Tájekoztatási Hivatala, 1956–8; available in translation as *The counter-revolutionary forces in the October events in Hungary 1–5* (volumes after 2 variously titled, including 5: *The counter-revolutionary conspiracy of Imre Nagy and his accomplices*) Budapest: Information Bureau of the Council of Ministers of the Hungarian People's Republic, 1957–1958; names 213 people killed by the rebels.

[594] UN General Assembly *Special Committee on the Problem of Hungary* (1957)

[595] UN General Assembly *Special Committee on the Problem of Hungary*(1957)

[596] **Video**: Revolt in Hungary Narrator: Walter Cronkite, producer: CBS (1956) – Fonds 306, Audiovisual Materials Relating to the 1956 Hungarian Revolution, OSA Archivum, Budapest, Hungary ID number: HU OSA 306–0–1:40

[597] Vincent E McHale (1983) *Political parties of Europe*, Greenwood Press, p. 508

[598] UN General Assembly *Special Committee on the Problem of Hungary*(1957)

[599] Fonds 306, Audiovisual Materials Relating to the 1956 Hungarian Revolution, OSA Archivum, Budapest, Hungary ID number: HU OSA 306–0–1:1

[600] *Hungary: workers' councils against Russian tanks* http://www.isj.org.uk/index.php4?id=250&issue=112 in *International Socialism (magazine)* Issue: 112 (Posted: 12 October 6)

[601] "Hungary '56: "the proletariat storming heaven" – Mouvement Communiste" http://libcom.org/library/hungary-56-proletariat-storming-heaven-mouvement-communiste. Libcom.org (19 July 2011). Retrieved on 2016-10-28.

[602] Andy Anderson 1956: The Hungarian Revolution http://libcom.org/history/articles/hungary-56 – 15. *The Workers' Councils* http://libcom.org/library/Hungary5615

[603] UN General Assembly *Special Committee on the Problem of Hungary* (1957)

[604] UN General Assembly *Special Committee on the Problem of Hungary* (1957)

[605] "When the Soviet Union nearly blinked" http://news.bbc.co.uk/2/hi/europe/6061852.stm, *BBC News*, 23 October 2006

[606] Declaration of the Government of the USSR on the Principles of Development and Further Strengthening of Friendship and Cooperation between the Soviet Union and other Socialist States http://www.fordham.edu/halsall/mod/1956soviet-coop1.html 30 October 1956, Printed in The Department of State Bulletin, XXXV, No. 907 (12 November 1956), pp. 745–47. Retrieved 19 October 2006.

[607] Mark Kramer, "New Evidence on Soviet Decision-making and the 1956 Polish and Hungarian Crises" (PDF) http://www.wilsoncenter.org/topics/pubs/ACF19B.pdf, Cold War International History Project Bulletin, page 368.

[608] The Institute for the History of the 1956 Hungarian Revolution: Part 3. Days of Freedom http://www.rev.hu/history_of_56/ora3/ora3_e.htm

[609] William Taubman: *Khrushchev: The Man and His Era* (2005), , p. 296.

[610] Sebestyen, Victor, *Ungernrevolten 1956: Tolv dagar som skakade världen* (2006), p. 286. (Swedish edition of *Twelve Days: The Story of the 1956 Hungarian Revolution*), . (Cites Borhi, *Hungary in the Cold War* (2004), pp. 243–49.)

[611] Mark Kramer, "New Evidence on Soviet Decision-making and the 1956 Polish and Hungarian Crises" (PDF) http://www.wilsoncenter.org/topics/pubs/ACF19B.pdf, Cold War International History Project Bulletin, page 369.

[612] Sebestyen, Victor, *Ungernrevolten 1956: Tolv dagar som skakade världen* (2006), p. 286.

[613] Sebestyen, Victor, *Ungernrevolten 1956: Tolv dagar som skakade världen* (2006), p. 286. (Cites Burlatsky, *Khrushchev and the first Russian Spring* (1991), pp. 88–94.)

[614] Johanna Granville, "New Insights on the 1956 Crisis" http://www.h-net.org/reviews/showrev.cgi?path=12620949617664, 2000–01

[615] Cold War International History Project: Working Notes from the Session of the CPSU CC Presidium on 1 November 1956 http//wilsoncenter.org. Retrieved 6 December 2008.

[616] Cold War International History Project (CWIHP), Report from A. Grechko and Tarasov in Berlin to N. A. Bulganin http://digitalarchive.wilsoncenter.org/document/110024.pdf?v=44e8834f7ae7294020d5e423a1c013a1, (by permission of the Woodrow Wilson International Center for Scholars) Retrieved 10 October 2006

[617] Andrzej Paczkowski, *Pół wieku dziejów Polski*, Wydawnictwo Naukowe PWN, Warszawa 2005, , p. 203

[618] Ł. Jastrząb, "Rozstrzelano moje serce w Poznaniu. Poznański Czerwiec 1956 r. – straty osobowe i ich analiza", Wydawnictwo Comandor, Warszawa 2006

[619] Wójtowicz, Norbert. *Ofiary "Poznańskiego Czerwca"*, Rok 1956 na Węgrzech i w Polsce. Materiały z węgiersko–polskiego seminarium. Wrocław październik 1996, ed. Łukasz Andrzej Kamiński, Wrocław 1996, pp. 32–41.

[620] Cold War International History Project (CWIHP), Working Notes from the Session of the CPSU CC Presidium on 3 November, 1956, with Participation by J. Kádár, F. Münnich, and I. Horváth http://digitalarchive.wilsoncenter.org/document/113648, (by permission of the Woodrow Wilson International Center for Scholars) Retrieved 8 October 2006

[621] UN General Assembly *Special Committee on the Problem of Hungary* (1957)

[622] Philip Short, *Mao: a life* (2001), p. 451.

[623] John Lewis Gaddis, *The Cold War: a new history* (2005), p. 109.

[624] Sebestyen, Victor, *Ungernrevolten 1956: Tolv dagar som skakade världen* (2006), p. 247.

[625] William Taubman: *Khrushchev: The Man and His Era* (2005), , p. 297.

[626] Mark Kramer, "New Evidence on Soviet Decision-making and the 1956 Polish and Hungarian Crises" (PDF) http://www.wilsoncenter.org/topics/pubs/ACF19B.pdf, Cold War International History Project Bulletin, pp. 373–74.

[627] Slobodan Stankovic, "Yugoslav Diplomat who Defied Soviet Leaders Dies" http://files.osa.ceu.hu/holdings/300/8/3/text/118-1-194.shtml , Radio Free Europe Research, 5 August 1982.

[628] Johanna Granville, *The First Domino: International Decision Making During the Hungarian Crisis of 1956.* https://www.academia.edu/23951275/The_First_Domino_International_Decision_making_during_the_Hungarian_Revolution_of_1956 Texas A & M University Press, 2004 (p. 103).

[629] *Legacy of Ashes: The History of the CIA* by Tim Weiner, pp. 150–51 (2008 Penguin Books edition)
[630] *Legacy of Ashes: The History of the CIA* by Tim Weiner, p. 153 (2008 Penguin Books edition)
[631] Hungarian Revolt, 23 October–4 November 1956 (Richard Lettis and William I. Morris, editors): Appendices The Hungary Question in the United Nations http://www.historicaltextarchive.com/books.php?op=viewbook&bookid=13&post=2#N_1_. Retrieved 3 September 2006.
[632] CNN: Géza Jeszenszky, Hungarian Ambassador, Cold War Chat (transcript) http://www.cnn.com/SPECIALS/cold.war/guides/debate/chats/jeszensky/. Retrieved 8 November 1998.
[633] UN General Assembly *Special Committee on the Problem of Hungary* (1957)
[634] Imre Nagy's Telegram to Diplomatic Missions in Budapest Declaring Hungary's Neutrality (1 November 1956) http://www.php.isn.ethz.ch/collections/colltopic.cfm?lng=en&id=20933&navinfo=15697 by permission of the Center for Security Studies at ETH Zürich and the National Security Archive at the George Washington University on behalf of the PHP network
[635] UN General Assembly *Special Committee on the Problem of Hungary* (1957)
[636] UN General Assembly *Special Committee on the Problem of Hungary* (1957)
[637] UN General Assembly *Special Committee on the Problem of Hungary* (1957)
[638] UN General Assembly *Special Committee on the Problem of Hungary* (1957)
[639] UN General Assembly *Special Committee on the Problem of Hungary* (1957)
[640] UN General Assembly *Special Committee on the Problem of Hungary* (1957)
[641] UN General Assembly *Special Committee on the Problem of Hungary* (1957)
[642] UN General Assembly *Special Committee on the Problem of Hungary* (1957)
[643] UN General Assembly *Special Committee on the Problem of Hungary* (1957)
[644] UN General Assembly *Special Committee on the Problem of Hungary* (1957)
[645] UN General Assembly *Special Committee on the Problem of Hungary* (1957)
[646] UN General Assembly *Special Committee on the Problem of Hungary* (1957)
[647] UN General Assembly *Special Committee on the Problem of Hungary* (1957)
[648] Mark Kramer, "The Soviet Union and the 1956 Crises in Hungary and Poland: Reassessments and New Findings", *Journal of Contemporary History*, Vol. 33, No. 2, April 1998, p. 210.
[649] Péter Gosztonyi, "Az 1956-os forradalom számokban", *Népszabadság* (Budapest), 3 November 1990
[650] Pravda (Moscow), 4 November [227/228]: "Without the Slightes Delays", Moscow
Imre Nagy turned out to be, objectively speaking, an accomplice of the reactionary forces. Imre Nagy cannot and does not want to fight the dark forces of reaction ... The Soviet Government, seeing that the presence of Soviet troops in Budapest might lead to further aggravation of the situation, ordered troops to leave Budapest, but ensuing events have shown that reactionary forces, taking advantage of the non-intervention of the Nagy Cabinet, have gone still further ... The task of barring the way to reaction in Hungary has to be carried out without the slightest delay -such is the course dictated by events ...
Retrieved 2007-10-8 Hungarian-history.hu http://www.hungarian-history.hu/lib/revolt/rev16.htm
[651]
[652] George Washington University: The National Security Archive, Communiqué on the Meeting of Representatives of the Governments and the Communist and Workers' Parties of Bulgaria, Czechoslovakia, Hungary, Romania and the Soviet Union http://www.gwu.edu/~nsarchiv/NSAEBB/NSAEBB76/doc11.pdf (Budapest, 6 January 1957), Retrieved 7 December 2008
[653] George Washington University: The National Security Archive, Minutes of the Meeting between the Hungarian and Chinese Delegations http://www.gwu.edu/%7Ensarchiv/NSAEBB/NSAEBB76/doc12.pdf in Budapest on 16 January 1957, Retrieved 7 December 2008
[654] *The 1956 Hungarian Revolution: A History in Documents* by Csaba Békés & Malcolm Byrne (Published by Central European University Press, 2002, , , 598 pages), p. 375, para 4: "... the (Kádár) regime had to find an explanation for the revolution and collapse of the old regime in October 1956 ... they chose to interpret the uprising as a conspiracy by anti-communist, reactionary forces. This is why they labeled many ordinary citizens' actions as crimes. Critical opposition attitudes were described as "a plot to overthrow the people's democratic regime", and workers and peasants who took part in the revolt were called "jailbirds, ragamuffins, and kulaks."

Armed resistance to occupying forces became "murder and wrecking state property." This kind of terminology became part of the official ideology of the regime toward the outside world." Also p. 375, footnote 40: "For a typical survey of propaganda intended for distribution abroad, see the so called "White Books" entitled *The Counter-Revolutionary Forces in the October Events in Hungary*, 4 vols., (Budapest: Information Bureau of the Council of Ministers of the Hungarian People's Republic, 1956–1957) ... The White Books published in the individual counties of Hungary in 1957–1958 summarized local "counter-revolutionary" events."

[655] Casardi, A. (17 April 1957) Report on Hungarian Refugees http://www.nato.int/nato_static/assets/pdf/pdf_archives_hungarian_revolution/20130904_C-M_57_65-ENG.PDF. *NATO*

[656] Békés, Csaba, Malcolm Byrne, János M. Rainer (2002). *Hungarian Tragedy*, p. L. Central European University Press: Budapest.

[657] UN General Assembly *Special Committee on the Problem of Hungary* (1957)

[658] UN General Assembly *Special Committee on the Problem of Hungary* (1957)

[659] International Committee of the Red Cross: ICRC action in Hungary in 1956 http://www.icrc.org/Web/Eng/siteeng0.nsf/html/57JN8C#a1. Retrieved 7 December 2008.

[660] Fryer, Peter (1997). *Hungarian Tragedy*, p. 10. Index Books: London.

[661] "On This Day 16 June 1989: Hungary reburies fallen hero Imre Nagy" http://news.bbc.co.uk/onthisday/hi/dates/stories/june/16/ British Broadcasting Corporation (BBC) reports on Nagy reburial with full honors. Retrieved 13 October 2006.

[662] Johns Hopkins University Professor Charles Gati, in his book *Failed Illusions: Moscow, Washington, Budapest, and the 1956 Hungarian Revolt* (see Further reading, below), agreed with a 2002 essay by Hungarian historian Csaba Bekes, "Could the Hungarian Revolution Have Been Victorious in 1956?". Gati states: "Washington implicitly acknowledging the division of the continent into two camps, understood that Moscow would not let go of a country bordering on neutral but pro-Western Austria and an independent Yugoslavia, so it shed ... tears over Soviet brutality, and exploited the propaganda opportunities ..." (p. 208)

[663] UN General Assembly *Special Committee on the Problem of Hungary* (1957)

[664] UN General Assembly *Special Committee on the Problem of Hungary* (1957)

[665] UN General Assembly (1957) *Special Committee on the Problem of Hungary* http://mek.oszk.hu/01200/01274/01274.pdf. Retrieved 14 October 2006.

[666] UN General Assembly *Special Committee on the Problem of Hungary* (1957)

[667] United Nations General Assembly, Thirteenth Session: Resolution 1312 (XIII) The Situation in Hungary (Item 59, p. 69 http://www.unhcr.org/refworld/docid/3b00f06b36.html (12 December 1958)

[668] ed. A. T. Lane. *Biographical dictionary of European labor leaders*. Volume 1. Greenwood Publishing Group, 1995. p. 20.

[669] Alsing Andersen http://www.gravsted.dk/person.php?navn=alsingandersen. Gravsted.dk. Retrieved on 28 October 2016.

[670] United Nations Yearbook. 1957. p. 63

[671] K. Danilov "The Provocation Continues". International Affairs, No. 8, Vol. 3, 1957, pp. 54–61

[672] . Retrieved 21 September 2008.

[673] Formal Address http://www.miniszterelnok.hu/mss/alpha?do=2&st=1&pg=2&m10_doc=546 of Prime Minister Ferenc Gyurcsány in the Hungarian Parliament (23 October 2006). Retrieved 21 September 2008.

[674] Statement with the Hungarian Prime Minister (11 October 2006) http://www.number10.gov.uk/Page10194 Retrieved 22 September 2008

[675] Melbourne/Stockholm 1956 (All facts) Olympic.org http://www.olympic.org/en/content/Olympic-Games/All-Past-Olympic-Games/Summer/Melbourne--Stockholm-1956/ Retrieved 29 August 2010.

[676] Radio Free Europe: Hungary: New Film Revisits 1956 Water-Polo Showdown http://www.rferl.org/featuresarticle/2006/05/0e5164bb-fd53-4562-88c5-9aac69e5845c.html. Retrieved 13 October 2006.

[677] Szabadság, szerelem (Children of Glory) http://european-films.net/content/view/603/57/ (film) 2006.

[678] Federal Reserve Bank of Minneapolis Community Development Project. "Consumer Price Index (estimate) 1800–" https://www.minneapolisfed.org/community/teaching-aids/cpi-

calculator-information/consumer-price-index-1800. Federal Reserve Bank of Minneapolis. Retrieved January 2, 2017.
[679] The following are references in English on the conflicting positions of *l'Unità* http://www.time.com/time/magazine/article/0,9171,808752,00.html, Antonio Giolitti and party boss Palmiro Togliatti http://www.time.com/time/magazine/article/0,9171,808824,00.html, Giuseppe Di Vittorio http://www.time.com/time/magazine/article/0,9171,868066,00.html and Pietro Nenni http://www.britannica.com/eb/article-219206/socialism.
[680] Sartre, Jean-Paul (1956), L'intellectuel et les communistes français https://www.humanite.fr/node/329963 Le Web de l'Humanite, 21 June 2005. Retrieved 24 October 2006.
[681] http://carlbeckpapers.pitt.edu/ojs/index.php/cbp/article/view/80
[682] https://web.archive.org/web/20070903000540/http://www.hungarian-history.hu/lib/dipl/dipl00.htm
[683] http://www.hungarian-history.hu/lib/dipl/dipl00.htm
[684] http://mek.oszk.hu/01200/01274/01274.pdf
[685] https://web.archive.org/web/20060807225525/http://www.hungary1956.com/docs/Urmenyhazi_HungarianRevolution_1956.pdf
[686] http://digitalarchive.wilsoncenter.org/collection/9/1956-polish-and-hungarian-crises
[687] http://www.rev.hu/
[688] http://osaarchivum.org/digitalarchive/av/
[689] https://archive.org/details/1956_Hungarian_Revolution_as_Depicted_in_Newsreels
[690] http://news.bbc.co.uk/onthisday/hi/dates/stories/november/4/newsid_2739000/2739039.stm
[691] http://libcom.org/library/hungary-56-andy-anderson
[692] https://archive.org/details/gov.archives.arc.2569633
[693] https://archive.org/details/gov.archives.arc.1683326
[694] https://archive.org/details/gov.archives.arc.2049945
[695] http://mek.oszk.hu/09600/09691/index.phtml
[696] http://nsarchive.gwu.edu/briefing-book/us-soviet-flashpoints/2017-05-10/hungary-1956-reviving-debate-over-us-inaction-during
[697] http://www.rferl.org/featuresarticle/2006/05/0e5164bb-fd53-4562-88c5-9aac69e5845c.html
[698] http://www.imdb.com/title/tt0468559/
[699] http://www.hungary1956.com/
[700] http://www.freedomfighter56.com/en_stories_2all.html
[701] https://web.archive.org/web/20080915210152/http://www.multiculturalcanada.ca/node/1521
[702] http://mek.oszk.hu/09400/09426/index.phtml
[703] //en.wikipedia.org/w/index.php?title=Template:History_of_Hungary&action=edit
[704] David 2009.
[705] Haydn 1910.
[706] Overall 1870.
[707] Chambers 1901.
[708] Eggenberger 1870.
[709] Nemes 2009.
[710] Büchler 1907.
[711] Britannica 1910.
[712] Heksch 1895.
[713] Shaw 1897.
[714] Lukacs 2012.
[715] Metro-Roland 2012.
[716] (about Berlin, Budapest, Prague, Warsaw)
[717] Hourihane 2012.
[718] Fenyo 1987.
[719] Történelmi Magyarország atlasza és adattára 1914, Budapest, 2001
[720] Nagy 2002.
[721] Deák 1968.
[722] Bodnár 1998.
[723] Bodnár 2001.
[724] http://hdl.handle.net/2027/uc2.ark:/13960/t9m32q949?urlappend=%3Bseq=123

[725] http://hdl.handle.net/2027/uc2.ark:/13960/t9m32rg8w?urlappend=%3Bseq=457
[726] http://hdl.handle.net/2027/uc2.ark:/13960/t0ft8v96d?urlappend=%3Bseq=94
[727] https://archive.org/stream/jewishencycloped03sing#page/416/mode/1up
[728] https://archive.org/stream/encyclopaediabri04chisrich#page/734/mode/1up
[729] //www.worldcat.org/oclc/14782424
[730] https://archive.org/stream/haydnsdictionary00hayd#page/214/mode/1up
[731] https://books.google.com/books?id=nTUQAAAAYAAJ&pg=PA42
[732] //www.jstor.org/stable/4205930
[733] //www.jstor.org/stable/1006574
[734] //www.jstor.org/stable/2500709
[735] https://books.google.com/books?id=S0_Vj7y9hDgC
[736] https://books.google.com/books?id=PPCJAgAAQBAJ&pg=PA72
[737] https://books.google.com/books?id=QjzYdCxumFcC&pg=PA94
[738] https://books.google.com/books?id=M_aMAgAAQBAJ&pg=PA141
[739] https://books.google.com/books?id=FtlMAgAAQBAJ&pg=PA451
[740] https://books.google.com/books?id=LSfhw-jzyE4C
[741] https://books.google.com/books?id=fB01Wl22GYkC
[742] https://books.google.com/books?id=QWM_AQAAMAAJ
[743] https://books.google.com/books?id=risPAQAAMAAJ

Article Sources and Contributors

The sources listed for each article provide more detailed licensing information including the copyright status, the copyright owner, and the license conditions.

Hungarian prehistory *Source:* https://en.wikipedia.org/w/index.php?oldid=805717879 *License:* Creative Commons Attribution-Share Alike 3.0 *Contributors:* A2-33, AKiwiDeerPin, Againme, Angr, BD2412, Baffle gab1978, Bamyers99, Blustler, Borsoka, Carnuntum, CommonsDelinker, Dthomsen8, Fakirbakir, Flobbadob, Florian Blaschke, Gorcat, HD86, Hibernian, Hidaspal, Hirabutor, Hortobagy, Hydraton31, Indigoeleven, JJMC89, Jageterix, John of Reading, Johnbod, Kay LaFay, Kintetsubuffalo, Koertefa, Llywrch, Look2See1, Magyar from Ural, Maswimelleu, Mogism, Moswento, Myasuda, Natg 19, Nedrutland, NicoScribe, Nikkimaria, Nizolan, Norden1990, Oldhouse2012, Richard Keatinge, Silverije, Smart Nomad, Taz, The Rambling Man, Torvalu4, TrixAreForKidsSillyRabbit, Tropylium, Ulric1313, Wario-Man, WereSpielChequers, 15 anonymous edits 1

Aquincum *Source:* https://en.wikipedia.org/w/index.php?oldid=807946227 *License:* Creative Commons Attribution-Share Alike 3.0 *Contributors:* 3ig-350125, A314268, Adam78, AlexanderVanLoon, Alfons2, Anastasia.Bukh, Attilios, Axeman89, BalkanAlliance, Bongwarrior, Caeruleancentaur, CaroleHenson, ChrisGualtieri, Civertan, Codrinb, D6, Daanschr, Darkstar1st, Deinocheirus, Dimitrii, Docu, Elisa.rolle, Esoltas, Eulogetos, Euratlas, Felix Folio Secundus, Gail, Gilliam, Groovenstein, Hobartimus, Iamthecheese44, Ian Pitchford, Iazyges, KIDB, Kfbs06, Kispál Zoltán, Korneld, Laurel Lodged, Magioladitis, Marcocapelle, Marcus Cyron, Mevagiss, Morningstar1814, Mysid, NawlinWiki, Neddyseagoon, Olivier, Omnipaedista, Oyfenthalt, Panairjdde∼enwiki, Paul S, Pegship, Psychonaut, RevelationDirect, Rhollenton, Rjdeadly, Rrius, SchreiberBike, SkiDragon, Szilágyi Ernő, Tbhotch, Thomas Antonius, Tomica, Tralala0, Twigletmac, Udimu, Waacstats, Woohookitty, 20 anonymous edits 32

Kingdom of Hungary (1526–1867) *Source:* https://en.wikipedia.org/w/index.php?oldid=805423575 *License:* Creative Commons Attribution-Share Alike 3.0 *Contributors:* 123Steller, AjaxSmack, Alfietucker, Alro, Aoidh, Apuldram, Aradic-es, Attilios, AvalerionV, Avaring, Awiseman, BDD, Baxter9, Bender235, Bgwhite, Bizso, Bozo1789, Brandmeister, Bzg1920, CanisRufus, Choalbaton, Codrinb, CommonsDelinker, Conducts, CsabaBabba, Cserlajos, Dbachmann, DocWatson42, EamonnPKeane, Editor2020, Esoltas, Fakirbakir, Frosty, Funnyface11, Gilo1969, Hebel, Hmains, Hobartimus, HydroBeaver, ITSENJOYABLE, Iaaasi, Indigoeleven, Iritakamas, Italia2006, J 1982, JaGa, Jaro88slav, Jfruh, John K, Joy, Juro, KIENGIR, KLBot2, Kenadra, Khoikhoi, KissL, Koertefa, Laslovarga, LilHelpa, Look2See1, Luis Molnar, Lulo.it, Magioladitis, Malcolmxl5, Marcocapelle, Mega Fixer Lee, Mermaid from the Baltic Sea, Michael Goodyear, Mix321, Mr Stephen, Mrkekson, Neutrality, Nmate, Norden1990, Oldhouse2012, Omnipaedista, PANONIAN, PZJTF, PaxEquilibrium, Pktlaurence, Qp10qp, RJFF, Reyk, Rgvis, Ritchie333, Rjecina, Rjwilmsi, Sadads, Samofi, Sct72, Ser Amantio di Nicolao, Silverhelm, SpellingGuru, Squash Racket, Squids and Chips, TRAJAN 117, TaBOT-zerem, The Anomebot2, ThecentreCZ, Thiseye, Tim!, Tomeczek, Toroko, Ulf Heinsohn, VinceB, Waynenoogen, WikiFlier, Wikid77, Wizzard, Woohookitty, Yopie, Zello, Zoupan, Zscout370, ۴, 49 anonymous edits 37

Buda Castle *Source:* https://en.wikipedia.org/w/index.php?oldid=803330610 *License:* Creative Commons Attribution-Share Alike 3.0 *Contributors:* 14GTR, 7&6=thirteen, 72, Adam Harangozó, Adam78, Algebraist, Andras0401, Andreas Kaganov, ApprenticeFan, Arch dude, Attilios, BD2412, Bermicourt, Billinghurst, Bkonrad, Civertan, ClueBot NG, Cold Season, D6, Dawnseeker2000, Dewritech, Diannaa, Donor001, Dourios, Dr.K., Dylandude6, Ebyabe, Egrian, Einstein2, Eleassar, Emmetfahy, EriFr, Eyesnore, Fakirbakir, Filederchest, Fluffernutter, GenQuest, George Ponderevo, Gfoley4, Globetrotter19, Gregorik, Gryffindor, Hmains, Hosszuka, Inwind, Jamesx12345, Jayjg, Jesi, Jllm06, John of Reading, Jorunn, KIDB, Kayninex, Kgf0, Khazar2, Kibi78704, Kispál Zoltán, Koertefa, Kummi, Like tears in rain, LilHelpa, Look2See1, Lotje, MIKHEIL, Mattisse, Matty.007, Mimihitam, Mogism, Necrothesp, Neurolysis-Auto, Nev1, Pjoef, Prof saxx, Qorilla, R00m c, RexNL, Richard Keatinge, Rjwilmsi, Sarmocid, SchreiberBike, Serols, Siggiboy81, Sigurdas, Soldier of the Empire, SpikeballUnion, Squash Racket, Stepheng3, Surtsicna, Szlgbp, TBloemink, Thiseye, Tiven2240, Tomica, Tripnoted, Túrelio, V79benno, Vegaswikian, Vozzz, Wai Hong, WereSpielChequers, Wikid77, WurmWoode, Zello, 80 anonymous edits 53

Ottoman Hungary *Source:* https://en.wikipedia.org/w/index.php?oldid=807598666 *License:* Creative Commons Attribution-Share Alike 3.0 *Contributors:* 123Steller, Aherunar, AjaxSmack, Alaexis, Alfons2, Angusmclellan, Anthony Appleyard, Asklepias, Attilios, Avaring, BD2412, Baristarim, Baxter9, Belligero, Bender235, Bestadvancer, Bhny, Bizovne, Blemse, Budija, Ceosad, Chamboz, Chitt66, ClueBot NG, CommonsDelinker, Comnenus, CoolKoon, Cplakidas, Dailogos, Darkercastel, Dbachmann, DeltaQuad, DragonTiger23, Emiellaiendiay, Emmetfahy, Fakirbakir, FocalPoint, Fz22, GRprefectures-have-been-dissolved, Gadget850, Good Olfactory, Ground Zero, Hairy Dude, Hasan-aga, Herostratus, Hmainsbot1, Hobartimus, ITSENJOYABLE, IkonicDeath, Inemanja, Inwind, Iritakamas, Itsmejudith, JHunterJ, JaGa, JoDonHo, John of Reading, Johnpacklambert, Joy, KLBot2, Kansas Bear, Kedadi, Khazar2, Khoikhoi, KissL, Koertefa, Koolokamba, Largerobanner, Laslovarga, Leegee23, Look2See1, Macrakis, Marcocapelle, MarekSS, Misibacsi, Mojo Hand, Moneycreator, Mukadderat, Nedim Ardoğa, Nihiltres, Norden1990, PANONIAN, PTSE, PottersWood, Reaper Eternal, Rgvis, Room429, Scythian1, ShakingSpirit, Someguy1221, Sorabino, Sun Creator, Taurion, Tbhotch, The Almightey Drill, Tobby72, Uzo20, WOSlinker, Wai Hong, Waxbean, West Bank Boy, Wrlicks, Yozer1, Тиверополник, 123 anonymous edits 115

Hungarian Revolution of 1848 *Source:* https://en.wikipedia.org/w/index.php?oldid=803957227 *License:* Creative Commons Attribution-Share Alike 3.0 *Contributors:* Alan, Ansh666, Anthony Appleyard, Anti-anyad, Arminden, Artemis Dread, Avpop, Bender235, Bgwhite, Blemse, Bolter21, Burtlerking, Bwatzuk, CTVRTLANIK 1975, Cadillac000, CambridgeBayWeather, ClueBot NG, Codrinb, CommonsDelinker, DaltonCastle, Debbiesw, Director, Edin Balgarin, Ehrenkater, Enginerfactories, Ericl, Fakirbakir, Fdewaele, Fitzcarmalan, Flyer22 Reborn, FrB.TG, German pop music, GoingBatty, GooglerW, Gorthian, Gubbubu, HaEr48, Hebel, Hebrides, Hugo999, J 1982, JeBonSer, John of Reading, Joy, Kaihsu, Kirglach, Koertefa, Konglich, KylieTastic, LilHelpa, Look2See1, Magioladitis, Marek69, Mccapra, Mogism, Niceguyedc, Norden1990, Oppashi, Orenburg1, Ospreys15, Paine Ellsworth, Peekzil, Peter-T, Pierpao, Pirtorlor, Pratyya Ghosh, R'n'B, RandomCritic, Rich Farmbrough, Rjensen, Rosalie Ivady, Rubldeck, Seasdas, SimonTrew, Snorvege, Supersaiyen312, Sylvain1975, TYelliot, Tim!, Tiptoety, Tobby72, Trappist the monk, Tumbsder, Tzowu, Vanjagenije, Vlachav, Walter Voterds, Whlushdred, Zezen, ZoleX, Zoupan, 142 anonymous edits 129

Austria-Hungary *Source:* https://en.wikipedia.org/w/index.php?oldid=807945094 *License:* Creative Commons Attribution-Share Alike 3.0 *Contributors:* 123Steller, 23 editor, 331dot, Acer, Aledownload, Arthur Brum, Ashley Pomeroy, Audaciter, BD2412, Baddygurl1986, Ban kavalir, Bananapeppers101, Battlesnake1, Bearsca, BlackcurrantTea, Blemse, Bobdog54, Bojovnik, Bokmanrocks01, Bolzanobozen, Brecapla000, Bsddy1234, Chewings72, Chris the speller, Cjrother, Cloudz679, ClueBot NG, CommonsDelinker, CoolKoon, Danukski, Dcirovic, Director, DocWatson42, Drewmutt, Ehrenkater, Elevatorrailfan, Enginerfactories, Ernio48, Favonian, Ferret, Filederchest, FkpCascais, Frietjes, GSS-1987, Gerersdorf, GrammarHead, GregorB, HFS-er, Hairy Dude, HangingCurve, Headbomb, Hebel, Hribovšek, J 1982, Jackfork, Jacquesverlaeken, Jbening, Jennica, Jerome Charles Potts, Jjj1238, JorisvS, KIENGIR, Koertefa, Kpc.nguyen, Lexutz, LilHelpa, Lipsifereg, Logicalgenius3, Look2See1, LouisAragon, Lálálá9999, Maatyn, Magioladitis, Marcocapelle, MarcusBritish, Marek69, Mxzbz, Mztourist, NCain99, Name goes here, Neil P. Quinn, NeroN BG, Nick Mitchell 98, Norden1990, Nyttend, Ogress, Oliszydlowski, PBS, PBS-AWB, Pavel Vozenilek, Permacultura, Pixelninja2000, PlyrStar93, Quebec99, R'n'B, RPH, Rgvis, Riverhugger, Rjensen, Romanian-and-proud, Rothorpe, Serols, Sheila1988, Shellwood, Sideshow Bob, Sigehelmus, Skinsmoke, Slazenger, Sphilbrick, Steve03Mills, The-, ThecentreCZ, Thomas H. White, Tom5551, Tommy130275, Trappist the monk, Tzolov, Tzowu, WaterlessLemon, Widr, Wikipelli, Will Pittenger, Yopie, Zoupan, ΘΕΟΔΩΡΟΣ, 96 anonymous edits 159

Hungary in World War II *Source:* https://en.wikipedia.org/w/index.php?oldid=804551591 *License:* Creative Commons Attribution-Share Alike 3.0 *Contributors:* 10metreh, 777sms, A Great Catholic Person, Airekp, Ale And Quail, Alfons2, Amire80, ArnoldPlaton, Avoided, Bahamut Star, Baxter9, Bender235, Benson85, Bermicourt, Bkonrad, Bogdangiusca, Brigade Piron, Brutaldeluxe, Btphelps, Capt Jim, CaptainFugu, Carlotm, Ceosad, Chefallen, Chris the speller, CityOfSilver, Closedmouth, ClueBot NG, CommonsDelinker, CoolKoon, DagosNavy, DaquannJenkums, Dart evader, Dbachmann, Dchris1990, Dcirovic, DocWatson42, Dodo19∼enwiki, DrFrench, Dubmill, Durova, Ehrenkater, Elekes Andor, Excirial, Frietjes, Gorthian, Ground Zero, Hamish59, HighKing, Hirschjoshua, Hobartimus, Imbris, ImperatorPublius, Indigoeleven, Iritakamas, J04n, JaGa, Jan D. Berends, Jdaloner, Jean-Jacques Georges, John of Reading, Joy, KPalicz, Khazar2, Kleuske, Koertefa, Konullu, Kostja1975, Leoni2, Lightmouse, Look2See1, Loriendrew, LuK3, M2545, Mathsci, MisterBee1966, Mkpumphrey, Mogism, Neun-x, Nick Number, Nigej, Number 57, Olegwiki, Pharaoh of the Wizards, Polonius1600, Project FMF, ProtossPylon, Ptbotgourou, Quinton Feldberg, RhinoMind, Rjwilmsi, Samira1, Sfan00 IMG, Srnec, Stianh22, Stj6, Storm Rider, Stumanusa, Tamaskapcsolat, Teutonic Tamer, That1user, The Anome, The Transhumanist, Themightyquill, TopAce∼enwiki, Treidoiunu, Valenciano, Valoem, VanishedUser sdu9aya9fasdsopa, Varlaam, Vmenkov, Webclient101, Widefox, Woohookitty, Xcommun, XrysD, Ykantor, 151 anonymous edits 239

Hungarian Revolution of 1956 *Source:* https://en.wikipedia.org/w/index.php?oldid=806759334 *License:* Creative Commons Attribution-Share Alike 3.0 *Contributors:* -sche, Alandeus, Albert Zalis, Alfie Gandon, Alfiuman, Ali.m.131, Amerijuanican, Anomalocaris, Anonimu, Apollo The Logician, Arjayay, Avala, Bender235, Berlin-George, Berty688, Bgwhite, BiggestSataniaFanboy89, Bilsonius, Biruitorul, Brandmeister, BreakfastJr, Buckshot06, Captain Ben Sisko, Charles Essie, Charles RB, Cjcaesar, ClueBot NG, CogitoErgoSum14, CommonsDelinker, Conradthebrave, DBruillard, Dafluff17, DagosNavy, Delicious Manager, Derzsi Elekes Andor, Dewritech, Discospinster, Djr13, Dolphin51, Dr Aaij, DrKay, Duncan Wad, Eduen, Edward, Einstein2, Elizium23, Emmasarfity, Emmetfahy, Equinox, Eteethan, Excirial, Finnusertop, FruzsE, Future Perfect at Sunrise, Garfield Garfield, GeneralizationsAreBad, GermanJoe, Gilliam, Gixce93, GoingBatty, Gunbirddriver, Hairy Dude, Hejligan, Howcheng, Igirlapplerocks, Illegitimate Barrister, Innotata, Iridescent, Isbromberg, Istvan, J 1982, JamesBWatson, Jaywubba1887, Jd2718, Jodosma, Jonathanawesomness, Jsanthara, K6ka, KConWiki, KFan II, KGirlTrucker81, Kintetsubuffalo, Kiril Simeonovski, Kissg, Koertefa, KylieTastic, Laci.d, Lekoren, Lietuvos Rytas Fan, LilHelpa, Lugia2453, M2545, Mannerheimo, Marcocapelle, Materialscientist, MiklosSz614, Millennium bug, Mogism, Mojoworker, Monopoly31121993, Morn, Morningstar1814, Morton9, Mr Stephen, Nagy zsuzsa89, Nihlus1, Norden1990, North Shoreman, Number 57, Oppashi, Oranges Juicy, Peyre, Pharaoh of the Wizards, Poeticbent, Premeditated Chaos, Qbek16, Qwertyus, RGloucester, RJANKA, RattleMan, Rjanag, RomanM82, Romanm, Rovibroni, Royalcourtier, Samat, SammyJL27, Sarvagyana guru, Serols, Sgr927, ShaziaM, Sluzzelin, Snowsuit Wearer, Sobreira, Solomon7968, Spaceshuttlediscovery, Srich32977, StjJackson, Supermoot, TCMemoire, Terrek, Textorus, The Northaptonshire pins, The eyewittness, TheFreeWorld, TheLeaper, Theatre worl, Theknowledgeguy69, TwoNyce, Ugog Nizdast, Vanamonde93, Vitéz42, Wanwa, WereSpielChequers, Whoop whoop pull up, Widr, Yerevantsi, 142 anonymous edits 259

Timeline of Budapest *Source:* https://en.wikipedia.org/w/index.php?oldid=798861791 *License:* Creative Commons Attribution-Share Alike 3.0 *Contributors:* Bender235, Borsoka, Clairehallstrom, Dcirovic, Einstein2, James500, M2545, Marek69, N.11.6, Norden1990, Rich Farmbrough, Tom.Reding 297

Image Sources, Licenses and Contributors

The sources listed for each image provide more detailed licensing information including the copyright status, the copyright owner, and the license conditions.

Image *Source:* https://en.wikipedia.org/w/index.php?title=File:Symbol_support_vote.svg *License:* Public Domain *Contributors:* Anomie, Fastily, Jo-Jo Eumerus ... 1

Image *Source:* https://en.wikipedia.org/w/index.php?title=File:Coat_of_Arms_of_Hungary.svg *Contributors:* - ... 1

Image *Source:* https://en.wikipedia.org/w/index.php?title=File:Flag_of_Hungary.svg *License:* Public Domain *Contributors:* SKopp ... 1

Figure 1 *Source:* https://en.wikipedia.org/w/index.php?title=File:Fastener.png *License:* Public Domain *Contributors:* Fakirbakir, OgreBot 2, Themightyquill ... 3

Figure 2 *Source:* https://en.wikipedia.org/w/index.php?title=File:Migration_of_the_Hungarians_(2016).jpg *Contributors:* User:Taz ... 4

Figure 3 *Source:* https://en.wikipedia.org/w/index.php?title=File:Gesta_Hungarorum_Anonymous.jpg *License:* Public Domain *Contributors:* User:Bogdan ... 5

Figure 4 *Source:* https://en.wikipedia.org/w/index.php?title=File:FeherSzarvas-ChroniconPictum.jpg *License:* Public Domain *Contributors:* Anonymus (P. Magister) ... 8

Figure 5 *Source:* https://en.wikipedia.org/w/index.php?title=File:Sajnovics_-_Demonstratio.jpg *License:* Public Domain *Contributors:* Csanády, Imz, Renard, Szenti Tamás, WayneRay ... 10

Figure 6 *Source:* https://en.wikipedia.org/w/index.php?title=File:Russia_Ignateva_Cave_Figure.JPG *License:* Creative Commons Attribution-Sharealike 3.0 *Contributors:* User:Kiwiodysee ... 11

Figure 7 *Source:* https://en.wikipedia.org/w/index.php?title=File:Hungarian_migration.png *License:* Public Domain *Contributors:* (author of original file), (author of modified file) ... 13

Figure 8 *Source:* https://en.wikipedia.org/w/index.php?title=File:Migration_of_Hungarians.jpg *License:* Creative Commons Attribution-Sharealike 3.0 *Contributors:* User:Fakirbakir ... 14

Figure 9 *Source:* https://en.wikipedia.org/w/index.php?title=File:Khazar_map1.PNG *License:* GNU Free Documentation License *Contributors:* Briangotts, Codrinb, Electionworld, Frode Inge Helland, Julieta39, Kjetil r, Look2See1, MGA73bot2, PANONIAN ... 15

Figure 10 *Source:* https://en.wikipedia.org/w/index.php?title=File:HetVezer-ChroniconPictum.jpg *License:* Public Domain *Contributors:* Anonymus (P. Magister) ... 17

Figure 11 *Source:* https://en.wikipedia.org/w/index.php?title=File:Picta.jpg *License:* Public Domain *Contributors:* Acoma, Copydays, Norden1990, Pe-Jo ... 19

Figure 12 *Source:* https://en.wikipedia.org/w/index.php?title=File:Arpad_Kepes_Kronika.jpg *License:* Public Domain *Contributors:* Imoti95, Mhmrodrigues, Norden1990, Qorilla ... 20

Figure 13 *Source:* https://en.wikipedia.org/w/index.php?title=File:Honfoglalas.gif *License:* Public Domain *Contributors:* Fz22 ... 22

Figure 14 *Source:* https://en.wikipedia.org/w/index.php?title=File:Osztjak_vejsze.jpg *License:* Public Domain *Contributors:* Jankó János (1868–1902) ... 23

Figure 15 *Source:* https://en.wikipedia.org/w/index.php?title=File:Szeged-Bojárhalom_női_sírlelet_1.JPG *License:* Public Domain *Contributors:* Csanády ... 24

Image *Source:* https://en.wikipedia.org/w/index.php?title=File:Commons-logo.svg *License:* logo *Contributors:* Anomie, Callanecc, CambridgeBayWeather, Jo-Jo Eumerus, RHaworth ... 31

Image *Source:* https://en.wikipedia.org/w/index.php?title=File:Aquincum_3_-_KKriszti.jpg *License:* Creative Commons Attribution-Sharealike 3.0 *Contributors:* User:KKriszti ... 32

Figure 16 *Source:* https://en.wikipedia.org/w/index.php?title=File:Aquincum-esp.jpg *License:* Public Domain *Contributors:* KIDB ... 33

Figure 17 *Source:* https://en.wikipedia.org/w/index.php?title=File:Aquincum_Amphitheatre.jpg *Contributors:* User:Elisa.rolle ... 34

Image *Source:* https://en.wikipedia.org/w/index.php?title=File:Flag_of_the_Habsburg_Monarchy.svg *License:* Public Domain *Contributors:* Sir Iain, earlier version by ThrashedParanoid and Peregrine981.ThrashedParanoid ... 37

Image *Source:* https://en.wikipedia.org/w/index.php?title=File:Coa_Hungary_Country_History_(19th_Century).svg *License:* Creative Commons Zero *Contributors:* Antemister, BrightRaven, Bubel, CommonsDelinker, DarwIn, David Liuzzo, Dbachmann, Madboy74, OgreBot 2, Sarang, Szilas 37

Image *Source:* https://en.wikipedia.org/w/index.php?title=File:Flag_of_Hungary_(15th_century,_rectangular).svg *License:* Public Domain *Contributors:* Sir Iain ... 38

Image *Source:* https://en.wikipedia.org/w/index.php?title=File:Flag_of_Hungary_(1867-1918).svg *License:* Public Domain *Contributors:* Thommy 38

Image *Source:* https://en.wikipedia.org/w/index.php?title=File:Coat_of_arms_of_Slovakia.svg *License:* GNU Free Documentation License *Contributors:* Tlusťa ... 39

Image *Source:* https://en.wikipedia.org/w/index.php?title=File:Flag_of_Slovakia.svg *License:* Public Domain *Contributors:* Achim1999, B1mbo, Cycn, Erlenmeyer, Fry1989, Herbythyme, Homo lupus, IP 84.5∼commonswiki, J 1982, Justass, Klemen Kocjancic, Leyo, Madden, Mattes, Mogelzahn, Mxn, Nightstallion, Peter Zelizňák, Pmsyyz, Pumbaa80, Ricordisamoa, Ruwolf, SKopp, Samah10, Sangjinhwa, Sarang, SiBr4, Srtxg, Str4nd, TFCforever, Torsch, Tvdm, Wiki-vr, Zscout370, 11 anonymous edits ... 40

Figure 18 *Source:* https://en.wikipedia.org/w/index.php?title=File:Central_europe_1572.png *License:* Creative Commons Zero *Contributors:* PANONIAN ... 41

Figure 19 *Source:* https://en.wikipedia.org/w/index.php?title=File:Central_europe_1683.png *License:* Creative Commons Zero *Contributors:* PANONIAN ... 43

Figure 20 *Source:* https://en.wikipedia.org/w/index.php?title=File:Growth_of_Habsburg_territories.jpg *License:* GNU Free Documentation License *Contributors:* Achim55, Auntof6, Bizso, BotMultichill, CSvBibra, Cplakidas, Fakirbakir, MGA73bot2, Spiridon Ion Cepleanu, Szajci, 9 anonymous edits 44

Figure 21 *Source:* https://en.wikipedia.org/w/index.php?title=File:KingdomOfHungary_Josephinische_Landesaufnahme_Original_Map_1782-1785.jpg *License:* Public Domain *Contributors:* Historische Militärkarte der österreichisch-ungarischen Monarchie ... 46

Figure 22 *Source:* https://en.wikipedia.org/w/index.php?title=File:Amerling_széchenyi.jpg *Contributors:* Zello ... 49

Figure 23 *Source:* https://en.wikipedia.org/w/index.php?title=File:Hungary_large_coa_1849.png *License:* Creative Commons Attribution-Sharealike 2.5 *Contributors:* Ádám Kovács at http://reviz.freeweb.hu/ (original author) ... 49

Figure 24 *Source:* https://en.wikipedia.org/w/index.php?title=File:Kossuth_Lajos_Prinzhofer.jpg *License:* Public Domain *Contributors:* user:Csanády ... 50

Image *Source:* https://en.wikipedia.org/w/index.php?title=File:Buda_Castle_with_Matthias_Church_(Ariel,night).jpg *License:* Creative Commons Zero *Contributors:* INeverCry, Tiven2240, Yann ... 53

Figure 25 *Source:* https://en.wikipedia.org/w/index.php?title=File:Buda_1493.jpg *License:* Public Domain *Contributors:* Michel Wolgemut, Wilhelm Pleydenwurff ... 55

Figure 26 *Source:* https://en.wikipedia.org/w/index.php?title=File:Mátyás_budai_vára.jpg *License:* Public Domain *Contributors:* Györgyi Géza 55

Figure 27 *Source:* https://en.wikipedia.org/w/index.php?title=File:Buda_látképe-XVI._sz.jpg *License:* Public Domain *Contributors:* Tolnai - korabeli kép alapján ... 56

Figure 28 *Source:* https://en.wikipedia.org/w/index.php?title=File:Var_rondellecivertanlegi.jpg *License:* Creative Commons Attribution-Sharealike 3.0 *Contributors:* Civertan ... 57

Figure 29 *Source:* https://en.wikipedia.org/w/index.php?title=File:Buda_Citerioris_Hungariae_Caput_Regni_avita_sedes._vulgo_Ofen_1617.jpg *License:* Public Domain *Contributors:* Braun & Hogenberg ... 58

Figure 30 *Source:* https://en.wikipedia.org/w/index.php?title=File:Die_Einnahme_von_Buda_1686.JPG *License:* Public Domain *Contributors:* User:Illustratedjc ... 59

Figure 31 *Source:* https://en.wikipedia.org/w/index.php?title=File:Ostrom1686.jpeg *License:* Public Domain *Contributors:* Zello ... 60

Figure 32 *Source:* https://en.wikipedia.org/w/index.php?title=File:Samuel_Mikoviny_001.jpg *License:* Public Domain *Contributors:* Sámuel Mikoviny ... 61

Figure 33 *Source:* https://en.wikipedia.org/w/index.php?title=File:Budapest_Budai_Várpalota.png *License:* Public Domain *Contributors:* Adam78, Fransvannes, Grunpfnul, Karelj, Lepeltier.ludovic, Red devil 666, 1 anonymous edits ... 62

Figure 34 *Source:* https://en.wikipedia.org/w/index.php?title=File:Johann_Ernst_Mansfeld_001.jpg *License:* Public Domain *Contributors:* Gryffindor, Judithcomm, Papergirl, Pe-Jo ... 62

Figure 35 *Source:* https://en.wikipedia.org/w/index.php?title=File:József_nádor_Barabás_Miklós.jpg *License:* Public Domain *Contributors:* Beroesz, Boo-Boo Baroo, Csanády, DarwIn, Dencey, Ecummenic, Einstein2, Mattes, Pe-Jo, Szilas, Themightyquill 64
Figure 36 *Source:* https://en.wikipedia.org/w/index.php?title=File:Budai_var01.jpg *License:* Public Domain *Contributors:* The original publisher was Edgar Schmidt, scanned by me 65
Figure 37 *Source:* https://en.wikipedia.org/w/index.php?title=File:Gyoergy_Kloesz_001.jpg *License:* Public Domain *Contributors:* Aschroet, Csanády, Gryffindor, Judithcomm, Szenti Tamás, Tambo 66
Figure 38 *Source:* https://en.wikipedia.org/w/index.php?title=File:Budai_var03.jpg *License:* Public Domain *Contributors:* Original publisher unknown, scanned by me 67
Figure 39 *Source:* https://en.wikipedia.org/w/index.php?title=File:Buda_Royal_Castle_western_courtyard_1880.jpg *License:* Public Domain *Contributors:* Globetrotter19, Gryffindor, VinceB 68
Figure 40 *Source:* https://en.wikipedia.org/w/index.php?title=File:Budai_var02.jpg *License:* Public Domain *Contributors:* Original publisher was Károly Divald the Younger (died in 1924), scanned by me 69
Figure 41 *Source:* https://en.wikipedia.org/w/index.php?title=File:Royal_Castle_Budapest_1926.JPG *License:* Public Domain *Contributors:* R. Balogh 70
Figure 42 *Source:* https://en.wikipedia.org/w/index.php?title=File:Budavári_Palota_10x15.jpg *Contributors:* Begoon, Gryffindor, OgreBot 2, Themightyquill 71
Figure 43 *Source:* https://en.wikipedia.org/w/index.php?title=File:Lanc_hid_-_Budapest_3_Febr_1946_Foto_Takkk_Hungary.jpg *License:* Public Domain *Contributors:* Photo taken by; készítette: id. Takács István (1946) Scanned by, lapolvasóval digitalizálta: Takkk (Takács István, 2008 72
Figure 44 *Source:* https://en.wikipedia.org/w/index.php?title=File:Buda_Castle_2365941876_12a03f263c.jpg *License:* Creative Commons Attribution 2.0 *Contributors:* http://www.flickr.com/photos/chad_k/ 73
Figure 45 *Source:* https://en.wikipedia.org/w/index.php?title=File:Buda--Castles01.jpg *License:* Creative Commons Attribution-Sharealike 2.5 *Contributors:* Adam78, Civertan, Csanády, Einstein2, Tacsipacsi, 1 anonymous edits 73
Figure 46 *Source:* https://en.wikipedia.org/w/index.php?title=File:Buda_castle_interior_church.JPG *License:* Public Domain *Contributors:* C1815 77
Figure 47 *Source:* https://en.wikipedia.org/w/index.php?title=File:Schedel_chapel.JPG *License:* Public Domain *Contributors:* Zello 78
Figure 48 *Source:* https://en.wikipedia.org/w/index.php?title=File:Zenta_Eloterem.png *Contributors:* Globetrotter19, Gryffindor, OgreBot 2 .. 82
Figure 49 *Source:* https://en.wikipedia.org/w/index.php?title=File:Fogadasi_Varoterem.png *Contributors:* Globetrotter19, Gryffindor, OgreBot 2 83
Figure 50 *Source:* https://en.wikipedia.org/w/index.php?title=File:Buda_Castle_nagyterem-mj.jpg *License:* Public Domain *Contributors:* Csanády, DrJunge, Globetrotter19, Gryffindor, M0tty, Szenti Tamás, Tambo 83
Figure 51 *Source:* https://en.wikipedia.org/w/index.php?title=File:Feher_Eloterem.png *Contributors:* Globetrotter19, Gryffindor, OgreBot 2 .. 84
Figure 52 *Source:* https://en.wikipedia.org/w/index.php?title=File:Budapest,_Kiralyi_Palota,_Koronazas_Eloterem.png *Contributors:* Globetrotter19, Gryffindor, OgreBot 2 85
Figure 53 *Source:* https://en.wikipedia.org/w/index.php?title=File:Kis_Tronterem.jpg *Contributors:* Globetrotter19, Gryffindor, OgreBot 2 86
Figure 54 *Source:* https://en.wikipedia.org/w/index.php?title=File:Circle_Teaszalon.png *Contributors:* Globetrotter19, Gryffindor, OgreBot 2 . 87
Figure 55 *Source:* https://en.wikipedia.org/w/index.php?title=File:Eloszoba_25.png *Contributors:* Globetrotter19, Gryffindor, OgreBot 2 87
Figure 56 *Source:* https://en.wikipedia.org/w/index.php?title=File:Budapest,_Kiralyi_Palota,_Dohanyzo_Szalon.png *Contributors:* Globetrotter19, Gryffindor, OgreBot 2 88
Figure 57 *Source:* https://en.wikipedia.org/w/index.php?title=File:Iroszoba.png *Contributors:* Globetrotter19, Gryffindor, OgreBot 2 89
Figure 58 *Source:* https://en.wikipedia.org/w/index.php?title=File:Tarsalkodo_Terem.png *Contributors:* Globetrotter19, Gryffindor, OgreBot 2 90
Figure 59 *Source:* https://en.wikipedia.org/w/index.php?title=File:Eloszoba_29.png *Contributors:* Globetrotter19, Gryffindor, OgreBot 2 90
Figure 60 *Source:* https://en.wikipedia.org/w/index.php?title=File:Királylépcső_bejárata.png *Contributors:* Globetrotter19, Gryffindor, OgreBot 2 91
Figure 61 *Source:* https://en.wikipedia.org/w/index.php?title=File:Kapolna_Buda_varpalota.jpg *Contributors:* Globetrotter19, Gryffindor, OgreBot 2 92
Figure 62 *Source:* https://en.wikipedia.org/w/index.php?title=File:Jozsefnador_palatin_Hungary_tombstone.jpg *License:* Creative Commons Attribution-ShareAlike 3.0 Unported *Contributors:* Akela3 94
Figure 63 *Source:* https://en.wikipedia.org/w/index.php?title=File:Nagy_Balterem.png *Contributors:* Globetrotter19, Gryffindor, OgreBot 2 ... 95
Figure 64 *Source:* https://en.wikipedia.org/w/index.php?title=File:Budapest,_Kiralyi_Palota,_Buffet_Csarnok.png *Contributors:* Globetrotter19, Gryffindor, OgreBot 2 96
Figure 65 *Source:* https://en.wikipedia.org/w/index.php?title=File:Budapest,_Királyi_Palota,_Habsburg_Nagyterem.png *Contributors:* Globetrotter19, Gryffindor, OgreBot 2 96
Figure 66 *Source:* https://en.wikipedia.org/w/index.php?title=File:BudapestDSCN3998.JPG *License:* Public Domain *Contributors:* Yoav Dothan 97
Figure 67 *Source:* https://en.wikipedia.org/w/index.php?title=File:Lepcsohaz.jpg *Contributors:* Globetrotter19, Gryffindor, OgreBot 2 98
Figure 68 *Source:* https://en.wikipedia.org/w/index.php?title=File:Szent_Istvan_Terem.png *Contributors:* Globetrotter19, Gryffindor, OgreBot 2 99
Figure 69 *Source:* https://en.wikipedia.org/w/index.php?title=File:Matyas_Terem_1903.jpg *Contributors:* Courcelles, Globetrotter19, Gryffindor, Pe-Jo 100
Figure 70 *Source:* https://en.wikipedia.org/w/index.php?title=File:I._Fejedelmi_eloterem_54.jpg *Contributors:* Globetrotter19, Gryffindor, Havang(nl), OgreBot 2 101
Figure 71 *Source:* https://en.wikipedia.org/w/index.php?title=File:Eloterem_58.jpg *Contributors:* Globetrotter19, Gryffindor, OgreBot 2 102
Figure 72 *Source:* https://en.wikipedia.org/w/index.php?title=File:Fogadoszoba_59.jpg *Contributors:* Globetrotter19, Gryffindor, OgreBot 2 . 103
Figure 73 *Source:* https://en.wikipedia.org/w/index.php?title=File:Iroszoba_60.png *Contributors:* Globetrotter19, Gryffindor 104
Figure 74 *Source:* https://en.wikipedia.org/w/index.php?title=File:Budapest,_Kiralyi_Palota,_I._Fejedelmi_Haloszoba.png *Contributors:* Globetrotter19, Gryffindor, Havang(nl), OgreBot 2 104
Figure 75 *Source:* https://en.wikipedia.org/w/index.php?title=File:I._Fejedelmi_Ebedlo_57.jpg *Contributors:* Globetrotter19, Gryffindor, Havang(nl), OgreBot 2 105
Figure 76 *Source:* https://en.wikipedia.org/w/index.php?title=File:Circle_Terem_56.jpg *Contributors:* Globetrotter19, Gryffindor, OgreBot 2 106
Figure 77 *Source:* https://en.wikipedia.org/w/index.php?title=File:Budapest,_Kiralyi_Palota,_Ebedlo.png *Contributors:* Globetrotter19, Gryffindor, OgreBot 2 107
Figure 78 *Source:* https://en.wikipedia.org/w/index.php?title=File:Mátyás_kút.JPG *License:* Creative Commons Zero *Contributors:* Myself .. 108
Figure 79 *Source:* https://en.wikipedia.org/w/index.php?title=File:Budapest_princ_Eugen_1.jpg *License:* Public Domain *Contributors:* Karelj 109
Figure 80 *Source:* https://en.wikipedia.org/w/index.php?title=File:Csikós_statue_by_György_Vastagh,_Hunyadi_Courtyard,_Royal_Palace._2009_BudapestDSCN3859.jpg *License:* Public Domain *Contributors:* Yoav Dothan 109
Figure 81 *Source:* https://en.wikipedia.org/w/index.php?title=File:Turul_and_Hungarian_flag.jpg *License:* GNU Free Documentation License *Contributors:* Ninane 110
Figure 82 *Source:* https://en.wikipedia.org/w/index.php?title=File:BudapestDSCN3839.JPG *License:* Public Domain *Contributors:* Yoav Dothan 111
Figure 83 *Source:* https://en.wikipedia.org/w/index.php?title=File:Várbelső.jpg *License:* Public Domain *Contributors:* Darinko 111
Figure 84 *Source:* https://en.wikipedia.org/w/index.php?title=File:Floor_plans_of_Buda_Castle_en.svg *License:* Creative Commons Zero *Contributors:* User:Goran tek-en, User:Zello 113
Figure 85 *Source:* https://en.wikipedia.org/w/index.php?title=File:Central_europe_1572.png *License:* Creative Commons Zero *Contributors:* PANONIAN 116
Figure 86 *Source:* https://en.wikipedia.org/w/index.php?title=File:Central_europe_1683.png *License:* Creative Commons Zero *Contributors:* PANONIAN 117
Figure 87 *Source:* https://en.wikipedia.org/w/index.php?title=File:Southern_destruction_in_the_Kingdom_of_Hungary.png *Contributors:* User:Fakirbakir 118
Figure 88 *Source:* https://en.wikipedia.org/w/index.php?title=File:Portyázó_törökök.jpg *License:* Public Domain *Contributors:* Criptorix, Magog the Ogre, OgreBot 2, Удивленный1 118
Figure 89 *Source:* https://en.wikipedia.org/w/index.php?title=File:1543-Siege_of_Estolnibelgrad_in_Hungary-Suleymanname.jpg *License:* Public Domain *Contributors:* Matrakci Nasuh 119
Figure 90 *Source:* https://en.wikipedia.org/w/index.php?title=File:Die_Einnahme_von_Buda_1686.JPG *License:* Public Domain *Contributors:* User:Illustratedjc 121
Figure 91 *Source:* https://en.wikipedia.org/w/index.php?title=File:Szechenyi_square_new_Pecs.JPG *License:* Creative Commons Attribution-ShareAlike 1.0 Generic *Contributors:* Jozsef TOTH 123
Figure 92 *Source:* https://en.wikipedia.org/w/index.php?title=File:Hungary_Eger_minaret.jpg *License:* Creative Commons Attribution-ShareAlike 3.0 Unported *Contributors:* Wojsyl 124
Figure 93 *Source:* https://en.wikipedia.org/w/index.php?title=File:Pasha_of_Buda.jpg *License:* Public Domain *Contributors:* Avaring 125

Figure 94 *Source:* https://en.wikipedia.org/w/index.php?title=File:Ottoman_hungary_coffeshop.jpg *License:* Public Domain *Contributors:* Avaring 125
Figure 95 *Source:* https://en.wikipedia.org/w/index.php?title=File:Ottoman_Hungary_dancer.jpg *License:* Public Domain *Contributors:* Informationswiedergutmachung, Magog the Ogre 126
Figure 96 *Source:* https://en.wikipedia.org/w/index.php?title=File:Ottoman_Hungary_slave_musician.jpg *License:* Public Domain *Contributors:* Avaring 126
Image *Source:* https://en.wikipedia.org/w/index.php?title=File:PD-icon.svg *License:* Public Domain *Contributors:* Alex.muller, Anomie, Anonymous Dissident, CBM, Jo-Jo Eumerus, MBisanz, PBS, Quadell, Rocket000, Strangerer, Timotheus Canens, 1 anonymous edits 127
Image *Source:* https://en.wikipedia.org/w/index.php?title=File:March15.jpg *License:* Public Domain *Contributors:* 1970gemini, Alensha, Alexandrin, Annenkov, Csanády, Daniel Baránek, Man vyi, Pe-Jo, Putnik, Themightyquill 129
Image *Source:* https://en.wikipedia.org/w/index.php?title=File:Croatia-1848.gif *License:* Public Domain *Contributors:* Triune Kingdom 130
Image *Source:* https://en.wikipedia.org/w/index.php?title=File:Flag_of_Serbian_Vojvodina.svg *License:* Creative Commons Attribution-Sharealike 3.0 *Contributors:* User:Jembezmamy 130
Image *Source:* https://en.wikipedia.org/w/index.php?title=File:Civil_Flag_of_Serbia.svg *License:* Public Domain *Contributors:* National Assembly of the Republic of Serbia (Serbian Parliament) 130
Image *Source:* https://en.wikipedia.org/w/index.php?title=File:Flag_of_Serbian_Vojvodina_(tricolour).png *License:* GNU Free Documentation License *Contributors:* Alan, BotMultichill, Cycn, Denniss, Fry1989, Homo lupus, MGA73bot2, Mattes, Ninane, Ricordisamoa, Svensson1, Torsch, Zoupan, Ранко Николић, 5 anonymous edits 130
Image *Source:* https://en.wikipedia.org/w/index.php?title=File:Austria-Hungary_civil_flag_1869-1918.svg *License:* Public Domain *Contributors:* Fetofs 130
Image *Source:* https://en.wikipedia.org/w/index.php?title=File:Slovak_Flag_(1848).svg *Contributors:* User:Oppashi 130
Image *Source:* https://en.wikipedia.org/w/index.php?title=File:Flag_of_Wallachian_Revolution_of_1848,_vertical_stripes.svg *Contributors:* Alex:D 130
Image *Source:* https://en.wikipedia.org/w/index.php?title=File:Flag_of_the_Ruthenian_National_Guard.svg *Contributors:* User:Oppashi 130
Image *Source:* https://en.wikipedia.org/w/index.php?title=File:Banner_of_the_Bohemian_Coat_of_Arms.svg *License:* Public Domain *Contributors:* Convert to SVG Tlusťa (see File:Small coat of arms of the Czech Republic.svg), copy to banner Sir Iain 130
Image *Source:* https://en.wikipedia.org/w/index.php?title=File:Flag_of_Bohemia.svg *License:* Public Domain *Contributors:* User:Urmas 130
Image *Source:* https://en.wikipedia.org/w/index.php?title=File:Wappen1-1-.gif *License:* Creative Commons Attribution-Sharealike 3.0 *Contributors:* Christian Agnethler 130
Image *Source:* https://en.wikipedia.org/w/index.php?title=File:Flag_of_Russia_(1696-1917).svg *License:* Creative Commons Attribution-Share Alike *Contributors:* Cathy Richards, Dannis243, Fry1989, Illegitimate Barrister, Sarang 130
Image *Source:* https://en.wikipedia.org/w/index.php?title=File:Flag_of_Hungarian_Revolution_of_1848.png *License:* Public Domain *Contributors:* Qorilla 130
Image *Source:* https://en.wikipedia.org/w/index.php?title=File:Flag_of_Poland.svg *License:* Public Domain *Contributors:* Anomie, Jo-Jo Eumerus, Mifter 130
Image *Source:* https://en.wikipedia.org/w/index.php?title=File:Flag_of_Germany.svg *License:* Public Domain *Contributors:* Anomie, Jo-Jo Eumerus 130
Image *Source:* https://en.wikipedia.org/w/index.php?title=File:Olasz_légió_zászló_1849_1.jpg *License:* Public Domain *Contributors:* Csanády, Themightyquill 130
Image *Source:* https://en.wikipedia.org/w/index.php?title=File:SlovenskaVlajka1848.png *License:* Creative Commons Attribution-Sharealike 3.0 *Contributors:* Nyiox 130
Image *Source:* https://en.wikipedia.org/w/index.php?title=File:Banner-Ruthenische-Nationalgarde-1848.JPG *License:* Public Domain *Contributors:* BotMultichill, Bukk, Deadstar, Ilyaroz, Mattes, Ninane, Oppashi 130
Figure 97 *Source:* https://en.wikipedia.org/w/index.php?title=File:Ferdinando_I_d'Austria.jpg *License:* Public Domain *Contributors:* Wilhelm Rupp, Prague 132
Figure 98 *Source:* https://en.wikipedia.org/w/index.php?title=File:Pilvax_Pest_Preiszler.jpg *License:* Public Domain *Contributors:* József Preiszler (?–?, 19. century) 135
Figure 99 *Source:* https://en.wikipedia.org/w/index.php?title=File:1848-49_Batthyany-kormany.jpg *License:* Public Domain *Contributors:* Barabás 135
Figure 100 *Source:* https://en.wikipedia.org/w/index.php?title=File:Petőfi_Nemzeti_Múzeum.jpg *License:* Public Domain *Contributors:* Csanády, Pe-Jo, Themightyquill 136
Figure 101 *Source:* https://en.wikipedia.org/w/index.php?title=File:A_szabadsajtó_első_terméke_Pesten_1848._március_15.JPG *License:* Public Domain *Contributors:* Hello world, Pe-Jo, Themightyquill 136
Figure 102 *Source:* https://en.wikipedia.org/w/index.php?title=File:Magyar_kokárda.png *License:* Creative Commons Attribution-Sharealike 3.0 *Contributors:* User:Khalai 139
Figure 103 *Source:* https://en.wikipedia.org/w/index.php?title=File:Barabás_Választási_menet.jpg *License:* Public Domain *Contributors:* Achim55, Csanády, Pe-Jo, Themightyquill 140
Figure 104 *Source:* https://en.wikipedia.org/w/index.php?title=File:Országgyűlés_megnyitása_1848.jpg *License:* Public Domain *Contributors:* Aputró, Bukk, Csanády, File Upload Bot (Magnus Manske), Hello world, Képíró Gépíró, Martin H., NBS, OgreBot 2, Themightyquill 141
Figure 105 *Source:* https://en.wikipedia.org/w/index.php?title=File:Jellasics_tamadasa_EN.jpg *License:* GNU Free Documentation License *Contributors:* Jellasics_tamadasa.jpg: Work of original author derivative work: SimonTrew (talk) 141
Figure 106 *Source:* https://en.wikipedia.org/w/index.php?title=File:Pákozdi_csata.jpg *License:* Public Domain *Contributors:* Zalder, F. (artist), Rauh, J. (lithographer) 142
Figure 107 *Source:* https://en.wikipedia.org/w/index.php?title=File:Buda_ostroma_1849._május_21.jpg *License:* Public Domain *Contributors:* Globetrotter19, Hello world, Pe-Jo 147
Figure 108 *Source:* https://en.wikipedia.org/w/index.php?title=File:Armee_Bulletin_V.jpg *License:* Public Domain *Contributors:* Csanády, Zhuyifei1999, Zoupan, 3 anonymous edits 148
Figure 109 *Source:* https://en.wikipedia.org/w/index.php?title=File:Than_tapiobicskei_utközet2_1849_aprilis_4.jpg *License:* Public Domain *Contributors:* Beyond silence, Csanády, Dencey∼commonswiki, Pe-Jo, Themightyquill, Иван Дулин, 1 anonymous edits 150
Figure 110 *Source:* https://en.wikipedia.org/w/index.php?title=File:Slovenskí_dobrovoľníci.jpg *License:* Public Domain *Contributors:* unknown, not stated in source 151
Figure 111 *Source:* https://en.wikipedia.org/w/index.php?title=File:Schlacht_von_Temesvar_am_9_August_1849.jpg *License:* Public Domain *Contributors:* Hello world 152
Figure 112 *Source:* https://en.wikipedia.org/w/index.php?title=File:Görgei_Artúr_by_Miklós_Barabás.jpg *License:* Public Domain *Contributors:* User:Csanády 154
Figure 113 *Source:* https://en.wikipedia.org/w/index.php?title=File:Windisch-Graetz.jpg *License:* Public Domain *Contributors:* user:Csanády 155
Figure 114 *Source:* https://en.wikipedia.org/w/index.php?title=File:Capitulaton_of_Hungarian_Army_at_Világos_1849.png *License:* Public Domain *Contributors:* István Szkicsák-Klinovszky (1820 – c. 1880) 156
Image *Source:* https://en.wikipedia.org/w/index.php?title=File:Flag_of_Austria-Hungary_1869-1918.svg *Contributors:* - 159
Image *Source:* https://en.wikipedia.org/w/index.php?title=File:Imperial_Coat_of_Arms_of_the_Empire_of_Austria.svg *License:* Creative Commons Attribution-Sharealike 3.0 *Contributors:* User:Sodacan 159
Image *Source:* https://en.wikipedia.org/w/index.php?title=File:Austro-Hungarian_Monarchy_(1914).svg *License:* Creative Commons Attribution-Sharealike 3.0,2.5,2.0,1.0 *Contributors:* TRAJAN 117 159
Image *Source:* https://en.wikipedia.org/w/index.php?title=File:Flag_of_Austria.svg *License:* Public Domain *Contributors:* User:SKopp 161
Image *Source:* https://en.wikipedia.org/w/index.php?title=File:Flag_of_Hungary_(1918-1919;_3-2_aspect_ratio).svg *License:* Creative Commons Zero *Contributors:* User:Thommy9 161
Image *Source:* https://en.wikipedia.org/w/index.php?title=File:Flag_of_the_Czech_Republic.svg *License:* Public Domain *Contributors:* special commission (of code): SVG version by cs:-xfi-. Colors according to Appendix No. 3 of czech legal Act 3/1993. cs 161
Image *Source:* https://en.wikipedia.org/w/index.php?title=File:Flag_of_the_Ukranian_State.svg *License:* Public Domain *Contributors:* Alex Tora 161
Image *Source:* https://en.wikipedia.org/w/index.php?title=File:Flag_of_Romania.svg *Contributors:* AdiJapan 161
Image *Source:* https://en.wikipedia.org/w/index.php?title=File:Flag_of_the_State_of_Slovenes,_Croats_and_Serbs.svg *License:* Public Domain *Contributors:* Orlovic: I drew this flag in photoshop, on the base of another version on the internet 161
Image *Source:* https://en.wikipedia.org/w/index.php?title=File:State_Flag_of_Serbia_(1882-1918).svg *License:* Creative Commons Attribution-ShareAlike 3.0 Unported *Contributors:* Guilherme Paula 161
Image *Source:* https://en.wikipedia.org/w/index.php?title=File:Flag_of_Italy_(1861-1946).svg *License:* Creative Commons Attribution-Sharealike 2.5 *Contributors:* F l a n k e r 161
Figure 115 *Source:* https://en.wikipedia.org/w/index.php?title=File:Pietzner,_Carl_(1853-1927)_-_Emperor_Franz_Josef_I_-_ca_1885.jpg *License:* Public Domain *Contributors:* CSvBibra, DIREKTOR, Eweht, G.dallorto, Nikola Smolenski, Raymond, Silar, 2 anonymous edits 162

Image *Source:* https://en.wikipedia.org/w/index.php?title=File:Austria_coat_of_arms_official.svg *License:* Public Domain *Contributors:* Original image from the Bundesministerium für Landesverteidigung, modified since then. Modified and uploaded by Gryffin ... 164
Figure 116 *Source:* https://en.wikipedia.org/w/index.php?title=File:Bécs_(12).jpg *License:* Public Domain *Contributors:* AndreasPraefcke, Anna reg, Darkweasel94, Derzsi Elekes Andor, Gugerell, OgreBot 2, Wieralee ... 167
Figure 117 *Source:* https://en.wikipedia.org/w/index.php?title=File:Parliament_Buildung_Hungary_20090920.jpg *License:* Creative Commons Attribution-Sharealike 3.0 *Contributors:* Ivanhoe ... 167
Figure 118 *Source:* https://en.wikipedia.org/w/index.php?title=File:Otevření_mostu_14._6._1904.jpg *License:* Public Domain *Contributors:* Cucumber, Daniel Baránek, Eweht, Gampe, Gryffindor, Infrogmation, John commons, Miaow Miaow, R-E-AL, Silar, ŠJů ... 170
Figure 119 *Source:* https://en.wikipedia.org/w/index.php?title=File:Rząca_Tadeusz,_Rynek_Główny_w_Krakowie.jpg *Contributors:* Tadeusz Rząca (1868-1928) ... 171
Figure 120 *Source:* https://en.wikipedia.org/w/index.php?title=File:Austria_Hungary_ethnic.svg *License:* Public Domain *Contributors:* Andrein 175
Figure 121 *Source:* https://en.wikipedia.org/w/index.php?title=File:Meyers_b12_s0486a.jpg *Contributors:* Jklamo, Leyo, Mapmarks, PM, Red Rooster, W!B:, 2 anonymous edits ... 176
Figure 122 *Source:* https://en.wikipedia.org/w/index.php?title=File:Andree48-2.jpg *License:* Public Domain *Contributors:* Grombo ... 176
Figure 123 *Source:* https://en.wikipedia.org/w/index.php?title=File:Literacy_in_Austria-Hungary_(1880).JPG *License:* Public Domain *Contributors:* own scan ... 177
Figure 124 *Source:* https://en.wikipedia.org/w/index.php?title=File:Austria1914physical.jpg *License:* Creative Commons Attribution 3.0 *Contributors:* Mariusz Paździora ... 177
Figure 125 *Source:* https://en.wikipedia.org/w/index.php?title=File:Sarajevo_1878.jpg *Contributors:* Bojovnik, Jacquesverlaeken, Smooth O, Stefan2, Zoupan ... 181
Figure 126 *Source:* https://en.wikipedia.org/w/index.php?title=File:BanknoteA-H.jpg *License:* Public Domain *Contributors:* ALE!, Burts, Chochopk, Drdoht, El bes, Foroa, GloriosoRocha, Julo, Man vyi, Marian99, Mindmatrix, Umherirrender, WikipediaMaster, 4 anonymous edits ... 182
Figure 127 *Source:* https://en.wikipedia.org/w/index.php?title=File:Railway_map_Austria-Hungary.png *License:* Public Domain *Contributors:* Globetrotter19, Kleeblatt187, Railwaystat, WFinch ... 185
Figure 128 *Source:* https://en.wikipedia.org/w/index.php?title=File:Hydrography_of_the_Pannonian_basin_before_the_river_and_lake_regulations_in_the_19th_century.jpg *Contributors:* Blemse ... 186
Figure 129 *Source:* https://en.wikipedia.org/w/index.php?title=File:Wagenfuhrer_1900_Vienna_Adriatic_Sea_canal.jpg *License:* Public Domain *Contributors:* Anna reg, Eleassar, Sporti ... 186
Figure 130 *Source:* https://en.wikipedia.org/w/index.php?title=File:1896-17_vasúti_építkezés_Klösz_György.JPG *License:* Public Domain *Contributors:* Antissimo, Beroesz, Csanády, Gareth, Pe-Jo, Szenti Tamás, Tambo ... 187
Figure 131 *Source:* https://en.wikipedia.org/w/index.php?title=File:KaiserFranzJoseph_Schiff.jpg *License:* Public Domain *Contributors:* FSII, Johann Jaritz, Otto Normalverbraucher ... 187
Figure 132 *Source:* https://en.wikipedia.org/w/index.php?title=File:Telefon_Hirmondo_-_Stentor_reading_the_day's_news.jpg *License:* Public Domain *Contributors:* World's Work ... 188
Figure 133 *Source:* https://en.wikipedia.org/w/index.php?title=File:A1TA_7097_Wandapp_aus_1890_Postmuseum_1941.gif *Contributors:* BambooBeast, Krd, Tangopaso ... .js, 188
Figure 134 *Source:* https://en.wikipedia.org/w/index.php?title=File:Teodor_Axentowicz_-_Pogrzeb_huculski.jpg *License:* Public Domain *Contributors:* Ahonc, Botaurus, Butko, Electron, Janbies, Leyo, Sanya3, Sceptic, Shakko, SofoPodilska, Thib Phil, Wst, Ykvach, Лобачев Владимир, Навка 199
Image *Source:* https://en.wikipedia.org/w/index.php?title=File:Flag_of_Italy.svg *License:* Public Domain *Contributors:* Anomie, Jo-Jo Eumerus 198
Image *Source:* https://en.wikipedia.org/w/index.php?title=File:Flag_of_Ukraine.svg *License:* Public Domain *Contributors:* Ahonc, Akhristov, Albedo-ukr, Andrew J.Kurbiko, Antonanton~commonswiki, Chase I, Cycn, Denelson83, Diánmondin, Dzordzm, Fred J, GoldenRainbow, Homo lupus, Ilyaroz, IvanOS, Jdx, Jon Harald Søby, Justass, Klemen Kocjancic, Kwasura, LIsnykMaria, Mattes, Maximaximax, Mormegil, Neq00, Odder, PsichoPuzo, Sangjinhwa, Sarang, SeNeKa~commonswiki, Serhio~commonswiki, SiBr4, Steinsplitter, TFerenczy, Tat1642, User000name, Zcout1993, ZooFari, Zscout370, МЕИ, Ранко Николић, 夢蝶葬花, 14 anonymous edits ... 199
Image *Source:* https://en.wikipedia.org/w/index.php?title=File:Flag_of_Serbia.svg *License:* Public Domain *Contributors:* ABF, Avala, B1mbo, Camervan, Cantons-de-l'Est, Cathy Richards, Creepfip, Cycn, Denelson83, EDUCA33E, Ebrahim, Erlenmeyer, Fry1989, Herbythyme, Homo lupus, Illegitimate Barrister, Imbris~commonswiki, Mats Stirlitz, Mattes, Mormegil, Nightstallion, Nikola Smolenski, Nuno Gabriel Cabral~commonswiki, Odder, OgreBot 2, PhilKnight, R-41~commonswiki, Rainman~commonswiki, Rodejong, Rokerismoravee, Sangjinhwa, Sarang, Sasa Stefanovic, SiBr4, Siebrand, TFCforever, ThomasPusch, Torsch, Túrelio, WhiteWriter, Zscout370, Абдулло-Довуд, Добромир Костадинов, Ранко Николић, 12 anonymous edits ... 199
Image *Source:* https://en.wikipedia.org/w/index.php?title=File:Flag_of_Croatia.svg *License:* Public Domain *Contributors:* Nightstallion, Elephantus, Neoneo13, Denelson83, Rainman, R-41, Minestrone, Lupo, Zscout370, MaGa (based on Decision of ... 199
Figure 135 *Source:* https://en.wikipedia.org/w/index.php?title=File:KuK_Infanterie_1898.jpg *License:* Public Domain *Contributors:* BotMultichill, Erwin Lindemann, KTo288, Spars ... 203
Figure 136 *Source:* https://en.wikipedia.org/w/index.php?title=File:Archduke_Eugen_Bosniaks.jpg *License:* Public Domain *Contributors:* Akimow, BošnjakArmin, Gryffindor, PRODUCER, Ras67 ... 205
Image *Source:* https://en.wikipedia.org/w/index.php?title=File:1913_Austro-Hungarian_order_banning_Serb_cultural_societies_in_Bosnia.jpg *License:* Public Domain *Contributors:* Anonimski, Prüm, Smooth O ... 206
Figure 137 *Source:* https://en.wikipedia.org/w/index.php?title=File:Gavrilo_Princip_captured_in_Sarajevo_1914.jpg *License:* anonymous-EU *Contributors:* Andros64, Anonimski, BokicaK, DIREKTOR, Gabriel VanHelsing, Paul Barlow, Prashanthns, Smooth O, Themightyquill, Tpbradbury ... 208
Figure 138 *Source:* https://en.wikipedia.org/w/index.php?title=File:1914-06-29_-_Aftermath_of_attacks_against_Serbs_in_Sarajevo.png *License:* Public Domain *Contributors:* Anonimski, Gabriel VanHelsing, Jacquesverlaeken, My-wiki-photos, Smooth O, Zoupan ... 209
Figure 139 *Source:* https://en.wikipedia.org/w/index.php?title=File:MÁV_armoured_train.jpg *Contributors:* Filederchest ... 210
Figure 140 *Source:* https://en.wikipedia.org/w/index.php?title=File:Szturm_Twierdzy_Przemysl_A._Ritter_von_Meissl.jpg *License:* Public Domain *Contributors:* R.v. Meissl 1867-1926 ... 215
Figure 141 *Source:* https://en.wikipedia.org/w/index.php?title=File:Sacrario_Militare_di_Redipuglia.jpg *License:* Public Domain *Contributors:* User:Dantadd ... 216
Figure 142 *Source:* https://en.wikipedia.org/w/index.php?title=File:Csíkpálfalva2.JPG *License:* Creative Commons Attribution 3.0 *Contributors:* Szabi237 ... 218
Figure 143 *Source:* https://en.wikipedia.org/w/index.php?title=File:Poprava_vůdců_rumburské_vzpoury_1918.jpg *License:* Public Domain *Contributors:* Catsmeat, Daniel Baránek, John commons, Miaow Miaow, Miraceti, TwoWings ... 220
Figure 144 *Source:* https://en.wikipedia.org/w/index.php?title=File:AustriaHungaryWW1.gif *License:* Public Domain *Contributors:* The Independent ... 224
Figure 145 *Source:* https://en.wikipedia.org/w/index.php?title=File:Dissolution_of_Austria-Hungary.png *License:* Creative Commons Attribution-ShareAlike 3.0 Unported *Contributors:* Österreich-Ungarns_Ende.png: AlphaCentauri derivative work: P. S. Burton (talk) ... 224
Figure 146 *Source:* https://en.wikipedia.org/w/index.php?title=File:Austria_hungary_1911_and_post_war_borders.jpg *License:* Public Domain *Contributors:* Numele1918 224
Image *Source:* https://en.wikipedia.org/w/index.php?title=File:Austria-Hungary_map_new.svg *License:* Public Domain *Contributors:* Austria-Hungary_map.svg: IMeowbot ... 225
Figure 147 *Source:* https://en.wikipedia.org/w/index.php?title=File:Austria-Hungary-flag-1869-1914-naval-1786-1869-merchant.svg *License:* Public Domain *Contributors:* PavelD ... 227
Figure 148 *Source:* https://en.wikipedia.org/w/index.php?title=File:Flag_of_Austria-Hungary_1869-1918.svg *Contributors:* - ... 227
Figure 149 *Source:* https://en.wikipedia.org/w/index.php?title=File:Naval_Ensign_of_Austria-Hungary_(1918).svg *License:* Public Domain *Contributors:* Austria-Hungary_Naval_Ensign1918.gif: Austria-Hungary derivative work: Hugh Jass (talk) ... 227
Figure 150 *Source:* https://en.wikipedia.org/w/index.php?title=File:War_flag_of_Austria-Hungary_(1918).svg *License:* Public Domain *Contributors:* B1mbo ... 228
Figure 151 *Source:* https://en.wikipedia.org/w/index.php?title=File:Royal_hungarian_maritime_flag.gif *License:* Public Domain *Contributors:* Royal Hungarian Maritime Flag ... 228
Figure 152 *Source:* https://en.wikipedia.org/w/index.php?title=File:Flag_of_the_Habsburg_Monarchy.svg *License:* Public Domain *Contributors:* Sir Iain, earlier version by ThrashedParanoid and Peregrine981.ThrashedParanoid ... 229
Figure 153 *Source:* https://en.wikipedia.org/w/index.php?title=File:Flag_of_Hungary_(1867-1918).svg *License:* Public Domain *Contributors:* Thommy ... 229
Figure 154 *Source:* https://en.wikipedia.org/w/index.php?title=File:Flag_of_Croatia-Slavonia_with_CoA.svg *License:* Creative Commons Attribution-Sharealike 3.0 *Contributors:* DIREKTOR (parts derived from User:Ex13's images) ... 230
Figure 155 *Source:* https://en.wikipedia.org/w/index.php?title=File:Imperial_Coat_of_Arms_of_the_Empire_of_Austria_(1815).svg *License:* Creative Commons Attribution-Sharealike 3.0 *Contributors:* User:Sodacan ... 230

Figure 156 *Source:* https://en.wikipedia.org/w/index.php?title=File:Wappen_Österreich-Ungarn_1916_(Klein).png *Contributors:* upload David Liuzzo ... 231
Figure 157 *Source:* https://en.wikipedia.org/w/index.php?title=File:Imperial_Coat_of_Arms_of_the_Empire_of_Austria.svg *License:* Creative Commons Attribution-Sharealike 3.0 *Contributors:* User:Sodacan ... 231
Figure 158 *Source:* https://en.wikipedia.org/w/index.php?title=File:Austria-Hungaria_transparency.png *License:* Public Domain *Contributors:* User:Hannes 2 ... 231
Figure 159 *Source:* https://en.wikipedia.org/w/index.php?title=File:Imperial_Coat_of_Arms_of_Austria.svg *License:* Creative Commons Attribution-Sharealike 3.0 *Contributors:* User:Sodacan ... 232
Figure 160 *Source:* https://en.wikipedia.org/w/index.php?title=File:Wappen_Österreichische_Länder_1915_(Mittel).png *License:* Public Domain *Contributors:* Upload David Liuzzo ... 232
Figure 161 *Source:* https://en.wikipedia.org/w/index.php?title=File:Coa_Hungary_Country_History_(1916).svg *License:* Creative Commons Zero *Contributors:* Madboy74 ... 233
Figure 162 *Source:* https://en.wikipedia.org/w/index.php?title=File:Coa_Hungary_Country_History_med_(1915).svg *License:* Creative Commons Zero *Contributors:* BrightRaven, Bubel, DarwIn, Jza84, Madboy74, Magyarcimerek, Mattes, Sarang, Szilas, W!B: ... 233
Image *Source:* https://en.wikipedia.org/w/index.php?title=File:Wikivoyage-Logo-v3-icon.svg *License:* Creative Commons Attribution-Sharealike 3.0 *Contributors:* User:AleXXw ... 237
Figure 163 *Source:* https://en.wikipedia.org/w/index.php?title=File:Miklós_Horthy_and_Adolf_Hitler_1938.jpg *License:* anonymous-EU *Contributors:* User:Luppus ... 240
Figure 164 *Source:* https://en.wikipedia.org/w/index.php?title=File:Magyarorszag_1920.png *License:* Creative Commons Attribution-Sharealike 3.0 *Contributors:* derivative work: CoolKoon (talk) Hungary1910-1920.png: () ... 241
Figure 165 *Source:* https://en.wikipedia.org/w/index.php?title=File:Pál_Teleki_01.jpg *License:* Public Domain *Contributors:* Unattributed .. 242
Figure 166 *Source:* https://en.wikipedia.org/w/index.php?title=File:TeritorialGainsHungary1920-41.svg *License:* Creative Commons Attribution-Sharealike 3.0 *Contributors:* User:ArnoldPlaton, User:PANONIAN, User:Rowanwindwhistler ... 243
Figure 167 *Source:* https://en.wikipedia.org/w/index.php?title=File:Hungary_1941_ethnic.svg *License:* Creative Commons Attribution-Sharealike 3.0 *Contributors:* User:ArnoldPlaton ... 244
Figure 168 *Source:* https://en.wikipedia.org/w/index.php?title=File:Kingdom_of_Hungary_1944_44_Varmegye.png *License:* Creative Commons Attribution-ShareAlike 3.0 Unported *Contributors:* XrysD ... 245
Figure 169 *Source:* https://en.wikipedia.org/w/index.php?title=File:Toldi.jpg *License:* Public Domain *Contributors:* Falkmart, High Contrast, KTo288, Membershiped, Rheo1905∼commonswiki, Smat, SuperTank17 ... 247
Figure 170 *Source:* https://en.wikipedia.org/w/index.php?title=File:Bundesarchiv_Bild_101I-680-8283A-12A,_Budapest,_marschierende_Pfeilkreuzler_und_Panzer_VI.jpg *License:* Creative Commons Attribution-Sharealike 3.0 Germany *Contributors:* Andy king50, BotMultichill, Brakeet, Denniss, Gandvik, Hohum, Kevjonesin, Martin H., Minderbinder, Themightyquill, 2 anonymous edits ... 248
Figure 171 *Source:* https://en.wikipedia.org/w/index.php?title=File:A_Harmadik_Birodalom_hadserege_a_Margit_hídon_-_1944.03.19.jpg *License:* Public Domain *Contributors:* Elekes Andor, Hungarikusz Firkász, Ipvivrnzl, Joostik, OgreBot 2, Pe-Jo, Svensson1 ... 249
Figure 172 *Source:* https://en.wikipedia.org/w/index.php?title=File:Hungarian_soldiers_in_the_Carpathians.jpg *License:* Creative Commons Attribution 3.0 *Contributors:* Slobodsky ... 250
Figure 173 *Source:* https://en.wikipedia.org/w/index.php?title=File:Hungarian_soldies_in_Denmark_2._World_War.JPG *License:* GNU Free Documentation License *Contributors:* BotMultichill, Giorgiomonteforti, MGA73bot2, RhinoMind, Sorenpeder, Thomas81, Valentinian, 4 anonymous edits 252
Image *Source:* https://en.wikipedia.org/w/index.php?title=File:Flag_of_German_Reich_(1935–1945).svg *Contributors:* - ... 253
Image *Source:* https://en.wikipedia.org/w/index.php?title=File:Flag_of_Hungary_(1920–1946).svg *Contributors:* - ... 253
Image *Source:* https://en.wikipedia.org/w/index.php?title=File:Flag_of_Italy_(1861-1946)_crowned.svg *License:* Creative Commons Attribution-Sharealike 2.5 *Contributors:* F l a n k e r ... 253
Image *Source:* https://en.wikipedia.org/w/index.php?title=File:Flag_of_the_Kingdom_of_Yugoslavia.svg *Contributors:* BotMultichill, Cycn, Eleassar, JuTa, Makaristos, Orzetto∼commonswiki, Permjak, R-41∼commonswiki, Rainman∼commonswiki, Sangjinhwa, SiBr4, Trần Nguyễn Minh Huy, 2 anonymous edits ... 253
Image *Source:* https://en.wikipedia.org/w/index.php?title=File:Flag_of_Finland.svg *License:* Public Domain *Contributors:* SVG drawn by Sebastian Koppehel ... 253
Image *Source:* https://en.wikipedia.org/w/index.php?title=File:Flag_of_First_Slovak_Republic_1939-1945.svg *License:* Public Domain *Contributors:* DarkEvil, PhiLiP ... 253
Image *Source:* https://en.wikipedia.org/w/index.php?title=File:Flag_of_Independent_State_of_Croatia.svg *License:* Public domain *Contributors:* public domain by User:Zscout370 ... 253
Image *Source:* https://en.wikipedia.org/w/index.php?title=File:Flag_of_the_Soviet_Union_(1923-1955).svg *Contributors:* - ... 253
Image *Source:* https://en.wikipedia.org/w/index.php?title=File:Chetniks_Flag.svg *Contributors:* Voytek s ... 253
Image *Source:* https://en.wikipedia.org/w/index.php?title=File:Yugoslav_Partisans_flag_1945.svg *Contributors:* - ... 253
Image *Source:* https://en.wikipedia.org/w/index.php?title=File:Flaga_PPP.svg *License:* Creative Commons Attribution-Sharealike 2.5 *Contributors:* Bastianow (Bastian) ... 254
Image *Source:* https://en.wikipedia.org/w/index.php?title=File:Flag_of_Poland_(1928-1980).svg *License:* Public Domain *Contributors:* User:Arvedui89 ... 254
Image *Source:* https://en.wikipedia.org/w/index.php?title=File:Flag_of_Bulgaria.svg *License:* Public Domain *Contributors:* SKopp ... 254
Image *Source:* https://en.wikipedia.org/w/index.php?title=File:U.S._flag,_48_stars.svg *Contributors:* - ... 254
Image *Source:* https://en.wikipedia.org/w/index.php?title=File:Flag_of_the_United_Kingdom.svg *License:* Public Domain *Contributors:* Anomie, Good Olfactory, Jo-Jo Eumerus, MSGJ, Mifter ... 254
Image *Source:* https://en.wikipedia.org/w/index.php?title=File:Canadian_Red_Ensign_1921-1957.svg *Contributors:* - ... 254
Image *Source:* https://en.wikipedia.org/w/index.php?title=File:Flag_of_France.svg *License:* Public Domain *Contributors:* Anomie, Fastily, Jo-Jo Eumerus ... 254
Image *Source:* https://en.wikipedia.org/w/index.php?title=File:Flag_of_Norway.svg *License:* Public Domain *Contributors:* Dbenbenn ... 254
Image *Source:* https://en.wikipedia.org/w/index.php?title=File:Flag_of_Denmark.svg *License:* Public Domain *Contributors:* Madden ... 254
Image *Source:* https://en.wikipedia.org/w/index.php?title=File:Flag_of_the_Netherlands.svg *License:* Public Domain *Contributors:* Zscout370 254
Image *Source:* https://en.wikipedia.org/w/index.php?title=File:Flag_of_Belgium_(civil).svg *License:* Public Domain *Contributors:* Allforrous, Andres gb.ldc, Bean49, Cathy Richards, David Descamps, Dbenbenn, Denelson83, Evanc0912, Fry1989, Gabriel trzy, Howcome, IvanOS, Jdx, Mimich, Ms2ger, Nightstallion, Oreo Priest, Pitke, Ricordisamoa, Rocket000, Rodejong, Sarang, SiBr4, Sir Iain, ThomasPusch, Warddr, Zscout370, 14 anonymous edits ... 254
Image *Source:* https://en.wikipedia.org/w/index.php?title=File:Naval_Ensign_of_Russia.svg *License:* Public Domain *Contributors:* User:SeNeKa, User:Zscout370 ... 255
Figure 174 *Source:* https://en.wikipedia.org/w/index.php?title=File:Bundesarchiv_Bild_183-N0827-318,_KZ_Auschwitz,_Ankunft_ungarischer_Juden.jpg *License:* Creative Commons Attribution-Sharealike 3.0 Germany *Contributors:* AdamBMorgan, BotMultichill, Catsmeat, Gertsam, Goesseln, Hannolans, Jarekt, LudwigSebastianMicheler, Man vyi, Mtsmallwood, Rowanwindwhistler, SlimVirgin, Svajcr, Tom5551, Yarl, 5 anonymous edits 256
Image *Source:* https://en.wikipedia.org/w/index.php?title=File:Hole_in_flag_-_Budapest_1956.jpg *License:* Attribution *Contributors:* The American Hungarian Federation ... 259
Image *Source:* https://en.wikipedia.org/w/index.php?title=File:Flag_of_the_Soviet_Union_(1955-1980).svg *License:* Creative Commons Attribution-ShareAlike 3.0 Unported *Contributors:* Cmapm ... 259
Image *Source:* https://en.wikipedia.org/w/index.php?title=File:Red_Army_flag.svg *License:* Public Domain *Contributors:* User:Zscout370 ... 259
Image *Source:* https://en.wikipedia.org/w/index.php?title=File:Emblema_KGB.svg *License:* Creative Commons Attribution-Sharealike 3.0 *Contributors:* jgaray ... 259
Image *Source:* https://en.wikipedia.org/w/index.php?title=File:Flag_of_Hungary_(1949-1956).svg *License:* Creative Commons Zero *Contributors:* Thommy ... 259
Image *Source:* https://en.wikipedia.org/w/index.php?title=File:Emblem_of_the_State_Protection_Authority.svg *License:* Creative Commons Zero *Contributors:* User:Oppashi, User:Thommy9 ... 259
Image *Source:* https://en.wikipedia.org/w/index.php?title=File:Flag_of_the_Hungarian_Revolution_(1956).svg *License:* Creative Commons Attribution-ShareAlike 3.0 Unported *Contributors:* User:Guilherme Paula ... 259
Image *Source:* https://en.wikipedia.org/w/index.php?title=File:Skull_and_crossbones.svg *Contributors:* Andux, Andy0101, AnselmiJuan, Bayo, BotMultichill, BotMultichillT, Coyau, D0ktorz, Derbeth, Eugenio Hansen, OFS, Franzenshof, Ies, J.delanoy, JMCC1, Jahoe, Juliancolton, Karelj, MarianSigler, Natr, Sarang, Shuhazmir, Sidpatil, Silsor, Stas1995, Stepshep, Str4nd, Sven Manguard, SweetCanadianMullet, The Evil IP address, Tiptoety, Túrelio, W!B:, Wknight94, 22 anonymous edits ... 259
Image *Source:* https://en.wikipedia.org/w/index.php?title=File:Warsaw_Pact_Logo.svg *License:* Creative Commons Attribution-Sharealike 3.0 *Contributors:* User:Fenn-O-maniC ... 260

Figure 175 *Source:* https://en.wikipedia.org/w/index.php?title=File:Rákosi_Mátyás_fortepan_56324.jpg *License:* Creative Commons Attribution-Sharealike 3.0 *Contributors:* Dencey, Monopoly31121993 263
Figure 176 *Source:* https://en.wikipedia.org/w/index.php?title=File:Nagy_Imre_fortepan_74215.jpg *License:* Creative Commons Attribution-Sharealike 3.0 *Contributors:* Agoston.hu, Gbarta, Pe-Jo 265
Image *Source:* https://en.wikipedia.org/w/index.php?title=File:Eugène_Delacroix_-_La_liberté_guidant_le_peuple.jpg *License:* Public Domain *Contributors:* 1970gemini, Aavindraa, Achim55, Alvaro qc, Anetode, Arnomane, Berrucomons, Better than Hustler, Bibi Saint-Pol, BotMultichill, Bzh-99, Cantons-de-l'Est, Crisco 1492, Dbenbenn, Didactohedron~commonswiki, DutchHoratius, Encephalon~commonswiki, FoeNyx, Graphium, Husky, J JMesserly, Jarekt, Jean-Frédéric, Julia W, Jérémy-Günther-Heinz Jähnick, Kelson, Mütty, Makthorpe, Marianika~commonswiki, Martin H., Mattes, Mglanznig, Miniwark, Mmxx, Nguyễn Lê, Olivier, Oursana, Paris 16, PawełMM, Pixel8tor, Plindenbaum, Pline, Pyb, RP88, Ranveig, Ravenpuff, Soerfm, Stewi101015, The art master, Thibaut120094, Thierry Caro, Thuresson, Trycatch, Tsui, Warburg, Wittylama, Zolo, たね, とある白い猫, 22 anonymous edits 267
Image *Source:* https://en.wikipedia.org/w/index.php?title=File:A_coloured_voting_box.svg *License:* Creative Commons Attribution-Sharealike 2.5 *Contributors:* Anomie, Jo-Jo Eumerus 268
Figure 177 *Source:* https://en.wikipedia.org/w/index.php?title=File:Sztálin_szobor_Budapest_1956.jpg *License:* Creative Commons Attribution-Sharealike 3.0 *Contributors:* Hello world, Monopoly31121993, Pe-Jo, RomanM82, Themightyquill 269
Figure 178 *Source:* https://en.wikipedia.org/w/index.php?title=File:Kossuth_Lajos_utca_a_Ferenciek_tere_felől_nézve._1956._október_25-e_délután,_-_Fortepan_24652.jpg *License:* Creative Commons Attribution-Sharealike 3.0 *Contributors:* Fæ, Pe-Jo, Rakás, RomanM82 270
Figure 179 *Source:* https://en.wikipedia.org *License:* Creative Commons Attribution-Sharealike 3.0 *Contributors:* Fæ, Pe-Jo, RomanM82 271
Figure 180 *Source:* https://en.wikipedia.org/w/index.php?title=File:Flyer._Imre_Nagy,_Head_of_goverment_-1956.10.27.tif *License:* Public Domain *Contributors:* Derzsi Elekes Andor, Rlevente 273
Figure 181 *Source:* https://en.wikipedia.org/w/index.php?title=File:Kossuth_Lajos_utca_-_Károly_(Tanács)_körút_sarok._Fortepan_23591.jpg *License:* Creative Commons Attribution-Sharealike 3.0 *Contributors:* Beroesz, Fæ, Pe-Jo, RomanM82 274
Figure 182 *Source:* https://en.wikipedia.org *License:* Creative Commons Attribution-Sharealike 3.0 *Contributors:* Fæ, Pe-Jo, RomanM82 276
Figure 183 *Source:* https://en.wikipedia.org *License:* Creative Commons Attribution-Sharealike 3.0 *Contributors:* Alexpl, Fæ, Globetrotter19, RomanM82 278
Figure 184 *Source:* https://en.wikipedia.org/w/index.php?title=File:1956_november_5._Eindhoven.jpg *License:* Creative Commons Attribution-Sharealike 3.0 *Contributors:* Hello world, Timmietovenaar 280
Figure 185 *Source:* https://en.wikipedia.org/w/index.php?title=File:1956-11-01_War_in_Egypt.ogv *Contributors:* Universal 281
Figure 186 *Source:* https://en.wikipedia.org *License:* Creative Commons Attribution-Sharealike 3.0 *Contributors:* Globetrotter19, Lklundin, Monopoly31121993, OgreBot 2, Revent, RomanM82, Sepultura 282
Figure 187 *Source:* https://en.wikipedia.org *License:* Creative Commons Attribution-Sharealike 3.0 *Contributors:* Beroesz, Fæ, Globetrotter19, RomanM82 283
Figure 188 *Source:* https://en.wikipedia.org/w/index.php?title=File:Erzsébet_(Lenin)_körút,_a_Royal_Szállóval_(ma_Corinthia_Hotel)_szemben._Fortepan_15317.jpg *License:* Creative Commons Attribution-Sharealike 3.0 *Contributors:* Fæ, Globetrotter19, Monopoly31121993, Pe-Jo, RomanM82 284
Figure 189 *Source:* https://en.wikipedia.org/w/index.php?title=File:Üllői_út_a_Nagykörút_felől_a_Vajdahunyad_utca_felé_nézve._Fortepan_24768.jpg *License:* Creative Commons Attribution-Sharealike 3.0 *Contributors:* Fæ, Globetrotter19, RomanM82 285
Figure 190 *Source:* https://en.wikipedia.org *License:* Public Domain *Contributors:* Docu, Fadesga, JustSomePics, WFinch 288
Figure 191 *Source:* https://en.wikipedia.org/w/index.php?title=File:60th_anniversary_of_Hungarian_Revolution_2016_stamp.jpg *License:* Public Domain *Contributors:* Hungarian Post Office 291
Figure 192 *Source:* https://en.wikipedia.org/w/index.php?title=File:Budapešť,_Hösök_tére,_pamětní_deska_1956.jpg *License:* Creative Commons Attribution 3.0 *Contributors:* Aktron, BotMultichillT, Csanády, Kilom691, Szenti Tamás, TamaSa52 292
Image *Source:* https://en.wikipedia.org/w/index.php?title=File:Open_Access_logo_PLoS_transparent.svg *License:* Creative Commons Zero *Contributors:* Adrignola, Aloneintheworld, AnonMoos, Closeapple, Le6cX6, JakobVoss, Josve05a, Renardo la vulpo, Sturm, Varnent 293
Image *Source:* https://en.wikipedia.org/w/index.php?title=File:Cscr-featured.svg *License:* GNU Lesser General Public License *Contributors:* Anomie 296

License

Creative Commons Attribution-Share Alike 3.0
//creativecommons.org/licenses/by-sa/3.0/

Index

Abda, Hungary, 256
Abgeordnetenhaus (Austria), 160
Absolute monarchy, 38
Abu Abdallah al-Jayhani, 6
Abu Tahir Marwazi, 6
Act Zluky, 223
Administrative divisions of the Kingdom of Hungary, 61, 225
Admiral, 223
Adolf Eichmann, 255
Adolf Hitler, 223, 240, 241
Adriatic Sea, 186, 191, 226
A. J. P. Taylor, 235
Akıncı, 116
Alajos Hauszmann, 67
Alajos Stróbl, 68
Alanic language, 15
Alans, 7
Alan Sked, 235
Alba Iulia, 44
Al-Bakri, 6
Albert Camus, 291
Albert Shaw (journalist), 306
Alevi, 124
Alexander Büchler, 306
Alfred Hillebrandt, 63
Alfred I, Prince of Windisch-Grätz, 65, 130, 154
Alfred Jodl, 257
Allen Dulles, 265, 266

Álmos, 9, 19, 20

Alois Aehrenthal, 210
Alps, 56
Amadeus Aba, 39
Anastas Mikoyan, 276
Anastylosis, 75
András Hegedüs, 269, 270, 284
András Róna-Tas, 6
Andrássy Avenue, 53, 301, 305
Andrees Allgemeiner Handatlas, 176
Andrzej Paczkowski, 324
Angelo Rotta, 250

Angel Sanz Briz, 250
Angyalföld, 271
Animal husbandry, 2
Anjou, 79
Annales iuvavenses, 6
Annals of Fulda, 6
Annals of Salzburg, 21
Annals of St. Bertin, 9
Anna of Foix-Candale, 57
Anonymus (chronicler), 6
Anschluss, 223, 242
Antisemitism, 180, 241
Anti-Serb riots in Sarajevo, 209
Anti-Serb riots of Sarajevo, 208
Antonio Giolitti, 290
Anton Vogl, 156
April laws, 52, 143
Aquincum, **32**, 298
Aquincum Civil Amphitheatre, 33
Aquincum Military Amphitheatre, 33
Aquincum Mithraeum (of Victorinus), 34
Aquincum Museum, 34, 301
Arad, Romania, 157, 184, 200
Archaeology, 2
Archbishopric of Moravia, 21
Archduchy of Austria, 117
Archduke Albrecht, Duke of Teschen, 157
Archduke Alexander Leopold of Austria, 64
Archduke Franz Ferdinand, 208
Archduke Franz Ferdinand of Austria, 179, 207
Archduke Friedrich, Duke of Teschen, 213
Archduke Joseph August of Austria, 106, 223
Archduke Joseph, Palatine of Hungary, 64, 94
Archduke Leopold Salvator of Austria, 179
Archduke Stephen, Palatine of Hungary, 38, 64, 144
Architrave, 102
Armando Diaz, 216
Armistice of Villa Giusti, 162, 217, 219
Army Group South, 252
Arnulf of Carinthia, 21

Árpád, 19, 20, 298
Árpád Bridge, 304

Árpád dynasty, 19
Árpáds, 99
Arrow Cross Party, 241, 249
Arrowslit, 76
Artillerymen, 60
Artisan, 56
Artists, 56
Artpool Art Research Center, 304
Artúr Görgey, 65, 130, 146, 150, 154, 155
Asiago plateau, 215
Assassination of Archduke Franz Ferdinand of Austria, 181
Assemblage (archaeology), 4
Aster Revolution, 221, 303
Astra Automobile & Waggon Factory, 184
Aszód, 184
A Tett, 302
Atlas (architecture), 98
Attila, 298
Attila the Hun, 9
Auschwitz concentration camp, 240, 255
Austria, 198, 252, 255
Austria-Hungary, 159, 160
Austrian Army, 287
Austrian Empire, 37, 40, 129–131, 161, 163, 165, 222, 224, 225
Austrian German, 159
Austrian Landwehr, 203
Austrian Littoral, 196, 225
Austrian resistance, 255
Austrian Silesia, 196, 225
Austrian State Treaty, 266
Austro-Daimler, 184
Austro-Hungaria, 41, 52
Austro-Hungarian annexation of Bosnia and Herzegovina, 206
Austro-Hungarian Army, 168, 205, 214
Austro-Hungarian campaign in Bosnia and Herzegovina in 1878, 181
Austro-Hungarian Compromise of 1867, 38, 66, 160, 161, 300
Austro-Hungarian concession (1901–1917), 226
Austro-Hungarian gulden, 38, 160
Austro-Hungarian krone, 160, 182
Austro-Hungarian Monarchy, 226
Austro-Hungarian Navy, 168, 223
Austro-Hungarian rule in Bosnia and Herzegovina, 161, 226
Austro-Prussian War, 165
Austro-Turkish War (1787–1791), 47
Automotive industry, 183
Avar Khaganate, 39
Avars (Carpathians), 26
Avgustyn Voloshyn, 244

Avram Iancu, 130
Axis powers, 239, 262
Axis Powers of World War II, 70
Bačka, 245
Baden (district of Austria), 287
Balatonalmádi, 93
Baldachin, 85
Banat, 144, 148, 178
Banat, Bačka and Baranja, 160, 161
Banat Bulgarians, 130
Baranja, 245
Baranya County (former), 225
Baroque, 53, 54
Baroque architecture, 61
Baroque Revival, 53
Barracks, 58
Bashkirs, 14
Bashkortostan, 13
Bastion, 57
Batthyány, 299
Battle of Asiago, 215
Battle of Brezalauspurc, 22
Battle of Buda (1686), 59, 121, 299
Battle of Buda (1849), 65, 299
Battle of Budapest, 70
Battle of Caporetto, 216
Battle of Debrecen, 251, 254
Battle of Galicia, 214
Battle of Isaszeg (1849), 150
Battle of Königgrätz, 166
Battle of Mohács, 38, 40, 41, 58, 115, 148
Battle of Nikolayevka, 253
Battle of Pákozd, 142, 144, 150
Battle of Păuliş, 254
Battle of Poznań (1945), 254
Battle of Solferino, 52
Battle of Stalingrad, 247, 253
Battle of Temesvár, 152, 153
Battle of the Dukla Pass, 254
Battle of the Piave river, 216
Battle of Turda, 254
Battle of Uman, 246, 253
Battle of Vienna, 117
Battle of Vittorio Veneto, 216
Battle of Voronezh (1942), 253
Battle of Voronezh (1943), 247
Battle of Zborov (1917), 215
Battle of Zenta, 69
Battles of the Isonzo, 215
Bavaria, 252
Bayezid II, 78
Bay of Kotor, 225
Beatrice of Naples, 56
Békés County, 271
Bektashi, 124

Béla Balázs Studio, 304
Béla Horváth, 249
Béla Imrédy, 242
Béla IV of Hungary, 54, 298
Béla Király, 271, 272
Béla Kun, 223, 303
Béla Miklós, 251
Belgium, 226, 254
Belgrade, 115, 225
Berehove, 243
Berlin, 257
Bertalan Szemere, 142, 145
BHÉV, 191
Bibliotheca Corviniana, 56
Biedermeier, 102
Bielsko-Biała, 190
BKV, 304, 305
Black Hand (Serbia), 208
Black Sea, 3
Blaha Lujza tér, 303
Blood In The Water match, 290
Bocskay, 122
Bohemia, 174, 178, 179
Bolond Istók, 301
Bolshevik Revolution, 215
Bolshie Tigany, 14
Bombing of Belgrade in World War II, 246
Boris Yeltsin, 292
Bor, Serbia, 255
Borsszem Jankó, 300
Bosnia and Herzegovina, 179, 181, 208, 209, 224, 226
Bosnia and Herzegovina (Austro-Hungarian condominium), 225
Bosniak, 122
Bosniaks, 205
Bosnian crisis, 161, 210
Bosnian-Herzegovinian Infantry, 205
Bosnian Muslims, 208
Bosnian people, 124
Bourgeoisie, 174
Boxer Rebellion, 226
Bozsik Stadion, 302
Brașov, 153
Bratislava, 37, 42, 131, 163, 189, 191, 193, 199, 299
Brest, Belarus, 278
Bride price, 26
Brijuni, 278
British Empire, 137
Brno, 178, 189, 190, 198
Bronze age, 297
Brusilov Offensive, 214
Bucharest, 217, 278
Buda, 37, 55, 58, 59, 116, 117, 120, 121, 139, 193, 282, 297, 298, 300

Buda Castle, 53, 298
Buda Health Center, 305
Budapest, 32, 45, 53, 54, 154, 159, 183, 189, 199, 229, 239, 251, 261, 297, 315
Budapest Business School, 300
Budapest Castle Hill Funicular, 54
Budapest City Archives, 305
Budapest Cog-wheel Railway, 300
Budapest-Déli Railway Terminal, 304
Budapest Festival Orchestra, 304
Budapest Fringe Festival, 305
Budapest Honvéd FC, 302
Budapesti Hírlap, 301
Budapest Keleti railway station, 301
Budapest Metro, 191, 301, 305
Budapest metropolitan area, 306
Budapest-Nyugati Railway Terminal, 301
Budapest Offensive, 254, 303
Budapest Open Access Initiative, 305
Budapest Opera Ball, 301
Budapest Philharmonic Orchestra, 300
Budapest Pride, 305
Budapest Stock Exchange, 182, 305
Budapest University of Technology and Economics, 263, 267
Budin Eyalet, 40, 117, 119, 298
Budva, 225
Buffer zone, 277
Bukovina, 196, 224
Bulgar language, 25
Bulgars, 7
Bunjevci, 130
Bureaucratic despotism, 277
Burgenland, 197, 225
Burgenland Croats, 130
Burgruine Kollmitz, 21
Buttress, 81
Byzantine Emperor, 2, 6, 20
Byzantine Empire, 3, 5
Byzantine literature, 1

Café Gerbeaud, 300
Calvinist, 198
Camarilla, 144
Canada, 254
Capetian House of Anjou, 113
Capitalism, 181
Capitalist state, 261
Captaincies of the Kingdom of Hungary, 41
Carbon dated, 4
Cardinal József Mindszenty, 273
Cardinal Mindszenty, 287, 293
Carlile Aylmer Macartney, 6, 235
Carl Lutz, 250
Carniola, 178
Carolingian Empire, 16

Carpathian Basin, 3, 4
Carpathian Military District, 282
Carpathian Mountains, 250
Carpathian Ruthenia, 243, 245
Carpatho-Ruthenia, 256
Carpatho-Ukraine, 244
Carrara marble, 97
Carriageway, 67
Carso, 215
Case Blue, 253
Castle, 54
Castrum, 33
Casus belli, 246
Category:City timelines, 297
Category:History of Austria, 164
Category:History of Hungary, 1, 39, 115, 130, 165, 260, 297
Category:History of Slovakia, 39
Category:Revolutions, 267
Caterinovca, 4
Catholic Church, 38
Catholic Church in Hungary, 264
Catholicism, 45
Catholics, 159, 197
Caucasus Mountains, 3, 24
Cave painting, 11
Celt, 297
Celts, 33
Central bank, 182
Central Croatia, 225
Central Hungary, 32
Central Powers, 162

České Budějovice, 190

C:File:Freedom Is Not Free Hungarian Freedom Fighters Monument.jpg, 293
CGIL, 290
Chamberss Encyclopaedia, 306
Chancel, 78
Chapel royal, 92
Charles II of Hungary, 78
Charles I of Austria, 70, 160, 179, 213
Charles I of Austrias attempts to retake the throne of Hungary, 223
Charles IV, Holy Roman Emperor, 200
Charles University, 200
Charles University in Prague, 178
Charles VI, Holy Roman Emperor, 45, 60
Chelyabinsk, 12
Chernivtsi, 198
Chernivtsi Oblast, 225
Chetniks, 253
Chief of Staff, 215
Chimenti Camicia, 80
China, 226

Chris Clark (historian), 319
Christianity, 242
Chronicle, 6
Chronicon Eberspergense, 9
Chuvash people, 15
Cifrapalota, 302
Cisleithania, 161, 163, 166, 220, 225, 229
Cistern, 80
CITEREFB.C3.BCchler1907, 327
CITEREFBerendUrba.C5.84czykWiszewski2013, 309–311, 313, 314
CITEREFBodn.C3.A1r1998, 327
CITEREFBodn.C3.A1r2001, 327
CITEREFBritannica1910, 327
CITEREFBrook2006, 311, 312
CITEREFCartledge2011, 312
CITEREFChambers1901, 327
CITEREFCsorba1997, 310, 313
CITEREFCurta2006, 309, 311, 312
CITEREFDavid2009, 327
CITEREFDe.C3.A1k1968, 327
CITEREFEggenberger1870, 327
CITEREFEngel2001, 310–313
CITEREFErtl2008, 309
CITEREFFenyo1987, 327
CITEREFFodor1975, 310–313
CITEREFGulya1997, 309
CITEREFHarmatta1997, 309
CITEREFHaydn1910, 327
CITEREFHeadlam1911, 317
CITEREFHeadlam1911b, 319
CITEREFHeksch1895, 327
CITEREFHourihane2012, 327
CITEREFJudah1997, 316
CITEREFKlima2004, 310
CITEREFKontler1999, 310, 313, 315
CITEREFKov.C3.A1cs2005, 309, 313
CITEREFKrist.C3.B31996, 309–313
CITEREFLang.C3.B32005, 309
CITEREFL.C3.A1szl.C3.B31996, 312–314
CITEREFLukacs2012, 327
CITEREFMacartney1953, 309, 310
CITEREFMarxEngels, 316, 317
CITEREFMetro-Roland2012, 327
CITEREFMoln.C3.A1r2001, 310, 312
CITEREFNagy2002, 327
CITEREFNemes2009, 327
CITEREFOverall1870, 327
CITEREFR.C3.B3na-Tas1999, 309–314
CITEREFRothenberg1976, 317
CITEREFShaw1897, 327
CITEREFSpinei2003, 309, 311–314
CITEREFSzabados2011, 311
CITEREFSz.C3.ADj2005, 310
CITEREFT.C3.B3th1998, 309, 311

CITEREFT.C3.B3th2005, 309, 310
CITEREFT.C3.BCrk2012, 309
CITEREFVeres2004, 310
CITEREFZimonyi2005, 309
City Park (Budapest), 299
Civil ensign, 226
Clerical fascism, 244
Climate change, 12
Cluj-Napoca, 152, 200
Coalition government, 216
Coat of arms of Austria-Hungary, 159, 230
Coat of arms of Budapest, 300
Coat of arms of Hungary, 37
Cockade, 139
Codices, 113
Cognate, 2
Cold War, 259, 266
Cold War International History Project, 295
Collective farms, 264
Combino Supra, 305
COMECON, 264
Committee of Liberation of the Hungarian National Uprising, 257
Common army, 203
Commons:Category:Aquincum, 35
Commons:Category:Austria-Hungary, 238
Commons:Category:Buda Castle, 114
Commons:Category:Budapest, 308
Commons:Category:Hungarian Revolution of 1848, 158
Commons:Category:Hungarian Revolution of 1956, 295
Commons:Category:Prehistory of Hungary, 31
Communist party, 261
Communist Party of Great Britain, 291
Composite monarchy, 48
Compromise of 1867, 52
Concentration camps, 264
Condoleezza Rice, 292
Confusion of tongues, 8
Congress of Berlin, 181, 204, 209
Constantine Porphyrogenitus, 6, 18
Constantine VII Porphyrogenitus, 2, 20
Constantinople, 16, 58, 122, 157
Constitutional crisis, 169
Constitutional monarchy, 143, 159, 161
Constitution of Hungary, 306
Containment, 266
Contra-Aquincum, 298
Copper age, 297
Copyright status of work by the U.S. government, 127
Corbel, 76
Corfu, 214
Corfu Declaration, 221
Corinthian order, 82

Cornus mas, 15
Corvée, 46
Corvin Áruház, 303
Count Anton Alexander von Auersperg, 178
Counter-Reformation, 42
Count Franz Conrad von Hötzendorf, 210
Count Franz Philipp von Lamberg, 144
Count Friedrich Ferdinand von Beust, 160, 166, 180
Count Kasimir Felix Badeni, 179
Count Leopold Berchtold, 210
County of Tyrol, 196, 225
Coup détat, 246
Cour dhonneur, 56
Cranium, 27
Crimean peninsula, 21
Crimean Tatar, 124
Crimean War, 189
Croatia, 179, 199, 209, 225
Croatian flag, 229
Croatian–Hungarian Settlement, 161, 163, 229
Croatian-Hungarian Settlement, 166
Croatian language, 38, 166, 178, 196
Croats, 179, 208
Crownland, 37
Crown of Saint Stephen, 100
Crown of St. Stephen, 68
Csepel, 191, 271, 284
Cultural hegemony, 47
Customs union, 168
Cvjetko Popović, 208
Czech language, 174, 195, 196
Czechoslovak government-in-exile, 254
Czechoslovak-Hungarian population exchange, 257
Czechoslovakia, 160, 221, 255, 264
Czechoslovak Legions, 215
Czechoslovak Republic (1918-1938), 243
Czech people, 130
Czech Republic, 198, 225
Czechs, 175, 178, 220

Dacha, 276
Dag Hammarskjöld, 281, 288
Dalmatia, 178, 179
Danube, 53, 56, 191
Danube–Tisza Interfluve, 121
Dates and numbers, 144, 148, 150
Daughter language, 2
De Administrando Imperio, 6, 18
Death camps, 255
Death march, 256
Death mask, 14
Debrecen, 191, 199, 274
Deer, 7
Defensive alliance, 206

Demands of Hungarian Revolutionaries of 1956, 261, 267
Democracy, 262
Denmark, 252, 254
Dentumoger, 18
Depreciation, 264
Depression (economics), 189
Dervish, 124
Destalinisation, 277
Destalinization, 265
Dezső Pais, 5
Diarchy, 19
Die Bosniaken Kommen (March), 205
Diet (assembly), 44
Diet of Budapest, 45
Diet of Hungary, 38, 131, 133, 145, 160, 163
Digital object identifier, 234
Dimitrov Square, 304
Diplomacy, 163
Disposable and discretionary income, 264
Disputed statement, 41, 244
Division of labour, 183
Dnieper, 15
Dniester, 18
Dobos torte, 301
Dohány Street Synagogue, 300
Döme Sztójay, 248
Donaudampfschiffahrtsgesellschaft, 192
Donets Basin, 251
Don River (Russia), 2, 16
Don River, Russia, 247
Double-headed eagle, 230
Dual Monarchy, 159, 163
Dubrovnik, 191
Duchy of Bavaria, 22
Duchy of Bukovina, 225
Duchy of Carinthia, 196, 225
Duchy of Carniola, 196, 225
Duchy of Salzburg, 196, 225
Duchy of Styria, 196, 225
Duna Plaza, 305
Dunaújváros, 283, 284
Dungeon, 56
Dwight D. Eisenhower, 279

Early modern period, 38
East Berlin, 277, 282
Eastern Bloc, 257, 260, 261, 266
Eastern Catholic, 159, 198
Eastern Catholic Churches, 176, 197
Eastern Front (World War I), 214, 219
Eastern Hungarian Kingdom, 40, 42, 116
Eastern Magyars, 18
Eastern Orthodox, 197, 198
Eastern Orthodox Church, 38
Eastern Orthodoxy, 116

East Francia, 3, 9
Economic and monetary union, 183
Eda I, 184
Edinburgh, 157
Edirne, 122
Edmund Veesenmayer, 249
Ed Sullivan, 290
Eduard Taaffe, 11th Viscount Taaffe, 174
Eduard Wagnes, 205
Edvard Rusjan, 184
Eger, 122, 124
Égig érő fa, 12
Egir Eyalet, 119
Eğri Eyalet, 40, 117
Egyetértés, 301
Eight-Nation Alliance, 226
Eindhoven, 280
Einsatzgruppe, 247
Eleanor Roosevelt, 288
Electric locomotive, 185
Electric power industry, 183
Elisabeth Bridge (Budapest), 302, 304
Elisabeth of Bavaria, 97
Elm, 2
Elvis Presley, 290
Embassy of Serbia, Budapest, 287, 292
Emmanuel Le Roy Ladurie, 291
Emperor Ferdinand Northern Railway, 189
Emperor Francis II, 133
Emperor of Austria, 48, 160, 163
Empire (style), 102
Empress Elisabeth of Austria, 69
Encyclopædia Britannica Eleventh Edition, 158, 306
Endnote aaa, 160
End of Communism in Hungary (1989), 257
Endonym, 6
Endre Bajcsy-Zsilinszky, 256
Enlargement of the European Union, 305
Enlightened absolutism, 46, 47
Enns (river), 252
Eötvös Loránd University, 63
Equestrian statue, 55
Eravisci, 33, 297
Ernő Gerő, 259, 265, 268, 285
Esegel, 20
Esti Budapest, 304
Esztergom, 117
Etelköz, 3, 18
Ethnic Germans, 175
Ethnic violence, 180
Ethnogenesis, 2, 5
Ethnonym, 5
Eurasian steppes, 4, 6

Europe, 131
European migrant crisis, 306
European Union, 74
Exposition Universelle (1900), 108
Extermination camp, 239
Eyalet, 58, 119
Eyalet of Budin, 119

Façade, 55
Facts on File, 307
False-flag operation, 246
Farkas Kempelen, 63
Fasori Gimnázium, 299
Feigned retreat, 26
Ferdinand I, Holy Roman Emperor, 38, 40, 41, 115
Ferdinand I of Austria, 130, 132, 144
Ferenc Deák, 52, 142, 143, 166
Ferenc Duschek, 146
Ferenc Gyurcsány, 74
Ferenc Kazinczy, 132
Ferenc Münnich, 278, 281
Ferenc Ryzsa, 256
Ferenc Szálasi, 239, 241, 250
Fife (instrument), 27
File:1913 Austro-Hungarian order banning Serb cultural societies in Bosnia.jpg, 206
Final solution, 248
Finance minister, 206
Finland, 253
Finnish language, 9
Finno-Ugrian languages, 11
Finno-Ugric languages, 1
Firework (Katy Perry song), 75
First Army (Hungary), 251
First Austrian Republic, 162, 222, 223
First Battle of Komárom (1849), 155
First Bulgarian Empire, 2, 6
First Czechoslovak Republic, 161, 162, 223
First industrial revolution, 183
First Vienna Award, 243, 244
Fiume, 191, 197
Five-Year Plans for the National Economy of the Soviet Union, 264
Flag of Austria-Hungary, 159
Flag of Hungary, 37, 259, 268
Flamboyant, 78
Flensburg government, 257
Florin Curta, 16
Folding screen, 103
Folklore, 2
Food industry, 183
Forecourt, 57
Foreign direct investment, 226
For Freedom and Truth, 283
Forints, 63

Fortifications, 60
Forty-Eighters, 157
Fourteen Points, 220
France, 223
Francis I, Holy Roman Emperor, 89
Francis II Rákóczi, 44
Francis I of Austria, 47
Francophone, 131
Frankfurt am Main, 317
Frank Wisner, 279
Franz Joseph I of Austria, 38, 66, 130, 131, 138, 144, 160, 164, 166, 300
Franz Liszt Academy of Music, 301
Freedom of assembly, 137
French Communist Party, 291
Friar, 60
Friar Julian, 13
Friedrich Born, 250
Friuli-Venezia Giulia, 225

Gábor Baross, 191
Gábor Demszky, 305
Gábor Klauzál, 142
Galicia (Eastern Europe), 163, 189, 199, 220
Galician autonomy, 163
Ganz company, 184, 185
Ganz Works, 299
Gardizi, 6
Gavrilo Princip, 208
Gellért Hill, 105, 298
Gendarmerie, 153, 249
Geographic coordinate system, 32, 53, 238
George Lichtenstein (musician), 157
George Mandel-Mantello, 250
George W. Bush, 292
Georg Lukács, 287
Georg Rukavina Baron von Vidovgrad, 149
Georgy Malenkov, 287
Georgy Zhukov, 269, 275
Gerard of Csanád, 298
German Army (German Empire), 218
German Austria, 223
German Confederation, 165
German Democratic Republic, 277
German Empire, 161
Germanisation, 157
German language, 37, 38, 41, 54, 159, 162, 164, 195
German occupation of Czechoslovakia, 244
German reunification, 292
Germans, 130
German Wikipedia, 306
Germany, 254
Gesta Hungarorum, 5, 6
Gesta Hunnorum et Hungarorum, 9
Gestapo, 257

Géza Jeszenszky, 280
Géza Lakatos, 249
Géza Losonczy, 287
Giant (mythology), 8
Giorgio Napolitano, 290
Giorgio Perlasca, 250
Giuseppe Di Vittorio, 290
Global spread of the printing press, 298
Gödöllő, 63, 191
Gödöllö artists colony, 302
Goldsmith, 25
Gorizia, 184, 215
Gorlice–Tarnów Offensive, 214
Gothic architecture, 54
Gott erhalte Franz den Kaiser, 159
Government of National Unity (Hungary), 250, 254, 255, 262
Gräf & Stift, 184
Grand Boulevard (Budapest), 301
Grand Prince of the Hungarians, 9, 19, 20
Grand Trianon, 223
Grand Vizier, 117
Grapes, 15
Graz, 189, 198, 287
Great Depression, 239, 240
Greater Bulgaria, 204
Greater Hungary (political concept), 250
Great Hungarian Plain, 115, 182, 192
Great Moravia, 3, 39
Great power, 161, 164
Great Turkish War, 41, 117
Gresham Palace, 302
Grisaille, 64
Guerrillas, 243
Gül Baba, 124
Gül Baba (poet), 124
Gundel, 301
Gunpowder, 60
Gunther E. Rothenberg, 236
Gyöngyösi utca (Budapest Metro), 305
Győr, 184, 185, 274
György Klapka, 130
György Zala (sculptor), 112
Gyors-hadtest, 246
Gyula Andrássy, 160, 174, 181, 204
Gyula Donáth, 110
Gyula Gömbös, 240
Gyula Jungfer, 110
Gyula Kristó, 7, 30
Gyula László, 11
Gyula Moravcsik, 5
Gyula Németh (linguist), 7
Gyula (title), 3, 19

Habsburg, 59, 299
Habsburg dynasty, 44, 131
Habsburg Hungary, 121
Habsburg Law, 223
Habsburg Monarchy, 37, 40, 42, 161, 189
Habsburgs, 41
Hajduk (soldiers), 116
Hajógyári Island, 192
Hall of Art, Budapest, 301
Hamazasp Babadzhanian, 282
Hand grenade, 208
Hannah Arendt, 277
Harald Feller, 250
Hartmann Schedel, 78
Havilah, 8
Haydns Dictionary of Dates, 306
Haynau, 156
Head of government, 140
Head of State, 238
Heavy industry, 183
Heavy machine guns, 216
Hegemony, 277
Heinrich Hentzi, 65
Heinrich Lammasch, 160, 221
Henryk Dembiński, 130
Herceg Novi, 226
Hercules, 57
Herodotus, 5
Heroes Square (Budapest), 302, 305
Herrenhaus (Austria), 160
Himnusz, 37
History of Austria, 164
History of Budapest, 297
History of Czechoslovakia, 40
History of Hungary, 1, 39, 99, 115, 130, 165, 260, 297
History of rail transport, 183
History of Slovakia, 39
History of Slovakia before the Slovaks, 39
History of the Jews in Hungary, 239
Hlučín Region, 225
Hofburg, 65
Hofkriegsrat, 61
Holy Alliance, 131
Holy Crown of Hungary, 166
Holy League (1684), 59, 121
Holy Roman Emperor, 54
Holy Roman Empire, 40, 42, 117
Holy See, 288
Horse-drawn tramway, 190
Horthy, 157
Hortobágy National Park, 108
House arrest, 248
House of Habsburg, 161, 226
House of Habsburg-Lorraine, 163
House of Keglević, 63
House of Magnates of Hungary, 160
House of Representatives of Hungary, 160

Hryhory Yakhymovych, 130
Hu:Heksch Sándor, 307
Humanists, 56
Hungarian Academy of Sciences, 300
Hungarian Communist Party, 256, 262, 287
Hungarian conquest of the Carpathian Basin, 1, 22
Hungarian Declaration of Independence, 150
Hungarian Democratic Republic, 161, 222, 223, 303
Hungarian flag, 229
Hungarian Front, 257
Hungarian Germans, 130
Hungarian Ground Forces, 282
Hungarian Honved, 203
Hungarian invasions of Europe, 9
Hungarian Kingdom, 154
Hungarian language, 1, 5, 10, 37, 38, 41, 54, 131, 133, 159, 163, 164, 195, 261
Hungarian National Bank, 264, 303
Hungarian National Defence Association, 240
Hungarian National Gallery, 84
Hungarian National Library, 97
Hungarian National Museum, 101, 299
Hungarian nobility, 45
Hungarian parliamentary election, 1945, 262
Hungarian Parliament Building, 261, 302
Hungarian pengő, 264
Hungarian people, 44, 130, 147, 166
Hungarian Peoples Republic, 259, 261, 304
Hungarian prehistory, 1
Hungarian Radio, 261, 303
Hungarian Republic of Councils, 303
Hungarian Revolutionary Army, 144
Hungarian Revolution of 1848, 38, 41, **129**, 256, 267, 299, 321
Hungarian Revolution of 1956, **259**, 304
Hungarian-Romanian War of 1919, 223
Hungarians in Romania, 144
Hungarian Slovene, 148
Hungarian Slovenes, 130
Hungarian Social Democratic Party, 256, 262
Hungarian Soviet Republic, 223, 303
Hungarian State Opera House, 301
Hungarian Technical and Transportation Museum, 302
Hungarian Wikipedia, 306
Hungarian Working Peoples Party, 261, 262
Hungarian Writers Union, 267
Hungary, 32, 53, 124, 199, 240, 241, 254, 297, 298, 315
Hungary during World War II, 262
Hungary in World War II, **239**
Hungary Millennium Celebrations, 301
Hunor and Magor, 7, 8
Huns, 1, 298

Hunter-gatherer, 2
Hyperinflation, 264, 322

Ibn Fadlan, 19
Ibn Rusta, 6, 20
Ignác Martinovics, 47, 131, 299
Ignateva Cave, 11
Illuminated Chronicle, 8, 17, 19, 20
Imperial and Royal, 166
Imperial Council (Austria), 160, 162
Imperial Diet (Austria), 145
Imperial Germany, 218
Imperial-Royal, 166
Imperial Russian Army, 214
Imre Nagy, 259, 265, 271, 287, 292
Imre Thököly, 40, 117
Independence, 131
Independent Smallholders, Agrarian Workers and Civic Party, 256, 262, 273
Independent State of Croatia, 253, 254
Indiana University Press, 237
Indro Montanelli, 320
Industrialization, 182
Infantry, 203
Inline engine (aviation), 184
Innsbruck, 190
International Gothic, 54
International Red Cross, 290
International Socialism (magazine), 323
International Standard Book Number, 28–31, 127, 158, 234, 235, 258, 293–295, 307
Internet Archive, 295
Interwar period, 241
Intimidation, 262
Invasion of Yugoslavia, 239, 245, 253, 262
Ionic order, 94
Iparterv, 304
Iranian languages, 12
Iron age, 297
Iron Gates, 191
Irredentist, 239
Islam, 162
Ismail ibn Ahmad, 22
Isonzo, 215
Issa Pliyev, 251
István Bárczy, 302
István Bethlen, 241
István Bibó, 283
István Burián, 217, 220
István Deák, 307
István Dobi, 284
István Fodor (archaeologist), 12
István Széchenyi, 49, 50, 133, 142, 191, 192
István Tarlós, 290, 306
Istvan Tisza, 179
István Tisza, 210, 217

ISU-152, 283
Italian Communist Party, 290
Italian language, 38, 195
Italian Peninsula, 165
Italians, 130
Italian Socialist Party, 291
Italy, 117, 198
It:Sacrario militare di Redipuglia, 216
Ivan Konev, 259, 282
Ivano-Frankivsk Oblast, 225
Ivan Paskevich, 130
Ivan Serov, 281
Ivo Andrić, 209
Iyrcae, 5

Jacobin (politics), 299
Jagiellonian University, 171
Jahjapasazáde Mehmed Pasha, 124
Jakovali Hasan Paša, 124
James A. Michener, 293
Janissaries, 124
János Batsányi, 132
János Damjanich, 130
János Fadrusz, 67
János Gundel, 300
János Hadik, 160
János Harmatta, 5
János Kádár, 259, 271, 278, 283, 286
János Pálffy, 61
János Sajnovics, 9, 10
János Szapolyai, 79
Jan Zachwatowicz, 74
Jasper, 23
Jean-Paul Sartre, 291
Jewish, 198
Jewish Encyclopedia, 306
Jews, 197
Jews and the Hungarian Revolution, 148
John Foster Dulles, 279
John Hunyadi, 56
John III Sobieski, 117
John I Zápolya, 115
John Lewis Gaddis, 324
John Lukacs, 307
John Malalas, 5
John Sigismund Zápolya, 40, 42
John the Merciful, 78
John Zápolya, 40, 41, 57
Joseph II, Holy Roman Emperor, 46, 131, 299
Josephinism, 46
Joseph Stalin, 264, 265
Josif Rajačić, 149
Josip Broz Tito, 278
Josip Jelačić, 130, 143
Jousts, 57
Józef Bem, 130, 153, 267

Jozef Tiso, 244
Józef Wysocki (general), 130
József Bem, 268
József Dudás, 272
József Eötvös, 142
József Mindszenty, 264, 279
József Róna, 108
Józsefváros, 283
JSTOR, 307
Judaism, 38, 197, 242
Jugendstil, 68
Julius Jacob von Haynau, 130, 157
July Ultimatum, 212

Kabars, 3, 20
Kaiserthum, 48
Kálmán Darányi, 241
Kálmán Tisza, 67
Kama River, 2, 12
Kamenets-Podolski, 247
Kamianets-Podilskyi Massacre, 247
Kanije Eyalet, 119
Kankalis, 18
Kaposvár, 271
Kara Mustafa Pasha, 117
Károly Lotz, 93
Kázmér Batthyány, 145
Keep, 54
Kempinski Hotel Corvinus, Budapest, 305
Kende, 3, 19
Kerch, 21
Key stone, 76
Keystone (architecture), 79
KGB, 259, 281
Khagan, 16
Khanty language, 10
Khanty people, 12, 23
Khazar Khaganate, 2, 11, 15
Khazars, 15
Khrushchev: The Man and His Era, 324
Kingdom of Bohemia, 117, 196, 225
Kingdom of Bulgaria, 254, 255, 262
Kingdom of Croatia and Slavonia, 163, 166
Kingdom of Croatia (Habsburg), 130
Kingdom of Croatia-Slavonia, 161, 179, 225, 230
Kingdom of Dalmatia, 163, 196, 225
Kingdom of Galicia and Lodomeria, 178, 180, 196, 225
Kingdom of Hungary, 39, 40, 44, 58, 115, 120, 131, 161, 163, 183, 222, 224, 225
Kingdom of Hungary (1000–1301), 39
Kingdom of Hungary (1301-1526), 115
Kingdom of Hungary (1301–1526), 38, 39
Kingdom of Hungary (1526–1867), **37**, 40
Kingdom of Hungary (1538-1867), 129, 130

Kingdom of Hungary (1538–1867), 117
Kingdom of Hungary (1867–1918), 38, 229
Kingdom of Hungary (1920-1946), 222, 257
Kingdom of Hungary (1920–1946), 223, 239
Kingdom of Hungary (1920–46), 162, 239, 253, 254
Kingdom of Italy, 161, 215, 253
Kingdom of Italy (1861-1946), 239
Kingdom of Italy (1861–1946), 224, 243, 262
Kingdom of Montenegro, 206
Kingdom of Romania, 161, 162, 224, 239, 253–255, 262
Kingdom of Serbia, 160, 206, 223
Kingdom of Yugoslavia, 162, 221, 223, 246, 253
King of East Francia, 21
King of Hungary, 21, 41, 42, 85, 160, 163, 300
King St. Stephen, 6
Kirovohrad Oblast, 3
Klemens von Metternich, 140
Köçek, 126
Kolozsvár, 100
Komárno, 154
Komárom, 154
Königsberg, 157
Kopřivnice, 184
Koran, 122
Korean War, 280
Košice, 191, 246
Kossuth Bridge, 304
Kossuth County, Iowa, 157
Kossuth Lajos square, 305
Kossuth Rádió, 283
Kozara Offensive, 253
Közmunkatanács, 300
Kraków, 171, 189, 198
Krisztinaváros, 97
Kuban River, 2, 14, 15
Kulmberg, 21
Kündür, 19

Labour service (Hungary), 255
Ladislaus I of Hungary, 27
Lady-in-waiting, 101
Laissez-faire, 137
Lajos Aulich, 130, 146
Lajos Batthyány, 130, 139, 142, 299
Lajos Kossuth, 50, 51, 130, 142, 301
Landsberg am Lech, 252
Landscape garden, 65
Lands of the Bohemian Crown, 166
Lands of the Crown of Saint Stephen, 161–163
Lands of the Crown of St. Stephen, 47
Landsturm, 203
Larch, 2
László Bárdossy, 246

László Csány, 146
László Hunyadi, 56
László Kontler, 10
László Rajk, 264, 267
László Szőgyény-Marich, Jr., 211
Latin, 64
Latin Catholic, 198
Latin Church, 197
Latin language, 37, 38
Laurin & Klement, 184
Laval Nugent von Westmeath, 154
Lázár Mészáros, 142, 146
League of Nations, 241
League of the Three Emperors, 206
Left Communists, 291
Leninist, 262
Leopard, 75
Leopold I, Holy Roman Emperor, 44
Leopold II, Holy Roman Emperor, 131
Leo the Wise, 6, 26
Lesser Poland Voivodeship, 225
Levedi, 18
Levedia, 2
Liberal autocracy, 159
Liberty Bridge, 306
Liberty Bridge (Budapest), 301
Liberty Statue (Budapest), 304
Library of Congress Country Studies, 127
Lib.ru, 321
Liechtenstein, 224
Light industry, 183
Limes, 33
Line 2 (Budapest Metro), 304
Line 2 reconstruction, 305
Line 4 (Budapest Metro), 306
Line (formation), 26
Linz, 198
List of countries and dependencies by area, 160
List of countries by population, 160
List of historical capitals of Hungary, 300
List of Prime Ministers of Hungary, 160
List of rulers of Hungary, 38, 298
List of World Heritage Sites in Hungary, 53
Liu Shaoqi, 278
Liutprand of Cremona, 6
Ljubljana, 178, 189, 215
Loan word, 2
Lodomeria, 220
Loggia, 56
Lohner-Werke, 184
Lokomotivfabrik der StEG, 185
Lokomotivfabrik Floridsdorf, 185
Lombards, 39
Lombardy, 226
Lorenzo de Monacis, 78
Loris Fortuna, 290

Los Angeles, California, 292
Louis II of Hungary and Bohemia, 115
Louis I of Hungary, 54, 202
Louis the German, 21
Lovran, 191
Lower Austria, 196, 225
Lower Danube, 3

Ľudovít Štúr, 130

Ludwig von Welden, 130, 155
Luftwaffe, 246
Luigi Cadorna, 215

Łukasz Andrzej Kamiński, 324

LUnità, 290
Lutheran, 43, 198
Lutheranism, 38
Lviv, 198
Lviv Oblast, 225
Lvov–Sandomierz Offensive, 254

M0 motorway, 305
MacArthur Park, 292
Macedonian Front, 214
Macedonia (theme), 16
Madeira, 223
Maeotian Swamp, 7
Magna Hungaria, 2
Magnate, 43, 44
Magomobil, 184
Magyar Írás, 303
Magyarization, 151, 179, 240
Magyar Optical Works, 303
Magyars, 1, 13, 14, 69
Magyar tribes, 2, 6
Malenkov, 278
Manfréd Weiss Steel and Metal Works, 301
Mansi people, 8
Mao Zedong, 278
March of Pannonia, 21
Marcomannia, 39
Marcus Aurelius, 32
Margaret Bridge, 301, 306
Margaret Island, 298, 300
Margraviate of Moravia, 196, 225
Maria Christina, Duchess of Teschen, 97
Mariánské Lázně, 190
Maria Theresa of Austria, 45, 61, 299
Marshall Plan, 264
Marshal of the Soviet Union, 282
Martial law, 131
Martin, Slovakia, 221
Marxism, 261
Matthew III Csák, 39

Matthias Church, 53, 298
Matthias Corvinus, 100, 298
Matthias Corvinus of Hungary, 55
Matthias Fountain, 68
Mattias Corvinus, 202
Mátyás Rákosi, 157, 263, 285
MÁVAG, 185, 210
Maximilian Fretter-Pico, 251
Maximilian II, Holy Roman Emperor, 40, 42
Maximilian I of Mexico, 206
Mayor of Budapest, 290, 300
Measures of national income and output, 182
Mecsek, 283
Medieval, 53
Medieval Hungary, 115
Medieval Kingdom of Hungary, 40
Medieval Royal Palace (Buda Castle), 71
Međimurje, 130, 245
Međimurje County, 225
Meditations, 32
Medrese, 122
Megyeri Bridge, 305
Mehmed-paša Sokolović, 122
Mekteb, 122
Ménrót, 7
Metternich, 138
Mevlevi, 124
Meyers Konversations-Lexikon, 176
Michael Korda, 293
Middle Ages, 38, 54, 78
Mihály Horváth, 146
Mihály Károlyi, 221, 303
Mihály Vörösmarty, 110
Mihály Zichy, 129
Mikhail Gorbachev, 292
Mikhail Suslov, 276, 287
Miklós Gimes, 287
Miklós Horthy, 70, 223, 239, 240, 303
Miklós Horthy, Jr., 249
Miklós Kállay, 247
Miklós Ligeti, 110
Miklós Radnóti, 256
Miklós Ybl, 66
Military District of Kaschau, 40
Military District of Preßburg, 40
Military Frontier, 46
Military justice, 220
Military of Hungary, 169
Militia, 261
Millennium Memorial, 302
Minaret, 124
Minister of Defence (Hungary), 146
Minister-President of Austria, 160
Minority group, 180
Misha Glenny, 179
Miskolc, 191, 267

Mladá Boleslav, 184
Modern architecture, 53
Molotov cocktail, 272
Mongol invasion of Europe, 298
Mongols, 26
Montenegro, 225, 226
Moravia, 189, 190
Moravians (ethnic group), 130
Mór Jókai, 132
Morning Star (UK newspaper), 291
Mór Perczel, 155
Mór Than, 150
Mosonmagyaróvár, 274, 275
Mosque, 122
Mosque of Pasha Qasim, 123
Mosques, 124
Moszkva tér (Budapest Metro), 304
Muageris, 5
Muhamed Mehmedbašić, 208
Multinational state, 161
Multiparty democracy, 262
Munich Agreement, 243
Museum of Fine Arts (Budapest), 302
Muslim, 162
Muslims, 197
Mutiny, 220

Nagykanizsa–Körmend Offensive, 252, 254
Napoleon III, 180
Nasr II, 6
Nasser, 279
Nation, 175
National flag, 226
Nationalization, 262
National Peasant Party (Hungary), 273
National Security Archive, 280, 295
National Széchényi Library, 74
National Theatre (Budapest), 305
NATO, 280
Natural science, 122
Nazi Germany, 223, 239, 243, 253–255, 262
NDH, 249
Nedeljko Čabrinović, 208
Nemzeti dal, 129, 139, 268
Nemzeti Szalon, 301
Neo-absolutism, 52
Neoclassical architecture, 65
Neolithic, 2, 12, 297
Neo-Renaissance, 66
Népszabadság, 304
Netherlands, 254, 280
New Imperialism, 160
New Public Cemetery, Budapest, 287
New York Palace (Budapest), 301
New York Public Library, 307
Nicholas I of Russia, 130, 131, 153

Nicolò Pacassi, 63
Nikita Khrushchev, 259, 265
Nomad, 2
Nóra Berend, 10
North Rail Bridge .28.C3.89szaki .C3.B6sszek.C3.B6t.C5.91 vas.C3.BAti h.C3.ADd.29, 305
Norway, 254
Norway national bandy team, 290
November Uprising, 153
Novi Sad, 191, 247
Nuclear war, 266
Nuncio, 250
Nunnery, 63
Nuremberg Chronicle, 55
Nyíregyháza, 191
Nyugat, 302

Obersturmbannführer, 255
Ob River, 11

Óbuda, 33, 297, 298, 300

Occupation of Vojvodina, 1941-1944, 246
Occupied Poland, 255
OCLC, 306
Octagon, 63
October Revolution, 303
Official language, 178
Oghur languages, 2, 25
Oghuz Turks, 22
One-party state, 241
Onogurs, 7
On the Personality Cult and its Consequences, 265
Opatija, 191
Open letter, 291
Operation Barbarossa, 239, 246, 253, 262
Operation Frühlingserwachen, 251
Operation Margarethe, 240, 248, 262, 303
Operation Panzerfaust, 249
Operation Spring Awakening, 254
Oradea, 191, 199
Orava (region), 226
Organisation of Militiamen, 143
Országos Pedagógiai Könyvtár és Múzeum, 301
Ostrava, 190
Ostrogozhsk–Rossosh Offensive, 253
Oszkár Jászi, 235
Ottoman architecture, 122
Ottoman Empire, 39, 41, 42, 58, 60, 115, 121, 157, 206, 226
Ottoman-Habsburg Wars, 121
Ottoman Hungary, 41, 42, **115**, 298, 299
Ottoman Sultan, 123

Ottoman Turks, 58
Otto Skorzeny, 70
Otto von Bismarck, 180, 206
Oxford English Dictionary, 321
Oxus, 20

Palace, 54
Palace Chapel (Buda Castle), 56
Palace of Versailles, 77, 223
Palatinal Crypt, 64, 93
Palatine (Kingdom of Hungary), 42, 64
Palatine of Hungary, 38
Paleolinguistics, 11
Paleolithic, 23
Pál Hunfalvy, 10
Pallas Athene, 56
Pál Maléter, 259, 272, 281, 287
Palmiro Togliatti, 290
Pál Teleki, 242, 246
Pál Vasvári, 132
Palynology, 2, 11
Pannonia, 298
Pannonia Inferior, 33
Pannonian basin, 186
Pannonia (Roman province), 32
Pan-Slavic, 204
Paris Peace Treaties, 1947, 257
Parliament, 168
Parliament of Hungary, 241
Partium, 225
Pasha, 119
Pasha of Buda, 298
Patent of Toleration, 46
Păuleni-Ciuc, 218
Paul-Henri Spaak, 288
Paul III Anton, Prince Esterházy, 142
Pavle Karadjordjevic, 246
Peace in the Valley, 290
Peçevi Arifi Ahmed Dede, 124
Pecheneg, 3
Pechenegs, 18
Pechora River, 11
Pécs, 122, 123, 191, 267, 283
Peoples Republic of Hungary, 257, 261–263
Permic languages, 11
Persia, 18
Personal union, 159, 164
Pest-Buda Musical Association, 299
Pest (city), 157, 282
Pest (county), 281
Pest, Hungary, 37, 64, 117, 131, 135, 139, 163, 166, 190, 297, 298, 300
Pesti Hírlap, 301
Péter Csák, 202
Peter Fryer, 291
Peter F. Sugar, 237

Peter II of Yugoslavia, 246
Péter Pázmány, 43
Péter Veres (politician), 268
Petőfi Bridge, 303
Petőfi Csarnok, 304
Petrovac (Montenegro), 225
Philip Short, 324
Piave (river), 216
Piedmont, 209
Piedmont-Sardinia, 157
Pietro Nenni, 290
Pilaster, 82
Pilisvörösvár, 93
Pit-house, 2, 23
Plenipotentiary, 157
Plzeň, 178, 190, 198
Pogroms, 180
Poland, 198, 226, 254
Poles, 130
Polish Armed Forces in the East, 254, 255
Polish Armed Forces in the West, 254
Polish language, 195
Polish-Lithuanian Commonwealth, 117
Polish October, 266, 275, 277
Polish Underground State, 254
Polish United Workers Party, 266
Politburo of the Central Committee of the Communist Party of the Soviet Union, 261, 275
Political prisoner, 287
Political rehabilitation, 266
Political repression, 248
Pontic steppes, 6
Pope Pius XII, 70
Popular revolt in late medieval Europe, 115
Population transfer in the Soviet Union, 264
Porajmos, 250
Portal:Austria, 164
Portal:Hungary, 1, 39, 115, 130, 165, 260, 297
Portal:Politics, 268
Portal:Slovakia, 40
Potsdam, 211
Poznań, 266, 277
Poznań 1956 protests, 266, 277
Pozsony, 189
Pragmatic Sanction, 45
Pragmatic Sanction of 1713, 166
Prague, 170, 178, 183, 189, 198
Prague Offensive, 255
Pravda, 285
Precision mechanics, 183
Predecessor state, 189
Prekmurje, 197, 225, 245
President of the Italian Republic, 291
Pressburg, 79
Prime minister, 168, 299

Prime Minister of the United Kingdom, 204
Prince Eugene of Savoy, 69
Princess Auguste of Bavaria (1875–1964), 106
Principality of Lower Pannonia, 39
Principality of Nitra, 39
Principality of Serbia, 149
Principality of Transylvania (1570–1711), 40, 42
Principality of Transylvania (1571–1711), 116
Principality of Upper Hungary, 43, 117
Prisoner of war, 130
Private school, 179
Prohorovo culture, 14
Propaganda, 275, 277
Protectorate of Bohemia and Moravia, 244
Protestantism, 45
Protestants, 42, 44, 197
Protocol of Sèvres, 279
Proto-Finno-Ugric language, 2, 12
Proto-Iranian language, 2, 24
Proto-Ugric, 11
Proto-Uralic language, 2, 11
Province of Belluno, 225
Provisional Government of the Fourth French Republic, 254
Prussia, 45, 52, 165
Prut, 18
Public domain, 158
Public holidays in Hungary, 131, 292
Pula, 191, 192
Punitive expedition, 215
Puppet state, 244
Putto, 93

Q28513, 237

Raba (automobile), 184
Rába (company), 185
Race (classification of human beings), 242
Ráckeve, 191
Radio Budapest, 268
Radio Free Europe, 265, 279, 280
Rail transport, 189
Rákóczi Bridge, 305
Rákóczis War of Independence, 38, 41, 44
Rákosi, 284
Rákosi bunker, 304
Randolph Braham, 257
Raoul Wallenberg, 250
Rastislav of Moravia, 21
Ráth Károly, 300
Ray S. Cline, 265
Red Army, 262
Red Cross, 287
Red ochre, 23
Red star, 272

Red Terror (Hungary), 303
Ref aaa, 161
Reflex bow, 26
Reformation, 123
Reformed, 38
Reformed Church in Hungary, 123
Regent, 157, 223, 246
Regent of Hungary, 303
Regino of Prüm, 6
Reinsurance Treaty, 206
Religious conversion, 242
Renaissance, 56, 298
Renaissance architecture, 100
Republic of German Austria, 222
Republic of German-Austria, 161
Republic of Ragusa, 63
Resistance in German-occupied Czechoslovakia, 255
Revolt, 261
Revolution, 267
Revolutionary council, 289
Revolutionary Workers-Peasants Government of Hungary, 281
Revolutions of 1848, 129, 131, 165, 189
Revolutions of 1848 in the Habsburg areas, 131
Revolutions of 1989, 257
Rhaeto-Romance languages, 196
Rib vault, 79
Richard Nixon, 266, 279
Right-wing politics, 240
Rijeka, 192
Risalit, 65
River Danube, 268
Robert Lansing, 221
Rococo, 63
Rollback, 266
Roma in Hungary, 240
Roman Catholic, 44, 159
Roman Catholic Church, 43
Roman Empire, 32
Romanesque Revival architecture, 99
Romania, 119, 179, 199, 200, 217, 225, 254
Romanian Land Forces, 217
Romanian language, 38, 195, 196
Romanians, 130, 178
Roman legion, 33
Rongyos Gárda, 243
Roterturm Pass, 153
Royal Geographical Society, 315
Royal Hungarian Army, 247, 248
Royal Hungarian Landwehr, 150
Royal Hungary, 59, 116, 117, 120
Royal Italian Army, 215
Rubiks Cube, 304
Rudas Baths, 122, 298
Ruđer Bošković, 315

Rudolf, Crown Prince of Austria, 206
Rudolf IV, Duke of Austria, 200
Ruling emperor, 133
Rumbach Street Synagogue, 300
Rus people, 16
Russia, 157
Russian Empire, 130, 161, 165, 215
Russian Liberation Army, 255
Russian Primary Chronicle, 6
Russian Revolution, 215
Russo-Turkish War (1877–1878), 204
Rustication (architecture), 75
Rusyn language, 196
Rusyn people, 148
Rusyns, 130
Ruthenian language, 38, 195, 196

S:1922 Encyclopædia Britannica, 234
Saami language, 10
Saami languages, 9
Sabir people, 7
Sabretache, 25
Saint Cyril the Philosopher, 21
Sainte-Chapelle, 78
Saint Margaret of Hungary, 298
Saint Methodius of Thessaloniki, 21
Saints Cyril and Methodius, 6
Saint Stephen of Hungary, 63
Salami tactics, 262
Saltovo-Mayaki, 16
Samanid Empire, 6
Samos Empire, 39
Sámuel Gyarmathi, 9
Sándor Petőfi, 129, 132, 139, 256, 267
Sándor Rónai, 284
Sandžak, 161, 206, 226
Sanjak, 119
Sanjak-bey, 120
Sanjak of Novi Pazar, 162
Sankt Pölten, 63
Sarajevo, 208
Sardinia-Piedmont, 52
Sarkel, 17
Sarmatians, 12
Satellite nation, 277
Satellite state, 265
Satu Mare, 191
Schönbrunn Palace, 102, 229
Schutzkorps, 209
Scythians, 1, 9
Sea of Azov, 6
Sebő Vukovics, 146
Second Army (Hungary), 247, 251, 255
Second Balkan War, 209
Second Czechoslovak Republic, 239, 243
Second French Empire, 52

Second industrial revolution, 183
Second Italian War of Independence, 165, 211
Second Polish Republic, 161, 162, 223
Second Republic of Hungary, 257
Second Vienna Award, 243, 245
Sediment, 15

Šejh Ali Dede, 124

Self-propelled artillery, 321
Senta, 108
Serbia, 179, 199, 209, 225, 226, 255
Serbian language, 38
Serbian Orthodox, 197
Serbian people, 130
Serbian Vojvodina, 130
Serbo-Croatian, 195, 197
Serb people, 122
Serbs, 179
Shaman, 27
Shtetls, 180
Sibiu, 153, 191
Siege of Buda (1530), 298
Siege of Buda (1540), 298
Siege of Buda (1541), 298
Siege of Buda (1849), 147
Siege of Budapest, 251, 254, 303, 304
Siege of Pest, 298
Siege of Przemyśl, 214, 215
Siege of Vienna, 116
Sigismund, Holy Roman Emperor, 54
Silesia, 226
Silesian Voivodeship, 225
Silversmith, 25
Simeon I of Bulgaria, 22
Simon of Kéza, 9
Siret River, 18

Şiria, Romania, 156

Sisters of Loreto, 63
Slavic languages, 178
Slavic peoples, 21
Slavic tribes, 3
Slavonia, 225
Slavs, 39
Slobozia, Moldova, 4
Slovak–Hungarian War, 244
Slovakia, 40, 42, 179, 199, 225, 243, 254
Slovak language, 38, 195
Slovak National Council (1848–1849), 130
Slovak National Uprising, 40
Slovak Republic (1939-1945), 244
Slovak Republic (1939–1945), 40, 239
Slovak Republic (1939–45), 249, 253, 255
Slovaks, 178

Slovaks in Czechoslovakia (1918–38), 40
Slovaks in Czechoslovakia (1948–89), 40
Slovak Socialist Republic, 40
Slovak Soviet Republic, 40
Slovak Uprising of 1848–49, 40
Slovene language, 38, 178, 195, 196
Slovene literature, 178
Slovenia, 225
Snaffle bit, 25
Social contract, 131
Social democracy, 273
Social equality, 178
Socialism, 262
Socialist Federal Republic of Yugoslavia, 264

Šokci, 130

Sokollu Mustafa Pasha, 298
Solidarity (UK), 295
Sopron, 191, 267, 274
Sosva River, 23
Southern Bug, 18
Southern Group of Forces, 282
Southern Transdanubia, 115
South Slavs, 116, 162
South Tyrol, 225
Soviet Armed Forces, 259
Soviet Army, 261, 262
Soviet (council), 277
Soviet Union, 239, 246, 253–255, 259, 261
Soviet Union national bandy team, 290
Spanish Civil War, 263
Sphere of influence, 179, 262
Spiš, 226
Sprachbund, 11
Sri Lanka, 289
Stables, 58
Stadion Constitution, 145
Stalin Monument in Budapest, 268
Stanford University Press, 293
Stanley Eric Reinhart, 252
State Department, 157
State of Slovenes, Croats and Serbs, 160, 161, 221, 223
State Protection Authority, 259, 261–263
State Religion, 138
Statistics, 245
Stephan Ludwig Roth, 153
Stephen, Duke of Slavonia, 54
Stephen I of Hungary, 26, 99
Stephen VII Báthory, 38
Steppes, 2
Stevan Knićanin, 130
Stirrup, 25
Structure and name, 159
St. Stephens Basilica, 300

Stucco, 65
Students union, 263
Subcarpathian Voivodeship, 225
Sublime Porte, 120
Subotica, 191, 199
Succession of states, 162
Successor state, 223
Suceava County, 225
Suez Canal, 204
Suez Crisis, 275, 279
Suleiman the Magnificent, 58, 298
Suleyman the Magnificent, 115
Sunni Islam, 116
Supreme Ruthenian Council, 130
Surrender at Világos, 156, 157
Surrender of Germany, 257
Sutomore, 225
Sutorina, 226
Svatopluk I of Moravia, 21
Swiss franc, 290
Switzerland, 224
Szabadság tér, 299
Szarvas, 272
Széchenyi Chain Bridge, 54
Széchenyi Lánchíd, 300
Szeged, 24, 191, 199, 267
Székesfehérvár, 117, 119
Széll Kálmán Square, 304
Széll Kálmán tér, 304
Szentendre, 191
Szent László Infantry Division, 252
Szigetvár, 124
Szolnok, 283
Szombathely, 191

T-54, 278
Tabán, 299, 303
Tactica of Emperor Leo VI the Wise, 6, 26
Táltos, 27
Tapani Salminen, 11
Tápióbicske, 150
Tatra (company), 184
Tear gas, 268
Technological change, 182
Teenage Dream (Katy Perry album), 75
Telamon, 91
Telefon Hírmondó, 194
Telephone exchange, 193
Temeşvar Eyalet, 117, 119
Template:Eastern Bloc sidebar, 261
Template:History of Austria, 165
Template:History of Hungary, 1, 39, 115, 131, 165, 260, 297
Template:History of Slovakia, 40
Template:Revolution sidebar, 268
Template talk:Eastern Bloc sidebar, 261

Template talk:History of Austria, 165
Template talk:History of Hungary, 1, 39, 115, 131, 165, 260, 297
Template talk:History of Slovakia, 40
Template talk:Revolution sidebar, 268
Teodor Axentowicz, 199
Ternopil Oblast, 225
Terrace (building), 60
Text corpus, 178
Thalers, 63
The 13 Martyrs of Arad, 157
The Blood of the Hungarians, 291
The Bridge at Andau, 293
The Castle of Buda (online database), 114
The Estates, 143
The Holocaust, 250
Theobald von Bethmann-Hollweg, 211
The Reformation, 43
The Revolutions of 1848 in France, 138
Thermae, 34
Third Army (Hungary), 246, 251
Third Hungarian Republic, 262, 304
Thomas Walker Arnold, 315
Thyssagetae, 5
Tibor Frank, 316
Tiger II, 248
Timeline of Budapest, **297**
Time (magazine), 289
Time Person of the Year, 289
Timişoara, 153
Timişoara, 191, 199
Tim Judah, 158
Tim Weiner, 322, 325
Tisza, 192
Tiszakécske, 270
Titoism, 263
Tivertsi, 21
Tobol River, 2
Toilet, 80
Toldi (tank), 247
Tony Blair, 290
Toquz Oghuz, 18
Torture, 262
Totalitarian, 242
Totem, 7
Transdanubia, 42, 143
Transleithania, 161, 163, 166, 225, 229
Transylvania, 42, 121, 144, 178, 197, 217, 224, 225, 245
Transylvanian Saxons, 130
Trapdoor, 80
Treaty of Brest-Litovsk, 216
Treaty of Eternal Friendship (1940), 246
Treaty of Karlowitz, 38, 41, 117
Treaty of Nagyvárad, 38, 41

Treaty of Saint-Germain-en-Laye (1919), 160, 161, 222, 224
Treaty of San Stefano, 181, 204
Treaty of Speyer (1570), 42
Treaty of Szatmár, 45
Treaty of Trianon, 160, 161, 222, 224, 240, 241, 243
Tree of life, 27
Trench warfare, 215
Trentino, 225
Trepanation, 27
Trialism in Austria-Hungary, 179
Trianon peace treaty, 245
Tricolour (flag), 229
Trieste, 192, 198, 220
Trifko Grabež, 208
Tripartite Pact, 246
Triple Alliance (1882), 206
Triple Entente, 212
Triune Kingdom, 163
Triune Kingdom of Croatia, Slavonia and Dalmatia, 163
Triune Kingdom of Croatia, Slavonia, and Dalmatia, 144, 179
Trnava, 63
Trotskyism, 263
Tumuli, 12
Tunisia, 289
Türbe, 124
Turin, 157
Turkic Khaganate, 7
Turkic languages, 2, 10
Turkic peoples, 2
Turkish Bath, 122
Turul, 69, 110
Tympanum (architecture), 68

UFAG, 184
Ugric languages, 1, 7
Ukraine, 178, 198, 225, 254
Ukrainian language, 178, 195, 196
Ukrainian Peoples Republic, 223
UNESCO, 191
Unified Empire under Attila, 5
Union (American Civil War), 157
Unitarian Church of Transylvania, 198
Unitarianism, 38
Unitary state, 165
United Kingdom, 161, 239, 242, 246, 254
United Nations Security Council, 279
United Nations Security Council Resolution 120, 279
United States, 161, 239, 254
United States of America, 292
United States Secretary of State, 279
University of Budapest, 299

University of Vienna, 200
Unsupported attributions, 150
Upper Austria, 196, 225
Upper Hungary, 150, 197, 244
Uprising of 1953 in East Germany, 277
Uralic languages, 2, 9
Ural Mountains, 2, 11
Uránia Hungarian Scientific Theatre, 302
Urbanization, 182
Urban planning, 66
Urbarium, 46
Urheimat, 2, 13, 14
Uruguay, 289
US Civil War, 157
US State Department, 292
Uyvar Eyalet, 40

Vác, 190, 299
Vanguard, 20
Varat Eyalet, 117, 119
Variety show, 290
Vaso Čubrilović, 208
Velvet Revolution, 40
Veneto, 226
Venice, 189, 216
Vérmező, 299
Victor Emmanuel III of Italy, 70
Victor Spinei, 16
Victory in Europe Day, 257
Vienna, 21, 42, 45, 66, 130, 138, 159, 190, 198, 222
Vienna Offensive, 255
Vienna Revolt, 139
Vienna Uprising, 154
Vigadó Concert Hall, 299, 300
Vinzenz Fischer, 82
Viticulture, 15
Vittorio Emanuele Orlando, 216
Vladislaus II of Bohemia and Hungary, 57
Voivode, 3, 17
Vojvodina, 149, 179, 197, 225
Volga Bulgars, 13
Volga River, 2
Vorarlberg, 196, 224, 225
Voronezh-Kastornensk operation, 253
Vörösmarty Square, 300
Vyacheslav Molotov, 275

Walter Cronkite, 323
War of the Austrian Succession, 61
War reparations, 264
Warsaw, 74
Warsaw Pact, 261, 265
Water polo, 290
Water polo at the 1956 Summer Olympics, 290
Wayback Machine, 238

WestEnd City Center, 305
Western Allied invasion of Germany, 254
Western Front (World War I), 215, 218
Western Slovakia, 150
Western world, 264
West Siberian Plain, 13
West Slavs, 162
West Ukrainian Peoples Republic, 161, 223
White Terror (Hungary), 303
Wiener Börse, 182
Wiener Neustadt, 185
Wiener Neustädter Lokomotivfabrik, 185
Wiener Zeitung, 152
Wikipedia:Avoid weasel words, 140
Wikipedia:Citation needed, 44, 60, 115, 117, 122, 123, 133, 134, 144, 149, 163, 180, 181, 184, 185, 216, 217, 241, 263, 264, 287, 298, 299, 301
Wikipedia:Link rot, 120
Wikipedia:Please clarify, 151
Wikisource:For Freedom and Truth, 283
Wilhelm II, German Emperor, 211
William Colby, 279
William Henry Overall, 306
William L. Langer, 236
William Taubman, 278, 324
Władysław Gomułka, 266, 278
Woodrow Wilson, 220, 324
Woodrow Wilson International Center for Scholars, 295
Workers council, 261, 272, 274, 287
Workers councils, 274
World Heritage Committee, 53
World Heritage Site, 53, 54, 191, 304
World War I, 160–162, 183, 212, 241
World War II, 239, 241, 261, 304

Young Bosnia, 208
Yugoslav Committee, 221
Yugoslavia, 253
Yugoslav Partisans, 253, 254
Yuri Andropov, 259, 281

Zagreb, 179, 191, 199, 300
Zakarpattia Oblast, 197, 225
Zala County (former), 225
Zeughaus, Buda, 65
Zigetvar Eyalet, 119
Zipser Germans, 130
Zodiac, 56
Zoltán Tildy, 262
Zwinger (fortification), 55
Zytan Schunherz, 256

www.ingramcontent.com/pod-product-compliance
Lightning Source LLC
Chambersburg PA
CBHW021141160426
43194CB00007B/646